MPRE Study Guide 2020

MPRE Study Guide including Comprehensive
Preparation Outline and Practice Questions

AmeriBar

Phone (800) 529-2651 • Fax (800) 529-2652

By AmeriBar

ISBN 9781694344618

TABLE OF CONTENTS

HOW TO USE THIS BOOK

This book contains everything you need to prepare for the Multistate Professional Responsibility Examination ("MPRE"). It is divided into three main sections: 1) the Introduction; 2) the Outline; and 3) Practice Questions.

Introduction

The first part of the book describes MPRE basics including the format of the exam and strategies.

Outline

The second part of the book is an outline of the legal subject-matter testable on the MPRE. The outline is divided into 12 chapters. Each chapter details a different topic. The end of each chapter contains a set of review questions.

Practice Questions

The final part of the book contains simulated MPRE questions. Every question contains an answer and explanation.

Working Through the Book

The best way to use this book is to go through it in order. First, learn about the MPRE. Second, learn the testable law. Third. the practice questions to refine your knowledge of the law.

MPRE BASICS

General Considerations

This Professional Responsibility outline covers material that has traditionally been tested on the MPRE. The MPRE is drafted by the National Conference of Bar Examiners (NCBE). It consists of 60 multiple choice questions. You will also be asked to complete 10 Test Center Review questions regarding your impressions of the testing conditions. The exam lasts two hours and five minutes.

The American Bar Association (ABA) has promulgated Model Rules of Professional Conduct, which are referred to herein as the "Rule(s)" and cited as the "Model Rules of Prof'l Conduct R. ___." Almost all states have adopted the Rules. The Rules are heavily tested on the MPRE. Accordingly, it is important to learn, know, and understand them.

The MPRE will also test legal principles other than those found in the Rules. The MPRE tests legal principles found in the ABA's Model Code of Judicial Conduct, which is referred to herein as the "Code" and cited as the "Model Code of Judicial Conduct." Another source of testable legal principles is the American Law Institute's *Restatement of the Law, 3d—Law Governing Lawyers*. It is referred to herein as the "Restatement" and cited as the "Restatement of the Law Governing Lawyers, Third, § ___." Finally, according to the National Conference of Bar Examiners (NCBE)

> [The MPRE also tests] controlling constitutional decisions and generally accepted principles established in leading federal and state cases and in procedural and evidentiary rules. The remaining items, outside the disciplinary context, are designed to measure an understanding of the generally accepted rules, principles, and common law regulating the legal profession in the United States; in these items, the correct answer will be governed by the view reflected in a majority of cases, statutes, or regulations on the subject. To the extent that questions of professional responsibility arise in the context of procedural or evidentiary issues, such as the availability of litigation sanctions or the scope of the attorney-client evidentiary privilege, the Federal Rules of Civil Procedure and the Federal Rules of Evidence will be assumed to apply, unless otherwise stated.

Some of those legal principles are described in this outline, as well as the outlines designed for Multistate Bar Examination preparation, including the Constitutional Law, Civil Procedure, and Evidence outlines.

The NCBE usually does not test local statutes or rules of court on the MPRE. However, be aware that some MPRE questions could "include the text of a local statute or rule that must be considered when answering that question." If you encounter such a question, use legal reasoning and analysis to apply the text of the given statute or rule in answering the question.

Coverage of the Outlines

This outline is intended to cover the main Rules and provisions of the Code and the Restatement that may be tested on the MPRE. Some of these legal principles may be more commonly tested than others. The other legal principles, however, remain subject to potentially being tested.

Due to the broad scope of the potentially testable issues and rules from sources beyond the Rules, Code, and Restatement, you might encounter a novel question not covered by these sources. Alternatively, you might encounter a question where the answer choice you anticipate is not presented to you. In those situations, use common sense, logic, and the process of elimination to select the best available answer choice. When attempting to eliminate incorrect answer choices, beware of answer choices that are factually accurate but legally incorrect.

MPRE STRATEGIES

Before taking a practice test or answering sample questions, you must learn:

- the testable provisions of the Rules, the Code, and the Restatement;
- the key words or phrases that may be used and underlined in the call of the question on the MPRE. Knowing the meaning of those words and phrases will enable you, when taking your own exam, to easily identify:
    - the type of question asked;
    - what the question is testing; and
    - what type of answer might be correct.

These words and phrases are described on the NCBE website, www.ncbex.org, and in NCBE testing materials. The NCBE provides MPRE Sample Questions, which are representative of the questions presented in an actual MPRE exam.

The multiple-choice questions on the MPRE always include four answer choices. Generally, there are two types of questions. One type simply provides a fact pattern and question and lists the four answer choices. Usually, this type of question is more common than the other type of question.

The other type of question provides a fact pattern and question, lists three or four statements, and then provides four answer choices asking which of the statements are correct. To answer this type of question, you will need to evaluate the statements and determine whether or not they are correct, and then choose the appropriate answer choice. The NCBE has not used this type of question in recent MPRE exams.

The fact patterns on the MPRE may include indented and quoted text. This text might be, for example, a person's verbal statement, contents of a document, or words used in a communication to the public. This type of information is at least as relevant as the rest of the fact pattern, and may contain facts that, when correctly analyzed under the controlling legal principles, will better enable you to select the correct answer.

Generally, most questions test one legal principle and/or its exception(s). Some questions might seem to test more than one legal principle, especially when the question arises in a factual context that relates to or is governed by other relevant legal principles. In this event, it is important to ascertain which legal principle is controlling when you are considering the answer choices and before you select an answer.

This is most likely to occur when the controlling legal principles are related, such as the duty of confidentiality in the context of a conflict of interest in representing multiple clients. Similarly, the legal principles governing the features of a retainer agreement and restrictions on contractually limiting liability for legal malpractice could apply simultaneously in a single factual situation.

Sometimes the same main legal principles are tested within different factual contexts, such as criminal, civil, or administrative proceedings. These types of legal principles include, for example, the duty of confidentiality and conflicts of interest in representing clients. Other legal principles, however, only apply in more limited contexts. For example, a few of the Rules regarding law firms only apply to a few specific contexts in which lawyers work together.

Some of the main issues and associated legal principles that are tested include:

- attorney advertising (including both media and content);
- competence in ordinary and emergency situations;
- conflicts of interest involving lawyers serving in the public and private sectors;
- disqualification of judges due to financial interests (including interests of immediate family and friends);
- false statements to anyone or any tribunal;
- fee sharing (division) with non-lawyers;
- assisting non-lawyers in the practice of law;
- agreements limiting malpractice liability;
- retainer agreements;
- contingency fees;
- publicity (literary) rights;
- prohibitions on attempting to influence judges and jurors;
- contacting unrepresented persons (e.g., using agents);
- public statements about judges (made by either lawyers or other candidates for judicial office);
- campaign contributions to judges or judicial candidates; and
- gifts to judges.

To succeed on the MPRE, you will need a practical working knowledge of how these legal principles apply to specific situations. For example, you should know how these legal principles apply to a lawyer's handling of personal funds, as well how those principles apply to funds received from clients and party-opponents. One important and testable issue is how to recognize and avoid the improper commingling of funds between the lawyer's general account and a client trust account.

Learning the controlling legal principles and how to pass the MPRE is more than an academic exercise. The MPRE tests issues that might arise in the real-life practice of law. For example, at least one state added the MPRE with the intent that it would reduce the problem of new attorneys violating the state's rules of professional ethics early in their careers after graduating from law school. In that sense, the MPRE's purpose could be considered as a preventative measure, and it serves an important function in making sure lawyers are educated about their professional responsibilities.

REVIEW QUESTIONS

1. The MPRE consists of:

    a) 50 questions, all of which count toward your final score.
    b) 60 questions, all of which count toward your final score.
    c) 50 questions, all but 10 of which count toward your final score.
    d) 60 questions, all but 10 of which count toward your final score.

2. The format of the MPRE includes:

    a) fact pattern questions with four possible answers from which you pick the best answer.
    b) true / false questions based on fact patterns from which you pick the best answer.
    c) fact pattern questions requiring short sentence answers.
    d) all of the above.

3. The MPRE tests:

    a) knowledge of state-specific ethics law regarding professional conduct.
    b) knowledge of established standards and rules related to a lawyer's professional conduct.
    c) reconciliation of personal ethical standards to model ethical rules.
    d) knowledge of proposed standards of professional conduct in the legal profession.

4. The sources of rules related to a lawyer's professional conduct that are tested on the MPRE include:

    a) generally established principles in the law of evidence and the Model Code of Judicial Conduct.
    b) generally established principles in the law of evidence and the ABA Model Rules of Professional Conduct.
    c) the ABA Model Rules of Professional Conduct and the Model Code of Judicial Conduct.
    d) generally established principles in the law of evidence, the Model Code of Judicial Conduct, and the ABA Model Rules of Professional Conduct.

5. An MPRE question sets forth a local rule governing the ethical conduct of a lawyer and asks for your analysis of the rule. You must analyze it using:

    a) the rules governing the locality in which the rule was promulgated.
    b) the state rules of professional responsibility.
    c) legal reasoning and analysis.
    d) ethical standards which follow local custom and usage.

6. On the MPRE, the phrase "subject to discipline" means the described conduct:

a) will result in an attorney or judge losing his or her license to practice law.

b) will subject the attorney or judge to a lawsuit.

c) shall result in sanction by the appropriate authority.

d) subjects the attorney or judge to discipline under the ABA Model Rules.

7. When the phrases "may" and "proper" are used in an MPRE question, the question is asking:

a) whether the court's permission is necessary before proceeding in an ethical manner.

b) if the conduct described is appropriate under local court rules.

c) if the conduct under consideration is professionally appropriate and would not subject the lawyer to discipline.

d) whether the conduct under consideration is a violation of the Canons of Ethics.

8. "Subject to litigation sanction," when used on the MPRE, means the conduct in question:

a) will subject the offending attorney to a dismissal of his client's case.

b) will subject the lay client to sanctions when the court discovers his unethical conduct.

c) will subject an attorney or an attorney's law firm to sanctions by the court.

d) will cause the judge to disqualify herself in order to avoid a conflict of interest and sanctions for continuing to preside over the litigation.

9. When appearing on the MPRE, the term "subject to disqualification" means:

a) the conduct described would subject a lawyer, but not the lawyer's firm, to disqualification as counsel in the case.

b) the conduct described would subject a lawyer, and/or the lawyer's firm, to disqualification as counsel in the case.

c) the conduct described would result in an immediate mistrial.

d) the conduct described would disqualify the attorney in question from ever practicing in that specific court.

10. If you see the term "subject to civil liability" on the MPRE, it means:

a) the conduct described could subject the lawyer or the lawyer's law firm to civil liability such as malpractice, breach of fiduciary duty, or misrepresentation.

b) the conduct described could subject the lawyer or the lawyer's firm to public sanction by the civil law authorities, such as censure, rebuke, or loss of license.

c) the conduct described could require the lawyer or the lawyer's firm to immediately withdraw from the case to maintain civility and avoid an appearance of impropriety.

d) the conduct described requires the judge to restore order in the court and find the offending attorney liable for contempt.

11. If you see the term "subject to criminal liability" on the MPRE, it means:

a) the conduct described bars the lawyer or firm from collecting fees in any case on which the lawyer or firm worked subsequent to the filing of a criminal charge against the lawyer or firm.

b) the conduct described, if proven to be true, automatically subjects the lawyer or the lawyer's firm to the same penalty imposed against their criminal defendant client.

c) the conduct described is a crime for which the attorney and/or the attorney's firm must be found liable as they are officers of the court and have presumptive knowledge of criminal law.

d) the conduct described could subject the lawyer or firm to criminal liability such as aiding and abetting a criminal action, fraud, or obstruction of justice.

12. The "disciplining authority" of an attorney is:

a) the attorney's supervisor within the law firm or, for a sole practitioner, the acting president of the local bar association.

b) the local bar association's membership sitting in their regulatory capacity.

c) the agency charged with regulating the legal profession, usually the state bar association.

d) the prosecutor in the judicial district.

13. An attorney is referred to as a "certified specialist" if the attorney has:

a) taken the proscribed number of continuing legal education credits in the specialization.

b) served as an understudy to a certified specialist in the relevant specialization for at least 24 months.

c) proven expertise to the chief justice of the state supreme court during an in-camera interview.

d) been granted the certification by the appropriate regulatory authority.

14. The terms "informed consent" and "consent after consultation":

a) have two separate and distinct meanings within the MPRE.

b) mean the same thing on the MPRE.

c) in criminal cases, have more serious ethical implications for an attorney due to the liberty interest of the client being at stake.

d) must be explained by an attorney to a client under arrest and subject to custodial interrogation. Failure to explain the terms is an ethical violation.

ANSWERS TO REVIEW QUESTIONS

Answer 1

The correct answer is choice D. 50 questions count. There are 10 additional experimental questions. You cannot determine which questions count toward your score. Therefore, you should answer all the questions.

Answer 2

The correct answer is choice A. You must pick the "best" answer from four possible choices in response to a fact pattern question.

Answer 3

The correct answer is choice B. The MPRE tests knowledge of established standards and rules related to a lawyer's professional conduct.

Answer 4

The correct answer is choice D. Generally established principles in the law of evidence, the Model Code of Judicial Conduct, and the ABA Model Rules of Professional Conduct are all testable on the MPRE.

Answer 5

The correct answer is choice C. General legal reasoning and analysis should be used to analyze local rules or statutes presented on the MPRE.

Answer 6

The correct answer is choice D. Attorneys and judges are subject to discipline under the ABA Model Professional Rules of Conduct or Model Code of Judicial Conduct.

Answer 7

The correct answer is choice C. An MPRE question testing the appropriateness of a lawyer's conduct may ask "May an attorney do X or Y?" Alternatively, the question may ask "Is it proper for an attorney to do X or Y?"

Answer 8

The correct answer is choice C. A litigation sanction is a sanction imposed by a court during the course of litigation upon an attorney and/or the attorney's firm for inappropriate conduct. Such sanctions may include, but are not limited to, contempt, fine, fees, or disqualification.

Answer 9

The correct answer is choice B. Disqualification refers to counsel and/or the firm's inability to continue representing a client due to their conduct in violation of a relevant ethical rule.

Answer 10

The correct answer is choice A. An attorney or firm subject to civil liability is subject to legal action in civil court for violating a duty owed to a client.

Answer 11

The correct answer is choice D. An attorney or firm subject to criminal liability is subject to legal action in criminal court for violating criminal laws.

Answer 12

The correct answer is choice C. In most states, the state bar association has regulatory authority, including disciplinary authority, over members of the bar.

Answer 13

The correct answer is choice D. The present method of certification as a specialist is established by the appropriate authority regulating the practice of law within a state.

Answer 14

The correct answer is choice B. The terms "informed consent" and "consent after consultation" have the same meaning on the MPRE.

MPRE OUTLINE

When studying the rules and standards governing lawyers' professional duties, you should pay special attention to whether a rule *requires* a lawyer to do something, or merely *recommends* or *permits* a lawyer to do something. The keywords "shall" and "must" indicate a required (or prohibited) action, while the keywords "should" and "may" indicate recommended or permitted actions.

I. REGULATION OF THE LEGAL PROFESSION

A. Power of Courts and Other Bodies to Regulate Lawyers

1) EXPRESS AUTHORITY

The Rules provide that the "ultimate authority over the legal profession is vested largely in the courts." Model Rules of Prof'l Conduct Preamble [10]. This authority is both *express* and *inherent*. Express authority includes enforcement of the Rules either in cases before the court, which could lead to disciplinary proceedings, or judicial review of determinations from disciplinary proceedings.

2) INHERENT AUTHORITY

In addition to express legal authority, courts also possess certain inherent powers to regulate lawyers. Accordingly, the authority of courts to regulate is not necessarily limited to the express scope of legal provisions (such as rules of professional conduct or court rules). The courts' inherent powers to regulate lawyers flow from various sources.

a) Officer of the Court

Lawyers are officers of the court and are subject to the courts' express and inherent authority to regulate them. Arguably, the Rules themselves provide a basis for a court's inherent authority to regulate lawyers. The Rules describe lawyers in many ways, including that they are "officer[s] of the legal system". Model Rules of Prof'l Conduct Preamble [1]

Specifically, as court officers, lawyers' legal and ethical responsibilities are not restricted to legal provisions, such as the Rules, that govern their conduct. Rather, the Rules and other legal provisions serve as the express basis of lawyers' responsibilities, but not as their limit. In other words, as court officers, lawyers must also fulfill additional inherent obligations and duties.

b) Professional Liability Standards

The courts' exercise of inherent authority has involved using the Rules in other ways, such as for guidance in establishing standards of legal malpractice liability, as illustrated below:

> As to whether ethical standards are admissible as some evidence of this standard of care, courts take four different approaches . . . . First, some courts hold that professional ethical standards conclusively establish the duty of care and any violation constitutes negligence per se. Second, a minority of courts finds that a

professional ethical violation establishes a rebuttable presumption of legal malpractice. Third, a large majority of courts treats professional ethical standards as evidence of the common law duty of care. Finally, one court has found professional ethical standards inadmissible as evidence of an attorney's duty of care.

Allen v. Lefkoff, Duncan, Grimes & Dermer, P.C., 265 Ga. 374, 453 S.E.2d 719 (1995). Such judicial treatment of the professional ethical standards is an example of the courts' exercise of the inherent power to regulate lawyers, rather than an example of the courts' express authority under the Rules. Using a Rule violation as the basis for civil liability is not an exercise of the courts' *express* power to regulate lawyers because the Rules "are designed to provide guidance to lawyers and to provide a structure for regulating conduct through disciplinary agencies. They are not designed to be a basis for civil liability. Nevertheless, since the Rules do establish standards of conduct by lawyers, a lawyer's violation of a Rule may be evidence of breach of the applicable standard of conduct." Model Rules of Prof'l Conduct Scope [20]. Therefore, the courts' use of the Rules as presumptions regarding civil liability, which is somewhat in conflict with the Rules themselves, could be considered the courts' exercise of its inherent power to regulate lawyers.

        c)   Additional Methods of Exercising Inherent Authority

Courts also exercise the inherent power to regulate lawyers when they take the following types of action (i.e., the following would be examples of the courts' inherent power if they are not acting pursuant to the Rules or any other express legal provision):

- holding lawyers in contempt of court;
- sanctioning lawyers by requiring them to relinquish legal fees; or
- dismissing an action.

B.   Admission to the Profession

A non-attorney individual may apply for admission to the bar of a jurisdiction. Also, an attorney in one jurisdiction can apply for admission to the bar in another jurisdiction. The admissions process requires an applicant to file forms on which the applicant must make certain statements or disclosures. The Rules require that these statements be *truthful* and that these disclosures be *complete*.

★   1)   <u>BAR ADMISSION</u>

★★   a)   False Statements or Nondisclosures

An applicant for admission to the bar must not (1) knowingly make a false statement of material fact; or (2) fail to disclose a fact necessary to correct a misapprehension known by the applicant to have arisen in the matter; or (3) knowingly fail to respond to a lawful demand for information from an admissions or disciplinary authority. However, an applicant does not need to disclose information otherwise protected by Rule 1.6 (referred to as the "Rule of Confidentiality"), which is addressed later. Model Rules of Prof'l Conduct R. 8.1.

C.   Regulation After Admission

Once a lawyer is admitted to the state bar, the lawyer becomes subject to regulation under the Rules by the professional authority of the jurisdiction. Violation of the Rules may result in disciplinary action by the disciplinary authority of the jurisdiction.

1)   ACTIONS SUBJECTING ATTORNEY TO DISCIPLINE

a)   Violating the Rules

(1) Lawyer's Acts

As a general matter, a lawyer is subject to discipline when violating, or attempting to violate, the Rules.

(2) Acts of Other

A lawyer is also subject to discipline for knowingly assisting or inducing another person to do so, or do so through the acts of a third person, as when a lawyer requests or instructs an agent to violate the Rules on the lawyer's behalf. Model Rules of Prof'l Conduct R. 8.4 cmt. [1].

b)   Criminal Actions

Although a lawyer is criminally liable for criminal law violations, a lawyer also faces professional consequences for offenses that indicate a lack of certain characteristics relevant to legal practice. Offenses involving violence, dishonesty, breach of trust, or serious interference with the administration of justice are in that category.

c)   Actions Involving Dishonesty

A lawyer may not engage in any conduct involving dishonesty, fraud, deceit, or misrepresentation.

2)   DISCIPLINARY MATTERS

★★   a)   Lawyer's False Statements or Nondisclosures

If a jurisdiction's professional authority commences proceedings against a lawyer, the lawyer must generally respond in writing. These forms or papers may require the lawyer to provide statements and disclosures with respect to a disciplinary matter. The Rules require that these statements be *truthful* and that these disclosures be *complete*.

A lawyer must not knowingly make a false statement of material fact in connection with a disciplinary matter. Also, a lawyer must not fail to disclose a fact necessary to correct a misapprehension known by the person to have arisen in the disciplinary matter, or knowingly fail to respond to a lawful demand for information from a disciplinary authority. This Rule does not require disclosure of information otherwise protected by the Rule of Confidentiality. Model Rules of Prof'l Conduct R. 8.1.

D.   Mandatory and Permissive Reporting of Professional Misconduct

A lawyer must report another lawyer's professional misconduct to a jurisdiction's professional authority.

★★★   1)   REPORTING PROFESSIONAL MISCONDUCT

          a)   Lawyer and Lawyer

A lawyer who knows that another lawyer has committed a violation of the Rules that raises a substantial question as to that lawyer's honesty, trustworthiness, and fitness to act as a lawyer *must* inform the appropriate professional authority. Model Rules of Prof'l Conduct R. 8.3(a).

          b)   Lawyer and Judge

Similarly, a lawyer who knows that a judge has committed a violation of the rules of judicial conduct that raises a substantial question as to the judge's fitness for office *must* inform the appropriate authority. Model Rules of Prof'l Conduct R. 8.3(b).

          c)   Exceptions

The Rule does not require disclosure of information otherwise protected by the Rule of Confidentiality or information gained by a lawyer or judge while participating in an approved lawyer assistance program. Model Rules of Prof'l Conduct R. 8.3(c).

★★★★   2)   WHAT CONSTITUTES PROFESSIONAL MISCONDUCT

Any violation of the Rules could constitute professional misconduct. Additionally, the Rules list several additional types of professional misconduct. Specifically, it is professional misconduct for a lawyer to:

- violate the rules: violate or attempt to violate the Rules, knowingly assist or induce another to do so, or do so through the acts of another;
- commit a crime: commit a criminal act that reflects adversely on the lawyer's honesty, trustworthiness or fitness as a lawyer in other respects;
- perpetrate falsehoods: engage in conduct involving dishonesty, fraud, deceit or misrepresentation;
- prejudice justice: engage in conduct that is prejudicial to the administration of justice;
- represent improper influence: state or imply an ability to influence improperly a government agency or official or to achieve results by means that violate the Rules or other law; or
- assist unethical judicial conduct: knowingly assist a judge or judicial officer in conduct that is a violation of applicable rules of judicial conduct or other law.

Model Rules of Prof'l Conduct R. 8.4(a)-(f).

E.   Unauthorized Practice of Law

As a general matter, a law school graduate who has not been admitted to the bar of a jurisdiction is not authorized to practice law in that jurisdiction until the graduate is admitted to the jurisdiction's bar. A lawyer who is admitted to practice law in one jurisdiction can only practice law in another jurisdiction in which the lawyer is not a member of the bar under certain limited circumstances provided by the Rules. The lawyer may violate the Rules by practicing law in another jurisdiction without proper authorization.

★★   1)   UNAUTHORIZED PRACTICE OF LAW

A lawyer must not practice law in a jurisdiction in violation of the regulation of the legal profession in that jurisdiction, or assist another in doing so. Model Rules of Prof'l Conduct R. 5.5(a). An exception applies under limited circumstances when a lawyer who is admitted to the bar of one state seeks to temporarily provide legal services in another state in which the lawyer is not admitted. Model Rules of Prof'l Conduct R. 5.5(c). This limited admission to practice is referred to as "admission pro hac vice."

Note that a lawyer may assist a person who is representing himself. A person is generally permitted to represent himself, and, therefore, a lawyer assisting such a person is not assisting in the unauthorized practice of law.

F.   Multijurisdictional Practice

Under certain limited circumstances, a lawyer who is admitted to the bar in one United States jurisdiction, and not disbarred or suspended from practice in any jurisdiction, may provide legal services on a temporary basis in another jurisdiction. Model Rules of Prof'l Conduct R. 5.5(c).

1)   ASSOCIATION WITH LAWYER IN OTHER JURISDICTION

One such circumstance is when legal services are undertaken in association with a lawyer who is admitted to practice in the other jurisdiction and who actively participates in the matter. Model Rules of Prof'l Conduct R. 5.5(c)(1).

2)   TRIBUNAL PROCEEDING

Another circumstance is when legal services are in, or reasonably related to, a pending or potential proceeding before a tribunal in the lawyer's jurisdiction or the other jurisdiction, if the lawyer, or a person the lawyer is assisting, is authorized by law or order to appear in such proceeding or reasonably expects to be so authorized. Model Rules of Prof'l Conduct R. 5.5(c)(2). Note that the Rules generally use the term tribunal when referring to a court or other similar decision-making authority such as the judicial body of an administrative agency.

3)   ALTERNATIVE DISPUTE RESOLUTION PROCEEDING

A third circumstance is when legal services are related to a potential arbitration, mediation, or other alternative dispute resolution proceeding. A court may authorize an attorney to appear if the services are related to the lawyer's practice in a jurisdiction in which the lawyer is admitted to practice. Model Rules of Prof'l Conduct R. 5.5(c)(3).

4) OTHER CIRCUMSTANCES

A final circumstance is when other legal services are reasonably related to the lawyer's practice in a jurisdiction in which the lawyer is admitted to practice. Model Rules of Prof'l Conduct R. 5.5(c)(4).

 G.   Fee Division with a Non-Lawyer

A lawyer or a law firm must not share legal fees with a non-lawyer, except under the following circumstances.

First, an agreement by a lawyer with the lawyer's firm, partner, or associate may provide for the payment of money, over a reasonable period of time after the lawyer's death, to the lawyer's estate or to one or more specified persons. Model Rules of Prof'l Conduct R. 5.4(a)(1).

Second, a lawyer who purchases the practice of a deceased, disabled, or disappeared lawyer may, pursuant to the provisions of the Rule regarding the sale of a law practice, pay to the estate or other representative of that lawyer the agreed-upon purchase price. Model Rules of Prof'l Conduct R. 5.4(a)(2).

Third, a lawyer or law firm may include non-lawyer employees in a compensation or retirement plan, even though the plan is based in whole or in part on a profit-sharing arrangement. Model Rules of Prof'l Conduct R. 5.4(a)(3).

Fourth, a lawyer may share court-awarded legal fees with a non-profit organization that employed, retained, or recommended employment of the lawyer in the matter. Model Rules of Prof'l Conduct R. 5.4(a)(4).

H.   Law Firm and other Forms of Practice

Several Rules govern the professional conduct of lawyers in law firms. A "law firm" may include a lawyer or lawyers in a law partnership, a sole proprietorship, a professional corporation, or some other association authorized to practice law. Model Rules of Prof'l Conduct R. 1.0(c). In addition, a "law firm" includes lawyers employed in the legal department of an organization (e.g., a corporation) or a legal services organization. *Id.*

I.   Responsibilities of Partners, Managers, Supervisory and Subordinate Lawyers

1)   LAW FIRMS AND ASSOCIATIONS

a)   Responsibilities of Partners and Supervisory Lawyers

(1) Measures of Complying with Rules

A partner in a law firm, or a lawyer who individually or together with other lawyers possesses comparable managerial authority in a law firm, must make reasonable efforts to ensure that the firm implements measures giving reasonable assurance that all lawyers in the firm conform to the Rules. Model Rules of Prof'l Conduct R. 5.1(a).

(a) Scope of Application

The foregoing Rule applies to lawyers having managerial authority over the professional work of more than one lawyer in a partnership, professional corporation, or other association authorized to practice law. Model Rules of Prof'l Conduct R. 5.1 cmt. [1]. It also includes lawyers having comparable managerial authority in a legal services organization or a law department of an enterprise or government agency. *Id.*

(2) Lawyer with Direct Supervisory Authority

A lawyer having direct supervisory authority over another lawyer must make reasonable efforts to ensure that the other lawyer conforms to the Rules of Professional Conduct. Model Rules of Prof'l Conduct R. 5.1(b).

(3) Supervisory Lawyer's Responsibility for Other Lawyer

A supervisory lawyer will be responsible for a subordinate lawyer's violation of an ethical rule if: (1) the supervisory lawyer orders or, with knowledge of the specific conduct, ratifies the conduct involved; or (2) the supervisory lawyer is a partner or has comparable managerial authority in the law firm in which the other lawyer practices, or has direct supervisory authority over the other lawyer, and knows of the conduct at a time when its consequences can be avoided or mitigated but fails to take reasonable remedial action. Model Rules of Prof'l Conduct R. 5.1(c).

★   b)   Responsibilities Regarding Non-Lawyer Assistants

As a general principle, a supervisory lawyer is also responsible for an action by a non-lawyer assistant that violates the Rules if either prong of the foregoing test is satisfied. Model Rules of Prof'l Conduct R. 5.3(c).

Specifically, a supervisory lawyer must make reasonable efforts to ensure that the non-lawyer's conduct is compatible with the professional obligations of the lawyer. Model Rules of Prof'l Conduct R. 5.3(b). A lawyer will be responsible for a non-lawyer's conduct that would constitute a violation of the Rules if engaged in by a lawyer if: (1) the lawyer orders or, with the knowledge of the specific conduct, ratifies the conduct involved; or (2) the lawyer is a partner or has comparable managerial authority in the law firm in which the person is employed, or has direct supervisory authority over the person, and knows of the conduct at a time when its consequences can be avoided or mitigated but fails to take reasonable remedial action. Model Rules of Prof'l Conduct R. 5.3(c). For example, a supervisory lawyer would be responsible for a paralegal's shredding of documents pursuant to the lawyer's instruction. Paralegals are paraprofessional legal assistants.

c)   Responsibilities of a Subordinate Lawyer

As a general principle, a lawyer may not escape responsibility for ethical violations simply because the lawyer acted at someone else's direction. Specifically, a lawyer is bound by the Rules even when the lawyer acted at the direction of another person. Model Rules of Prof'l Conduct R. 5.2(a). A subordinate lawyer does not violate the Rules, however, if that lawyer acts in accordance with a supervisory lawyer's reasonable resolution of a question of professional duty. Model Rules of Prof'l Conduct R. 5.2(b).

d)   Professional Independence of a Lawyer

★   (1) Forming Partnership with Non-Lawyer

A lawyer cannot form a partnership with a non-lawyer if *any* activities of the partnership consist of the practice of law. Model Rules of Prof'l Conduct R. 5.4(b).

                         (2) Lawyer's Professional Judgment

★ A lawyer must not permit a person who recommends, employs, or pays the lawyer to render legal services for another, to direct or regulate the lawyer's professional judgment in rendering such legal services. Model Rules of Prof'l Conduct R. 5.4(c). For example, if a parent pays for the legal services of a child, the lawyer cannot permit the parent to direct or regulate the lawyer's professional judgment.

                         (3) Involvement of Non-Lawyer

★ A lawyer must not practice with, or in the form of, a professional corporation or association authorized to practice law for a profit, if a non-lawyer:

- owns any interest therein, except that a fiduciary representative of the estate of a lawyer may hold the stock or interest of the lawyer for a reasonable time during administration;
- is a director or officer thereof, or occupies the position of similar responsibility in any form of association; or
- has the right to direct or control the professional judgment of a lawyer.

Model Rules of Prof'l Conduct R. 5.4(d).

J.   Restrictions on Right to Practice

The Rules govern the type and nature of contractual restrictions that can be imposed upon a lawyer within a relationship between the lawyer and others.

★★   1)   <u>RESTRICTIONS ON RIGHT TO PRACTICE</u>

a)   Employment or other Relationship

A lawyer must not participate in offering or making a partnership, shareholders, operating, employment, or other similar type of agreement that restricts the right of a lawyer to practice after termination of the relationship, except an agreement concerning benefits upon retirement. Model Rules of Prof'l Conduct R. 5.6(a).

b)   Settlement of a Client Controversy

A lawyer must not participate in offering or making an agreement in which a restriction on the lawyer's right to practice is part of the settlement of a client controversy. Model Rules of Prof'l Conduct R. 5.6(b).

REVIEW QUESTIONS

15. Authority to regulate attorney conduct comes from:

   a) a state's supreme court's published rules of attorney conduct.

   b) mandatory membership in the state bar association which requires adherence to its charter and bylaws.

   c) the Rules of Professional Conduct, express and inherent judicial powers, and all courts' supervisory roles over attorneys acting as officers of the court.

   d) the ABA's charter and bylaws.

16. The ABA's Rules of Professional Conduct are:

   a) the starting point of legal responsibilities.

   b) the end goal of legal responsibilities.

   c) the mandatory path to acting in a legally responsible manner.

   d) the recommended path to acting in a legally responsible manner.

17. A lawyer may not be involved in any conduct involving:

   a) gambling, vice, or morally reprehensible activities.

   b) public intoxication resulting in disturbing the peace.

   c) government-identified terrorist organizations.

   d) dishonesty, fraud, deceit, or misrepresentation.

18. A lawyer must reply to all disciplinary actions against her:

   a) within two business days of receiving notice of them.

   b) truthfully and completely.

   c) immediately and without excuse.

   d) personally and not through legal counsel.

19. A lawyer must report another lawyer's alleged professional misconduct involving:

   a) honesty, trustworthiness, and fitness to act as a lawyer.

   b) questionable moral judgment.

   c) the lawyer's family problems.

   d) the lawyer's contemplation of filing bankruptcy.

20. The following action constitutes professional misconduct:

   a) being arrested for a crime that does not involve dishonesty.

   b) being convicted of driving while under the influence of alcohol or drugs.

   c) inducing another attorney to engage in a highly risky business venture.

   d) attempting to violate the Rules of Professional Conduct but not actually violating them.

21. A person is authorized to practice law when they are:

a) admitted to the state bar.
b) sworn in by the Chief Justice of the state Supreme Court.
c) appearing for the first time in practice before a court.
d) in actual possession of a license to practice law.

22. An attorney filing a Motion to Appear Pro Hoc Vice is an attorney's request to:

    a) appear before a court to contest a client's appearance on vice charges.
    b) bring the person(s) alleged to be involved in a vice crime before the court for questioning.
    c) appear before and practice in a court in a jurisdiction in which the attorney is not admitted.
    d) appear before a disciplinary committee to contest alleged misconduct.

23. Fee splitting by a lawyer with a non-lawyer is strictly prohibited under the following except:

    a) the lawyer and non-lawyer are married and share all income equally.
    b) the lawyer and non-lawyer have executed a fee splitting agreement and filed the same as a matter of public record and provided a copy to the appropriate disciplinary authority for review.
    c) the non-lawyer is a licensed securities dealer or investment advisor working to further the financial interests of the lawyer and the lawyer's clients.
    d) the lawyer pays the estate of a deceased lawyer a sum negotiated as the purchase price for the deceased lawyer's practice.

24. A lawyer with supervisory authority over another lawyer is responsible for the subordinate lawyer's violation of the Rules of Professional Conduct:

    a) even if the supervising lawyer is unaware of the unethical conduct as the supervising lawyer is always responsible for the actions of a subordinate lawyer.
    b) in all circumstances due to the supervising lawyer's role as a supervisor.
    c) if the supervising lawyer knows of or ratifies the unethical conduct, or if the supervising lawyer has direct supervisory authority over the subordinate lawyer and knows of the unethical conduct at a time when the supervisory lawyer could avoid or mitigate the unethical conduct but fails to do so.
    d) even if the supervising lawyer is assured in writing by the subordinate lawyer that the subordinate lawyer's actions are in full compliance with the Rules of Professional Conduct.

25. A subordinate lawyer is bound by Rules of Professional Conduct even when directed by a supervising lawyer, but the subordinate lawyer will not be subject to discipline for violating those rules when:

    a) the subordinate lawyer informs the supervising lawyer of the possible violation of ethical rules but proceeds with the action.
    b) the subordinate lawyer informs the supervising lawyer of the possible violation of

ethical rules and the supervising lawyer threatens to terminate the lawyer's employment unless the lawyer proceeds with the action.

c) the subordinate lawyer acts in accordance with the supervising lawyer's reasonable resolution of a question of professional duty.

d) the supervising lawyer takes full responsibility in writing for all actions and consequences of the subordinate lawyer's actions.

26. No third-party may direct a lawyer's professional, independent decision-making process and, therefore, a lawyer may not:

a) enter into a business relationship with a non-lawyer if the business involves the practice of law or enter into any business form if a non-lawyer owns any interest in the business.

b) invest in any business run by a non-lawyer that provides legal products or services outside of the lawyer's own practice.

c) earn profit from a business the lawyer sold prior to being licensed to practice law but in which the lawyer, as part of the sale agreement, is to be paid a percentage of future profits by the new owner, a non-lawyer.

d) marry an accountant who has sole control of the law firm's financial matters.

27. When a third-party pays for a lawyer to represent a client, the lawyer must:

a) give adequate consideration to the third-party's opinion but make independent decisions with respect to actions taken for the client.

b) give no consideration to the paying third-party who is not the client.

c) abide by the client's wishes unless the client is a minor and the third-party is the minor's parent with authority and control over the client.

d) abide by the third party's direction insofar as it does not harm the client.

28. If a lawyer enters into an agreement that restricts the lawyer's ability to practice law as a condition of a settlement in a breach of contract action with another local law firm, the lawyer is:

a) not violating ethical rules because the lawyer may choose when and where to practice law.

b) violating ethical rules because the lawyer may not enter into any agreement that may restrict the lawyer's ability to practice law.

c) violating ethical rules because the lawyer may not enter into any agreement that may restrict the ability to practice law, except a retiring attorney may agree to limit the right to practice law in exchange for retirement benefits from the law firm.

d) not violating ethical rules because the attorney is exercising a constitutional right to free association.

ANSWERS TO REVIEW QUESTIONS

Answer 15

The correct answer is choice C. Authority to regulate attorney conduct comes from three sources: 1) the Rules of Professional Conduct, 2) inherent judicial powers, and 3) all courts' regulatory roles over attorneys acting as officers of the court.

Answer 16

The correct answer is choice A. The ABA Rules of Professional Conduct are the starting point for legal responsibilities of a lawyer.

Answer 17

The correct answer is choice D. A lawyer may not be involved in any conduct involving dishonesty, fraud, deceit, or misrepresentation.

Answer 18

The correct answer is choice B. A lawyer must reply truthfully and completely to all disciplinary actions against her.

Answer 19

The correct answer is choice A. A lawyer's alleged professional misconduct involving honesty, trustworthiness, and fitness to act as a lawyer must be reported by another lawyer aware of the alleged professional misconduct.

Answer 20

The correct answer is choice D. Violating or attempting to violate the Rules of Professional Responsibility, knowingly assisting or inducing another lawyer to do so, or knowingly assisting or inducing a judge to violate the Code of Judicial Conduct always constitutes professional misconduct.

Answer 21

The correct answer is choice A. A person is authorized to practice law within a jurisdiction when they are admitted to that jurisdiction's bar.

Answer 22

The correct answer is choice C. An attorney who files a Motion to Appear Pro Hoc Vice requests that the court allow the attorney to appear and practice before that court for a limited time and purpose if the attorney is not admitted to practice in that jurisdiction.

Answer 23

The correct answer is choice D. Fee splitting by a lawyer with non-lawyers is allowed if the lawyer pays the estate of a deceased lawyer a sum negotiated as the purchase price for the deceased lawyer's practice, payments to non-lawyers are made over time after a lawyer's death as part of the estate, or non-lawyer employees are paid in a compensation or retirement plan based in part on a profit-sharing arrangement.

Answer 24

The correct answer is choice C. A lawyer with supervisory authority over another lawyer is responsible for the subordinate lawyer's violation of the Rules of Professional Conduct if: 1) the supervising lawyer knows of or ratifies the unethical conduct; or 2) if the supervising lawyer has direct supervisory authority over the subordinate lawyer and knows of the unethical conduct at a time when the supervisory lawyer could avoid or mitigate the unethical conduct but fails to do so.

Answer 25

The correct answer is choice C. A subordinate lawyer will not be subject to discipline for violating the Rules of Professional Conduct if the subordinate lawyer acts in accordance with the supervising lawyer's reasonable resolution of a question of professional duty.

Answer 26

The correct answer is choice A. No third-party may direct a lawyer's professional, independent decision-making process; therefore, a lawyer may not enter into a business relationship with a non-lawyer if the business involves the practice of law or enter into any business form if a non-lawyer owns any interest in the business.

Answer 27

The correct answer is choice B. The fact that a third-party refers or even pays for legal services for another person does not allow the lawyer to follow the direction of that third-party who is not the lawyer's client.

Answer 28

The correct answer is choice C. A lawyer may not enter into an agreement that may restrict the lawyer's ability to practice law, except a retiring attorney may agree to limit the right to practice law in exchange for retirement benefits from the law firm.

II.   THE CLIENT-LAWYER RELATIONSHIP

A.   Formation of Client-Lawyer Relationship

1)   MUTUAL AGREEMENT

A client-lawyer relationship is created when a person expresses to a lawyer the person's intent that the lawyer provide legal services for the person, and the lawyer expresses to the person consent to provide legal services. Restatement of the Law Governing Lawyers, Third, § 14(1)(a).

As a general matter, a lawyer usually can exercise discretion in deciding whether to represent a person who requests the lawyer's representation. This principle, however, is subject to exceptions, such as when a court orders a lawyer to represent a criminal defendant. Restatement of the Law Governing Lawyers, Third, § 14(2).

a)   Accepting Appointments

Under the Rules, a lawyer must not seek to avoid appointment by a tribunal to represent a person, except for good cause. Good cause would exist if:

- representing the client is likely to result in violation of the Rules or other law;
- representing the client is likely to result in an unreasonable financial burden on the lawyer; or
- the client or the cause is so repugnant to the lawyer as to be likely to impair the client-lawyer relationship or the lawyer's ability to represent the client.

Model Rules of Prof'l Conduct R. 6.2.

b)   Detrimental Reliance

Another way a client-lawyer relationship might form is if, after a client requests representation, the lawyer does not express any opposition to being hired and it would have been reasonable for the lawyer to have declined this representation. In such a situation, the lawyer would be obligated to represent the client who reasonably and detrimentally relied upon being represented by the lawyer and consequently did not procure the services of another lawyer. Restatement of the Law Governing Lawyers, Third, § 14(1)(b).

The Restatement summarizes this requirement by stating that a client-lawyer relationship arises when a person manifests to the lawyer the person's intent that the lawyer provide legal services for the person and the lawyer fails to manifest a lack of consent to do so, but the lawyer knows or reasonably should know that the person reasonably relies on the lawyer to provide the services. *Id.*

(1) Example

Suppose a potential client contacts a domestic relations law firm. In response to the client's request for legal representation at an emergency child custody hearing in two weeks, a lawyer takes the potential client's paperwork and assures the client not to worry about the hearing. During the next 11 days, neither the lawyer nor the law firm contacts the potential client, who does not contact them or any other lawyers. The lawyer calls the potential client on the 12th day and declines the representation. In this situation, a court could find that a client-lawyer relationship exists based on the lawyer's delayed expression of an absence of intent to be retained.

2)   ETHICAL CONSIDERATIONS FOR ACCEPTING CLIENTS

Some of the Rules provide guidance as to when a lawyer can accept or reject representation of a client. A lawyer should know, consider, and apply these Rules when making a discretionary decision whether to accept or reject the representation of a potential client. For example, a lawyer should reject representation of a client if the lawyer lacks the requisite legal competence to handle the matter. Model Rules of Prof'l Conduct R. 1.1. Similarly, the Rules prohibiting lawyers from counseling a client to engage in, or assisting a client with, criminal or fraudulent conduct relate to whether or not a lawyer may represent a client. Model Rules of Prof'l Conduct R. 1.2(a). Also, the Rules regarding conflict of interest are controlling with respect to whether a lawyer may represent a client if doing so would result in a conflict of interest. Model Rules of Prof'l Conduct Rs. 1.7-1.12.

A lawyer can accept representation of a client even if the lawyer thinks that the client will not succeed in a matter. Accordingly, a lawyer should not reject representation of a potential client on the basis of the lawyer's personal opposition to the client's legal position. However, a lawyer should reject representation of a potential client if the matter is completely baseless. Model Rules of Prof'l Conduct R. 3.1.

★   B.   Scope, Objective, and Means of the Representation

1)   SCOPE OF REPRESENTATION AND ALLOCATION OF AUTHORITY

a)   General Considerations

Both the lawyer and client have authority and responsibility with respect to the objectives and means of the legal representation. In order to analyze the allocation of authority between client and lawyer, one would use the "objectives versus means" test. Annotated Model Rules of Professional Conduct, Rule 1.2, p. 36 (Sixth ed., ABA Center for Professional Responsibility).

(1) Client Decides Objectives of Representation

The client has ultimate authority to determine the objectives to be served by legal representation. For example, the client makes the final decision about whether to commence a cause of action or settle a civil matter.

A lawyer must abide by a client's decisions concerning the objectives of representation. Model

Rules of Prof'l Conduct R. 1.2(a). In a criminal case, the lawyer must abide by the client's decision, after consultation with the lawyer, regarding:

- what plea will be entered,
- whether to waive a jury trial, and
- whether the client will testify. Id.

(2) Lawyer Decides Means for Objectives

The lawyer must consult with the client regarding the means (e.g., technical, legal, and tactical matters) for pursuing the client's objectives. A lawyer ultimately decides the means for pursuing the objectives.

(3) Lawyer Has Implied Authority to Act for Client

The lawyer may act as is impliedly authorized to represent the client. Model Rules of Prof'l Conduct R. 1.2(a).

b) Client with Diminished Capacity

When a client's capacity to make adequately considered decisions in connection with representation is diminished, whether because of minority status, mental impairment, or for some other reason, the lawyer must, as far as reasonably possible, maintain a normal client-lawyer relationship with the client. Model Rules of Prof'l Conduct R. 1.14(a).

If a lawyer reasonably believes that the client has diminished capacity, is at risk of substantial physical, financial or other harm unless action is taken, and cannot adequately act in the client's own interest, the lawyer may take reasonably necessary protective action, including consulting with individuals or entities that have the ability to take action to protect the client and, in appropriate cases, seeking the appointment of a guardian *ad litem*, conservator, or guardian. Model Rules of Prof'l Conduct R. 1.14(b).

Information relating to the representation of a client with diminished capacity is protected by the Rule regarding confidentiality. When taking reasonably necessary protective action, the lawyer is impliedly authorized under the Rule of confidentiality to reveal information about the client to the extent reasonably necessary to protect the client's interests. *Id.* Model Rules of Prof'l Conduct R. 1.14(c).

C. Decision-Making Authority – Actual and Apparent

1) ALLOCATION OF AUTHORITY

A client and a lawyer may generally agree as to which of them will make certain decisions, and the client may instruct the lawyer during representation. Restatement of the Law Governing Lawyers, Third, § 21(1)-(2). A lawyer may use any lawful means to advance the client's objectives. *Id.* at § 21(3).

a)   Authority Always Reserved to Client

A client in a civil matter always has authority to decide on settlement of a claim and whether to appeal. *Id.* at § 22(1). A defendant in a criminal case has authority to decide on making a plea, having a jury trial, testifying, and whether to appeal. *Id.*

b)   Authority Always Reserved to Lawyer

A lawyer has authority, which neither a client agreement nor instruction can trump: 1) to decline performing, counseling, or assisting with acts that the lawyer reasonably believes to be unlawful; and 2) to take actions or make decisions in the representation that the lawyer reasonably believes are required by law or court order. *Id.* at § 23(1).

2)   WHEN LAWYER HAS ACTUAL OR APPARENT AUTHORITY

a)   Lawyer's Actual Authority

A lawyer has actual authority to act for a client when:

- the act is always reserved to the lawyer (as described above);
- the client has actually authorized the lawyer to act; or
- the client has ratified (subsequently consented to) the act.

Id. at § 26.

b)   Lawyer's Apparent Authority

A lawyer has apparent authority to act for a client if a tribunal or the third party *reasonably assumes* that the lawyer is authorized to do the act based on the client's expressions of such authorization. *Id.* at § 27 (emphasis added).

★   **D.   Counsel and Assistance Within the Bounds of the Law**
★

As a general matter, a lawyer's assistance to a client cannot go beyond the limits of the law. A lawyer cannot counsel a client to engage in, or assist a client in, conduct that the lawyer knows is criminal or fraudulent. Model Rules of Prof'l Conduct R. 1.2(d). However, a lawyer may discuss the legal consequences of any proposed course of conduct with a client. *Id.* A lawyer may also counsel or assist a client to make a good faith effort to determine the validity, scope, meaning, or application of the law. *Id.*

★★★   **E.   Termination of the Client-Lawyer Relationship**

1)   DECLINING OR TERMINATING REPRESENTATION

Termination or withdrawal of legal representation may be either mandatory (i.e., required) or permissive (i.e., voluntary).

a) Discharge by Lawyer--Mandatory Withdrawal

Generally, a lawyer cannot represent a client or, if representation has commenced, *must* withdraw from the representation of a client if:

- the representation will result in violation of the Rules or other law;
- the lawyer's physical or mental condition materially impairs the lawyer's ability to represent the client; or
- the lawyer is discharged.

Model Rules of Prof'l Conduct R. 1.16(a).

b) Discharge by Lawyer--Permissive Withdrawal

An alternative to mandatory withdrawal by a lawyer is permissive withdrawal. The lawyer *may* withdraw from representation in some circumstances. For example, a lawyer can withdraw representation if:

- withdrawal can be accomplished without material adverse effect on the client's interests;
- the client persists in a course of action involving the lawyer's services that the lawyer reasonably believes is criminal or fraudulent;
- the client has used the lawyer's services to perpetrate a crime or fraud;
- the client insists upon taking action that the lawyer considers repugnant or with which the lawyer has a fundamental disagreement;
- the client fails substantially to fulfill an obligation to the lawyer regarding the lawyer's services and has been given reasonable warning that the lawyer will withdraw unless the obligation is fulfilled;
- the representation will result in an unreasonable financial burden on the lawyer or has been rendered unreasonably difficult by the client; or
- other good cause exists for withdrawal.

Model Rules of Prof'l Conduct R. 1.16(b).

(1) Obligation to Tribunal

A lawyer must comply with applicable law requiring notice to or permission of a tribunal when terminating a representation, and when ordered to do so by a tribunal, a lawyer must continue representation notwithstanding good cause for terminating the representation. Model Rules of Prof'l Conduct R. 1.16(c). In other words, a tribunal (e.g., court) may refuse to allow an attorney to withdraw from a representation.

(2) Discharge by Client

The client-lawyer relationship can be terminated at the will of a client; however, a lawyer may be entitled to quasi-contract damages (i.e., unjust enrichment and promissory estoppel). Model Rules of Prof'l Conduct R. 1.16 cmt. [4].

(3) Duties upon Discharge

As a general matter, the client's position should not be jeopardized by withdrawal. A lawyer must take steps to the extent reasonably practicable to protect a client's interests, such as:

- giving reasonable notice to the client,
- allowing time for employment of other counsel,
- surrendering files, papers and property to which the client is entitled, and
- refunding any advance payment (i.e., retainer) of a fee that has not been earned or incurred.
- Model Rules of Prof'l Conduct R. 1.16(d).

A lawyer may retain papers relating to the client to the extent permitted by other law. *Id.*

F.   Client-Lawyer Contracts

1)   GENERAL RULE

The Restatement provides that a contract between a client and lawyer regarding their relationship, including a contract modifying an existing contract, usually can be enforced by either of them if the contract meets all applicable requirements. Restatement of the Law Governing Lawyers, Third, § 18(1). The client, however, may be able avoid the contract under certain circumstances.

a)   Exception for Subsequent Formation or Modification

If the contract or modification is made more than a reasonable time after the lawyer has commenced representation of a client, the client can avoid the contract *unless* the lawyer shows that the contract and circumstances of its formation were fair and reasonable to the client. *Id.*

b)   Exception for Post-Representation Formation

If the contract is made after the lawyer has finished providing services, the client can avoid the contract if the client was not informed of the facts needed to evaluate the appropriateness of the lawyer's compensation or other benefits conferred on the lawyer by the contract. *Id.*

c)   Interpretation of Contract – Reasonable Person Standard

A tribunal should construe a contract between a client and a lawyer as a reasonable person in the client's circumstances would have construed it. Restatement of the Law Governing Lawyers, Third, § 18(2).

2)   AGREEMENTS LIMITING CLIENT OR LAWYER DUTIES

a)   Lawyer and Client Can Limit Lawyer's Duties

A client and lawyer may agree to reasonably limit a duty the lawyer would otherwise owe to the client if: 1) the client is adequately informed and consents; and 2) the terms of the limitation are reasonable given the circumstances. Restatement of the Law Governing Lawyers, Third, § 19(1).

b)   Lawyer Can Waive Client's Duties

A lawyer may also agree to waive a client's duty to pay or other duty owed to the lawyer. Restatement of the Law Governing Lawyers, Third, § 19(2).

G.   Communications with Client

1)   DUTY TO INFORM AND CONSULT WITH CLIENT

In general, reasonable communication between a lawyer and client is necessary for the client to participate effectively in the representation. Model Rules of Prof'l Conduct R. 1.4 cmt. [1]. In particular, a lawyer must:

- promptly inform the client of any decision or circumstance for which the client's informed consent is required;
- reasonably consult with the client about the means by which the client's objectives are to be accomplished;
- keep a client reasonably informed about the status of the matter, including significant developments relating to the representation;
- promptly comply with reasonable requests for information and copies of significant documents to keep the client so informed; and
- consult with the client about any relevant limitation on the lawyer's conduct when the lawyer knows that the client expects assistance not permitted by the Rules or other law.

Model Rules of Prof'l Conduct R. 1.4(a).

Additionally, a lawyer must explain a matter to the extent reasonably necessary to enable the client to make an informed decision regarding the representation. Model Rules of Prof'l Conduct R. 1.4(b).

H.   Fees

1)   FEE AGREEMENTS

a)   General Principles

Fees for legal services are set by agreement between the lawyer and client. The agreement must be in writing and clearly set forth the terms of the representation. The fee must be reasonable under the totality of the circumstances, including the time, skill, and labor required. The fee should be set at the commencement of the representation or shortly thereafter. The fee cannot be unconscionable.

b)   Reasonable Fee Requirement

A lawyer cannot make an agreement for, charge, or collect an unreasonable fee or unreasonable amount for expenses. The factors to be considered when determining the reasonableness of a fee include, but are not limited to:

- the time and labor required;
- the novelty and difficulty of the questions involved;
- the skill required to perform the legal service properly;
- the likelihood, if apparent to the client, that the acceptance of the particular employment will preclude other employment by the lawyer;
- the fee customarily charged in the locality for similar legal services;
- the amount involved and the results obtained;
- the time limitations imposed by the client or by the circumstances;
- the nature and length of the professional relationship with the client;
- the experience, reputation, and ability of the lawyer doing the work; and
- whether the fee is fixed or contingent.

Model Rules of Prof'l Conduct R. 1.5(a).

★

c)   Communications Regarding Fees

Generally, the scope of the representation, the basis or rate of the fee, and the expenses for which the client will be responsible must be communicated to the client, preferably in writing, before or within a reasonable time after commencing the representation. Model Rules of Prof'l Conduct R. 1.5(b). This Rule, however, does not apply when a lawyer regularly represents a client and charges the same basis or rate each time. *Id.* In either case, any changes in the basis or rate of the fee or expenses must be communicated to the client. *Id.*

★★★

2)   CONTINGENCY FEES

a)   Prohibited for Criminal and Domestic Matters

Contingency fees are generally permissible, except in criminal or domestic relations cases. Model Rules of Prof'l Conduct R. 1.5(c)-(d). Specifically, a lawyer must not enter into an arrangement for, charge, or collect: (1) a contingent fee for representing a defendant in criminal case; or (2) any fee in a domestic relations matter, the payment or amount of which is contingent upon the securing of a divorce or upon the amount of alimony or support, or property settlement in lieu thereof. Model Rules of Prof'l Conduct R. 1.5(d).

b)   Contingency Fee Agreements

A contingent fee agreement must be in writing and signed by the client and must state the method by which the fee is to be determined, including:

- the percentage or percentages that will accrue to the lawyer in the event of settlement, trial, or appeal;
- litigation and other expenses to be deducted from the recovery, and
- whether such expenses are to be deducted before or after the contingent fee is calculated.

Model Rules of Prof'l Conduct R. 1.5(c).

The agreement must clearly notify the client of any expenses for which the client will be liable, regardless of whether the client is the prevailing party. *Id.* Upon conclusion of a contingent fee matter, the lawyer must provide the client with a written statement describing the outcome of the matter and, if there is a recovery, showing the remittance to the client and the method of its determination. *Id.*

★   3)   <u>FEE SPLITTING WITH OTHER LAWYERS</u>

Under the Rules, a division of a fee between lawyers who are not in the same firm is permissible only if:

- the division is in proportion to the services performed by each lawyer or each lawyer assumes joint responsibility for the representation;
- the client agrees to the arrangement, including the share each lawyer will receive, and the agreement is confirmed in writing; and
- the total fee is reasonable.

Model Rules of Prof'l Conduct R. 1.5(e).

I.   Sale of Law Practice

A lawyer or law firm can sell or purchase a law practice under the following circumstances:

- the seller ceases to engage in the private practice of law, or in the area of practice that has been sold, in the geographic area or in the jurisdiction in which the practice has been conducted;
- the entire practice, or the entire area of practice, is sold to one or more lawyers or law firms;
- client fees are not increased by reason of the sale;
- the seller gives written notice to each of the seller's clients regarding: (1) the proposed sale; (2) the client's right to retain other counsel or to take possession of the file; and (3) the fact that the client's consent will be presumed if the client takes no action within ninety days of receipt of the notice. If a client cannot be provided with notice, representation of the client may be transferred to the

purchaser only upon entry of a court order.

Model Rules of Prof'l Conduct R. 1.17.

REVIEW QUESTIONS

29. A lawyer does not have to represent any client unless appointed by a court to do so in a criminal case. Even then, the lawyer may refuse to represent the client for good cause shown if:

    e) the lawyer knows, beyond all reasonable doubt, that the client is guilty.

    f) the lawyer will lose potential business in the community.

    g) the client or the cause is so repugnant to the lawyer as to likely impair the lawyer-client relationship or representation of the client, or representing the client would violate the Rules of Professional Conduct or the law, or cause the lawyer undue financial burden.

    h) other lawyers in the firm unanimously oppose the lawyer's representation of a particular defendant.

30. A lawyer should reject representation of a client if:

    a) the client has committed a heinous act that offends the lawyer.

    b) the client asks the lawyer to seek payment for legal fees from friends and family members more than one time.

    c) the client's flirtatious spouse repeatedly distracts the lawyer's attention from the client.

    d) the position of the client is legally baseless.

31. The ultimate authority to determine the objectives of any legal representation rests with:

    a) the lawyer.

    b) the client.

    c) the lawyer and client together.

    d) the person paying the lawyer's fees.

32. In a criminal case, the lawyer must abide by the client's decision regarding:

    a) how to cross-examine a hostile witness personally known to the client.

    b) whether the client will testify and whether to waive a jury trial.

    c) whether to engage in reciprocal discovery after the defendant's discovery motion is granted.

    d) the percentage of fees to be paid if the client pleads guilty by reason of mental disease or defect.

33. If an attorney represents a client with diminished capacity, the lawyer must attempt to maintain a normal lawyer-client relationship with the client. If the lawyer reasonably believes the client is at risk of substantial physical, financial, or other harm, the lawyer may take reasonably necessary protective action such as seeking a guardian or conservator. When taking protective action, a lawyer is:

    a) implicitly authorized to reveal information about the client, but only to the extent reasonably necessary to protect the client's interest.

b) implicitly authorized to request a court to remove the lawyer from the representation and appoint an attorney with specialty expertise to handle the matters involving the client's diminished capacity.

c) explicitly authorized to take all reasonable actions to protect the client.

d) explicitly authorized to hire additional professionals and attorneys to address the special needs of the client.

34. When a lawyer discusses with a client a course of criminal conduct being contemplated by the client, the lawyer:

   a) must advise the client to cease such communications lest the lawyer be forced to turn the client over to a law enforcement authority.

   b) may discuss with a client the nature and ramifications of the proposed criminal conduct.

   c) should dissuade the client from profiting or otherwise improving the client's legal situation by such conduct.

   d) may ignore such proposed criminal conduct as the discussion of any such conduct is protected by the lawyer-client privilege.

35. A lawyer must withdraw or decline representation of a client if:

   a) the client's physical or mental condition impairs representation.

   b) the lawyer's physical or mental condition impairs representation.

   c) the client files a complaint against the lawyer with a disciplinary authority.

   d) the lawyer was previously romantically involved with the client.

36. A lawyer may withdraw from representing a client if:

   a) good cause for withdrawal exists or, even if good cause for withdrawal does not exist, the lawyer's withdrawal from representation has no material adverse effect on the client's interest.

   b) the lawyer secures another client who pays substantially more and will require greater time and attention.

   c) legal representation becomes more difficult due to the client's bad temperament.

   d) the client fails to appear for appointments with the lawyer.

37. If ordered by a court, a lawyer must continue representation of a client:

   a) unless the client's cause sincerely offends the lawyer.

   b) notwithstanding good cause for terminating the representation.

   c) but not if the client refuses to pay for the lawyer's services.

   d) only if the client posts a bond to pay for the court-ordered services.

38. A client can terminate the lawyer-client relationship at any time, but the lawyer may be entitled to:

a) quasi-contract damages or compensation for services rendered, and the client's position must not be jeopardized.

b) full compensation for the agreed upon contract amount or the balance of the retainer if the client unjustifiably breached the employment contract.

c) nothing because the lawyer failed to bring the client's case to a close.

d) a fair and reasonable compensation package as determined by the court.

39. After being discharged by a client, a lawyer has duty to:

a) take reasonable steps to protect the client's interest, including turning over files to the client to aid in continued representation and returning the balance of any retainer.

b) have no further contact with the client to avoid any potential conflict of interest with a new lawyer.

c) take reasonable steps to collect all past due fees which will enable the lawyer to close the file and not sue the client thereby hindering the client's legal position.

d) notify all potential adverse parties that the lawyer no longer represents the client and that the lawyer is available for representation, barring any conflict of interest.

40. A client may be able to avoid a lawyer-client contract if:

a) the client can show the lawyer's conduct and performance were beneath the standard of a reasonable lawyer under the same or similar circumstances.

b) a reasonable person would interpret the contract as fair and reasonable but for the lawyer's failing to disclose its terms and conditions.

c) it is formed after the lawyer has finished providing services and the client was not informed of the facts needed to evaluate the appropriateness of the lawyer's compensation or benefits through the contract.

d) a judicial representative tells the client that the contract can be avoided.

41. A lawyer and client can agree to limit the lawyer's duties if the client is:

a) provided with a written list of limited services the lawyer will and will not provide.

b) adequately informed and consents to the limitation, and the terms of the limitation are reasonable in the circumstances.

c) a prepaid legal services client and the limited duties are previously set forth in the prepaid legal services contract.

d) paying only a fee-for-services basis, and the list of available services is limited in writing.

 42. A lawyer cannot charge a client a fee:

a) if the client cannot afford any legal representation because the rules mandate attorneys provide such clients pro bono representation upon presentation.

b) if the client declares bankruptcy after the initiation of the legal representation.

c) if there is no written fee agreement as required under the Statute of Frauds.

d) without the client's agreement to do so.

43. Contingency fees are permissible:

a) if the fee agreement is in writing, is signed by the client, and includes the percentages earned by the lawyer under all circumstances and whether expenses are deducted before or after the contingent fee is calculated.

b) only in personal injury cases when the lawyer for the injured party has executed lien agreements with medical and related service providers who are thereby guaranteed payment prior to the lawyer's contingency fee.

c) when the lawyer and client have engaged in an arm's length negotiation over the contingency fees which are set forth in a clear writing understandable by a non-lawyer.

d) in divorce cases only if both parties to the divorce agree to them and the amount is limited to avoid unjust hardship on either party.

44. Fee splitting between lawyer in different firms is permitted if:

a) the court approves the fees after conclusion of the case and considers the nature and scope of each attorney's representation.

b) the client has previously waived any conflict of interest by the lawyers in both firms.

c) the client has contracted in writing with both lawyers and allocated the percentage of fees to each based upon a reasonable assessment of each attorney's satisfactory performance in the matter.

d) division is in proportion to services performed by each lawyer or each lawyer assumes joint liability for representation, the client agrees to the arrangement in writing, and the total fee is reasonable.

ANSWERS TO REVIEW QUESTIONS

Answer 29

The correct answer is choice C. A lawyer, when appointed by a criminal court to represent a client, may refuse to represent the client for good cause shown if representation would violate the Rules of Professional Conduct or the law, or cause the lawyer undue financial burden, or the client or the cause is so repugnant to the lawyer as to likely impair the lawyer-client relationship or representation of the client.

Answer 30

The correct answer is choice D. A lawyer should reject representation of a client if the client's position is legally baseless. Further, a lawyer should reject representation of a client if the lawyer lacks the legal competence to handle the client's case, or if the client asks a lawyer to counsel on committing a criminal act.

Answer 31

The correct answer is choice B. The client possesses the ultimate authority to determine the objectives of any legal representation by a lawyer.

Answer 32

The correct answer is choice B. If the client is charged with a violation of criminal law, the lawyer must abide by the client's decision regarding whether the client will testify and whether the client will waive a jury trial.

Answer 33

The correct answer is choice A. When representing a client with diminished capacity, a lawyer may take reasonably necessary protective action and is implicitly authorized to reveal information about the client but only to the extent reasonably necessary to protect the client's interest.

Answer 34

The correct answer is choice B. When a lawyer discusses with a client a course of criminal conduct being contemplated by the client, the lawyer may discuss the nature and ramifications of the proposed criminal conduct.

Answer 35

The correct answer is choice B. A lawyer must withdraw or decline representation of a client if the lawyer's physical or mental condition impairs representation. Further, a lawyer must withdraw or decline representation of a client if the representation violates the law or the Rules of Professional Conduct, or the client discharges the lawyer.

Answer 36

The correct answer is choice A. A lawyer may withdraw from representing a client if good cause for withdrawal exists or even if good cause does not exist but the lawyer's withdraw from representation has no material adverse effect on the client's interest.

Answer 37

The correct answer is choice B. If ordered by a court, the lawyer must continue to represent a client notwithstanding good cause for terminating the representation.

Answer 38

The correct answer is choice A. A client can terminate the lawyer-client relationship at any time, but the lawyer may be entitled to quasi-contract damages or compensation for services rendered, and the client's position must not be jeopardized by the termination of legal services.

Answer 39

The correct answer is choice A. A lawyer who is discharged by a client must take reasonable steps to protect the client's interest, including turning over files to the client to aid in continued representation and returning the balance of any retainer.

Answer 40

The correct answer is choice C. A client may be able to avoid a lawyer-client contract if it is formed after the lawyer has finished providing services and the client was not informed of the facts needed to evaluate the appropriateness of the lawyer's compensation or benefits through the contract.

Answer 41

The correct answer is choice B. A lawyer's duties may be limited if the lawyer and client agree to limitations, and the client is adequately informed and consents to the limitations, and the terms of the limitation are reasonable in the circumstances.

Answer 42

The correct answer is choice D. A lawyer cannot charge a client a fee without the client's agreement to do so. The rules include provisions concerning what amounts to a reasonable fee agreement, including payments for services rendered that take into account services expected, the skills of the lawyer, the nature and difficulty of the case, and the reasonableness of expenses.

Answer 43

The correct answer is choice A. Contingency fees are permissible if the fee agreement is in writing, is signed by the client, and includes the percentages earned by the lawyer in all circumstances and whether expenses are deducted before or after the contingent fee is calculated.

Answer 44

The correct answer is choice D. Fee splitting between lawyers in different firms is permitted if division is in proportion to services performed by each lawyer or each lawyer assumes joint liability for representation, the client agrees to the arrangement in writing, and the total fee is reasonable.

★★★★ III.   CLIENT CONFIDENTIALITY

The principle of client-lawyer confidentiality is given effect by related bodies of law: the attorney-client privilege, the work product doctrine, and the rule of confidentiality established in professional ethics. Model Rules of Prof'l Conduct R. 1.6 cmt. [3]. The evidentiary attorney-client privilege is based upon the Federal Rules of Evidence, and work product immunity is an exception to the evidentiary privilege under the Federal Rules of Civil Procedure. The duty of confidentiality is distinct from the evidentiary privilege in that it exists in the client-lawyer relationship and is based upon the Rules and/or the Restatement. These three concepts will be separately addressed below.

★★★ A.   Attorney-Client Privilege

For purposes of the MPRE, the Federal Rules of Evidence and the Federal Rules of Civil Procedure govern the scope of the attorney-client evidentiary privilege.

1)   WHEN STATE LAW OF EVIDENTIARY PRIVILEGES APPLIES

State law of evidentiary privileges usually applies in a state court that is applying state law. Generally, federal constitutional law, statutes, rules, or common law will govern privileges applied by federal courts. Fed. R. Evid. 501. An exception to this rule applies in civil cases when state law supplies the rule of decision regarding an element of a claim or defense; in that event, the evidentiary privilege must be determined based on state law. *Id.* This might occur, for example, when a federal court is sitting in diversity jurisdiction in a civil case and applying state law. In that event, an evidentiary privilege could be determined based on state law.

Although the MPRE will probably not test the foregoing principles, it is useful to know that there are different types of privileges. Those principles are relevant because they indicate that even under the Federal Rules of Evidence, the following general legal principles of evidentiary privileges can apply. Therefore, although state-specific evidentiary privileges won't be tested, it is necessary to know these general principles for the MPRE.

2)   GENERAL LAW OF EVIDENTIARY PRIVILEGES

a)   Privileged Communications

A person or an entity may communicate with a lawyer as a potential or existing client. If the communication is a casual one not conducted for the purpose of obtaining legal advice or representation, it is not considered confidential. If that communication is made to obtain legal representation or advice, it is confidential and therefore legally privileged from disclosure. That privilege exists even if the potential or existing client communicated with someone reasonably believed to be, but who in fact was not, a lawyer. The privilege applies irrespective of whether the lawyer provided any advice or representation to the person.

b)   Holder of the Privilege

Generally, a *client* holds the privilege of confidential communications with the client's lawyer.

The client usually may exercise that privilege by preventing anyone from disclosing to any third party, or testifying about, the confidential communication. Generally, the privilege continues even after the death of the client or lawyer. A lawyer is obligated to assert the privilege to protect a client who cannot assert it for a valid reason, such as incapacity or death.

c) General Exceptions to the Privilege

The privilege exists unless: (1) the client waives confidentiality as to one or more issues; or (2) the client or the lawyer breaches a duty that is owed to the other.

The privilege does not apply:

- to physical evidence that the client provides to the lawyer;
- to documents preexisting the attorney-client relationship; or
- if the lawyer's services were requested to assist in planning or committing a crime or a fraud.

(1) Examples

(a) Not Privileged

A routine report that a company's non-attorney employee prepared for the company's executive or according to company policy does not become privileged because the company provided the report to its lawyer for the purpose of litigation.

(b) Privileged

If a lawyer hires a physician to examine a patient, a confidential communication from the patient to the physician, which is subsequently conveyed to the lawyer, is subject to the attorney-client privilege because the physician acted as the lawyer's agent.

B. Work Product Doctrine

Work product immunity may protect a lawyer from the requirement of disclosing to a third party some of the information that the lawyer acquired while preparing for litigation. Federal Rule of Civil Procedure 26(b)(3) provides qualified immunity, which means that work product materials are only subject to discovery if the party requesting them proves: (1) a substantial need for the materials; and (2) an inability to obtain a substantial equivalent of those materials by another method.

A lawyer will have absolute immunity from disclosing work product documents that include the lawyer's "mental impressions, conclusions, opinions, or legal theories" regarding litigation. Fed. R. Civ. P. 26(b)(3).

★★★ ### C. Professional Obligation of Confidentiality

The professional obligation of confidentiality is separate and distinct from the attorney-client evidentiary privilege. For purposes of the MPRE, the Rules and/or the Restatement govern the professional obligation of confidentiality in the client-lawyer relationship.

1)   DUTIES TO PROSPECTIVE CLIENT

A person who discusses with a lawyer the possibility of forming a client-lawyer relationship with respect to a matter is a prospective client. Model Rules of Prof'l Conduct R. 1.18(a).

Even when no client-lawyer relationship ensues, a lawyer who has had discussions with a prospective client must not use or reveal information learned in the consultation, except as Rule 1.9, regarding conflict of interests, would permit with respect to a former client's information. Model Rules of Prof'l Conduct R. 1.18(b).

2)   CONFIDENTIALITY OF INFORMATION

A lawyer must never reveal information relating to the representation of a client *unless*:

- the client gives informed consent;
- the disclosure is impliedly authorized in order to carry out the representation; or
- the disclosure is permitted under the Rules.

Model Rules of Prof'l Conduct R. 1.6(a).

This general Rule is referred to elsewhere in this outline as the Rule of Confidentiality. Several other Rules refer to or relate to this Rule of Confidentiality.

D.   Disclosures Expressly or Impliedly Authorized by Client

1)   CLIENT-AUTHORIZED DISCLOSURE

Under certain circumstances, a client can authorize disclosure of confidential information that is otherwise subject to the previously described attorney-client evidentiary privilege.

The Rule of Confidentiality provides that a lawyer can reveal information relating to the representation of a client if the client provides either informed express or implied consent. Model Rules of Prof'l Conduct R. 1.6(a).

a)   Express Consent

Express consent exists after a lawyer provides the client sufficient information to enable the client to recognize the waiver's impact, and the client approves of the waiver.

b)   Implied Consent

Implied consent means that, even without obtaining a client's express approval of waiving the protections of the Rule of Confidentiality, a lawyer can disclose confidential client information for the purposes of representing the client. For example, a lawyer may reveal such confidential client information in order to obtain a "satisfactory conclusion" of a matter for the client. Model Rules of Prof'l Conduct R. 1.6 cmt. [5].

★★   **E.**   **Other Exceptions to the Confidentiality Rule**

A lawyer may disclose confidential information under certain additional circumstances. Particularly, a lawyer may reveal information relating to the representation of a client to the extent the lawyer reasonably believes necessary:

- to prevent reasonably certain death or substantial bodily harm;
- to prevent the client from committing a crime or fraud that is reasonably certain to result in substantial injury to the financial interests or property of another and in furtherance of which the client has used or is using the lawyer's services;
- to prevent, mitigate, or rectify substantial injury to the financial interests or property of another that is reasonably certain to result, or has resulted, from the client's commission of a crime or fraud, in furtherance of which the client has used the lawyer's services;
- to secure legal advice about the lawyer's compliance with the Rules;
- to establish a claim or defense in a dispute between the lawyer and the client;
- to establish a defense to a criminal charge or civil claim against the lawyer based on conduct in which the client was involved,
- to respond to allegations in any proceeding concerning the lawyer's representation of the client;
- to comply with other law or a court order; or
- to detect and resolve conflicts of interest arising from the lawyer's change of employment or from changes in the composition or ownership of a firm, but only if the revealed information would not compromise the attorney-client privilege or otherwise prejudice the client.

Model Rules of Prof'l Conduct R. 1.6(b).

REVIEW QUESTIONS

45. Communications made between a client or potential client and a lawyer are:

    a) confidential, except if the lawyer has a conflict of interest with a pre-existing client and must disclose the visit and communications by the potential client to the pre-existing client.

    → b) confidential and legally privileged from disclosure, regardless of whether the lawyer provides advice or representation.

    c) confidential, except to the extent that the confidential communication is previously known to the lawyer, and the lawyer advises the potential client that the lawyer already knew the information.

    d) not confidential because without a representation agreement, no attorney-client relationship is established.

46. The privilege of confidential communication does not apply when:

    → a) the client waives confidentiality as to any issue or the client or lawyer breaches a duty owed to the other.

    b) the client provides a written confession of a crime to a lawyer.

    c) the lawyer is representing a client who has previously been convicted of perjury.

    d) the lawyer is fired by the client who refused to pay for services rendered.

47. Attorney work-product immunity protects lawyers from disclosing some information acquired or created during preparation for litigation. Qualified immunity extends to work product materials. However, otherwise protected materials are discoverable if the party seeking discovery shows:

    a) manifest injustice would occur if the immunity were allowed to stand and the party seeking the material was denied access to it.

    → b) both substantial need for the material and inability to obtain the substantial equivalent of the materials by another method.

    c) the work product was developed for the purpose of obtaining an unfair advantage at trial.

    d) a clear and present danger that without such information the party will suffer irreparable harm.

48. A lawyer has absolute immunity for disclosing work-product as to the lawyer's:

    → a) mental impressions, conclusions, opinions, or legal theories regarding litigation.

    b) calculations concerning damages to be sought from the opposing party.

    c) adverse witness list.

    d) fees charged to the client.

49. A lawyer owes a professional obligation of confidentiality to a prospective client and cannot reveal information relating to possible representation of the client:

a) unless the client reveals the information to the lawyer to prevent discovery of a crime or fraud.

b) without the client's explicit or implicit consent or unless otherwise consistent with the Rules.

c) except if the lawyer clearly informs the client, in writing and prior to any client statement, that confidentiality attaches upon engagement of the attorney.

d) if the client explicitly or implicitly retains the lawyer.

ANSWERS TO REVIEW QUESTIONS

Answer 45

The correct answer is choice B. Communications made between a client or potential client and a lawyer are confidential and, therefore, legally privileged from disclosure, regardless of whether the lawyer provides advice or representation.

Answer 46

The correct answer is choice A. The privilege of confidential communication does not apply if the client waives confidentiality as to any issue or the client or lawyer breaches a duty owed to the other. Further, the privilege does not apply to physical evidence supplied by the client to the lawyer, to documents preexisting the attorney-client relationship, or if the lawyer's services were requested to assist in planning or committing a crime or a fraud.

Answer 47

The correct answer is choice B. Qualified immunity extends to work product materials, but they are discoverable if the party seeking discovery shows both substantial need for the material and inability to obtain the substantial equivalent of the material by another method.

Answer 48

The correct answer is choice A. A lawyer has absolute immunity for disclosing work-product as to the lawyer's mental impressions, conclusions, opinions, or legal theories regarding litigation.

Answer 49

The correct answer is choice B. A lawyer owes a professional obligation of confidentiality to a prospective client and cannot reveal information relating to possible representation of the client without the client's explicit or implicit consent or unless otherwise consistent with the Rules.

IV.   CONFLICTS OF INTEREST

A practicing lawyer often encounters conflicting responsibilities. Many ethical problems arise from a conflict between a lawyer's responsibilities to clients, to the legal system, and to the lawyer's own interest. The Rules often provide guidelines for resolving these conflicts.

A.   Current Client Conflicts – Multiple Clients and Joint Representation

1)   MULTIPLE CLIENTS

a)   General Rule--Client 1 v. Client 2

Generally, a lawyer cannot represent a client if the representation involves a concurrent conflict of interest. Model Rules of Prof'l Conduct R. 1.7(a). A concurrent conflict of interest exists if: (1) the representation of one client will be directly adverse to another client; or (2) there is a significant risk that the representation of one or more clients will be materially limited by the lawyer's responsibilities to another client, a former client, a third person, or by the lawyer's personal interest. *Id.*

(1) Exceptions

The lawyer may, however, engage in representation involving a concurrent conflict of interest if:

- the lawyer reasonably believes that the lawyer will be able to provide competent and diligent representation to each affected client;
- the representation is not prohibited by law;
- the representation does not involve the assertion of a claim by one client against another client represented by the lawyer in the same litigation or other proceeding before a tribunal; and
- each affected client gives informed consent, in writing, to this representation.

Model Rules of Prof'l Conduct R. 1.7(b).

2)   JOINT REPRESENTATION

When a lawyer represents multiple clients in a single matter, the consultation must include an explanation of the common representation and the risks involved. Model Rules of Prof'l Conduct R. 1.7 cmt. [18]. Special considerations exist, however, when representing criminal defendants. Generally, a lawyer should decline to represent more than one criminal co-defendant. Model Rules of Prof'l Conduct R. 1.7 cmt. [23].

a)   Aggregate Settlement

A lawyer who represents two or more co-clients must not participate: (1) in making an aggregate settlement of the civil claims of or against the clients; or (2) in a criminal case, an aggregated agreement as to guilty or *nolo contendere* pleas, unless each client gives informed consent in a writing signed by the client. Model Rules of Prof'l Conduct R. 1.8(g). The lawyer's disclosure must include the existence and nature of all the claims or pleas involved and of the participation of each person in the settlement. *Id.*

B.   Current Client Conflicts - Lawyer's Personal Interest or Duties

A lawyer whose personal interest might negatively impact the lawyer's relationship with a potential client may decline representation of the potential client. Model Rules of Prof'l Conduct R. 1.7. For example, a lawyer may decline representing a potential client who seeks to bring a civil action against a childhood friend of the lawyer. The relationship with the childhood friend may adversely affect the lawyer's ability to provide detached representation.

C.   Former Client Conflicts

★★★   1)   DUTIES TO FORMER CLIENTS

a)   General Rule--Client v. Former Client

A lawyer who represented a client in a matter must not later represent another person in the same or a substantially related matter in which that person's interests are materially adverse to the interests of the former client, unless the former client gives informed written consent. Model Rules of Prof'l Conduct R. 1.9(a).

b)   Former Firm

A lawyer must not knowingly represent a person in the same or a substantially related matter in which a firm that the lawyer was formerly associated with had previously represented a client: (1) whose interests are materially adverse to that person; and (2) about whom the lawyer had acquired information protected by the Rule of Confidentiality and Rule 1.9(c), discussed below, that is material to the matter, unless the former client gives informed written consent. Rules of Prof'l Conduct R. 1.9(b).

c)   Use of Former Client's Information

A lawyer who represented a client in a matter, or whose present or former firm represented a client in a matter, must not later (1) use information relating to the representation to the disadvantage of the former client or (2) reveal information relating to the representation except as the Rules would permit or require or when the information has become generally known. Model Rules of Prof'l Conduct R. 1.9(c).

★★   d)   Former and Current Government Officers and Employees

A lawyer who served as a public officer or government employee is subject to Rule 1.9(c) discussed above regarding a lawyer's duties with respect to a former client's information. Model Rules of Prof'l Conduct R. 1.11(a). Additionally, a lawyer who served as a public officer or government employee must not represent a client in connection with a matter in which the lawyer participated personally and substantially unless the appropriate government agency gives its informed written consent to the representation. *Id.*

D.   Prospective Client Conflicts

A lawyer may encounter a situation in which a prospective client made confidential communications, and then later a person with materially adverse interests seeks the lawyer's representation in the matter. The lawyer cannot represent the second person under these circumstances. In particular, a lawyer cannot represent a client with interests materially adverse to those of a prospective client in the same or a substantially related matter if the lawyer received information from the prospective client that could be significantly harmful to the person in the matter. Model Rules of Prof'l Conduct R. 1.18(c). This provision is subject to the following exception.

When the lawyer has received disqualifying information under the circumstances in the preceding paragraph, the lawyer **may represent the client if:**

- Both the affected client and the prospective client give their informed written consent; or
- In the situation of a law firm, the lawyer who received the information took reasonable measures to avoid exposure to more disqualifying information than was reasonably necessary to determine whether to represent the prospective client; and

  o   The disqualified lawyer is timely screened from any participation in the matter and is apportioned no part of the fee from the matter; and
  o   Written notice is promptly given to the prospective client.

Model Rules of Prof'l Conduct R. 1.18(d).

E.   Imputed Conflicts

When two lawyers have a special relationship, the conflicts of one lawyer may be ascribed to the other lawyer.

★★   1)   LAWYERS ASSOCIATED IN A FIRM

While lawyers are associated in a firm, none of them can knowingly represent a client when any one of them practicing alone would be prohibited from doing so because of a conflict of interest. Model Rules of Prof'l Conduct R. 1.10(a). The conflict of one lawyer in the firm is *imputed* to all lawyers in the firm.

                     a)   Exceptions

There are two exceptions when a conflict of one lawyer in a firm will not be imputed to another lawyer in the firm.

(1) No Significant Risk of Limiting Representation

A conflict of one lawyer in a firm is not imputed to other lawyers in the firm when the disqualified lawyer's prohibition is based on a personal interest and would not present a significant risk of materially limiting the representation of the client by the firm's remaining lawyers. *Id.*

★★   <center>(2) Screening</center>

A conflict of one lawyer in a firm is not imputed to other lawyers in the firm when the prohibition arises out of the disqualified lawyer's association with a prior firm and the disqualified lawyer is adequately screened from the case as follows:

- The disqualified lawyer must be timely screened from any participation in the matter and be apportioned no part of the fee from it; and
- Written notice must promptly be provided to any affected former client. The notice must include: a description of the screening procedures employed; a statement of the firm's and the screened lawyer's compliance with these Rules; a statement that review may be available before a tribunal; and an agreement by the firm to respond promptly to any written inquiries or objections by the former client about the screening procedures; and
- Certifications of compliance with the screening requirements and procedures must be provided to the former client by the screened lawyer and by a partner of the firm at reasonable intervals, upon the former client's written request, and upon termination of the screening procedures. *Id.*

2) LAWYER DISSOCIATED FROM A FIRM

When a lawyer has terminated an association with a firm, the firm is not prohibited from representing a person with interests materially adverse to those of a client represented by the formerly associated lawyer and not currently represented by the firm, unless: (1) the matter is the same or substantially related to that in which the formerly associated lawyer represented the client; and (2) any lawyer remaining in the firm has information protected by the Rule of Confidentiality and Rule 1.9(c), regarding a lawyer's duties with respect to a former client's information, that is material to the matter. Model Rules of Prof'l Conduct R. 1.10(b).

3) WAIVER

An imputed conflict of interest may be waived by the affected client's informed written consent. Model Rules of Prof'l Conduct R. 1.10(c).

★   **F.   Acquiring an Interest in Litigation**

A lawyer cannot acquire a proprietary interest in a cause of action or subject matter of litigation that the lawyer is conducting for a client. Model Rules of Prof'l Conduct R. 1.8(i). The lawyer may, however: (1) acquire a lien authorized by law to secure the lawyer's fee or expenses; and (2) contract with a client for a reasonable contingent fee in a civil case. *Id.*

★   **G.   Business Transactions with Client**

1)   LIMITATIONS ON BUSINESS TRANSACTIONS WITH CLIENT

Generally, a lawyer may pursue a business transaction with, or adverse to, a client only under limited circumstances. Specifically, a lawyer cannot enter into such a transaction or knowingly acquire an ownership, possessory, security, or other pecuniary interest adverse to a client *unless*:

- The transaction is fair and reasonable to the client, fully disclosed in writing to the client in a manner that can be reasonably understood; and
- The client is advised in writing of the desirability of seeking independent counsel and is given a reasonable opportunity to do so; and
- The client provides informed written consent to the transaction and the lawyer's role in the transaction, including whether the lawyer is representing the client in the transaction.

Model Rules of Prof'l Conduct R. 1.8(a).

2)   USE OF CLIENT'S INFORMATION

A lawyer must not use information relating to representation of a client to the client's disadvantage unless the client gives informed consent, except as permitted or required by these Rules. Model Rules of Prof'l Conduct R. 1.8(b).

★★   ### 3)   LIMITATION ON GIFTS

A lawyer must not solicit any substantial gift from a client, including a testamentary gift, or prepare on behalf of a client an instrument giving the lawyer or a person related to the lawyer any substantial gift, unless the lawyer or other recipient of the gift is related to the client. Model Rules of Prof'l Conduct R. 1.8(c). Related persons include a spouse, child, grandchild, parent, grandparent, or other relative or individual with whom the lawyer or the client maintains a close familial relationship. *Id.*

4)   MEDIA OR LITERARY RIGHTS

Prior to the conclusion of representation of a client, a lawyer cannot make or negotiate an agreement giving the lawyer literary or media rights to a portrayal or account based in substantial part on information relating to the representation. Model Rules of Prof'l Conduct R. 1.8(d).

5)   FINANCIAL ASSISTANCE TO CLIENT

★★ A lawyer must not provide financial assistance to a client in connection with pending or contemplated litigation, *except* that a lawyer may advance court costs and expenses of litigation, the payment of which may be contingent upon the outcome of the matter; and a lawyer representing an indigent client may pay court costs and expenses of litigation on behalf of the client. Model Rules of Prof'l Conduct R. 1.8(e).

6)   SEXUAL RELATIONS WITH CLIENT

As a general principle, a lawyer may not coerce, intimidate, or take advantage of any client in an attempt to have sexual relations. This rule is intended to prohibit sexual exploitation by a lawyer in the course of professional representation.

Specifically, a lawyer must not have sexual relations with a client unless a consensual sexual relationship existed between them when the client-lawyer relationship commenced. Model Rules of Prof'l Conduct R. 1.8(j).

★   H.   Third-Party Compensation and Influence

In practice, a third party might pay for a lawyer to represent a client, which may create a conflict of interest if the third party's interests in the representation are not the same as the client's. A lawyer cannot accept compensation from someone other than the client unless:

- The client gives informed consent;
- There is no interference with the lawyer's independence of professional judgment or with the client-lawyer relationship; and
- The information relating to representation of a client is protected as required by the Rule of Confidentiality.

Model Rules of Prof'l Conduct R. 1.8(f).

★   I.   Lawyers Currently or Formerly in Government Service

The disqualification of lawyers associated in a firm with former or current government lawyers is governed by Rule 1.11 discussed above. Model Rules of Prof'l Conduct R. 1.10(d).

When a lawyer who served as a public officer or employee of the government is disqualified from representation, no lawyer in a firm with which that lawyer is associated may knowingly undertake or continue representation in such a matter unless: (1) the disqualified lawyer is timely screened from any participation in the matter and is apportioned no part of the fee; and (2) written notice is promptly given to the appropriate government agency to enable it to ascertain compliance with these provisions. Model Rules of Prof'l Conduct R. 1.11(b).

J.   Former Judge. Arbitrator, Mediator, or other Third-Party Neutral

Generally, a lawyer must not represent anyone in connection with a matter in which the lawyer participated personally and substantially: (1) as a judge or other adjudicative officer, or law clerk to such a person, or 2) as an arbitrator, mediator, or other third-party neutral, *unless* all parties to the proceeding give informed written consent. Model Rules of Prof'l Conduct R. 1.12(a).

REVIEW QUESTIONS

50. A lawyer can enter into a business transaction with a client under limited circumstances if:

    a) both the lawyer and the client seek independent counsel with regard to the proposed business transaction and are both advised that it does not present a conflict of interest.

    b) the transaction is fair and reasonable to the client and fully disclosed in writing, and the client is advised in writing of the desirability of seeking independent counsel and is given an opportunity to do so, and the client agrees in writing to the transaction.

    c) the client waives, in writing, any possible conflict of interest to the extent that it might impede either the business transaction or the lawyer's ability to demonstrate independent judgment.

    d) the lawyer agrees to not represent the client in any future matters including those related to the business transaction.

51. A lawyer cannot receive or solicit any gift from a client:

    a) unless the lawyer is related to the client or has a close family relationship with the client.

    b) unless the gift is trivial, a token, or otherwise has no value.

    c) unless the lawyer is romantically involved with the client.

    d) unless the gift is received from a client's trust and the client has no control over the trust.

52. A lawyer cannot make or negotiate literary or media rights to a portrayal of the representation of a client:

    a) except if the client agrees in writing and is represented by independent counsel in negotiations of the rights with the lawyer.

    b) under any circumstances.

    c) unless the client receives preferential rights.

    d) except if the client is placed in the most favorable light possible in the portrayal.

53. A lawyer cannot provide financial assistance to a client related to pending or contemplated litigation:

    a) except for court costs and expenses which may be advanced contingent on the outcome of a matter, or court costs and expenses for an indigent client.

    b) unless the client's assets are currently unavailable and the lawyer is assigned an interest in the assets plus reasonable interest for the time period the lawyer advances funds.

    c) except if the client is a minor and has attachable assets available to pay the attorney upon reaching majority.

    d) except for advances on an estate in probate if the estate has guaranteed all legal fees related to the probate.

54.   A lawyer may not have sexual relations with a client during the course of representation:

    a) unless the sexual relationship is consensual.
    b) unless the sexual relationship existed without any instigation by the lawyer.
    c) unless the sexual relationship existed when the client/lawyer relationship commenced.
    d) under any circumstances.

55.   A lawyer's representation of two clients simultaneously presents a conflict of interest when:

    a) both clients object to the lawyer's actions in representing the other client.
    b) one client objects to the lawyer's actions in representing the other client.
    c) the interests of the clients are directly adverse.
    d) the lawyer perceives a possible conflict.

56.   Generally, a lawyer should not represent more than one codefendant in a criminal matter. However, if a lawyer does undertake joint representation of criminal defendants:

    a) the lawyer cannot participate in making an aggregate agreement for guilty or no contest pleas unless each client signs informed consents that explain each client's participation in the agreement.
    b) the lawyer must inform the court prior to entering the pleas so that the judge can advise each client to retain separate counsel and avoid a conflict of interest.
    c) each codefendant is entitled to know the complete terms and conditions of any plea agreement reached by the other codefendant prior to entering their plea.
    d) the lawyer must prorate legal fees so as not to charge either of the codefendants more than the other.

57.   A lawyer has a conflict of interest when:

    a) continued representation of a client will adversely impact the lawyer's ability to attract more clients.
    b) there is a significant risk that representation of one or more clients will be materially limited by the lawyer's previously scheduled personal matters.
    c) a lawyer believes a client is lying beyond a reasonable doubt and the lies impede the lawyer's ability to represent the client with a clear conscience.
    d) One client's interest is directly adverse to another client's interest or there is a significant risk that representation of a client will be limited by responsibilities to another client.

58.   A lawyer cannot represent a new client in the same or a substantially related matter relating to a former client if that new client's interests are materially adverse to the interests of the former client unless:

    a) the former client gives written informed consent.
    b) both the former and current client give written informed consent.
    c) the lawyer obtains signed, written waivers of confidentiality from both clients.

d) the former client gives verbal informed consent.

59. When a lawyer who formerly served as a government agency employee or officer is disqualified from representation of a client:

   a) the lawyer and any member of the lawyer's firm can represent the client if there is written informed consent given by the client to the firm and the lawyer's former government employer.

→ b) no lawyer in the lawyer's firm can be involved in the representation unless the disqualified lawyer is screened from any representation in the matter, gets no fee from the matter, and notice is given to the former government agency of the representation.

   c) the lawyer's firm is wholly disqualified from representing the client.

   d) the government agency that formerly employed the lawyer can release the lawyer, in writing, from any conflict of interest.

60. If a lawyer wants to represent a client but previously served as an arbitrator, mediator, or judge in a matter in which the client was once involved, there is a conflict of interest and the lawyer cannot represent the client unless:

→ a) all parties involved in the matter give informed consent in writing to the representation.

   b) the lawyer and the lawyer's firm agree to never represent an interest adverse to any of the parties involved in the matter.

   c) a neutral magistrate reviews the matter and, after all parties are given an opportunity to be heard on the matter, holds that the lawyer may represent the client.

   d) there is a written offer, acceptance, and consideration between the parties waiving the conflict.

ANSWERS TO REVIEW QUESTIONS

Answer 50

The correct answer is choice B. A lawyer can enter into a business transaction with a client under limited circumstances if the transaction is fair and reasonable to the client and fully disclosed in writing, and the client is advised in writing of the desirability of seeking independent counsel and is given an opportunity to do so, and the client agrees in writing to the transaction.

Answer 51

The correct answer is choice A. A lawyer cannot receive or solicit any gift from a client unless the lawyer is related to the client or unless the lawyer has a close family relationship with the client.

Answer 52

The correct answer is choice B. Prior to the conclusion of representation of a client, a lawyer cannot make or negotiate literary or media rights to a portrayal of the representation of a client.

Answer 53

The correct answer is choice A. A lawyer cannot provide financial assistance to a client related to pending or contemplated litigation except for court costs and expenses which may be advanced contingent on outcome of the matter or to pay court costs and expenses for an indigent client.

Answer 54

The correct answer is choice C. A lawyer may not have sexual relations with a client during the course of representation unless the sexual relationship existed when the client/lawyer relationship commenced.

Answer 55

The correct answer is choice C. A lawyer's representation of two clients simultaneously presents a conflict of interest if the interests of the clients are directly adverse.

Answer 56

The correct answer is choice A. Generally, a lawyer should not represent more than one codefendant in a criminal matter. However, if the lawyer does represent more than one criminal codefendant, the lawyer cannot participate in making an aggregate agreement for guilty or no contest pleas unless each client signs informed consents that explain each client's participation in the agreement.

Answer 57

The correct answer is choice D. A lawyer has a conflict of interest if representation of one client is directly adverse to another client's interest, or there is a significant risk that representation of one or more clients will be materially limited by the lawyer's responsibilities to another party, person, or the lawyer's own interest. An exception exists if the lawyer reasonably believes the lawyer will be able to provide competent representation to each affected client, the representation is not prohibited by law, the representation does not involve assertion of a direct claim by one client against another client, and each affected client provides informed written agreement to representation.

Answer 58

The correct answer is choice A. A lawyer cannot represent a new client in the same or a substantially related matter relating to a former client if that new client's interests are materially adverse to the interests of the former client unless the former client gives written informed consent.

Answer 59

The correct answer is choice B. If a lawyer who formerly served as a government agency employee or officer is disqualified from representation of a client, no lawyer in the lawyer's firm can be involved in the representation unless the disqualified lawyer is screened from any representation in the matter, gets no fee from the matter, and notice is given to the former government agency of the representation.

Answer 60

The correct answer is choice A. If a lawyer wants to represent a client but previously served as an arbitrator, mediator, or judge in a matter in which the client was once involved, there is a conflict of interest and the lawyer cannot represent the client unless all parties involved in the matter give informed consent in writing to the representation.

V.   COMPETENCE, MALPRACTICE, AND OTHER CIVIL LIABILITY

★★   **A.   Maintaining Competence**

1)   DUTY OF COMPETENCE

A lawyer has a duty to act competently with regard to legal representation. Generally, a lawyer must apply the 1) diligence, 2) learning and skill, and 3) mental, emotional, and physical ability reasonably necessary for the performance of the legal service requested.

2)   OBLIGATION TO MAINTAIN COMPETENCE

A lawyer has an obligation to not only have the competence to handle a matter, but also to maintain competence through ongoing learning or continuing legal education and keeping abreast of ongoing changes in the law. In some jurisdictions, such study and education is voluntary. In other jurisdictions, the professional authority makes such study and education mandatory.

The duty to maintain competence also includes keeping informed of the benefits and risks associated with relevant technology. For example, a lawyer may be required to protect confidential electronic client information in a commercially reasonable manner.

★★   **B.   Competence Necessary to Undertake Representation**

1)   COMPETENCE REQUIREMENT

A lawyer must provide competent representation to a client. Model Rules of Prof'l Conduct R. 1.1. Competent representation requires the legal knowledge, skill, thoroughness, and preparation reasonably necessary for the representation. *Id.* Accordingly, a lawyer should only accept employment from a client if the lawyer has the ability to competently handle the client's matter, or can, through reasonable preparation, gain the necessary competence to handle the matter.

If a lawyer were to represent a client without being competent to do so, this could jeopardize both the client's matter and the lawyer's professional status (potential Rules violations and/or malpractice).

2)   GAINING COMPETENCE

A lawyer who lacks competence in a matter can become competent by learning and preparing to practice the type of law involved. This effort should be reasonable so that it does not impose unreasonable cost and delay upon a client. A lawyer may consider whether "it is feasible to refer the matter to, or associate or consult with, a lawyer of established competence." Model Rules of Prof'l Conduct R. 1.1 cmt. [1]. For example, a lawyer can gain competence by working with another lawyer in the same firm who is competent with respect to the matter. Similarly, with a client's consent, a lawyer can gain competence by working with another lawyer who is not in the same firm as the lawyer.

a)   Emergency Situations

In an emergency, however, a lawyer may give advice or assistance in a matter in which the lawyer does not ordinarily possess the relevant legal skill (i.e., competence). This can occur when "referral to or consultation or association with another lawyer would be impractical." Model Rules of Prof'l Conduct R. 1.1 cmt. [3]. This situation might arise, for example, when a dying person wants to make a will and does not have time to find a probate lawyer. In that event, a lawyer should limit the assistance to what is "reasonably necessary in the circumstances" to avoid placing a client's interest at risk. *Id.*

★★
C.   Exercise of Diligence and Care

A lawyer must act with reasonable diligence and promptness in representing a client. Model Rules of Prof'l Conduct R. 1.3. Common exam questions involve lawyers procrastinating in different aspects of their practice. As previously mentioned, a lack of diligence can give rise to disciplinary action or civil liability.

D.   Civil Liability to Client Including Malpractice

★★
1)   GENERAL CONSIDERATIONS

Some attorney professional misconduct may result in disciplinary proceedings, as well as potential civil liability. For example, a lawyer's failure to timely file a pleading within the controlling statute of limitations that results in a client's loss of a cause of action violates the Rule regarding diligence and also could give rise to a civil legal malpractice action.

a)   Enforcement Proceedings

An alleged violation of the Rules must be reported to the relevant professional authority, which has the authority to bring an enforcement proceeding against a lawyer. A lawyer admitted to practice in a jurisdiction is subject to the disciplinary authority of the jurisdiction, regardless of where the lawyer's conduct occurs. Model Rules of Prof'l Conduct R. 8.5(a). A lawyer not admitted to practice law in a jurisdiction is subject to the disciplinary authority of the jurisdiction if the lawyer provides or offers to provide any legal services in the jurisdiction. *Id.* A lawyer can be subject to the disciplinary authority of multiple jurisdictions for the same conduct. *Id.*

The enforcement proceeding should satisfy constitutional due process requirements to the extent that its outcome could adversely affect the lawyer's property interest in the license to practice law.

b)   Civil Liability

Civil liability for violating the Rules includes tort liability for a legal malpractice cause of action and civil liability for a contract law cause of action. For example, a lawyer whose conduct violated the Rules regarding competence in handling a client's matter might also have violated a representation agreement with the client, which might support a breach of contract claim.

(1) Legal Malpractice

Some states have codified a legal malpractice claim, which is a negligence tort claim with common law origins. Generally, a lawyer's violation of the Rules involving some actionable negligence can support a malpractice action. Usually, in addition to establishing the negligence elements of duty, breach, causation, and damages, a client must also prove that the client would have prevailed in the underlying cause of action that was adversely affected by the lawyer's professional misconduct.

E.   Civil Liability to Non-Clients

1)   GENERAL DUTY

A lawyer's duty to a client does not completely outweigh the duty to not injure a nonclient. With a few exceptions, a lawyer is subject to liability to a client or nonclient when a nonlawyer would be liable in similar circumstances. Restatement (Third) of The Law Governing Lawyers § 56. Thus, if a lawyer aids the client in the commission of a tort on a nonclient, the client-lawyer relationship would not provide a shield from liability. A lawyer has some defenses and exceptions to liability to nonclient claims if the lawyer acts merely as an advocate of a client:

- A lawyer has an absolute privilege to publish matters concerning a nonclient if: 1) the publication occurs in communications prior to or during a proceeding before a tribunal; 2) the lawyer participates as counsel in that proceeding; and 3) the matter is published to a person who may be involved in the proceeding, and the publication has some relation to the proceeding;

- A lawyer representing a client in a civil proceeding or procuring criminal proceedings by a client is not liable to a nonclient for wrongful use of civil proceedings or for malicious prosecution if the lawyer has probable cause for acting, or if the lawyer acts primarily to help the client obtain proper adjudication of the client's claim in that proceeding; and

- A lawyer who advises or assists a client to make or break a contract or to enter or dissolve a legal relationship is not liable to a nonclient for interference with a contract or a legal relationship if the lawyer acts to advance the client's interests without using wrongful means. *Id.* § 57.

2)   SPECIFIC DUTY

A lawyer owes a duty to use care to a nonclient when and to the extent that:

- The lawyer or a client invites the nonclient to rely on the lawyer's opinion or legal services, the nonclient does so rely, and the nonclient is not too remote from the lawyer to be entitled to protection;

- The lawyer knows that a client intends to primarily benefit a nonclient by the lawyer's services; that such duty would not significantly impair the lawyer's performance of obligations to the client; and the absence of such duty would make enforcement of those obligations to the client unlikely; and

- The lawyer's client is a trustee, guardian, executor, or fiduciary acting primarily to perform similar functions for the nonclient; the lawyer knows that appropriate action is necessary to prevent or rectify the breach of fiduciary duty owed by the client to the nonclient where the breach is a crime or fraud, or the lawyer assisted in the breach; the nonclient is not reasonably able to protect its rights; and such duty would not significantly impair the performance of the lawyer's obligations to the client. *Id.* § 51.

★★   **F.   Limiting Liability for Malpractice**

A lawyer may not make an agreement prospectively limiting malpractice liability unless the client is independently represented by counsel in making the agreement.

Additionally, a lawyer cannot settle a claim with a client for malpractice unless the client is informed, in writing, of the ability to obtain independent counsel.

G.   Malpractice Insurance and Risk Prevention

Insurance companies offer malpractice insurance to lawyers. A lawyer is not required to obtain malpractice insurance.

1)   INSURANCE POLICY MAY PROTECT LAWYER FROM LIABILITY

A lawyer may protect himself from financial liability for malpractice by obtaining malpractice insurance. An insurance company issues the policy, which provides coverage in exchange for the payment of premiums.

a)   Common Aspects of Insurance Policy

Usually, a legal malpractice insurance policy:

- applies when the insured makes a claim to the insurer (e.g., malpractice lawsuit);
- provides that the insurer will defend the insured;
- covers damages awarded to a plaintiff, such as a former client; and
- may have coverage exclusions (e.g., for pre-existing malpractice).

2)   RISK PREVENTION SEEKS TO DECREASE LIABILITY EXPOSURE

A lawyer should take steps to prevent the risk of legal malpractice actions. Such steps include complying with all applicable law and ethical standards while practicing law. A malpractice insurance provider may inform the insured about risk prevention. For example, the insurer could provide a booklet addressing risk prevention to the insured. The insurer could provide a malpractice insurance application requiring that an applicant describe the applicant's system for identifying prospective clients who present potential problems (e.g., conflicts of interest) that could give rise to legal malpractice actions against the applicant. The applicant could decrease liability exposure by using that system in order to make more informed decisions about whether to represent prospective clients.

REVIEW QUESTIONS

61. A lawyer not admitted to practice in a jurisdiction is subject to the disciplinary authority of that jurisdiction:

    a) if the lawyer provides or offers to provide legal services in that jurisdiction.

    b) if the lawyer provides consultation to a lawyer licensed to practice in that jurisdiction.

    c) if the lawyer represents himself as a non-licensed lawyer and only offers suggestions.

    d) if the lawyer refers a potential client to a licensed lawyer for a fee.

62. A lawyer may be subject to disciplinary proceedings:

    a) in only the jurisdiction in which the lawyer is licensed.

    b) in more than one jurisdiction for the same conduct.

    c) only if evidence supports a finding of a violation of the Rules beyond a reasonable doubt.

    d) if reported by another lawyer.

63. Civil liability for violating the Rules includes:

    a) automatic forfeiture of a lawyer's license to practice.

    b) causes of action alleging legal malpractice and breach of contract.

    c) statutory fines for repeat violations.

    d) suspension of a lawyer's license to practice law.

64. A legal malpractice claim is a negligence tort claim that is codified in many states. The elements of such a claim are:

    a) duty, breach, causation, damages, and that the lawyer knowingly and intelligently committed the malpractice and failed to self-report the violation.

    b) duty, breach, causation, damages, and that the client would have prevailed in the underlying cause of action that was adversely affected by the lawyer's professional misconduct.

    c) duty, breach, causation, damages.

    d) duty, breach, causation, damages, and that the lawyer knowingly and intelligently committed the malpractice and profited or otherwise benefitted from the actions to the detriment of the client.

65. A lawyer has a duty of professional competence in representation of a client which means that:

    a) the lawyer must possess and maintain competence with regard to those matters of legal representation that the attorney advertises as an area of practice.

    b) the lawyer must possess minimum competency to perform the legal services requested.

    c) the lawyer need only maintain continuing legal education relating to legal ethics.

    d) the lawyer possesses and maintains competence in all legal representation, applies reasonable diligence in that representation, and maintains such competence through legal education.

66. Competent representation requires the legal skill, knowledge, thoroughness and preparation needed for the representation. A lawyer should only accept representation if the lawyer can:

   a) apply similar areas of law in which the lawyer is competent to address the client's issues.
   b) project competency to uphold both faith and stability of the legal system while simultaneously engaging other counsel.
    c) competently handle the client's matter or through reasonable preparation can obtain the necessary competence to handle the matter.
   d) file any necessary lawsuit to protect the client's interests, comply with the Statute of Limitations, and refer the client to competent counsel.

67. With respect to a malpractice claim, a lawyer may not:

   a) advise a client of the difficulty of proving a malpractice claim.
   b) reveal possible malpractice concerns with a client which would undermine confidence and trust in the attorney-client relationship.
   c) contract with a client to limit malpractice liability nor attempt to settle a potential malpractice claim without advising the client in writing to obtain independent counsel with respect to the claim and its settlement.
   d) reply to an inquiry from the relevant disciplinary authority concerning a reported incident of malpractice until the complaining client has waived attorney-client confidentiality which prevents an attorney from fully and freely replying.

ANSWERS TO REVIEW QUESTIONS

Answer 61

The correct answer is choice A. A lawyer not admitted to practice in a jurisdiction is subject to the disciplinary authority of that jurisdiction if the lawyer provides or offers to provide legal services in that jurisdiction.

Answer 62

The correct answer is choice B. A lawyer may be subject to disciplinary proceedings in more than one jurisdiction for the same conduct.

Answer 63

The correct answer is choice B. Civil liability for violating the Rules includes causes of action alleging legal malpractice and breach of contract.

Answer 64

The correct answer is choice B. A legal malpractice claim is a negligence tort claim and is codified in some states. The elements of such a claim are duty, breach, causation, damages, and that the client would have prevailed in the underlying cause of action that was adversely affected by the lawyer's professional misconduct.

Answer 65

The correct answer is choice D. A lawyer has a duty of professional competence in representation of a client which means the lawyer must possess and maintain competence with regard to all legal representation, apply all reasonable diligence to perform the legal services requested, and is obliged to maintain competence via legal education.

Answer 66

The correct answer is choice C. A lawyer should only accept representation if the lawyer can competently handle the client's matter or through reasonable preparation can obtain the necessary competence to handle the matter.

Answer 67

The correct answer is choice C. A lawyer may not contract with a client to limit malpractice liability nor attempt to settle a potential malpractice claim without advising the client in writing to obtain independent counsel with respect to the claim and its settlement.

VI.   LITIGATION AND OTHER FORMS OF ADVOCACY

A.   Meritorious Claims and Contentions

★   1)   <u>LAWYER CANNOT BRING FRIVOLOUS CLAIM</u>

A lawyer's claims and contentions must have merit. A lawyer can never bring or defend a proceeding, or assert any contention, unless it is grounded in a non-frivolous legal or factual basis. However, a lawyer may make good faith arguments for an extension, modification, or reversal of existing law. Model Rules of Prof'l Conduct R. 3.1.

2)   <u>FEDERAL RULE OF CIVIL PROCEDURE 11</u>

Issues regarding pleadings governed by Federal Rule 11 are usually tested under the subject of Civil Procedure. However, these issues could also arise on the MPRE in relation to meritorious claims and contentions.

a)   Signature Requirement

Every pleading, motion, or other paper of a party represented by an attorney must be *signed* by at least one attorney of record. For a *willful* violation of Federal Rule 11 (failing to sign a pleading or motion), an attorney may be subjected to *disciplinary* action. Incidentally, similar action may be taken if scandalous or indecent matter is inserted.

b)   Representations

When an attorney signs and files a paper with a court, that attorney makes several representations.

(1) No Improper Purpose

An attorney represents that the contentions set forth in a paper filed with the court are not presented for an improper purpose, such as to harass or to cause unnecessary delay or needless increase in the cost of litigation.

(2) Legal Grounding

An attorney represents that the legal contentions set forth in a paper filed with the court are warranted by existing law, or by a non-frivolous argument for the extension, modification, or reversal of existing law.

(3) Evidentiary Support

An attorney represents that the allegations and other factual contentions set forth in a paper filed with the court have evidentiary support or, if specifically so identified, are likely to have evidentiary support after a reasonable opportunity for further investigation or discovery.

(4) Denials

An attorney represents that the denials of factual contentions set forth in a paper filed with the court are warranted on the evidence or are reasonably based on a lack of information or belief.

c)   Process for Sanctions

A court may sanction an attorney for violating Federal Rule 11. If a court finds that a lawyer violated the Federal Rule 11 representations, then the court may impose an appropriate sanction upon the responsible lawyers, law firms, or parties. The court must give a lawyer notice and a reasonable opportunity to respond.

The court may impose sanctions either by motion or on the court's own initiative.

(1) By Motion

A party may file a motion for sanctions. A motion for sanctions must describe the specific conduct alleged to violate Federal Rule 11.

(a) Opportunity to Correct

Before filing a motion for sanctions, a party must provide an opportunity to correct or withdraw the complained-of action. A motion for sanctions must first be served on the parties in the action. It should not be filed with the court at that time. Service of the motion on the parties provides the attorney alleged to have violated the rule with an opportunity to correct the alleged violation. If the complained-of action is not corrected or withdrawn within 21 days after service of the motion on the parties, then the motion may be filed with the court.

(b) Expenses and Fees Available

If warranted, a court may award, to the party prevailing on the motion, the reasonable expenses and attorney's fees incurred in presenting or opposing the motion.

(2) On Court's Initiative

A court may enter, on its own initiative, an order describing specific conduct that appears to violate Federal Rule 11. The court may direct the lawyer, law firm, or party to withdraw or correct the violative contentions or show cause why it has not violated Federal Rule 11.

d)   Nature of Sanctions

A sanction imposed for violation of Federal Rule 11 is limited to that which is sufficient to deter repetition of the conduct or comparable conduct by others. The sanction may include directives of a nonmonetary nature and an order to pay a penalty to court. A court may also order an attorney violating Federal Rule 11 to pay, to the moving party, reasonable attorney's fees and expenses incurred as a direct result of the violation.

B.   Expediting Litigation

A lawyer must make reasonable efforts to expedite litigation consistent with the interests of a client. Model Rules of Prof'l Conduct R. 3.2. This obligation goes hand-in-hand with the lawyer's duty of diligence.

★★   **C.   Candor to the Tribunal**

An attorney must act with openness and honesty to a tribunal. A "tribunal" is a court, an arbitrator in a binding arbitration proceeding, a legislative body, an administrative agency, or any other body acting in an adjudicative capacity. Model Rules of Prof'l Conduct R. 1.0.

1)   FALSE REPRESENTATIONS ARE PROHIBITED

A lawyer cannot knowingly make false statements, fail to disclose binding legal authority, or provide false evidence to a tribunal.

a)   False Statements

A lawyer cannot make a false statement of material fact or law to a tribunal, or fail to correct a false statement of material fact or law the lawyer previously made to the tribunal.

b)   Binding Legal Authority

A lawyer cannot fail to disclose to the tribunal legal authority in the controlling jurisdiction known to the lawyer to be *directly adverse* to the position of the client and not disclosed by opposing counsel.

c)   False Evidence

A lawyer cannot knowingly offer false evidence. If a lawyer, the lawyer's client, or a witness called by the lawyer has offered material evidence and the lawyer comes to know of its falsity, the lawyer must take reasonable remedial measures, including, if necessary, disclosure to the tribunal. The lawyer may refuse to offer evidence, other than the testimony of a defendant in a criminal matter, that the lawyer reasonably believes is false. Model Rules of Prof'l Conduct R. 3.3(a).

2)   LAWYER'S SUBSEQUENT REMEDIAL MEASURES

A lawyer who represents a client in an adjudicative proceeding and who knows that the client intends to engage in, is engaging in, or has engaged in criminal or fraudulent conduct related to the proceeding, must take reasonable remedial measures, including, if necessary, disclosure to the tribunal. Model Rules of Prof'l Conduct R. 3.3(b).

a)   Duration of Duties

The duty to take reasonable remedial measures continues until the proceeding's conclusion and applies even if compliance requires disclosure of information otherwise protected by the Rule of Confidentiality. Model Rules of Prof'l Conduct R. 3.3(c).

3)   DISCLOSURE OF MATERIAL FACTS IN *EX-PARTE* PROCEEDINGS

In an *ex-parte* proceeding, a lawyer must disclose all known material facts to the tribunal that will enable the tribunal to make an informed decision. Model Rules of Prof'l Conduct R. 3.3(d).

D.   Fairness to Opposing Party and Counsel

The concepts of civility, courtesy, and decorum are not just pleasant notions about polite behavior among professionals. Those concepts have practical application in maintaining the appropriate level of professional propriety in the conduct of legal proceedings.

A lawyer must be fair to an opposing party and counsel. The fairness required under the ethical rules impacts the lawyer's conduct in all phases of litigation.

1)   EVIDENCE

a)   Access to Evidence

A lawyer cannot obstruct a party's access to evidence or material having potential evidentiary value.

b)   Falsification of Evidence

A lawyer cannot falsify evidence, counsel or assist a witness to testify falsely, or offer an inducement to a witness that is prohibited by law.

c)   Discovery Requests

A lawyer cannot make a frivolous discovery request or fail to make a reasonably diligent effort to comply with a legally proper discovery request by an opposing party.

d)   Request to Not Disclose Relevant Information

A lawyer cannot request that a person other than a client refrain from voluntarily giving relevant information to another party unless the person is a relative or an agent of a client, and the lawyer reasonably believes that the person's interests will not be adversely affected by refraining from giving such information.

2)   TRIAL

In trial, a lawyer cannot allude to any matter that the lawyer does not reasonably believe is relevant or that will not be supported by admissible evidence. A lawyer cannot assert personal knowledge of facts in issue except when testifying as a witness or state a personal opinion as to the justness of a cause, the credibility of a witness, the culpability of a civil litigant, or the guilt or innocence of an accused. However, some courts permit an attorney to assert that a witness lied if that assertion is supported by the facts.

3) DISOBEY RULES OF TRIBUNAL

A lawyer cannot knowingly disobey an obligation under the rules of a tribunal except for an open refusal based on an assertion that no valid obligation exists.

4) THREATS

a) Criminal Charges

A lawyer cannot present (or threaten to present) criminal charges in order to obtain an advantage in a civil matter.

b) Disciplinary Charges

A lawyer cannot present (or threaten to present) disciplinary charges under the ethical rules in order to obtain an advantage in a civil matter.

Model Rules of Prof'l Conduct R. 3.4.

As allowed by law, a lawyer may pay for a witness's reasonable expenses, but the lawyer may not pay the witness for the witness's testimony. An expert witness, however, may be paid for the expert's time in testifying, but the fee paid to the expert must be a non-contingent fee. *Id.*, cmt. [3].

E. Impartiality and Decorum of the Tribunal

★★   1) IMPROPER CONTACT WITH COURT AND JURORS

A lawyer must avoid improper contact with court officials and jurors. A lawyer cannot communicate or attempt to influence a judge, juror, prospective juror, or other judicial official. Even after a trial is concluded, a lawyer cannot communicate with a juror if the juror has demonstrated a desire not to communicate. Of course, a lawyer is always prohibited from engaging in conduct intended to disrupt a tribunal.

Model Rules of Prof'l Conduct R. 3.5.

★   F. Trial Publicity

1) NO PREJUDICIAL EXTRAJUDICIAL STATEMENTS

A lawyer who is participating, or has participated, in the investigation or litigation of a matter must not make an extrajudicial (out of court) statement that the lawyer knows or reasonably should know will be disseminated by means of public communication and will have a substantial likelihood of materially prejudicing an adjudicative proceeding in the matter. Model Rules of Prof'l Conduct R. 3.6(a).

a)   Exception for Responsive Statement

A lawyer may make a statement that a reasonable lawyer would believe is required to protect a client from the substantial undue prejudicial effect of recent publicity not initiated by the lawyer or the lawyer's client. Such a statement must be limited to the information necessary to mitigate the recent adverse publicity. Model Rules of Prof'l Conduct R. 3.6(c).

★★ **G.   Lawyer as Witness**

Generally, a lawyer should not represent a client in a matter in which the lawyer might need to testify. Specifically, a lawyer cannot act as advocate at a trial in which the lawyer is likely to be a necessary witness unless:

- the testimony relates to an uncontested issue;
- the testimony relates to the nature and value of legal services provided; or
- the lawyer's disqualification would be a substantial hardship to the client.

Model Rules of Prof'l Conduct R. 3.7(a).

REVIEW QUESTIONS

68. A lawyer should not represent a client if the lawyer is likely to be a necessary witness except when:

    a) the lawyer's testimony relates to an uncontested issue, the lawyer's testimony relates to value of services provided, or the lawyer's disqualification would work a substantial hardship on the client.

    b) the client expressly waives any claim against the lawyer as a result of the testimony proving harmful to the client.

    c) the lawyer is confident that the lawyer's testimony will not reveal any attorney-client privileged information.

    d) a neutral magistrate hears the testimony in camera and determines the lawyer as a witness is necessary to the client.

69. A lawyer should behave with:

    a) the proper manners demonstrated by other lawyers, judges and elected officials.

    b) due respect and in accordance with the local rules and customs of the court before which the lawyer is practicing.

    c) civility, courtesy, and decorum which are legal standards that must be respected.

    d) the reasonable manners expected of anyone in a position of trust and authority.

70. A lawyer must act in fairness to opposing parties and counsel, meaning a lawyer, among other things:

    a) cannot unlawfully obstruct access to evidence, or destroy or alter anything of evidentiary value, make a frivolous discovery request or obstruct a valid discovery request, nor assist in false testimony or make any unlawful inducement to a witness.

    b) cannot make objections throughout a trial that lengthen the trial and delay a decision.

    c) cannot file lengthy and detailed motions that make opposing counsel's work more difficult than a reasonably competent attorney of similar education and experience might otherwise do.

    d) cannot act in a zealous manner that the lawyer knows will enflame the passions of the opposing party.

71. The rule requiring a lawyer to act with impartiality and make only meritorious claims and contentions allows the lawyer to:

    a) bring a proceeding in which there are serious questions about the laws or facts underlying the case.

    b) make good faith arguments for reversals, modification, or extensions of existing law.

    c) challenge a prior court ruling against a client where the judge held the client in contempt.

    d) file claims based solely on the word of the client if the client has financial means to support a suit.

72. A lawyer makes the following representations when making a filing:

   a) the filing conforms to the proper document size and all court rules relating to its formatting.
   b) the lawyer has verified the veracity of the client's statements which are the basis of the filing.
   c) there is no improper purpose, the filing rests on a legal grounding, and there is evidentiary support for the filing.
   d) no reasonable denials of factual contentions are warranted on the evidence.

73. Improper filings may be the subject of:

   a) sanctions requested by opposing counsel or imposed by the court sufficient to deter repetition of the offensive conduct or comparable conduct by others.
   b) sanctions requiring payment of fines and jail time.
   c) review and rejection by the court which can force counsel to refile properly.
   d) lost profits due to the fact that an attorney may have to redo work and absorb the added expense.

74. A lawyer's duty of candor requires that the lawyer:

   a) exhibit a calm demeanor and respectful tone before the court.
   b) must be blunt and direct when speaking to the court.
   c) disclose controlling cases or law directly opposed to a client's interest, even if opposing counsel fails to disclose them.
   d) withhold controlling cases or law detrimental to a client's interest if opposing counsel fails to disclose them.

75. A lawyer must take subsequent remedial measures if the lawyer knows or reasonably believes that the client will take criminal or fraudulent actions related to the proceedings. Such subsequent remedial measures include:

   a) disclosure of such conduct to the court and even disclosure of confidential information.
   b) withdrawing from representation of the client.
   c) notifying adverse parties of the client's actions so that the adverse parties can protect themselves.
   d) documenting the client's words and actions as proof and the lawyer's own words and actions attempting to prevent the client from causing further harm.

ANSWERS TO REVIEW QUESTIONS

Answer 68

The correct answer is choice A. A lawyer should not represent a client if the lawyer is likely to be a necessary witness except if the lawyer's testimony relates to an uncontested issue, the lawyer's testimony relates to value of services provided, or the lawyer's disqualification would work a substantial hardship on the client.

Answer 69

The correct answer is choice C. A lawyer should behave with civility, courtesy, and decorum which are legal standards that must be respected.

Answer 70

The correct answer is choice A. A lawyer must act in fairness to opposing parties and counsel, meaning a lawyer, among other things, cannot unlawfully obstruct access to evidence, or destroy or alter anything of evidentiary value, make a frivolous discovery request or obstruct a valid discovery request, nor assist in false testimony or make any unlawful inducement to a witness.

Answer 71

The correct answer is choice B. The rule requiring a lawyer to act with impartiality and make only meritorious claims and contentions allows the lawyer to make good faith arguments for reversals, modification, or extensions of existing law.

Answer 72

The correct answer is choice C. When making a filing, a lawyer represents that there is no improper purpose, the filing rests on a legal grounding, and there is evidentiary support for the filing.

Answer 73

The correct answer is choice A. Improper filings may be the subject of sanctions requested by opposing counsel or imposed by the court sufficient to deter repetition of the offensive conduct or comparable conduct by others.

Answer 74

The correct answer is choice C. A lawyer's duty of candor requires that the lawyer disclose controlling cases or law directly opposed to a client's interest, even if opposing counsel fails to disclose them.

Answer 75

The correct answer is choice A. A lawyer must take subsequent remedial measures if the lawyer knows or reasonably believes that the client will take criminal or fraudulent actions related to the proceedings. Such subsequent remedial measures include disclosure of such conduct to the court and even disclosure of confidential information.

VII.   COMMUNICATIONS WITH PERSONS OTHER THAN CLIENTS

★   **A.   Truthfulness in Statements to Others**

1)   NO FALSE STATEMENTS OF FACT

A lawyer must never knowingly make a false statement of material fact or law to a third person. A misrepresentation may qualify as a false statement of material fact. A lawyer makes a prohibited misrepresentation if the lawyer affirms another person's statement that the lawyer knows is false, even if the lawyer does not specifically say something false.

For example, suppose a client and lawyer are having lunch together when they are approached by an opponent's attorney. If the client tells the attorney a material fact that the attorney knows is false, and the attorney nods in affirmation, the act of nodding could be interpreted as a false statement of fact.

2)   NO FAILURE TO DISCLOSE MATERIAL FACT ASSISTING CRIME

A lawyer must never fail to disclose a material fact when disclosure is necessary to avoid assisting a criminal or fraudulent act by a client, unless disclosure is prohibited by the Rule of Confidentiality. Model Rules of Prof'l Conduct R. 4.1. The rule only applies when the disclosure is required to prevent a fraudulent or criminal act by the client. Therefore, a lawyer has no general affirmative duty to inform an opposing party of relevant facts.

3)   DISTINGUISHING STATEMENTS MADE DURING NEGOTIATIONS

Some statements made during negotiations are not treated as statements of fact. For example, estimates of price or value, and a party's intentions as to an acceptable settlement offer of a claim are ordinarily in this category. For example, a lawyer can tell opposing counsel that a client wouldn't accept a settlement offer below $1,000,000, even if the lawyer knows this is not truth.

★   **B.   Communications with Represented Persons**

In representing a client, a lawyer must not communicate about the subject of the representation with a person the lawyer knows to be represented by another lawyer in the matter, unless the lawyer has the other lawyer's consent or is authorized to do so by law or a court order. Model Rules of Prof'l Conduct R. 4.2.

★★   **C.   Communications with Unrepresented Persons**

In dealing on behalf of a client with a person who is not represented by counsel, a lawyer must not state or imply that the lawyer is disinterested. When the lawyer knows or reasonably should know that the unrepresented person misunderstands the lawyer's role in the matter, the lawyer must make reasonable efforts to correct the misunderstanding. The lawyer must not give legal advice to an unrepresented person, other than the advice to secure counsel if the lawyer knows, or reasonably should know, that the interests of such a person are, or have a reasonable possibility of becoming, in conflict with the interests of the client. Model Rules of Prof'l Conduct R. 4.3.

D.   Respect for Rights of Third Persons

1)   HARASSING OTHERS

In representing a client, a lawyer must not use means that have no substantial purpose other than to embarrass, delay, or burden a third person, or use methods of obtaining evidence that violate the legal rights of such a person. Model Rules of Prof'l Conduct R. 4.4(a).

2)   INADVERTENT DISCLOSURE OF INFORMATION

Special problems are presented when a document is inadvertently sent by a non-client to a lawyer. The document can be sent in various ways including mail, fax, email, or other electronic modes. Model Rules of Prof'l Conduct R. 4.4 cmt. [2].

Specifically, a lawyer who receives a document related to the representation of the lawyer's client and knows or reasonably should know that the document was inadvertently sent must promptly notify the sender. Model Rules of Prof'l Conduct R. 4.4(b).

If the inadvertently sent document contains confidential or privileged information about an opposing party (the sender or the sender's client), the receiving lawyer should "promptly notify the sender in order to permit that person to take protective measures." Model Rules of Prof'l Conduct R. 4.4 cmt. [2].

If the document includes confidential or privileged information, the sender may request a protective order from the relevant court. If the court declines to issue the protective order, the receiving party could possibly use the information against the sender and/or the sender's client. The law is unsettled as to whether the privilege is lost after accidental disclosure and whether the court should protect the sender from the consequences of such disclosure. A consideration that could affect the court's decision on this issue is whether the sender took reasonable precautions to prevent the inadvertent disclosure.

REVIEW QUESTIONS

76. Can a lawyer communicate about a legal matter with a person involved in the matter who is known to be represented by an attorney?

    a) Never.
    b) No, unless authorized by the law or a court order.
    c) Yes, if the attorney has the informed consent of the represented party.
    d) Yes, if the attorney has the other lawyer's consent or is authorized by law or court order.

77. A lawyer who obtains confidential information through an inadvertent disclosure by a third party must:

    a) prudently use the information to the client's benefit if not doing so would prejudice or harm the client's case and possibly result in malpractice.
    b) acknowledge receipt of the information in writing to the third party.
    c) notify the third party sender if the lawyer knows or should know the information was inadvertently sent.
    d) seek a court's protective order to allow fair use of the inadvertent disclosure.

ANSWERS TO REVIEW QUESTIONS

Answer 76

The correct answer is choice D. In representing a client, a lawyer must not communicate about the subject of the representation with a person the lawyer knows to be represented by another lawyer in the matter, unless the lawyer has the other lawyer's consent or is authorized to do so by law or a court order.

Answer 77

The correct answer is choice C. A lawyer who obtains confidential information through an inadvertent disclosure by a third party must notify the third party sender if the lawyer knows or should know the information was inadvertently sent.

VIII. DIFFERENT ROLES OF THE LAWYER

A lawyer performs various functions in several different capacities. For example, as an advocate, a lawyer zealously represents a client's interest. As an advisor, a lawyer provides a client with an informed understanding of legal rights and responsibilities and explains practical implications.

A. Lawyer as Advisor

In representing a client, a lawyer must exercise independent professional judgment and provide candid advice. In providing advice, a lawyer may refer not only to law but to other considerations such as moral, economic, social, and political factors that may be relevant to the client's situation. Model Rules of Prof'l Conduct R. 2.1.

B. Lawyer as Evaluator

As an evaluator, a lawyer examines a client's legal affairs and reports about them to the client.

1) EVALUATION FOR USE BY THIRD PERSONS

A lawyer may provide an evaluation of a matter affecting a client for the use of someone other than the client if the lawyer reasonably believes that making the evaluation is compatible with other aspects of the lawyer's relationship with the client. Model Rules of Prof'l Conduct R. 2.3(a).

When the lawyer knows, or reasonably should know, that the evaluation is likely to affect the client's interests materially and adversely, the lawyer must not provide the evaluation unless the client gives informed consent. Model Rules of Prof'l Conduct R. 2.3(b).

Information relating to the evaluation is otherwise protected by the Rule of Confidentiality. Model Rules of Prof'l Conduct R. 2.3(c).

C. Lawyer as Negotiator

As negotiator, a lawyer seeks a result advantageous to the client. However, the lawyer must deal honestly with others.

D. Lawyer as Arbitrator, Mediator, or other Third-Party Neutral

In addition to acting as a representative, a lawyer may serve as a third-party neutral, a nonrepresentational role helping the parties to resolve a dispute or other matter. A lawyer serves as a third-party neutral when the lawyer assists two or more people who are not clients of the lawyer to reach a resolution of a dispute or other matter that has arisen between them. Service as a third-party neutral may include service as an arbitrator, a mediator, or in such other capacity as will enable the lawyer to assist the parties to resolve the matter. Model Rules of Prof'l Conduct R. 2.4(a).

A lawyer serving as a third-party neutral must inform unrepresented parties that the lawyer is not representing them. When the lawyer knows or reasonably should know that a party does not understand the lawyer's role in the matter, the lawyer must explain the difference between the lawyer's role as a third-party neutral and a lawyer's role as one who represents a client. Model Rules of Prof'l Conduct R. 2.4(b).

★   **E.   Prosecutors and other Governmental Lawyers**

1)   <u>SPECIAL RESPONSIBILITIES OF PROSECUTORS DURING CASE</u>

A prosecutor possesses special responsibilities regarding the prosecution of a criminal action. The prosecutor in a criminal case must:

- refrain from prosecuting a charge that the prosecutor knows is not supported by probable cause;
- make reasonable efforts to assure that the accused has been advised of the right to, and the procedure for obtaining, counsel, and has been given reasonable opportunity to obtain counsel;
- not seek to obtain from an unrepresented accused a waiver of important pretrial rights, such as the right to a preliminary hearing;
- make timely disclosure to the defense of all evidence or information known to the prosecutor that tends to negate the guilt of the accused or mitigates the offense, and, in connection with sentencing, disclose to the defense and to the tribunal all unprivileged mitigating information known to the prosecutor, except when the prosecutor is relieved of this responsibility by a protective order of the tribunal;
- not subpoena a lawyer in a grand jury or other criminal proceeding to present evidence about a past or present client unless the prosecutor reasonably believes:

(1)   the information sought is not protected from disclosure by any applicable privilege;

(2)   the evidence sought is essential to the successful completion of an ongoing investigation or prosecution; and

(3)   there is no other feasible alternative to obtain the information.

Model Rules of Prof'l Conduct R. 3.8(a)-(e).

2)   <u>DUTY OF PROSECUTOR TO DISCLOSE INFORMATION CONCERNING CONVICTION</u>

a)   New Credible and Material Evidence

When a prosecutor knows of new credible and material evidence creating a reasonable likelihood that a convicted defendant did not commit the offense, the prosecutor must promptly disclose the evidence to an appropriate court or authority. If the conviction was obtained in the prosecutor's jurisdiction, then the prosecutor must promptly disclose the evidence to the defendant unless a court authorizes delay. Additionally, the prosecutor must undertake further investigation, or make reasonable efforts to cause an investigation, to determine whether the defendant was convicted of an offense that the defendant did not commit.

b) Clear and Convincing Evidence

When a prosecutor knows of clear and convincing evidence establishing that a defendant in the prosecutor's jurisdiction was convicted of an offense that the defendant did not commit, the prosecutor must seek to remedy the conviction.

3) DUTY OF PROSECUTOR TO REFRAIN FROM MAKING EXTRAJUDICIAL COMMENTS

Except for statements that serve a legitimate law enforcement purpose, a prosecutor must refrain from making extrajudicial comments that have a substantial likelihood of heightening public condemnation of the accused. A prosecutor must also exercise reasonable care to prevent investigators, law enforcement personnel, employees, or other persons assisting or associated with the prosecutor in a criminal case from making an extrajudicial statement that the prosecutor would be prohibited from making.

★★ **F.   Lawyer Appearing in Non-Adjudicative Proceeding**

A lawyer representing a client before a legislative body or administrative agency in a non-adjudicative proceeding must: 1) disclose that the appearance is in a representative capacity; and 2) conform to the Rules regarding Candor toward the Tribunal, Fairness to Opposing Party and Counsel, and Impartiality and Decorum of the Tribunal. Model Rules of Prof'l Conduct R. 3.9.

★★ **G.   Lawyer Representing an Entity or other Organization**

An organization is an entity such as a business, company, corporation, or other entity. A lawyer can represent an individual or an organization. Special rules apply to representing an organization as a client.

1) GENERAL DUTY TO ORGANIZATION

When a lawyer represents an organization, the lawyer owes a fiduciary duty to the *organization* itself. Such a duty is paramount to any duty to the individual officers, directors, or employees of the organization. Accordingly, a lawyer employed or retained by an organization represents the organization acting through its duly authorized constituents. Model Rules of Prof'l Conduct R. 1.13(a).

2) VIOLATIONS OF LEGAL OBLIGATIONS OR LAWS

If a lawyer for an organization knows that an officer, employee or other person associated with the organization is engaged in action, intends to act, or refuses to act in a matter related to the representation that is a violation of a legal obligation to the organization, or a violation of law that reasonably might be imputed to the organization, and that is likely to result in substantial injury to the organization, the lawyer must proceed as is reasonably necessary in the best interest of the organization. Model Rules of Prof'l Conduct R. 1.13(b).

Unless the lawyer reasonably believes that it is not necessary in the best interest of the organization to do so, the lawyer *must* refer the matter to higher authority in the organization, including, if warranted by the circumstances, to the highest authority that can act on behalf of the organization (such as the board of directors) as determined by applicable law. *Id.*

3) ADVERSE ORGANIZATION AND CONSTITUENTS

In dealing with an organization's directors, officers, employees, members, shareholders or other constituents, a lawyer must explain the identity of the client when the lawyer knows or reasonably should know that the organization's interests are adverse to those of the constituents with whom the lawyer is dealing. Model Rules of Prof'l Conduct R. 1.13(f).

4) DUAL REPRESENTATION

A lawyer representing an organization may also represent any of its directors, officers, employees, members, shareholders or other constituents, subject to the provisions of the Rule regarding conflicts of interest involving current clients. If the organization's consent to the dual representation is required by that Rule, the consent must be given by an appropriate official of the organization other than the individual who is to be represented, or by the shareholders. Model Rules of Prof'l Conduct R. 1.13(g).

REVIEW QUESTIONS

78. A lawyer may serve in the role of negotiator, mediator, arbitrator, or some other form of third-party neutral while assisting two or more people who are not clients to reach a resolution of a dispute. In such a capacity, the lawyer must:

    a) advise all parties of their constitutional rights under the proceedings.

    b) inform unrepresented parties that the lawyer is not representing them and explain the role of a third-party neutral.

    c) discuss the possible admissions and denials the parties may make and the effect each may have on the proceeding and the party.

    d) reach a successful conclusion that avoids a formal trial.

79. A prosecutor must:

    a) refrain from prosecuting a charge that's not supported by reasonable suspicion.

    b) make timely disclosure to the defense of all evidence that mitigates the offense or tends to negate the guilt of the accused.

    c) prosecute all crimes and misdemeanors supported by some credible evidence with the knowledge that the discovery process is likely to reveal further useful information.

    d) make reasonable efforts to meet with the accused and the accused's counsel prior to trial in order to negotiate a plea agreement and reduce unnecessary public expenditures on legal fees and costs.

80. When representing an organization, a lawyer owes a fiduciary duty to:

    a) the Board of Directors, which is ultimately responsible for all aspects of the organization.

    b) the CEO responsible for all day-to-day operations of the organization.

    c) the organization itself and not any officer or director.

    d) all persons employed by the organization who will be affected by the lawyer's representation.

81. If a lawyer representing an organization has knowledge that an employee of the organization intends to act, or will act, in a manner that is detrimental to the organization, the lawyer must:

    a) advise the person considering acting in a manner detrimental to the organization that, as a lawyer for the organization, the lawyer will not allow the person to take such action.

    b) proceed as is reasonably necessary in the best interest of the organization.

    c) notify the individual that the lawyer will take legal action against the individual to prevent any possible action that is detrimental to the organization.

    d) inform the person's superior that the person's employment should be terminated prior to the person taking action detrimental to the organization.

82. A lawyer may agree to "dual representation" (representing both an organization and a representative of the organization) if:

    a) the lawyer representing the organization has another lawyer in the same firm represent the representative of the organization.

    b) there are no conflicts of interests and, if consent is required under a conflict of interest rule, it is given by an appropriate representative of the organization or the shareholders.

    c) the dual representation is presented to a neutral magistrate for review and the court determines there is no conflict.

    d) the lawyer is paid by both the organization and the representative of the organization, but from separate sources of funding to avoid commingling of client funds.

ANSWERS TO REVIEW QUESTIONS

Answer 78

The correct answer is choice B. In the role of negotiator, mediator, arbitrator, or some other form of third-party neutral while assisting two or more people who are not clients to reach a resolution of a dispute, a lawyer must inform unrepresented parties that the lawyer is not representing them and explain the role of a third-party neutral.

Answer 79

The correct answer is choice B. Prosecutors must make timely disclosure to the defense of all evidence that mitigates the offense or tends to negate the guilt of the accused.

Answer 80

The correct answer is choice C. When representing the organization, a lawyer owes a paramount fiduciary duty to the organization itself and not to any particular person within the organization.

Answer 81

The correct answer is choice B. A lawyer representing an organization must proceed as is reasonably necessary in the best interest of the organization if the lawyer has knowledge that any employee of an organization intends to act or will act in a manner that is detrimental to the organization.

Answer 82

The correct answer is choice B. If there are no conflicts of interest and, if required, consent is given by an appropriate representative of the organization or the shareholders, a lawyer may undertake dual representation of both an organization and a representative of the organization.

IX.   SAFEKEEPING FUNDS AND OTHER PROPERTY

A.   Establishing and Maintaining Client Trust Accounts

1)   CLIENT TRUST ACCOUNTS

When a lawyer holds property of clients or third persons in connection with legal representation, the lawyer must keep that property *separate* from the lawyer's own property. Model Rules of Prof'l Conduct R. 1.15(a). For exam purposes, the implicated property is usually money in a bank account. For example, unearned retainers must be placed in a separate client trust account. A lawyer must deposit into this client trust account legal fees and expenses that have been paid in advance, to be withdrawn by the lawyer only as fees are earned or expenses incurred. Model Rules of Prof'l Conduct R. 1.15(c). Separate trust accounts may be warranted when administering estates or acting in another similar fiduciary capacity.

a)   Account Located in State of Office

Funds must be kept in a separate client trust account in the state where the lawyer's office is located, or elsewhere with the consent of the client or third person.

b)   Complete Records Must be Kept for Five Years

A lawyer must keep complete records of client trust account funds and other property. The records must be preserved for five years after termination of the legal representation.

c)   Limited Exception for Paying Bank Service Charges

A lawyer can deposit the lawyer's own funds in a client trust account for the sole purpose of paying bank service charges on that account, but only in an amount necessary for that purpose. Model Rules of Prof'l Conduct R. 1.15(b). Under other circumstances, though, mixing the lawyer's own funds with client funds in a client trust account is not permitted and can result in prohibited commingling of those funds. Model Rules of Prof'l Conduct R. 1.15 cmt. [2].

★★★★ B.   Safekeeping Funds and other Property of Clients

★★★ 1)   SEPARATION OF PROPERTY

A lawyer should hold property of others with the care required of a professional fiduciary. As a general matter, securities should be kept in a safe deposit box, except when some other form of safekeeping is warranted by special circumstances.

C.   Safekeeping Funds and other Property of Third Persons

Attorneys often receive money from third parties from which the lawyer's fee will ultimately be paid. For example, a lawyer may receive a settlement check, from which the lawyer's fee will be paid. Upon receiving funds or other property in which a client or third person has an interest, a lawyer must promptly notify the client or third person. Model Rules of Prof'l Conduct R. 1.15(d).

Unless the Rules, the law, or an agreement provides otherwise, a lawyer must promptly deliver to the client or third person any funds or property the client or third person is entitled to receive and, upon request by the client or third person, must promptly provide a full accounting regarding such property. *Id.*

★★ **D.   Disputed Claims**

      1)   <u>TYPES OF DISPUTES</u>

The following types of disputes can arise regarding claims upon property contained in client trust funds:

- The lawyer and the client might disagree about the amount of funds in the account that the lawyer can keep as earnings for services provided to the client.

- The lawyer might disagree with the client's creditor regarding the amount of funds to which the creditor claims it is entitled pursuant to the client's alleged obligation.

- The client's creditor might disagree with the client regarding their respective claims to the funds in the account.

      2)   <u>CONTROL OF FUNDS</u>

          a)   Funds Must Be Separate

When in the course of representation a lawyer is in possession of property in which two or more people claim interests, the property must be kept separate by the lawyer until the dispute is resolved. Model Rules of Prof'l Conduct R. 1.15(e). One of the people claiming an interest in the property can be the lawyer. *Id.*

          b)   Undisputed Funds Must Be Promptly Returned

In the event of a disputed claim, the lawyer must promptly distribute the remaining, undisputed portion of the property. *Id.*

          c)   Lawyer can Withhold Funds for Fees if Risk Exists

If there is risk that the client may divert funds without paying the fee, the lawyer is not required to remit the portion from which the fee is to be paid. However, a lawyer may not hold funds to coerce a client into accepting the lawyer's contention.

          d)   Dispute Between Client and Third Party

A lawyer may be obligated to protect a third-party's lawful claims upon a client's funds or property, which the lawyer possesses, from a client's wrongful interference. *Id.*, cmt. [4]. In that event, if the third-party's claim is not frivolous, the lawyer may not release the funds or property to the client until resolution of the competing claims occurs. *Id.* The lawyer may not assume to decide a dispute between the third party and the client. *Id.* However, the lawyer can file an action to have a court resolve their dispute when substantial grounds exist for the dispute. *Id.* For example, suppose a client is awarded damages in a civil action that have been transferred to the lawyer for distribution to the client. If a third-party creditor possesses a lien on those funds, the lawyer must protect the funds. *Id.*

REVIEW QUESTIONS

83. A lawyer must hold client funds as a fiduciary and keep them separate from the lawyer's own funds. However,

   a) retainers are up-front payments to the lawyer who may access them as needed for business purposes.

   b) a lawyer must provide a full accounting of the client's funds within two business days of such a demand by the client.

   c) a lawyer need not set aside funds that are in dispute with a client as the lawyer can always return the funds when the dispute is settled.

   d) a lawyer can deposit the lawyer's own funds in a client trust account for the sole purpose of paying bank service charges on that account.

ANSWERS TO REVIEW QUESTIONS

Answer 83

The correct answer is choice D. A lawyer must hold client funds as a fiduciary and keep them separate from the lawyer's own funds. However, a lawyer can deposit the lawyer's own funds in a client trust account for the sole purpose of paying bank service charges on that account.

X.   COMMUNICATION ABOUT LEGAL SERVICES

★★★★ **A.   Advertising and other Public Communications About Legal Services**

Historically, ethical rules prohibited lawyers from advertising their services. Today, lawyers are permitted to conduct limited advertising.

★★★   1)   <u>COMMUNICATIONS CONCERNING A LAWYER'S SERVICES</u>

      a)   Must Be Truthful

A lawyer cannot make a false or misleading communication about the lawyer or the lawyer's services. Model Rules of Prof'l Conduct R. 7.1. A communication is false or misleading if it contains a material misrepresentation of fact or law, or omits a fact necessary to make the statement considered as a whole not materially misleading. *Id.*

      b)   Unjustified Expectations

A lawyer may not include statements of fact or opinion that would create an unjustified expectation. An example of such a statement is that "opposing counsel shiver when they hear that I represent the plaintiff." *Id.*, cmt. [3].

      c)   Unfair Comparisons

An advertisement may not include unfair comparisons to other lawyers. *Id.*

★★★   2)   <u>ADVERTISING</u>

Subject to the requirement of truthful (and not false or misleading) statements and the limitations upon soliciting prospective clients, a lawyer may communicate information about the lawyer's services through any media. Model Rules of Prof'l Conduct Rs. 7.1, 7.2(a), 7.3.

      a)   Contents of Advertisements

Most types of advertisements must contain the name and office address of the lawyer or law firm responsible for the contents of the advertisement. Model Rules of Prof'l Conduct R. 7.2(d). Additionally, an advertisement may not mention a client *unless* the client is regularly represented by that lawyer or firm and the client consents in advance. Model Rules of Prof'l Conduct R. 7.1, cmt. [1].

      b)   Keeping Copies of Advertisements

In many jurisdictions, a lawyer must keep copies of written or electronic advertisements for two years. The copies must be produced on demand from the state regulatory authorities.

      c)   Place of Advertisements

In many jurisdictions, a court may consider the location of the advertisement in determining its permissibility. For example, an advertisement located in a hospital will generally not be permitted because of the potentially vulnerable nature of the patients.

3) FIRM NAMES AND LETTERHEAD

a) Not False or Misleading

A lawyer must not use a firm name, letterhead, or other professional designation that is false or misleading. Model Rules of Prof'l Conduct R. 7.1, cmts. [1], [5]. A trade name may be used by a lawyer in private practice if, for example, it does not imply a connection with a government agency or with a public or charitable legal services organization and is not otherwise false or misleading. *Id.*

b) Partner Serving in Public Office

The name of a lawyer holding a public office cannot be used in the name of a law firm, or in communications on its behalf, during any substantial period in which the lawyer is not actively and regularly practicing with the firm. Model Rules of Prof'l Conduct R. 7.1, cmt. [8].

c) Representation as Partnership

Lawyers may state or imply that they practice in a partnership or other organization only when that is the fact. Model Rules of Prof'l Conduct R. 7.1, cmt. [7].

d) Law Firm May Use Same Name in Multiple Jurisdictions

A law firm with offices in more than one jurisdiction may use the same name or other professional designation in each jurisdiction. Model Rules of Prof'l Conduct R. 7.1, cmt. [6].

★ B. Solicitation – Direct Contact with Prospective Clients

"Solicitation" means a lawyer's communication: 1) to a person that the lawyer knows or reasonably should know needs legal services; and 2) that offers to provide, or reasonably can be understood as offering to provide, legal services. Model Rules of Prof'l Conduct R. 7.3(a).

1) LIVE PERSON-TO-PERSON SOLICITATION IS PROHIBITED

Unlike advertising, as a general rule, live solicitation is prohibited. A lawyer may not by live person-to-person contact, solicit professional employment when earning money a significant motive for doing so. Model Rules of Prof'l Conduct R. 7.3(b).

a) Definition of Live Person-to-Person Contact

"Live person-to-person contact" means in-person, face-to-face, live telephone, and other real-time person-to-person communications where the person has a direct encounter without time for consideration. *Id.*, cmt. [2]. For example, such contact does not include text messages, chat rooms, or other written communications that one may easily disregard. *Id.*

b)   Exceptions as to Lawyers or Persons in Relationship with Lawyer

The prohibition is not applicable if the person solicited:

- is a lawyer; or
- has a family, close personal, or prior business or professional relationship with the lawyer or law firm; or
- routinely uses for business purposes the lawyer's type of legal services.

Model Rules of Prof'l Conduct R. 7.3(b).

c)   When Communication Is Not a Solicitation

A lawyer's communication is not a solicitation if:

- it is in response to a request for information; or
- it is directed to the public (e.g., billboard, website, TV commercial); or
- it is generated in response to Internet searches.

Id., cmt. [1].

2)   OTHER SOLICITATION PERMISSIBLE

Solicitation that is not live person-to-person, is permissible. Therefore, solicitation by direct mail or electronic mail or by other electronic means that do not involve live person-to-person contact may be permissible, if not otherwise prohibited. *Id.*, cmt. [3].

a)   Exception to Allowable Solicitations

A lawyer may not solicit professional employment if: 1) the target of the solicitation has made known to the lawyer a desire not to be solicited; or 2) the solicitation involves coercion, duress, or harassment. Model Rules of Prof'l Conduct R. 7.3(c).

3)   SOLICITATION BY THIRD PARTIES

If the solicitation is carried out by a third party, it will be attributed to the lawyer if the elements of solicitation are otherwise present and the communication was directed by the lawyer. ABA Model Rules of Prof'l Conduct R. 7.3(a).

C.   Prepaid or Group Legal Service Plans

A lawyer may participate in a prepaid or group legal service plan operated by an organization not owned or directed by the lawyer that uses live person-to-person contact to enroll members or sell subscriptions for the plan to people who are not known to need legal services in a matter covered by the plan. Model Rules of Prof'l Conduct R. 7.3(e).

★   **D.   Referrals**

1) PAYMENT FOR RECOMMENDING A LAWYER'S SERVICES

A lawyer must not compensate, promise, or give anything of value to another person as payment for recommending the lawyer's services. Model Rules of Prof'l Conduct R. 7.2(b). This Rule is subject to the following exceptions:

a) Reasonable Costs of Advertisements or Communications

A lawyer may pay the reasonable costs of advertisements or communications. Model Rules of Prof'l Conduct R. 7.2(b)(1).

b) Legal Service Plans and Certain Lawyer Referral Services

A lawyer may pay the usual charges of a legal service plan or a not-for-profit or qualified lawyer referral service. Model Rules of Prof'l Conduct R. 7.2(b)(2).

c) Purchase of Law Practice

A lawyer can pay for a law practice that the lawyer acquires. Model Rules of Prof'l Conduct R. 7.2(b)(3).

d) Reciprocal Referral Agreement

A lawyer can refer clients to another lawyer or a non-lawyer professional per to an agreement (not otherwise prohibited by the Rules) providing for the other person to refer clients or customers to the lawyer if: 1) the reciprocal referral agreement is not exclusive; and 2) the client is informed of the agreement's existence and nature. Model Rules of Prof'l Conduct R. 7.2(b)(4).

e) Gift Neither Reasonably Expected Nor Intended to Be Payment

A lawyer may give a nominal gift as a token of appreciation that is neither reasonably expected nor intended to be payment for recommending the lawyer's services. Model Rules of Prof'l Conduct R. 7.2(b)(5).

E. Communications of Fields of Practice and Specialization

1) FIELDS OF PRACTICE

A lawyer may communicate the fact that the lawyer does or does not practice in particular fields of law. Model Rules of Prof'l Conduct R. 7.2, cmt. [9].

a) Patent Lawyers

A lawyer admitted to engage in patent practice before the United States Patent and Trademark Office may, for example, use the designation "Patent Attorney" or a similar designation. Model Rules of Prof'l Conduct R. 7.2, cmt. [10].

b) Admiralty Lawyers

A lawyer engaged in Admiralty practice may, for example, use the designation "Admiralty," "Proctor in Admiralty," or a similar designation. *Id.*

2)   SPECIALIZATION

Generally, a lawyer is permitted to assert that the lawyer is a "specialist" in particular fields, but the assertion must not be "false and misleading." A lawyer must not state or imply that a lawyer is *certified* as a specialist in a particular field of law unless: 1) the lawyer has been certified as a specialist by an organization that has been approved by an appropriate state authority or accredited by the ABA; and 2) the name of the certifying organization is clearly identified in the communication. Model Rules of Prof'l Conduct R. 7.2(c), cmt. [9].

REVIEW QUESTIONS

84. A lawyer is permitted to conduct limited advertising in public communications which may include:

    a) statements of fact or opinion that create unjustified expectations in potential clients or unfair comparisons to other lawyers.

    b) declarations of win, losses, or ties in court proceedings.

    c) statements declaring the lawyer's relationships with judges or other heads of tribunals or elected officials.

    → d) statements of fact as to the attorney's name, business address, phone number, website, and hours.

85. A lawyer may make a written, recorded, or electronic communication advertisement to the public as long as the advertisement:

    → a) contains the lawyer's name and office address, is kept for two years, and is produced on demand by regulatory authorities.

    b) declares the lawyer's expertise and mentions other clients who regularly are represented and rely upon that expertise.

    c) is preapproved by the regulatory authority so as to avoid potential liability.

    d) is filed with the regulatory authority at least five business days prior to publication and not found too libelous, slanderous, or false in any manner.

86. A lawyer cannot give anything of value to another person or entity for recommending their services, except:

    a) a business card.

    → b) the reasonable costs of advertising or communications, the usual charge of a legal service plan or lawyer referral service approved by the state's legal regulatory agency, or the cost of a law practice the lawyer purchases.

    c) an invitation to the lawyer's or law firm's annual holiday dinner and party where gifts are anonymously exchanged by all attendees.

    d) a promise to give discounted rates based on future clients' referrals.

87. Reciprocal referral agreements (RRA) are:

    a) allowed if the RRA is exclusive.

    → b) allowed if the client is informed of the existence and nature of the agreement and the agreement is not exclusive.

    c) never allowed.

    d) always allowed because to hold otherwise would restrain trade.

88. Solicitation by a lawyer is:

    a) permitted under all circumstances.

    b) prohibited if the lawyer's financial gain is the significant motivation.

→ c) prohibited unless the potential client is a lawyer or a close personal friend or a family member.

d) prohibited under all circumstances.

89. A lawyer's communications cannot state that a lawyer is a specialist unless:

a) the lawyer has undertaken continuing legal education for at least three years exclusively in the area of specialty and can provide proof of the same to the licensing authority that may grant such certification.

b) the lawyer is certified as such by at least one appointed judge who has observed the lawyer's practice, demeanor, knowledge, education, and experience before the court and determined that the lawyer has attained a proficient competency in the requisite specialty.

c) the lawyer is certified by the highest court in the state or federal judiciary with jurisdiction to hear such specialty cases.

→ d) the lawyer is certified as such by an organization approved by a state authority authorized to grant such certifications or by an ABA accredited agency, and the name of the certifying organization is clearly stated in the communication.

ANSWERS TO REVIEW QUESTIONS

Answer 84

The correct answer is choice D. A lawyer is permitted to conduct limited advertising in public communications which may include statements of fact as to the attorney's name, business address, phone number, website, and hours. However, the advertisement may not make statements of fact or opinion that create unjustified expectations in potential clients or unfair comparisons to other lawyers, declarations of wins, losses, or ties in court proceedings, or statements declaring the lawyer's relationships with judges or other heads of tribunals or elected officials.

Answer 85

The correct answer is choice A. A lawyer may make a written, recorded, or electronic communication advertisement to the public as long as the advertisement contains the lawyer's name and office address, is kept for two years, and is produced on demand by regulatory authorities.

Answer 86

The correct answer is choice B. A lawyer cannot give anything of value to another person or entity for recommending their services, except the reasonable costs of advertising or communications, the usual charge of a legal service plan or lawyer referral service approved by the state's legal regulatory agency, or the cost of a law practice they purchase.

Answer 87

The correct answer is choice B. Reciprocal referral agreements are allowed if the RRA is not exclusive and the client is informed of the existence and nature of the agreement.

Answer 88

The correct answer is choice C. Solicitation by a lawyer is prohibited unless the potential client is a lawyer or a close personal friend or a family member.

Answer 89

The correct answer is choice D. A lawyer's communications cannot state that a lawyer is a specialist unless the lawyer is certified as such by an organization approved by a state authority authorized to grant such certifications or by an ABA accredited agency, and the name of the certifying organization is clearly stated in the communication.

XI.   LAWYERS' DUTIES TO THE PUBLIC AND THE LEGAL SYSTEM

A.   Voluntary *Pro Bono* Service

Every lawyer has a professional responsibility to provide legal services to those unable to pay. A lawyer should aspire to render at least 50 hours of *pro bono publico* (i.e., free to the public) legal services per year. Model Rules of Prof'l Conduct R. 6.1.

1)   SUBSTANTIAL MAJORITY OF SERVICES

In fulfilling this responsibility, the lawyer should provide a substantial majority of the 50 hours of legal services without fee or expectation of fee to persons of limited means or to charitable, religious, civic, community, governmental, and educational organizations in matters that are designed primarily to address the needs of persons of limited means. *Id.*

2)   FOCUS OF VOLUNTARY SERVICE

In fulfilling this *pro bono* service responsibility, lawyers should provide legal services to:

- persons with limited means free of charge or at a substantially reduced fee; or
- participation in activities for improving the law, legal system, or legal profession; or
- charitable, religious, civic, governmental, and educational organizations free of charge or at a substantially reduced fee.

When a lawyer provides *pro bono* legal services to an organization, the lawyer's legal services and financial support should primarily aid the organization in addressing the needs of persons with limited means. The legal services could also further the group's organizational purposes if the payment of standard legal fees would significantly deplete the organization's economic resources.

B.   Accepting Appointments

A lawyer must not seek to avoid appointment by a tribunal to represent a person except for good cause, such as:

- when representing the client is likely to result in violation of the Rules or other law;
- when representing the client is likely to result in an unreasonable financial burden on the lawyer; or
- if the client or the cause is so repugnant to the lawyer as to be likely to impair the client-lawyer relationship or the lawyer's ability to represent the client.

C.   Serving in Legal Services Organizations

A lawyer may serve as a director, officer, or member of a legal services organization even if the organization serves people who have adverse interests to the lawyer's clients. However, the lawyer cannot knowingly participate in a decision or action of the organization if: 1) participating in the decision or action is incompatible with the lawyer's obligations to a client; or 2) the decision or action could have a materially adverse effect on the representation of a client of the organization whose interests are adverse to a client of the lawyer.

D.   Law Reform Activities Affecting Client Interests

A lawyer may serve as a director, officer, or member of an organization involved in reform of the law even though the reform may affect the interests of a client of the lawyer. A lawyer serving in this capacity does not have a client-lawyer relationship with the organization. When the lawyer knows that a client's interests may be materially benefitted by a decision in which the lawyer participates, the lawyer must disclose the fact but does not need to identify the client.

E.   Criticism of Judges and Adjudicating Officials

Lawyers contribute to improving the administration of justice by expressing their honest and candid opinions on the professional or personal fitness of persons being considered for election or appointment to judicial office. However, "a lawyer must not make a statement that the lawyer knows to be false or with reckless disregard as to its truth or falsity concerning the qualifications or integrity of a judge, adjudicatory officer, or candidate for election or appointment to judicial or legal office." Model Rules of Prof'l Conduct R. 8.2(a).

To maintain the fair and independent administration of justice, lawyers are encouraged to continue traditional efforts to defend judges and courts unjustly criticized.

F.   Political Contributions to Obtain Engagements or Appointments

Lawyers have a right to participate fully in the political process, which includes making and soliciting political contributions to candidates for judicial and other public office. However, a lawyer or law firm must not accept a governmental legal engagement or an appointment by a judge if the lawyer or law firm makes a political contribution or solicits political contributions for the purpose of obtaining or being considered for that type of legal engagement or appointment.

1)   POLITICAL CONTRIBUTION

The term "political contribution" means any gift, subscription, loan, advance, or deposit of anything of value made directly or indirectly to a candidate, incumbent, political party, or campaign committee to influence or provide financial support for election to or retention in judicial or other government office. Political contributions in initiative and referendum elections are not included. Furthermore, the term does not include any uncompensated services.

2)   GOVERNMENT LEGAL ENGAGEMENT/JUDICIAL APPOINTMENT

The term "government legal engagement" means any engagement to provide legal services that a public official has the direct or indirect power to award. The term "appointment by a judge" means an appointment to a position such as referee, commissioner, special master, receiver, guardian, or other similar position that is made by a judge. However, these terms do not include:

- substantially uncompensated services;
- engagements or appointments made on the basis of experience, expertise, professional qualifications, and cost following a request for proposal or other process that is free from influence based upon political contributions; and
- engagements or appointments made on a rotational basis from a list compiled without regard to political contributions.

G.   Improper Influence on Government Officials

It is professional misconduct for a lawyer to state or imply an ability to improperly influence a government agency or official.

H.   Assisting Judicial Misconduct

It is professional misconduct for a lawyer to knowingly assist a judge or judicial officer in conduct that is a violation of applicable rules of judicial conduct or other law.

I.   Impropriety Incident to Public Service

1)   LAWYERS AS JUDICIAL CANDIDATES

A lawyer who is a candidate for judicial office must comply with the applicable provisions of the Model Code of Judicial Conduct. Model Rules of Prof'l Conduct R. 8.2(b). Some of the Code's provisions are described in the next section of this outline.

REVIEW QUESTIONS

90. A lawyer involved with an organization that is developing or reforming the law must:

    a) refrain from representing any client who may benefit or be harmed by the lawyer's actions.

    b) disclose to the organization that the lawyer has a client who may benefit from the activity.

    c) register as a lobbyist and disclose the same to all current and potential clients to allow them to decide if such actions are to their detriment or against their interests.

    d) avoid invalidating a law if such invalidation would have a negative impact or unintended consequence on other laws.

91. Lawyers who are declared judicial candidates:

    a) are not subject to the Model Code of Judicial Conduct, as they have not been sworn onto the bench.

    b) must disclose such candidacy to current and potential clients as appointment to the bench may force them to recuse themselves from further representation and hinder effective and consistent representation of the client.

    c) must not appear before the court for which they are a judicial candidate to avoid an appearance of impropriety.

    d) are subject to the Model Code of Judicial Conduct, even before they ascend to the bench.

92. Every lawyer has a professional responsibility to provide pro bono services and aspire to provide at least 50 hours of pro bono service to the public. A substantial majority of that time must go toward:

    a) those identified by the state bar association as eligible charitable or civic organizations or by the court as needy individuals.

    b) charitable contributions in lieu of pro bono hours as not all licensed attorneys are capable of providing legal representation.

    c) those unable to afford an attorney or to charitable or civic organizations addressing the needs of persons with limited means.

    d) pro bono service to government agencies in order to reduce the overall cost of public services, including legal services.

ANSWERS TO REVIEW QUESTIONS

Answer 90

The correct answer is choice B. A lawyer involved with an organization that is developing or reforming a law must disclose to the organization that the lawyer has a client who may benefit from the activity.

Answer 91

The correct answer is choice D. Lawyers who are declared judicial candidates are subject to the Model Code of Judicial Conduct, even before they ascend to the bench.

Answer 92

The correct answer is choice C. A substantial majority of pro bono legal services must go toward those unable to afford an attorney or to charitable or civic organizations addressing the needs of persons with limited means.

★★★ **XII.   JUDICIAL CONDUCT**

Judicial ethics are governed by the Model Code of Judicial Conduct's Canons and Rules.

A.   Maintaining the Independence and Impartiality of the Judiciary

A judge must uphold and promote the independence, integrity, and impartiality of the judiciary. Model Code of Judicial Conduct Canon 1. A judge must avoid impropriety and the appearance of impropriety. *Id.* Moreover, a judge or candidate for judicial office must not engage in activity that is inconsistent with the judiciary's independence, integrity, and impartiality. Model Code of Judicial Conduct Canon 4.

1)   COMPLIANCE WITH THE LAW

A judge must comply with the law. Model Code of Judicial Conduct Rule 1.1. Specifically, a judge or other judicial candidate in a public election must comply with all applicable laws and regulations concerning elections, campaigns, and fund raising. Model Code of Judicial Conduct Rule 4.2(A)(2).

2)   PROMOTING CONFIDENCE IN THE JUDICIARY

A judge must act in a way that promotes public confidence in the judiciary's independence, integrity, and impartiality. Model Code of Judicial Conduct Rule 1.2.

a)   Independence, Integrity, and Impartiality Defined

Independence means a judge's freedom from controls or influence beyond those set by law. Model Code of Judicial Conduct Terminology. Integrity means honesty, fairness, uprightness, and soundness of character. *Id.* "Impartially" or "impartial" means a lack of prejudice or bias in favor of, or against, specific parties or types of parties, as well as keeping an open mind when considering issues that could come before a judge. *Id.*

b)   Avoiding Impropriety and the Appearance of Impropriety

A judge must avoid impropriety and the appearance of impropriety. Model Code of Judicial Conduct Rule 1.2. Actual improprieties include illegal conduct, conduct in violation of court rules, and conduct in violation of the Code. *Id.*, cmt. 5. Also, impropriety means conduct that undermines a judge's independence, integrity, or impartiality. Model Code of Judicial Conduct Terminology.

A judge's improper conduct (i.e., improprieties), as well as conduct that creates the appearance of impropriety, adversely affects public confidence in the judiciary. Model Code of Judicial Conduct Rule 1.2 cmt. 2. Because a judge is in the public eye, the judge should accept the Code's greater limitations upon conduct than those applicable to regular citizens, such as limits upon judicial speech. *Id.*

(1) Test for Appearance of Impropriety

The appearance of impropriety exists when the judge's "conduct would create in reasonable minds a perception that the judge violated the Code or engaged in other conduct" that reflects negatively on the judge's impartiality, honesty, temperament, or fitness. Model Code of Judicial Conduct Rule 1.2 cmt. 5.

3) AVOIDING ABUSE OF THE PRESTIGE OF JUDICIAL OFFICE

A judge must not abuse the prestige of judicial office to advance the personal or economic interests of the judge or others. Model Code of Judicial Conduct Rule 1.3. A judge must not allow others to abuse the prestige of judicial office to advance their personal or economic interests. *Id.*

a)   Improper Use of Judicial Office

A judge engages in improper conduct by attempting to use or using the judge's position to gain personal advantage or deferential treatment. *Id.*, cmt. 1. For example, a judge may not refer to the judge's official status to obtain favorable treatment in encounters with law enforcement officers. *Id.* Likewise, a judge cannot use official judicial letterhead to obtain an advantage in carrying on the judge's personal business affairs. *Id.* Generally, a judge can serve as a reference or provide a letter or recommendation for someone that the judge personally knows, provided that the judge complies with the above provisions. Model Code of Judicial Conduct Rule 1.3 cmt. 2.

B.   Performing Judicial Duties Impartially, Competently, and Diligently

A judge must perform judicial duties impartially, competently, and diligently. Model Code of Judicial Conduct Canon 2.

1) GIVING PRECEDENCE TO THE DUTIES OF JUDICIAL OFFICE

A judge's judicial duties take precedence over all the judge's other activities. Model Code of Judicial Conduct Rule 2.1. Judicial duties include all the duties of the judge's office prescribed by law. *Id.* A judge must conduct extrajudicial and personal activities so as to reduce the risk of conflicts that would result in their disqualification from participation in proceedings. *Id.*, cmt. 1.

2) IMPARTIALITY AND FAIRNESS

A judge must uphold and apply the law. Model Code of Judicial Conduct Rule 2.2. The judge must perform all judicial duties fairly and impartially. *Id.* In order to ensure fairness and impartiality, the judge must manifest objectivity and open-mindedness. *Id.*, cmt. 1. The judge must interpret and apply the law regardless of whether the judge approves of the law. Model Code of Judicial Conduct Rule 2.2 cmt. 2.

3) BIAS, PREJUDICE, AND HARASSMENT

A judge must not manifest bias or prejudice, or engage in harassment. Model Code of Judicial Conduct Rule 2.3(B). A judge must not permit court staff to do so. *Id.* A judge must require lawyers to refrain from manifesting bias or prejudice, or engaging in harassment.

4) EXTERNAL INFLUENCES ON JUDICIAL CONDUCT

A judge must decide cases based on the law and facts, regardless of whether specific laws or parties are popular or unpopular. Model Code of Judicial Conduct Rule 2.4 cmt. 1.

a) Public Clamor or Fear of Criticism May Not Sway Judges

A judge must not be swayed by public clamor or fear of criticism. Model Code of Judicial Conduct Rule 2.4(A).

b) Certain Relationships or Interests May Not Influence Judges

A judge must not allow family, social, financial, political, or other relationships or interests to influence the judge's judicial conduct or judgment. Model Code of Judicial Conduct Rule 2.4(B). For example, a judge cannot allow any relationship to affect the judge's impartiality in judicial decision-making.

c) No Conveying that One Occupies Position to Influence Judges

A judge may not convey the impression that anyone can influence the judge. Model Code of Judicial Conduct Rule 2.4(C). For example, a judge should prevent a close friend from indicating that the friend can influence the judge.

5) COMPETENCE, DILIGENCE, AND COOPERATION

a) Requirements of Competence and Diligence

A judge must perform administrative and judicial duties competently and diligently. Model Code of Judicial Conduct Rule 2.5(A). "Competence in the performance of judicial duties requires the legal knowledge, skill, thoroughness, and preparation reasonably necessary to perform" a judge's judicial responsibilities. Model Code of Judicial Conduct Rule 2.5 cmt. 1. A judge should supervise and monitor cases in ways that eliminate or reduce dilatory practices, avoidable delays, and unnecessary costs. Model Code of Judicial Conduct Rule 2.5 cmt. 4.

b) Requirement of Cooperation

The judge must cooperate with other judges and court officials in the administration of court business. Model Code of Judicial Conduct Rule 2.5(B).

6) ENSUREING THE RIGHT TO BE HEARD

The right of people to be heard in a court is a key aspect of a fair and impartial justice system. Model Code of Judicial Conduct Rule 2.6 cmt. 1. Observance of procedures protecting the right to be heard is necessary to protect a litigant's substantive rights. *Id.*

a)   Judge Must Provide the Right to Be Heard

A judge must provide every person who has a legal interest in a proceeding, or that person's lawyer, the right to be heard in the proceeding according to law. Model Code of Judicial Conduct Rule 2.6(A).

b)   Judge May Encourage Settlement of Disputed Matters

A judge may encourage parties to a proceeding and their lawyers to settle matters in dispute. Model Code of Judicial Conduct Rule 2.6(B). However, the judge may not act in a way that coerces any party into settlement of disputed matters. *Id.* Such improper conduct by the judge could undermine a party's legal right to be heard.   Model Code of Judicial Conduct Rule 2.6 cmt. 2.

A judge should consider the effect that participation in settlement discussions can have on the judge's objectivity and impartiality and the appearance of judicial objectivity and impartiality. Model Code of Judicial Conduct Rule 2.6 cmt. 2.

7)   RESPONSIBILITY TO DECIDE

A judge must hear and decide matters assigned to the judge. Model Code of Judicial Conduct Rule 2.7. Disqualification may be required to protect the rights of litigants or to preserve public confidence in the judiciary's independence, integrity, and impartiality. *Id.*, cmt. 1. A judge should not use disqualification to avoid matters that involve difficult, unpopular, or controversial issues. *Id.*

8)   DECORUM, DEMEANOR, AND COMMUNICATION WITH JURORS

A judge must require order and decorum in proceedings before the judge. Model Code of Judicial Conduct Rule 2.8(A). A judge must be patient, dignified, and courteous to jurors, litigants, witnesses, lawyers, court officials, court staff, and others with whom the judge deals in an official capacity. Model Code of Judicial Conduct Rule 2.8(B). The judge must require similar conduct of lawyers, court officials, court staff, and others subject to the judge's direction and control. *Id.*

9)   JUDICIAL STATEMENTS ON IMPENDING AND PENDING CASES

Some restrictions on judicial speech are essential to the maintenance of the judiciary's independence, integrity, and impartiality. Model Code of Judicial Conduct Rule 2.10 cmt. 1.

a)   Definition of Impending Matter and Pending Matter

An impending matter is one that is imminent or anticipated to occur soon, but has not yet begun. Model Code of Judicial Conduct Terminology. A pending matter is one that has begun, but has not yet reached final disposition. *Id.* A matter remains pending through any appellate process until its final disposition. *Id.*

b)   Public Statement Appearing to Impair Fairness

A judge must not make a statement, or permit a court officer to make a statement, about a case that might reasonably be expected to impair fairness. Model Code of Judicial Conduct Rule 2.10(A),(C).

c)   Any Statement Inconsistent with Impartiality

A judge must not make any statement, or permit a court officer to make a statement, inconsistent with the impartial performance of judicial duties. Model Code of Judicial Conduct Rule 2.10(B).

d)   Permissible Statements

A judge may make some statements about a case including:

- explaining court procedures;
- commenting about a case in which the judge is a litigant; and
- responding to an allegation regarding the judge's conduct.

Model Code of Judicial Conduct Rule 2.10.

10)   SUPERVISORY DUTIES

a)   Court Staff

A judge must require court staff, court officials, and others subject to the judge's direction and control to act in a way consistent with the judge's duties pursuant to the Code. Model Code of Judicial Conduct Rule 2.12(A).

b)   Judge with Supervisory Authority

A judge with supervisory authority for the judicial performance of other judges must take reasonable measures to ensure that these judges properly perform their judicial responsibilities, including their prompt disposition of matters before them. Model Code of Judicial Conduct Rule 2.12(B).

11)   ADMINISTRATIVE APPOINTMENTS

a)   General Limitations on Judge's Power of Appointment

A judge must act impartially in making administrative appointments. Model Code of Judicial Conduct Rule 2.13(A)(1). A judge must avoid favoritism, nepotism, and unnecessary appointments. Model Code of Judicial Conduct Rule 2.13(A)(2).

b)   Election Contribution Limit on Judge's Power of Appointment

A judge must not appoint a lawyer to a position if the judge either knows that the lawyer, or the lawyer's domestic partner or spouse, has contributed more than a specified dollar amount within the specified number of years prior to the judge's election campaign, or learns of such a contribution. Model Code of Judicial Conduct Rule 2.13(B).

(1) Exceptions to Limits on Judge's Appointments

The limitation on a judge's power of appointment based on an contribution applies *unless*:

- the position is substantially uncompensated;
- the lawyer has been selected in rotation from a list of available and qualified lawyers compiled without regard to their having made political contributions; or
- the judge finds that no other lawyer is competent, willing, and able to accept the position. *Id.*

c) Judge May not Approve Compensation Greater than Fair Value

A judge must not approve compensation of appointees greater than the fair value of services rendered. Model Code of Judicial Conduct Rule 2.13(B).

12) DISABILITY AND IMPAIRMENT

a) When Judge Must Take Action about Impairment

A judge must take appropriate action when the judge has a reasonable belief that the performance of another judge or a lawyer is impaired by alcohol, drugs, or an emotional, mental, or physical condition. Model Code of Judicial Conduct Rule 2.14.

(1) What Constitutes Appropriate Action

Appropriate action may include a confidential referral to a lawyer or judicial assistance program. *Id.* "Appropriate action" means action intended and reasonably likely to assist the impaired judge or lawyer in handling the problem and prevent harm to the justice system. *Id.*, cmt. 1.

13) RESPONDING TO JUDICIAL AND LAWYER MISCONDUCT

a) Another Judge's Code Violation

A judge having knowledge that another judge has committed a violation of the Code that raises a substantial question about the other judge's trustworthiness, honesty, or fitness for judicial office must inform the appropriate authority. Model Code of Judicial Conduct Rule 2.15(A).

A judge who receives information indicating a substantial likelihood that another judge has committed a violation of the Code must take appropriate action. Model Code of Judicial Conduct Rule 2.15(C).

b)   A Lawyer's Rules Violation

A judge having knowledge that a lawyer has committed a violation of the Rules that raises a substantial question as to the lawyer's trustworthiness, honesty, or fitness as a lawyer in other regards must inform the appropriate authority. Model Code of Judicial Conduct Rule 2.15(B).

A judge who receives information indicating a substantial likelihood that a lawyer has committed a violation of the Rules must take appropriate action. Model Code of Judicial Conduct Rule 2.15(D).

14)   COOPERATION WITH DISCIPLINARY AUTHORITIES

a)   Requirement of Judge's Cooperation

A judge must cooperate and be honest and candid with lawyer and judicial disciplinary agencies. Model Code of Judicial Conduct Rule 2.16(A).

b)   Prohibition of Judge's Retaliation

A judge may not retaliate against a person known or suspected to have cooperated or assisted with an investigation of a lawyer or a judge. Model Code of Judicial Conduct Rule 2.16(B).

★★   C.   **Ex Parte Communications**

An *ex parte* communication is a communication made to a judge for or by one party outside the presence of the other party. To the extent reasonably possible, communications with a judge must include all parties or their lawyers. Model Code of Judicial Conduct Rule 2.9 cmt. 1.

1)   GENERALLY, NO EX-PARTE COMMUNICATION BY JUDGE

Subject to certain exceptions, a judge must not initiate, permit, or consider *ex parte* communications, or consider other communications made to the judge outside the presence of the parties, regarding an impending or pending matter. Model Code of Judicial Conduct Rule 2.9(A).

a)   Scope of General Prohibition on Ex Parte Communications

Generally, the foregoing rule against a judge's involvement with *ex parte* communications applies to such communications with people other than the proceeding's participants, such as law teachers and other attorneys. Model Code of Judicial Conduct Rule 2.9(A) cmt. 3. However, the judge may consult with ethics advisory committees and outside counsel about compliance with the Code. Model Code of Judicial Conduct Rule 2.9(A) cmt. 7.

b)   When Judge May Engage in Ex Parte Communications

Certain exceptions to the general rule exist permitting specific *ex parte* communications:

(1) Scheduling, Administrative, or Emergency Purposes

When circumstances require it, *ex parte* communications for scheduling, administrative, or emergency purposes, which do not deal with substantive matters, are allowed, provided:

- No Procedural or Tactical Advantage

  the judge reasonably believes that no party will gain a substantive, procedural, or tactical advantage as a result of the *ex parte* communication; and

- Notice and Opportunity to Respond

  the judge makes provision promptly to notify all other parties of the substance of the *ex parte* communication, and affords the parties an opportunity to respond.

Model Code of Judicial Conduct Rule 2.9(A)(1).

★   (2) Disinterested Expert's Advice

A judge may obtain the written advice of a disinterested expert on the law applicable to a proceeding before the judge, if the judge: (1) notifies the parties of the person to be consulted and the subject matter of the advice to be procured; and (2) provides the parties a reasonable opportunity to object and respond to the notice and to the advice received. Model Code of Judicial Conduct Rule 2.9(A)(2).

(3) Court Officials, Court Staff, and other Judges

Generally, a judge may consult with court officials and court staff whose functions are to assist the judge in conducting the judge's adjudicative responsibilities, or with other judges. Model Code of Judicial Conduct Rule 2.9(A)(3).

(a) Limits on Consultation with other Judges

Although a judge may consult with another judge on a pending matter, the judge must avoid *ex parte* discussions about a case with other judges who have been disqualified from hearing it, and with judges who have appellate jurisdiction over it. *Id.*, cmt. 5.

(4) Parties and their Lawyers

A judge may, with the consent of the parties, confer separately with the parties and their lawyers in an effort to mediate or settle matters pending before the judge. Model Code of Judicial Conduct Rule 2.9(A)(4).

(5) Authorized by Law

A judge may initiate, permit, or consider any *ex parte* communications when expressly authorized by law to do so. Model Code of Judicial Conduct Rule 2.9(A)(5). For example, the judge may have such authority when serving on therapeutic or problem-solving courts, drug courts, or mental health courts. *Id.*, cmt. 4. In that capacity, the judge may have a more interactive role with parties, social workers, treatment providers, probation officers, and others. *Id.*

2) INADVERTENT RECEIPT OF EX-PARTE COMMUNICATIONS

If a judge inadvertently receives an unauthorized *ex parte* communication concerning the substance of a matter, then the judge must make provision promptly to notify the parties of the communication's substance and afford the parties with an opportunity to respond. Model Code of Judicial Conduct Rule 2.9(B).

3) CANNOT INVESTIGATE AND IS LIMITED TO EVIDENCE/FACTS

A judge may not investigate facts in a matter independently. Model Code of Judicial Conduct Rule 2.9(C). The judge must consider only the evidence presented and those facts that may properly be judicially noticed. *Id.*

4) ENSURE COMPLIANCE ABOUT EX-PARTE COMMUNICATIONS

A judge must make reasonable efforts, including providing appropriate supervision, to ensure that the Code's provision regarding *ex parte* communications is not violated by court officials, court staff, and others subject to the judge's direction and control. Model Code of Judicial Conduct Rule 2.9(D).

★★★ D. Disqualification

A judge has a duty to disqualify herself from any participation in a proceeding in which the judge's impartiality might reasonably be questioned. Model Code of Judicial Conduct Rule 2.11(A). This duty applies whether or not a party files a motion to disqualify the judge. *Id.*, cmt. 2.

1) WHEN IMPARTIALITY MIGHT REASONABLY BE QUESTIONED

Generally, the Code requires disqualification in a proceeding in which the judge's impartiality might reasonably be questioned, regardless of whether any of the following specific provisions apply. *Id.*, cmt. 1. The judge's impartiality might reasonably be questioned in the following types of circumstances.

a) Personal Bias or Prejudice

Disqualification is required if the judge has a personal bias or prejudice regarding a party's lawyer or a party. Model Code of Judicial Conduct Rule 2.11(A)(1).

b) Personal Knowledge

Disqualification is required if the judge has personal knowledge of facts that are in dispute in the proceeding. *Id.*

★   c)   Certain Types of Connections to Proceedings

Disqualification is required if the judge knows that the judge, the judge's domestic partner/spouse, or a person within a third degree of relationship to either of them, or the domestic partner or spouse of such a person is:

- a party to the proceeding, or an officer, director, managing member, general partner, or trustee of a party;
- a lawyer in the proceeding;
- a person who has more than a *de minimis* interest that could be substantially affected by the proceeding; or
- likely to be a material witness in the proceeding.

Model Code of Judicial Conduct Rule 2.11(A)(2).

★   d)   Economic Interests

Disqualification is required if the judge knows that the judge, individually or as a fiduciary, or the judge's domestic partner, spouse, parent, or child, or any other member of the judge's family residing in the judge's household, has an economic interest in the subject matter in controversy or in a party to the proceeding. Model Code of Judicial Conduct Rule 2.11(A)(3).

(1) De Minimis Interest

Generally, an economic interest means ownership of more than a *de minimis* equitable or legal interest. Model Code of Judicial Conduct Terminology. In the context of interests regarding a judge's disqualification, "*de minimus*" means a minor interest that could not present a reasonable question about the judge's impartiality. *Id.*

e)   Contributions to Judge's Campaign

Disqualification is required when the judge learns or knows by means of a timely motion that a party's lawyer, a party, or the party's lawyer's law firm has, within the prior certain number of years, made contributions to the judge's campaign in an amount that is more than a specified dollar amount. Model Code of Judicial Conduct Rule 2.11(A)(4).

f)   Statement by Judge Regarding Issue

Disqualification is required if the judge has made a public statement that commits, or appears to commit, the judge to rule in a specific way or to reach a specific result in the proceeding or controversy. Model Code of Judicial Conduct Rule 2.11(A)(5). This rule does not apply to such a public statement made in a court proceeding, judicial opinion, or decision. *Id.*

★   g)   Judge Served as Lawyer

Disqualification is required if the judge served as a lawyer in the matter. Model Code of Judicial Conduct Rule 2.11(A)(6)(a).

                     h)   Judge was Associated with Lawyer

Disqualification is required if the judge was associated with a lawyer who participated substantially in the matter during that association. *Id.*

                     i)   Judge Served in Governmental Employment

Disqualification is required if the judge served in governmental employment and in this capacity participated substantially and personally as a public official or lawyer regarding the proceeding. Model Code of Judicial Conduct Rule 2.11(A)(6)(b). The judge must also be disqualified if the judge served in governmental employment and publicly expressed in that capacity an opinion regarding the merits of the matter in controversy. *Id.*

                     j)   Judge Served as Material Witness

Disqualification is required if the judge served as a material witness concerning the matter. Model Code of Judicial Conduct Rule 2.11(A)(6)(c).

                     k)   Judge Presided as Judge

Disqualification is required if the judge previously presided as a judge over the matter in another court. Model Code of Judicial Conduct Rule 2.11(A)(6)(d).

★   2)   JUDGE'S PERSONAL AND FIDUCIARY ECONOMIC INTERESTS

A judge must keep informed regarding the judge's personal and fiduciary economic interests. Model Code of Judicial Conduct Rule 2.11(B). Also, the judge must make a reasonable effort to keep informed about the personal economic interests of the judge's domestic partner or spouse and minor children residing in the judge's household. *Id.*

★   3)   WAIVER OF DISQUALIFICATION

A judge subject to disqualification pursuant to the Code, other than for bias or prejudice, may disclose the basis of the judge's disqualification and may ask the parties and their lawyers to consider, outside the presence of court personnel and the judge, whether to waive disqualification. Model Code of Judicial Conduct Rule 2.11(C). If, after the disclosure, the lawyers and parties agree, without participation by court personnel and the judge, that the judge should not be disqualified, then the judge may participate in the proceeding. *Id.*

           4)   NECESSITY MAY OVERRIDE DISQUALIFICATION

This general rule of disqualification is subject to exceptions in case law and in the Code:

> The rule of necessity may override the rule of disqualification. For example, a judge might be required to participate in judicial review of a judicial salary statute, or might be the only judge available in a matter requiring immediate judicial action, such as a hearing on probable cause or a temporary restraining order.

Model Code of Judicial Conduct Rule 2.11 cmt. 3.

E.   Extrajudicial Activities

A judge must conduct personal and extrajudicial activities so as to minimize the risk of conflict with judicial obligations. Model Code of Judicial Conduct Canon 3.

Extrajudicial activities include certain types of conduct by the judge that occurs outside of the judge's judicial office. Several Code provisions fall under this category.

1)   LIMITATIONS ON JUDGE'S EXTRAJUDICIAL ACTIVITIES

A judge may participate in extrajudicial activities, other than those prohibited by law or the Code. Model Code of Judicial Conduct Rule 3.1.

a)   Interfering with Proper Performance of Judicial Duties

A judge must not participate in extrajudicial activities that will interfere with the proper performance of the judge's judicial duties. Model Code of Judicial Conduct Rule 3.1(A).

b)   Leading to Frequent Disqualification

A judge must not participate in extrajudicial activities that will lead to frequent disqualification of the judge. Model Code of Judicial Conduct Rule 3.1(B).

c)   Undermining Independence, Integrity, or Impartiality

A judge must not participate in extrajudicial activities that would appear to a reasonable person to undermine the judge's independence, integrity, or impartiality. Model Code of Judicial Conduct Rule 3.1(C).

(1) Discriminatory Conduct; Expressions of Prejudice or Bias

Discriminatory conduct and expressions of prejudice or bias by a judge, even outside the judge's judicial or official actions, are likely to appear to a reasonable person to call into question the judge's impartiality and integrity. *Id.*, cmt. 3. Examples include remarks or jokes that demean individuals based upon their gender, sex, race, religion, ethnicity, national origin, age, disability, sexual orientation, or socioeconomic status. *Id.*

d)   Appearing to be Coercive

When participating in extrajudicial activities, a judge may not engage in conduct that would appear to a reasonable person to be coercive. Model Code of Judicial Conduct Rule 3.1(D).

e)   Using Court Resources

When engaging in extrajudicial activities, a judge must not make use of court staff, premises, equipment, stationery, or other resources, except for incidental use for activities that concern the legal system, the law, or the administration of justice, or unless the law allows such additional use. Model Code of Judicial Conduct Rule 3.1(E).

2)   APPEARANCES BEFORE GOVERNMENTAL BODIES AND CONSULTATION WITH GOVERNMENT OFFICIALS

a)   Generally, No Appearances at Public Hearings or Consultation

As a general rule, a judge must not appear voluntarily at a public hearing before, or otherwise consult with, an executive or legislative body or official except:

- on matters concerning the law, the legal system, or the administration of justice;
- on matters about which the judge obtained expertise or knowledge during the judge's official duties; or
- when acting *pro se* in a matter involving the judge's economic or legal interests, or when the judge is acting as a fiduciary.

Model Code of Judicial Conduct Rule 3.2.

3)   APPOITNMENTS TO GOVERNMENTAL POSITIONS

A judge must not accept appointment to a governmental committee, commission, board, or other governmental position unless the position concerns the law, the legal system, or the administration of justice. Model Code of Judicial Conduct Rule 3.4.

For example, a judge may not serve on the board of a public educational institution, unless the institution is a law school. However, service on the board of a public law school or any private educational institution would usually be permitted.

4)   TESTIFYING AS CHARACTER WITNESS

Except when a judge is duly summoned, a judge must not testify as a character witness in an administrative, judicial, or other adjudicatory proceeding or otherwise vouch for the character of a person in a legal proceeding. Model Code of Judicial Conduct Rule 3.3.

a)   Abuse of Prestige of Office by Testifying as Character Witness

If a judge testifies as a character witness without being subpoenaed to testify, then the judge abuses the prestige of judicial office in order to advance someone else's interests. *Id.*, cmt. 1.

5)   USE OF NONPUBLIC INFORMATION

A judge must not intentionally disclose or use, for any purpose unrelated to the judge's judicial duties, nonpublic information acquired in a judicial capacity. Model Code of Judicial Conduct Rule 3.5. This is not intended to affect a judge's ability to act on information as necessary to protect the safety or health of a judge, a member of the judge's family, other judicial officers, or court personnel if consistent with the Code's other provisions. *Id.*, cmt. 2.

6)   AFFILIATION WITH DISCRIMINATORY ORGANIZATIONS

A judge may not hold membership in an organization that engages in invidious discrimination on the grounds of race, gender, sex, religion, ethnicity, national origin, or sexual orientation. Model Code of Judicial Conduct Rule 3.6(A). Moreover, a judge cannot use the benefits or facilities of an organization if the judge knows, or should know, that the organization engages in invidious discrimination. However, a judge may attend an event in a facility of such an organization when the judge's attendance is an isolated event that could not reasonably be perceived as an endorsement of the organization's practices. Model Code of Judicial Conduct Rule 3.6(B)

a)   Prohibited Membership Gives Appearance of Impropriety

A judge's membership in an organization that engages in invidious discrimination gives rise to perceptions "that the judge's impartiality is impaired." *Id.*, cmt. 1. This issue relates to matters of federal constitutional law.

A judge must resign immediately from an organization upon learning that the organization engages in invidious discrimination. Model Code of Judicial Conduct Rule 3.6 cmt. 3.

7)   PARTICIPATION IN EDUCATIONAL, RELIGIOUS, CHARTABLE, FRATERNAL, OR CIVIC ORGANIZATIONS AND ACTIVITIES

Generally, judges may engage in non-profit educational, religious, charitable, fraternal, or civic extrajudicial activities, even when those activities do not involve the law. Model Code of Judicial Conduct Rule 3.1 cmt. 1 (20).

a)   Activities Sponsored by Organizations or Governmental Entities

Generally, subject to the other, earlier addressed limitations upon a judge's participation in extrajudicial activities, a judge may engage in activities sponsored by organizations or governmental entities concerned with the law, the legal system, or the administration of justice. Model Code of Judicial Conduct Rule 3.7.

b)   Activities of Non-Profit Organizations

Generally, subject to the other, earlier addressed limitations upon a judge's participation in extrajudicial activities, a judge may engage in activities of non-profit educational, religious, charitable, fraternal, or civic organizations.

c) Judge Can Participate in Activities of Organizations or Entities

Generally, relative to the foregoing types of organizations or entities, a judge may participate in activities such as these:

- soliciting contributions only from members of the judge's family, or from judges over whom the judge lacks authority;
- soliciting membership, but only if the organization or entity is concerned with the law, the legal system, or the administration of justice;
- participating in an event of an organization or entity that serves a fund-raising purpose, but only if the event concerns the law, the legal system, or the administration of justice;
- serving as an officer, director, trustee, or advisor of an entity, unless it is likely that the organization or entity will be engaged in proceedings before the judge or the court of which the judge is a member, or another court under its appellate jurisdiction.

Model Code of Judicial Conduct Rule 3.7(A)(2)-(4), (6).

8) APPOINTMENTS TO FIDUCIARY POSITIONS

a) Fiduciary for Family Member under Limited Circumstances

Usually, a judge may not accept appointment to serve in a fiduciary position. Model Code of Judicial Conduct Rule 3.8(A). However, an exception to this prohibition applies for the estate, trust, or person of the judge's family, and then only when such service will not interfere with the proper performance of judicial duties. *Id.* A fiduciary position includes executor, administrator, trustee, guardian, attorney in fact, or other personal representative. *Id.*

b) When Judge May Not Serve as Fiduciary

A judge may not serve in a fiduciary position if the judge as fiduciary will likely be involved in proceedings that would normally come before the judge. Model Code of Judicial Conduct Rule 3.8(B). Alternatively, a judge may not serve in a fiduciary position if the trust, estate, or ward becomes involved in adversary proceedings in the court on which the judge serves, or another court under its appellate jurisdiction. *Id.*

9) SERVICE AS ARBITRATOR OR MEDIATOR

Unless expressly authorized by law, a judge may not act as an arbitrator or a mediator or perform other judicial functions separate from the judge's official duties. Model Code of Judicial

Conduct Rule 3.9(C). However, a judge may participate in arbitration, mediation, or settlement conferences conducted as part of assigned judicial duties. *Id.*, cmt. 1.

10)   PRACTICE OF LAW

A judge may not practice law. Model Code of Judicial Conduct Rule 3.10. A judge may not serve as a lawyer, even to represent a member of the judge's family. *Id.* However, the judge may act *pro se* by representing himself. *Id.* Also, the judge may, without compensation, provide legal advice to, and draft or review documents for, a member of the judge's family. *Id.*

11)   FINANCIAL, BUSINESS, OR REMUNERATIVE ACTIVITIES

a)   Permitted Financial Activities

★   (1) Holding and Managing Investments

Generally, a judge may hold and manage the judge's investments and those of the judge's family members. Model Code of Judicial Conduct Rule 3.11(A).

(2) Serving in Certain Capacities in Business Entities

Generally, a judge may not serve as a director, officer, manager, general partner, employee, or advisor of any business entity. Model Code of Judicial Conduct Rule 3.11(B). However, a judge may participate in or manage: 1) a business closely held by the judge or members of the judge's family; or 2) a business entity mainly involved in investment of the judge's financial resources and those of the judge's family members. *Id.*

b)   When a Judge May Not Engage in Permitted Financial Activities

A judge may not hold and manage investments or participate in or manage certain business entities if such activity will:

- interfere with proper performance of judicial duties;
- lead to the judge's frequent disqualification;
- "involve the judge in frequent transactions or continuing business relationships with lawyers or other persons likely to come before the court on which the judge serves"; or
- result in other violations of the Code.

Model Code of Judicial Conduct Rule 3.11(C).

12)   COMPENSATION FOR EXTRAJUSIDICAL ACTIVITIES

Generally, a judge may accept reasonable compensation for extrajudicial activities allowed by the Code or other law. Model Code of Judicial Conduct Rule 3.12. However, the judge may not accept such compensation if this acceptance "would appear to a reasonable person to undermine the judge's independence, integrity, or impartiality." *Id.*

13) ACCEPTANCE AND REPORTING OF GIFTS, LOANS, BEQUESTS, BENEFITS, OR OTHER THINGS OF VALUE

If a judge accepts something of value, such as a gift, without paying fair market value for it, then a risk exists that a reasonable person could view it as intended to influence the judge's decision in some case. Model Code of Judicial Conduct Rule 3.13 cmt. 1. The following limitations are placed upon a judge's acceptance of certain things of value according to the degree of the risk that the acceptance would appear to undermine the judge's independence, integrity, or impartiality. *Id.*

a) When Judge Must Not Accept Something of Value

Generally, a judge must not accept a gift, loan, bequest, benefit, or other thing of value "if acceptance is prohibited by law or would appear to a reasonable person to undermine the judge's independence, integrity, or impartiality." Model Code of Judicial Conduct Rule 3.13(A).

b) When Judge May Accept Something of Value without Reporting It

Unless otherwise prohibited, a judge may accept certain types of items without publicly reporting such acceptance.

★   (1) Items with Little Intrinsic Value

A judge may accept items with little intrinsic value, such as certificates, plaques, greeting cards, and trophies.

(2) Things from Those for Whom Disqualification is Required

A judge may accept gifts, loans, bequests, benefits, or other things of value from relatives, friends, or other persons, including lawyers, whose interest or appearance in a proceeding impending or pending before the judge would require the judge's disqualification.

(3) Ordinary Social Hospitality

A judge may accept ordinary social hospitality, such as an invitation to a festive party for a special occasion.

★   (4) Financial or Commercial Opportunities and Benefits

A judge may accept financial or commercial benefits and opportunities, if the same benefits and opportunities or loans are made available on identical terms to people other than judges.

(5) Prizes and Rewards Given in Public Contests

A judge may accept prizes and rewards given to participants or competitors in random contests, drawings, or other events that are open to people other than judges.

(6) Fellowships, Scholarships, and Similar Items

A judge may accept fellowships, scholarships, and similar benefits and awards.

(7) Resource Materials Provided by Publishers

A judge may accept resource materials provided by publishers for free and for official use (e.g., magazines, journals, books, audiovisual materials).

(8) Awards, Gifts, or Benefits

A judge may accept awards, gifts, or benefits associated with the profession, business, or other separate activity of a domestic partner, spouse, or other family member of a judge living in the judge's household that incidentally benefit the judge.

Model Code of Judicial Conduct Rule 3.13(B)(1)-(8).

c)   When Judge May Accept Things of Value with Reporting

Unless otherwise prohibited, a judge may accept certain additional types of items, but the judge must publicly report their acceptance:

★
(1) Gifts Incident to Public Testimonial

A judge must report accepted "gifts incident to a public testimonial";

(2) Invitations for Free Attendance of Certain Events

A judge must report accepted invitations to a judge and the judge's domestic partner, spouse, or guest to attend without charge: 1) an event related to a bar-related function or another activity regarding the law, the legal system, or the administration of justice; or 2) an event connected with any of the judge's charitable, educational, fraternal, religious, or civic activities, if the identical invitation is given to non-judges who are involved in similar ways in the same activity; and

(3) Things of Value from Certain Types of Parties or Attorneys

A judge must report accepted gifts, loans, bequests, benefits, or other things of value, if their source is a party or an attorney who has appeared or is likely to appear before the judge in a court, or whose interests have or could come before the judge in a court. Model Code of Judicial Conduct Rule 3.13(C)(1)-(3).

14)   REIMBURSEMENT OF EXPENSES, WAIVERS OF FEES/CHARGES

a)   General Considerations about Certain Reimbursement/Waiver

A judge may participate in permissible extrajudicial activity, such as attending a legal educational program sponsored by an educational, civic, fraternal, religious, or charitable organization. Model Code of Judicial Conduct Rule 3.14 cmt. 1.

b) When Judge May Accept Certain Reimbursements/Waivers

Unless otherwise prohibited, a judge may accept reimbursement of reasonable and necessary expenses for food, travel, lodging, or other incidental expenses, or a waiver of fees or charges for registration, tuition, and similar items, from sources besides the judge's employer, if the expenses or charges are connected with the judge's participation in permissible extrajudicial activities. Model Code of Judicial Conduct Rule 3.14(A).

(1) Limitation on Permissible Reimbursement

Reimbursement of a judge's expenses for necessary food, travel, lodging, or other incidental expenses is limited to the actual costs reasonably incurred by the judge and, when suitable to the occasion, by the judge's domestic partner, spouse, or guest. *Id.* Model Code of Judicial Conduct Rule 3.14(B).

c) Public Reporting Requirement

A judge who accepts reimbursement of expenses or waivers of fees or charges on behalf of the judge or the judge's domestic partner, spouse, or guest must publicly report such acceptance. Model Code of Judicial Conduct Rule 3.14(C).

15) PUBLIC REPORTING REQUIREMENTS

Generally, a judge must publicly report the amount of certain permissible reimbursements and other things of value received by the judge.

a) Public Documents

The judge files a report in order to make it public. The judge must file the report as a public document in the court on which the judge serves or another office designated by law. Model Code of Judicial Conduct Rule 3.15(D).

b) Public Report Contents

If public reporting is required, then a judge must report:

- the description of any gift, loan, bequest, benefit, or other thing of value accepted;
- the activity for which the judge received any compensation; and
- the source of reimbursement of expenses or waiver of fees or charges.

Model Code of Judicial Conduct Rule 3.15(B).

c) Timing of Public Report

A judge must make a required public report at least annually. Model Code of Judicial Conduct Rule 3.15(C). However, a judge must make a required public report about reimbursement of expenses or waiver of fees or charges within 30 days after the end of the event or program for which the judge received such reimbursement or waiver.

d)   What Must Be Publicly Reported

A judge must publicly report the amount or value of:

- compensation received by the judge for permissible extrajudicial activities;
- permissible gifts and other things of value received by a judge, unless their value does not exceed a specified dollar amount; and
- permissible reimbursement of expenses and waiver of fees or charges, unless it does not exceed a specified dollar amount.

Model Code of Judicial Conduct Rule 3.15(A)(3).

REVIEW QUESTIONS

93. The Model Code of Judicial Conduct's first canon requires a judge to uphold and promote the judiciary's:

    a) independence, integrity, and impartiality.
    b) independence, trustworthiness, and compliance with the law.
    c) honesty, trustworthiness, and impartiality.
    d) compliance with the law.

94. When a judge acts impartially, the judge has:

    a) no opinion on a case or controversy before the court.
    b) no feelings for, against, or in any manner, toward the parties or their attorneys.
    c) a lack of prejudice or bias in favor of, or against a party, as well as an open mind about all issues that come before the court.
    d) a respectful understanding of personal biases and prejudices and an ability to control them in any case or controversy.

95. "Impropriety" means:

    a) only violations of the law
    b) any speech that may offend
    c) any conduct that adversely affects public confidence in the judiciary
    d) decisions that embarrass other public officials

96. Whether a judge's conduct creates an appearance of impropriety is determined by:

    a) a judicial ethics panel composed of attorneys and judges.
    b) whether a reasonable person would perceive the judge to have violated the Code or otherwise acted in a manner that reflects negatively on the judge's impartiality, temperament, honesty, or fitness.
    c) a preponderance of the evidence submitted to the appropriate review authority.
    d) the state Supreme Court acting in its oversight and regulatory capacity of the judiciary.

97. If a judge's father-in-law attempts to impress and influence others with the judge's position, the judge must:

    a) advise court security officers to bring the father-in-law before the court to be formally notified that such conduct constitutes contempt of court and is an actionable offense.
    b) notify law enforcement officers that the father-in-law is interfering with court operations, which is an actionable offense.
    c) take reasonable action to not allow the father-in-law to abuse the prestige of judicial office in order to advance personal or economic interests.
    d) direct the judge's spouse to exercise all necessary control over the spouse's father to

prevent detracting from the prestige of the judge and the court.

98. Which of the following is not an example of abuse of the prestige of judicial office:

a) purchasing an expensive set of used leather office furniture for your chambers, posted for sale by a retiring partner of a local law firm

b) mentioning your position as a judge to the tax appraisal official inspecting your new house.

c) replying on official letterhead to several publishers who expressed interest in publishing your spouse's memoirs.

d) having the title "Judge of the Superior Court" printed above your name on your personal stationary.

99. By accepting the position of judicial office, an individual:

a) must withdraw from any other business, financial, or other opportunity that could present a conflict of interest before the court.

b) gives up the right to participate in any other aspect of governmental activity that might lead to a conflict of interest or disqualification from a case or controversy.

c) must advise family members and close friends not to engage in any activity which may compromise the integrity, honor, and impartiality of the judicial office by association.

d) must conduct any extrajudicial and personal activities so as to reduce the risk of conflict or disqualification.

100. If a judge disapproves of a law that comes before the court, the judge must:

a) notify all parties to the proceeding of the predisposition and consider any reasonable objection and request recusal from counsel.

b) be automatically recused from the case to avoid any appearance of impropriety.

c) interpret and apply the law regardless of any personal feelings, and the judge must manifest objectivity and open-mindedness in doing so.

d) keep personal views private and rule as the judge believes to be proper.

101. Judge Martin, while listening to testimony in a civil rights case tried to a jury, was concerned about the derogatory language being used by multiple witnesses in the case. The Judge stopped the proceedings abruptly. In open court, the Judge banned the further use of twelve sexual, ethnic, and sexual orientation terms that were generally found offensive and derogatory. Despite having heard the terms used by witnesses, several jurors were appalled that the Judge used such language and asked to be dismissed from jury duty. Judge Martin:

a) displayed poor judgment and taste by repeating the derogatory language from the bench and is subject to sanction.

b) demonstrated bias and prejudice by using such terms when the judge knew or should have known they would be offensive to jurors and, therefore, is subject to sanction.

c) is not precluded from making legitimate references to factors such as sex, ethnicity, marital status, and sexual orientation when they are pertinent to an issue in the case.

d) violated the Code by allowing others in court to use offensive language.

102. The juvenile court judge recently hired a clerk who is a 69-year-old woman who served in the same position in a local probate court for many years. The law clerk is generally quiet, but has demonstrated little tolerance for loud or poorly dressed adolescents. The juvenile court judge:

   a) should remind the new clerk that adolescents are going to challenge rules and conformity.

   b) should direct the new clerk that the clerk is held to the judicial standard of not manifesting bias or prejudice based on age or socioeconomic status.

   c) must fire the clerk for discrimination.

   d) should advise all adolescents in the court to maintain a respectful tone of voice and to dress respectfully when coming to court.

103. Judge Martin lives next door to a religious school and, although not affiliated with the religion, the judge's spouse is the school administrator. A highly charged and publicized case has come before the court asking the judge to decide if religious schools should be entitled to select state educational funding. Teachers from the religious school are picketing in front of the courthouse, and several parents of students have approached the judge's spouse to express their positions and question whether the spouse can adequately perform school duties if the judge does not decide the case "properly." Under the Code:

   a) the judge's spouse subjects the judge to undue influence and, therefore, the judge must be recused from the case.

   b) the judge cannot allow either public clamor or fear of criticism, or any family relationship or interest, to influence judicial judgment.

   c) the judge and the judge's spouse must be screened from each other while the case is pending.

   d) the judge must instruct the judge's spouse to inform anyone attempting to influence the spouse that such attempts are a violation of the Code under which they may be prosecuted.

104. The youngest judge to be appointed to the circuit court bench is also one of the most eligible single professionals according to the local newspaper. As a lawyer, the judge dated frequently and has previously indicated that the judge does not believe in marriage. Performing marriage ceremonies and presiding over divorces are now part of the judge's duties. The judge:

   a) must not allow social or other relationships or interests to influence judicial conduct or judgment.

   b) should be disqualified from performing marriage ceremonies and presiding over divorces.

   c) must be disqualified from performing marriage ceremonies and presiding over divorces.

d) so as to avoid the appearance of bias, prejudice, or harassment based on marital status, the judge must publically proclaim the intent to accommodate the various views of marriage that others who may appear before the judge in court will espouse.

105. A judge has just been appointed to the bench. The judge's two children attend a private religious school that requires all parents to devote at least 16 hours each semester to religious-based public service work. The judge must:

a) inform the school that the judge may be limited in availability to perform certain religious-based public service work as the judge must conduct extrajudicial and personal activities so as to reduce the risk of conflicts that would result in disqualification from participating in proceedings.

b) decline the appointment if the judge intends to continue to perform the religious-based public service work as it is a conflict that will inevitably result in the judge's disqualification from proceedings.

c) refuse to perform the religious-based public service work, even if it means the children will not be allowed to attend the school, as the judge's obligation to support the Constitution and laws require keeping a clear separation of church and state activities.

d) find another school for the children if the school refuses to excuse the judge from service that could present the appearance of impropriety in favoring one religion over another.

106. A judge is the chief judge of the local circuit and has extensive administrative responsibilities. The judge's newest staff member, Steven, is married to the judge's niece. Steven does not demonstrate the cooperative spirit modeled by the judge and has demonstrated a temper to several attorneys. The judge has ignored repeated verbal complaints about Steven, who has failed to properly maintain several active court files in the last month. Steven's actions are responsible for delays in several criminal hearings over the last two months. Steven also appears to have lost several court files that required costly replication by attorneys and the court. Morale among court staff is deteriorating, but the judge refuses to take action. The judge:

a) has not violated the Code as personnel matters are within the discretion of the Chief Judge and fall outside of the Code's purview.

b) has not violated the Code, which is designed to address professional legal problems.

c) has violated the Code by not performing administrative duties competently and diligently, causing avoidable delays and unnecessary costs.

d) has violated the Code by not cooperating with attorneys who rely on the judge's ability to administer the court effectively.

107. A judge believes that the parties in a divorce action are making unreasonable demands and acting openly hostile toward each other. The parties could only agree that they both trust the judge to hear their discrete matters relating to the divorce. The judge proposes to the

attorneys to offer the parties a single opportunity to settle matters in the judge's chambers. If the parties could not reach an agreement, the judge would consider a motion to transfer the case to another judge for a hearing. The judge:

    a) violated the Code by coercing the parties should they not reach a settlement.

    b) violated the Code by denying the parties the right to be heard in a fair and impartial hearing.

    c) did not violate the Code because the judge was using the position to conserve judicial resources.

    d) did not violate the Code because the judge did not coerce any party into settlement of a disputed manner but, rather, considered the effect that participation in a settlement discussion may have on the judge's objectivity and impartiality.

108. A judge does not like publicity and attempts to avoid it if possible. A controversial adoption case, in which the prospective adoptive parents are both female, comes before the court. The judge elects to be disqualified from the case on "personal" grounds. The judge:

    a) does not have to hear and decide matters that cause personal angst. The judge's action does not violate the Code.

    b) must hear the case unless the Code or other law requires the judge's disqualification from the matter.

    c) does not have to hear the case if doing so may bring the judge's personal opinions and views into the public light and bring undue attention to the court and the parties.

    d) must hear the case because disqualification, without further explanation, brings the integrity of the entire judiciary into question.

109. A particular witness for the defendant in a bench trial is using vulgar language in answering questions on direct examination. The prosecutor objects to the use of such language. Defense counsel insists that the language is an important aspect of defense strategy and is an accurate representation of events surrounding the crime. Defense counsel also argues that, as this is a bench trial, no jurors are being offended. The judge should:

    a) overrule the objection because a judge cannot dictate defense strategy.

    b) overrule the objection because the judge can direct the witness to choose language more carefully.

    c) sustain the objection because court order and decorum must be maintained regardless of whether the proceeding is before a judge or jury.

    d) sustain the objection because the trial is open to the public and anyone, including minors, may enter the courtroom and be offended to hear such language in a court of law.

110. A resident alien is accused of making terroristic threats against government officials. Despite being told to do so by the bailiff, the defendant and the defendant's family members refuse to rise to their feet when the judge enters or exits the courtroom. Some jurors, court staff, and visitors are visibly offended by these actions. The judge:

a) must require all persons before the court to demonstrate respect in accordance with the customs and traditions of the American judicial system.

b) should advise defense counsel privately that the defendant's actions and the actions of friends, family, and supporters are disrespectful, disruptive, and may result in sanctions.

c) must inform the protesters in open court that their actions are disruptive and will result in sanctions if they continue.

d) must show patience, dignity, and courtesy to the defendant and others in the court who, while not abiding by custom or showing respect to the court, are not disrupting proceedings or the court by their actions.

111. A case with serious political implications is before a judge. Among themselves, the court staff has expressed strong opinions on both sides of the issue. The judge is aware of several comments made by the staffers. The judge must:

a) admonish court staff to only make such statements outside of the courthouse and never to the parties, their attorneys, or to declared witnesses.

b) not substantially interfere with the constitutional rights of citizens who are not judges to engage in free speech just because they are employed in the judicial branch of government.

c) admonish court staff to not make statements, even nonpublic ones, that might substantially interfere with a fair trial or hearing, even though such admonishment may restrict speech.

d) remind court staff that their comments may make the judge and the court look bad and, therefore, they should be more discrete.

112. In chambers with counsel for both parties present, a judge politely, but firmly, admonishes a juror for making off-color comments to other jurors about a witness. The admonished juror asks to be excused from jury service, but the judge refuses the request. The juror promptly files a formal complaint about the judge alleging harassment and providing the local newspaper with a copy of the complaint. The judge dismisses the juror from the case and the judge comments to the newspaper that "the allegation is false, and I'll let the proper authorities come to their own conclusions." The judge's comment to the newspaper is:

a) not allowed under the Code as the only place for comment by the judge is a hearing on the complaint.

b) allowed under the Code because a judge may directly respond to allegations about the judge's conduct in a matter.

c) not allowed under the Code because the judge is presiding over the case at the time.

d) allowed under the Code which requires a judge to maintain order in the court, and the actions by the juror were potentially disruptive to proceedings and needed to be quashed.

113. A judge's drug court is controversial but has proven moderately effective in rehabilitating

drug users. The judge's law clerk was a published editor of the law clerk's law school's law review. The law clerk's comment used sound legal reasoning to support the medicinal use of marijuana. While in the court's employment, unbeknownst to the judge, the law clerk authors a widely published article supporting the legalization of drugs and an end to the 'war on drugs'. The law clerk concludes with a commitment to work toward the repeal of restrictive drug laws. The article draws widespread condemnation from law enforcement and prosecutors who have appeared before the judge. The judge:

a) must respect the law clerk's First Amendment right to freedom of speech as long as the judge does not make such a commitment to work toward the repeal of restrictive drug laws.

b) must take appropriate action toward the law clerk as the judge must require the court staff, subject to direction and control of the court, to refrain from making prohibited comments such as pledges, promises, or commitments that are inconsistent with the judge's impartial performance of adjudicative duties.

c) must balance the court's tolerance toward drug users in an attempt to rehabilitate them with the need to maintain an unbiased and neutral court, including court staff.

d) must step down from the bench for failing to maintain control over the law clerk who made a prohibited statement that has resulted in ill will and reduced trust in the court.

114. A family law judge gets married to an attractive television anchorperson. The wedding is a large social event for members of the bench, bar, and media. At the wedding reception, an attorney, who is known to be a habitual drinker, is clearly intoxicated. In front of a criminal law judge, the attorney makes several inappropriate comments about the young anchorperson. The criminal law judge concurs and also makes a vulgar and disparaging comment about the anchorperson. A third judge, a probate judge, overhears the criminal law judge making the comment. With respect to the comments:

a) The criminal law judge must take appropriate action with respect to the attorney, and the probate law judge must take appropriate action with respect to the criminal law judge.

b) Neither the criminal law judge nor the attorney violated any Code with respect to their respective comment or actions as neither were acting in an official capacity.

c) Given the circumstances and situation, consideration and tolerance should be extended to the judges and lawyers who do not have the same social outlets as persons outside the legal and judicial system.

d) As the family law judge neither heard, nor was informed of the comments made by the criminal law judge and the attorney, the comments were innocuous and no harm was caused to the judiciary or any attorney. Thus, there was no Code violation.

115. An attorney's temper flares once too often in front of a judge, who slams a gavel onto the bench and holds the attorney in contempt of court. The judge fines the attorney $1,000 and orders the attorney to be held in the county jail for 24 hours "or until cooled off." The attorney's temper erupts again with a string of expletives toward the judge, who then orders the attorney to be held in jail for ten days. The judge has known the attorney for

over a decade, but the judge has a duty to maintain order and respect in the court. The prosecutor is the first of several attorneys who file a complaint against the attorney with the state disciplinary agency. When called before the agency to answer questions, the judge, believing the attorney was punished sufficiently, states "the record speaks for itself" and respectfully declines to answer any questions that might jeopardize the attorney's license to practice law. The judge:

a) acted reasonably by referring the disciplinary agency to a complete record of the incident and knowing other attorneys would answer any questions.

b) did not violate the Code because the judge presented a full and complete record of the incident to the disciplinary agency for review and has nothing further to add.

c) violated the Code by sanctioning the attorney with the knowledge that the attorney would also be sanctioned by the disciplinary committee, thereby unjustly punishing the attorney twice for the same conduct.

d) violated the Code by failing to cooperate with the disciplinary agency.

116. While delivering a brief to the court, an attorney's law clerk sees the judge assigned to the case in the hallway. The law clerk greets the judge and comments that the attorney's client, a criminal defendant, is a childhood friend, a choirboy, and a Rhodes scholar. The judge is annoyed by the law clerk's inappropriate communication. The judge retorts, "that's strange, I thought he was a burglar."

a) The judge's comment is an ex parte communication in violation of the Code.

b) The judge's comment is clearly intended as a sarcastic remark toward a non-lawyer and, therefore, is not an ex parte communication.

c) The law clerk's comment is an ex parte communication that is imparted to the clerk's employer. The attorney has violated the Code.

d) The law clerk is immune from discipline because the law clerk is not an attorney.

117. Concerned about a complex legal issue relating to state antitrust law, a judge asks for written advice on a point of law from a law school professor with extensive practice experience in the area. The judge makes sure the professor had no connection to any party or attorney in the case. The judge provides all counsel with copies of the correspondence and the professor's response. The judge:

a) did not violate the Code by consulting the professor as the judge afforded all counsel the opportunity to review communications and to object and respond to the communications.

b) did not violate the Code as a judge may seek a disinterested expert's advice on the law applicable to a proceeding before the judge.

c) violated the Code by engaging in an ex parte communication with a disinterested expert without notifying the parties of the person to be consulted and the subject matter to be discussed and providing the parties with a reasonable opportunity to object and respond to the notice and to the advice received.

d) violated the Code by initiating an ex parte communication with an expert not pre-approved by the parties.

18. A judge, who is nearly deaf without the use of hearing aids, was standing in an office hallway when an attorney in the case about to be heard rushed into the office and began talking to the judge. The judge looked at the attorney and nodded respectfully while the attorney spoke for several minutes. When the attorney stopped speaking the judge thanked the attorney and motioned to the door. The judge never heard a word the attorney said as the judge's hearing aids were turned off at the time. The judge:

a) permitted an ex parte communication because the judge knew the attorney was about to be heard in a case before the judge and allowed the attorney to speak outside the presence of the other party or their lawyer.

b) did not permit an ex parte communication if the judge, after turning the hearing aid on, promptly notified all parties of the incident and afforded them an opportunity to respond.

c) did not engage in an ex parte communication because the judge heard nothing.

d) permitted an ex parte communication and, regardless of whether the judge heard the communication, must report the attorney to the appropriate disciplinary authority.

119. In a copyright infringement case, a judge is confused about some of the testimony concerning how a computer program is developed. Not wanting to appear ignorant, the judge searches the internet to learn more about computer programming and even asks a relative, a novice programmer, for some information. The judge:

a) did not violate the Code because the judge only initiated research after one party opened the door to explaining how computer programs are developed.

b) violated the Code by independently investigating facts and not considering only the evidence presented and those facts that could be judicially noticed.

c) violated the Code by not informing all parties and counsel that the judge performed independent research and allowing them to object and respond with their own additional information for consideration.

d) did not violate the Code as judges have a duty to make informed decisions and ensure a fair trial, even if counsel fails to present sufficient evidence for such an informed decision.

120. A case involving a hostile takeover of a local company with statewide government contracts is before a judge who will retire after the conclusion of the case. The judge, the parties, and the attorneys all know that the judge's great-step-nephew (son of the judge's step-sister's son) is the registered agent and a 10% stockholder in the company. All parties agree that they are comfortable with the judge hearing the case. The judge:

a) must be disqualified due to the fact that a person within the third degree of relationship to the judge or the judge's spouse is a person with more than a de minimis interest that could be substantially affected by the proceeding.

b) can hear the case as the judge has made complete disclosure of a familial connection to the proceeding and all parties agree there is no conflict or interest or reason for judicial disqualification.

c) can hear the case because the great-step-nephew is outside of the judge's immediate family and does not reside in the judge's household.

    d) need not be disqualified as a 10% stock interest, even owned by a person within the judge's immediate household, is only a de minimis interest.

121. If a judge serves as an assistant district attorney prior to ascending to the bench, the judge cannot:

    a) preside over any criminal trial which was filed by the State during the judge's tenure at the District Attorney's office.

    b) hear a case on appeal if it is argued that a member of the District Attorney's office committed malpractice during the judge's tenure at the District Attorney's office.

    c) preside over any criminal trial in which the judge personally handled the motions for continuance filed by the District Attorney's office in the case.

    d) preside over any criminal trial in which the judge was involved in evaluating evidence in the discovery process during the judge's tenure at the District Attorney's office.

122. A judge comes from a rich family. Each of the judge's five children living at home has a trust account established to accommodate gifts from relatives. The judge oversees dozens of stock investments in all of the trusts. The judge:

    a) should appoint an executor to independently oversee the investments so as to avoid any appearance of impropriety and avoid disqualification in a case involving an aspect of the investments or companies in which the children own stock.

    b) must be divested of all responsibility for the stock investments in the trusts because, as the trusts are established for minors, it is really the judge, as a parent, who is in control of the stock.

    c) can invest or oversee investments as an appointment to the bench does not prohibit one from investing wisely.

    d) must make a reasonable effort to keep informed about the personal economic interests of the judge's children who reside in the same household in order to know when the circumstances for disqualification arise.

123. A judge had a clear reason to be disqualified from hearing a probate case because the judge drafted the will of the decedent years earlier. The validity of the will is not being challenged. The judge disclosed the basis for disqualification to counsel in chambers. The judge then asked counsel to leave chambers and consider whether counsel wanted to waive disqualification. The judge's actions were:

    a) in violation of the Code if there was a clear and present possibility that the will may come into contest during the probate proceeding.

    b) in accordance with the Code as the judge disclosed the basis for disqualification and asked the lawyers to consider, outside the presence of the judge and court personnel, whether they would agree to waive the judge's disqualification.

    c) in violation of the Code if the judge did not present reasons for disqualification in writing to all counsel to allow them an opportunity to respond in writing.

d) in accordance with the Code because the judge is the only judge within a reasonable distance who could hear the case and to allow disqualification would work a hardship on the parties and delay distribution of the proceeds.

124. A judge had a clear reason to be disqualified from acting on a prosecutor's request for an arrest warrant for a violent, convicted felon. The judge was the former defense attorney for the subject of the arrest warrant. The felon was a known flight risk and was seen on video committing an armed robbery. However, no other judge is available, nor could one be available for at least two days. The judge signs the warrant. The judge's actions are:

a) in violation of the Code since the judge should have been disqualified due to having represented the person subject to the warrant.

b) in accordance with the Code since the judge, while subject to disqualification, could be disqualified from any subsequent proceedings at which jeopardy would attach and thereby ensure the defendant's rights were protected.

c) in accordance with the Code since the judge, while subject to disqualification, acted under the rule of necessity because without the warrant there was good reason to believe the subject of the warrant would flee the jurisdiction.

d) in violation of the Code since disqualification under such circumstances is mandatory to protect the attorney-client privilege.

125. A judge can participate in any extrajudicial activity as long as it does not inhibit the judge's ability to independently, fairly, and judiciously conduct the judge's official activities.

a) True. A judge's ability to independently, fairly, and judiciously conduct the affairs of court is the cornerstone of judicial integrity and independence and as long as the judge's conduct does not impede the judge's ability to so act, extrajudicial conduct is allowed.

b) True. Rising to the bench does not require a judge to give up all extrajudicial activities and, in fact, some should be specifically encouraged such as teaching the law.

c) False. There are some extrajudicial activities that are prohibited by law, that interfere with the proper exercise of judicial duties, that lead to frequent disqualification, and that undermine judicial independence, integrity, and impartiality, and such conduct cannot be tolerated.

d) False. Just as the appearance of impropriety is not allowed for judges, the appearance of engaging in extrajudicial activities that may inhibit a judge's ability to independently, fairly, and judiciously conduct the judge's official activities is also prohibited.

126. While giving a public speech to the local League of Women Voters, a judge strongly criticizes recent panels of jurors who, the judge believes, failed to follow the law. The judge contends that these recent jurors failed to recognize that the law requires the

prosecutor to bring charges that the jurors may not agree with, but that if the evidence supports a finding of guilt beyond a reasonable doubt, then the oath sworn as a juror gives no choice but to find the defendant guilty. The judge concludes by urging the audience to "keep what I said in mind if you're ever called to jury duty in my court." The judge's choice of words were:

a) coercive in the mind of a reasonable person and, therefore, had no place in extrajudicial activity.

b) strongly worded but not likely to overpower the minds of the people listening to a speech outside of the courtroom.

c) harsh, but it was clear that the judge was simply venting in one of the few available forums to do so.

d) a reasonable interpretation of the law and subject to interpretation and consideration by any reasonable person.

127. A judge is called upon by a class reunion committee to assist in getting other classmates to attend a reunion, which would also serve as a forum for a 40-minute continuing legal education seminar during a luncheon. The judge agrees and instructs three law clerks to contact a list of attorneys, none of whom ever practiced in front of the judge, to urge them to attend. The judge:

a) did not violate the Code since the judge made sure none of the attorneys ever practiced in front of the judge.

b) violated the Code by engaging in extrajudicial activities that made use of court staff or other resources.

c) did not violate the Code since any attorney who attended the event would engage in continuing legal education which members of the judiciary can support.

d) violated the Code by contacting licensed attorneys for no purpose relevant to a matter before the court.

128. A probate court judge is concerned about threatened legislative cuts to the funding of state park operations. The judge meets with the chairwoman of the state House of Representatives' Committee on Public Affairs to gain knowledge about the Committee's proposed cuts. During a long meeting, the judge repeatedly advises the chairwoman that cuts to such programs would result in lawsuits by numerous entities and that the judge finds it difficult to believe any judge would support the proposed actions. The judge points out that the judge would not hear such a suit in probate court. The judge:

a) violated the Code by using the meeting to determine legislative intent prior to the passage of legislation, thereby giving the judge insider knowledge that could allow the judge to use influence to sway legislation.

b) did not violate the Code as engaging in information gathering from a public official is not prohibited while on the bench.

c) did not violate the Code because the judge was acting as a good steward of the environment and, as such, was acting in an allowable fiduciary capacity.

d) violated the Code by voluntarily consulting with a legislative official.

129. A judge is appointed to an executive branch body that makes recommendations on improvements to the human services system. The body also votes to award grants funded by legislative appropriations, but the judge abstains from all discussions and votes concerning specific grants. The judge's service on the body:

   a) does not violate the Code because the position only indirectly affects the justice system.

   b) violates the Code because the body's purpose does not concern the law, the legal system, or the administration of justice.

   c) violates the Code as appointments to the body are under the control of the executive branch and it is improper for a judge to serve as an appointee from another branch of government.

   d) does not violate the Code because the judge could use the position to award legislative appropriations to fund improvements that may affect the judicial system.

130. A judge may testify as a character witness if:

   a) a judge in a senior court asks the judge to appear before that court to give testimony.

   b) a motion is properly filed with the judge's court, and a hearing is held to determine if the judge has a conflict by testifying. If no conflict exists, the judge may testify.

   c) a legal subpoena has been issued and served upon the judge.

   d) only if a fellow judge requests character witness testimony.

131. For seven generations the Zygmont family has had a living member inducted into the Organizacion Marquee de Guerra, a fraternal organization that raises money for disabled veterans. Judge Zygmont is currently the family member inducted into the organization. The Judge is asked to serve on the organization's Executive Committee. In that capacity, the Judge has reason to review the charter and founding documents. The Judge discovers that the charter limits membership on the Executive Committee to only men, even though women have been members of the organization for two generations. The Judge brings this to the attention of the Committee. Judge Zygmont:

   a) may maintain membership as, despite the document, the organization does not discriminate in its membership.

   b) must resign membership immediately as the organization engages in invidious discrimination that gives rise to the perception that the judge's impartiality is impaired.

   c) may maintain membership but must work to ensure the discriminatory language is removed from all organization documents promptly.

   d) must resign the position on the Executive Committee because the organization's document supports an illegal act, namely, discrimination.

132. A judge belongs to a non-profit charitable organization that raises money for building public parks and has been appointed to its donations committee which is responsible for raising money from the public. The judge:

    a) must resign from the committee because the organization's letterhead lists all committee members.

    b) must resign from the committee as association with it may appear to exert pressure on others to make donations.

    c) may solicit contributions from anyone other than attorneys and parties who have appeared or currently appear in court.

    d) may remain on the committee as long as the judge only solicits contributions from family members or other judges over whom the judge has no authority.

133. A judge of a state's highest court is the only person with the knowledge, education, and experience, in the judge's family, to serve as guardian for an uncle who suffers from multiple mental and physical disabilities. Without the judge's assistance, the uncle will likely become a ward of the state and be institutionalized. The uncle's expenses are paid from a well-funded trust that has been in litigation by other family members for several years but the judge has steadfastly avoided any participation in the litigation. The judge:

    a) can serve as guardian under a hardship exception to the Code as no other person is willing or able to do so.

    b) can serve as guardian so long as the judge steadfastly continues to avoid any participation in the ongoing litigation.

    c) cannot serve as guardian because the uncle's trust litigation is in a court under the judge's appellate jurisdiction.

    d) cannot serve as guardian due to the fact that the duties will require the judge to act in the best interest of the uncle and regularly take funds from a trust that is under litigation.

134. A local judge, prior to ascending to the bench, was a recognized expert in mediation of high-profile divorce cases. Another judge in a neighboring state is overseeing a messy divorce between movie stars and has asked the local judge to take a few vacation days and mediate the case pro bono. The local judge:

    a) may, at the request of a fellow member of the judiciary, assist with the case.

    b) may not engage in any mediation other than as part of assigned judicial duties.

    c) may never mediate a case because doing so would amount to practicing law.

    d) may mediate the case as it is outside of the state.

135. A judge was a probate lawyer for nearly 20 years prior to ascending to the bench. The judge's younger sister needs a simple will drafted and asks to pay the judge to do it. The judge:

    a) can perform legal work but only for family members that reside within the household.

    b) cannot practice law while an active member of the judiciary.

    c) can perform legal work involving drafting or reviewing legal documents or providing legal advice for family members, but the judge may not accept compensation for such work.

    d) cannot practice law but may accept free legal services for family members from lawyers who do not practice in the judge's court.

136. A judge's family owns a brokerage firm. Family members may invest, trade, and receive services including advice at no cost if they provide any significant service to the family business. The judge regularly attends the firm's management meetings and provides business advice for the firm but does not represent it. The judge manages personal household financial matters. The judge:

   a) is not violating the Code because the judge's participation and management is in a closely held family business.

   b) is violating the Code by serving in a management capacity of a business interest while sitting on the bench.

   c) is violating the Code by holding and managing the investments of others.

   d) is not violating the Code if the judge fully disclosed involvement prior to being appointed to the bench.

137. A judge's family owns a brokerage firm. Family members may invest, trade, and receive services including advice at no cost if they provide any significant service to the family business. The judge regularly attends the firm's management meetings and provides business advice for the firm but does not represent it. The judge manages personal household financial matters. The judge's brother is the firm's marketing director and aggressively and successfully recruits new business from the legal community and advises them that the judge is a member of the firm. The judge:

   a) may continue involvement with the firm as long as the judge's brother clearly and conspicuously advises potential new clients who are lawyers of the judge's involvement.

   b) may continue involvement with the firm but must keep apprised of all firm clients who are attorneys so the judge may inquire of any potential conflict of interest should an attorney appear before the judge.

   c) may not continue involvement with the firm unless its marketing strategy clearly advises in writing to all attorneys who are potential clients that the judge may be disqualified in their cases if they invest with the firm.

   d) may not continue to participate in or manage the firm's business if such activities will involve the judge with attorneys or other persons likely to come before the court on which the judge serves.

138. A judge is a former Olympic boxer. The judge serves as a referee in Olympic boxing trials and is paid a stipend plus per diem expenses for travels and work around the nation. The judge:

   a) cannot accept compensation for extrajudicial activities as they create a perception that the judiciary is poorly compensated and is subject to bribery.

   b) may not accept compensation if such acceptance would appear to a reasonable person to undermine the judge's independence, integrity, or impartiality.

   c) can only accept a set fee for services to avoid an appearance of padding expenses.

d) can accept only token compensation and set per diems as allowed under federal law.

139. A judge and the judge's spouse volunteer time over many years to help build a local civic center. The judge and the judge's spouse are offered free season tickets once the civic center is completed. Free season tickets are also offered to a few other key supportive persons and their spouses.

   a) The tickets may be accepted but must be publicly reported.
   b) The tickets may not be accepted unless they are paid for as they have substantial value and very few people were offered free tickets.
   c) The tickets may not be accepted, and the offer must be publicly reported.
   d) The tickets may be accepted, but the judge must pay taxes upon their value.

140. A judge decides a case against a local bank. Two years pass. In need of a second mortgage, the judge applies for and receives a loan from the same bank at a very favorable interest rate. Suspicious, the judge asks a bank officer why the rate was so low and is told it is due to an "exceptional credit score and reputation for honesty." The judge accepts the loan. The judge:

   a) has to report the loan as the bank had an interest that came before the judge in a court.
   b) does not have to report the loan as a similar loan would be given to a person with a similar credit score and reputation.
   c) does not have to report the loan because the judge previously ruled against the bank and could not now be said to have benefitted from an adverse ruling.
   d) has to report the loan to the extent that it is below the published rate afforded to the general public.

141. A judge and the judge's spouse attend a neighboring state's bar association annual weekend meeting. The judge agrees to give a presentation on extradition and waiver at the meeting. While at the weekend conference, the judge and the judge's spouse are wined and dined at several expensive restaurants along with legal product vendors and the neighboring state's bar association officials. The judge and the judge's spouse:

   a) are guests at all the events and could accept the hospitality of their hosts without reservation when they are not allowed to pay their bills.
   b) may accept reimbursement from the neighboring state's bar association but only for actual costs reasonably incurred by the judge and the judge's spouse.
   c) must pay their own way and cannot be reimbursed for expenses incurred at a foreign jurisdiction's events.
   d) may accept reimbursement for the judge's actual costs but not for those of the judge's spouse who was a guest and not a presenter.

142. A judge is a known wine connoisseur and regularly receives a bottle or two of fine wine as a gift or reimbursement. In reporting these things, the judge:

   a) complied with the Code if the judge notified the chief judge of the court, in writing, within five business days of receiving the gift or reimbursement and stated what was received, why it was received, and from whom it was received.

b) complied with the Code if the judge filed a public document in court stating the source and activity from which the judge received the wine as a gift or reimbursement but, due to the extensive nature of the judge's wine cellar and its value, the judge did not describe the wine in order to preserve privacy.

c) complied with the Code if the judge filed a report as a public document in court and stated the value of the thing received so that a public record existed for tax reporting and conflict of interest purposes.

d) complied with the Code if the judge filed a report as a public document in court and provided a description of the gift or reimbursement, the activity for which the judge received it, and the source of the reimbursement.

143. A judge must make required public reports about reimbursement of expenses and waiver of fees or charges:

a) at least bi-annually but within 60 days of the event or program for which the judge received a reimbursement or waiver.

b) always within 30 days of the event or program for which the judge received a reimbursement or waiver.

c) always within 60 days of the event or program for which the judge received a reimbursement or waiver.

d) at least annually.

ANSWERS TO REVIEW QUESTIONS

Answer 93

The correct answer is choice A. The Model Code of Judicial Conduct's first canon requires a judge to uphold and promote the judiciary's independence, integrity, and impartiality.

Answer 94

The correct answer is choice C. A judge acts impartially if the judge has a lack of prejudice or bias in favor of, or against a party, as well as an open mind about all issues that come before the court.

Answer 95

The correct answer is choice C. Any conduct that adversely affects public confidence in the judiciary is considered an impropriety.

Answer 96

The correct answer is choice B. A judge's conduct creates an appearance of impropriety if the conduct would create in reasonable minds a perception that the judge violated the Code or engaged in other conduct that reflects negatively on the judge's impartiality, honesty, temperament, or fitness.

Answer 97

The correct answer is choice C. A judge must not allow others to abuse the prestige of judicial office in order to advance their personal or economic interests.

Answer 98

The correct answer is choice A. Purchasing used furniture, albeit expensive and from a retiring partner of a local law firm, if offered for sale to the public, advances neither the personal nor economic interests of the judge or others and, therefore, is not an abuse of the prestige of judicial office.

Answer 99

The correct answer is choice D. A judge's judicial duties take precedence over all his other activities, and to ensure he can perform his duties he must conduct any extrajudicial and personal activities so as to reduce the risk of conflict or disqualification.

Answer 100

The correct answer is choice C. A judge must uphold and apply the law while performing judicial duties fairly and impartially. A judge must manifest objectivity and open-mindedness regardless of whether the judge approves of the law in question.

Answer 101

The correct answer is choice C. While a judge must perform duties without bias, prejudice, or harassment with respect to race, gender, sex, religion, ethnicity, national origin, disability, age, marital status, sexual orientation, political affiliation, or socioeconomic status, a judge may make legitimate references to factors when they are pertinent to an issue in the case.

Answer 102

The correct answer is choice B. A judge must not permit court officials, court staff, or others subject to the judge's direction and control to manifest bias or prejudice, to engage in harassment, including but not limited to bias, prejudice, or harassment based on race, gender, sex, religion, ethnicity, national origin, disability, age, marital status, sexual orientation, political affiliation, or socioeconomic status.

Answer 103

The correct answer is choice B. Judges must decide cases based on the law and facts, regardless of whether the laws or facts are unpopular or popular. Similarly, judges should not be swayed by public clamor or fear of criticism, nor should they allow family or financial relationships or interests to influence their official conduct or judgment.

Answer 104

The correct answer is choice A. A judge must not allow social or other relationships or interests to influence the judge's judicial conduct or judgment.

Answer 105

The correct answer is choice A. In order to ensure that judges are available to do their judicial duties, they must conduct their extrajudicial and personal activities so as to reduce the risk of conflicts that would result in disqualification from participating in proceedings. Judges are not required to refrain from participating in or supporting a religious institution of their choice, However, they must reduce the risk of conflicts such participation or support may cause.

Answer 106

The correct answer is choice C. A judge must perform administrative and judicial duties competently and diligently as well as supervise and monitor cases in ways that eliminate or reduce dilatory practices, avoidable delays, and unnecessary costs. By ignoring a known administrative personnel problem under the judge's control that has delayed cases, added to costs, and diminished the decorum and demeanor of the court, the judge has violated the Code.

Answer 107

The correct answer is choice D. A judge must provide the parties to a legal proceeding with the right to be heard, but a judge may also encourage, without coercion, parties and their lawyers to settle disputed matters, and the judge may participate in a settlement discussion. However, a judge must also consider the effect participation in a settlement discussion may have on the judge's objectivity and impartiality. Here, the judge offered to hear the parties, including their discrete matters, in chambers, in an effort to settle the case. The judge only offered to consider the case if any party made such a motion after the attempt to settle the case failed. Such an offer does not amount to coercion.

Answer 108

The correct answer is choice B. A judge must hear and decide matters that come before the court unless the Code or law requires disqualification to protect the rights of litigants and preserve public confidence in the judiciary's independence, integrity, and impartiality. A judge should not use disqualification to avoid matters that involve difficult, unpopular, or controversial issues.

Answer 109

The correct answer is choice C. A judge must maintain order and decorum in all proceedings before the judge.

Answer 110

The correct answer is choice D. A judge must be patient, dignified, and courteous to jurors, litigants, witnesses, lawyers, court officials, court staff, and others with whom the judge deals in an official capacity. This includes persons who may not share the judge's or the judicial system's values or traditions.

Answer 111

The correct answer is choice C. Certain restrictions on judicial speech are essential to the maintenance of the judiciary's independence, integrity, and impartiality with regard to pending and impending matters before the court. A judge must not make any statement that might substantially interfere with a fair trial or hearing. The judge must also require court staff and others subject to the judge's direction and control to refrain from making statements that the judge would be prohibited from making.

Answer 112

The correct answer is choice B. While a judge may not make a public statement that might reasonably be expected to impair the fairness of or affect the outcome of a pending or impending matter, a judge may respond to allegations about the judge's conduct in a matter.

Answer 113

The correct answer is choice B. The judge must require that court staff, court officials, and others subject to the judge's direction and control act in a way consistent with the judge's duties pursuant to the Code, including the prohibition on making comments such as pledges, promises, or commitments that are inconsistent with the judge's impartial performance of adjudicative duties.

Answer 114

The correct answer is choice A. A judge must take appropriate action when the judge has a reasonable belief that the performance of another judge or lawyer is impaired by alcohol, drugs, or an emotional, mental, or physical condition. Appropriate action may include a confidential referral to an assistance program. The attorney's apparent alcohol problem should give the criminal law judge reasonable belief that the attorney may be impaired. A judge having knowledge that another judge has committed a violation of the Code that raises a substantial question about the other judge's trustworthiness, honesty, or fitness for judicial office must inform the appropriate authority.

Answer 115

The correct answer is choice D. A judge must cooperate and be honest and candid with lawyer and judicial disciplinary agencies.

Answer 116

The correct answer is choice A. Subject to certain exceptions, a judge must not initiate, permit, or consider ex parte communications, or consider other communications made to the judge outside the presence of the parties regarding an impending or pending matter. The rule applies to communications with people other than the proceeding's participants, such as law teachers and other attorneys.

Answer 117

The correct answer is choice C. A judge may only obtain the advice of a disinterested expert on the law applicable to a proceeding before the court if the judge: (1) notifies the parties of the person to be consulted and the subject matter to be discussed; and (2) provides the parties a reasonable opportunity to object and respond to the notice and to the advice received.

Answer 118

The correct answer is choice C. An ex parte communication is a communication made to a judge for or by one party outside the presence of the other party. A critical element is missing here, namely, communication, which requires the judge to have heard what the attorney said outside the presence of opposing counsel. The judge could not consider what could not be heard.

Answer 119

The correct answer is choice B. A judge may not investigate facts in a matter independently. The judge must consider only the evidence presented and those facts that may properly be judicially noticed.

Answer 120

The correct answer is choice A. A judge must be disqualified from any participation in a proceeding in which the judge's impartiality might reasonably be questioned. A judge's duty not to hear or decide matters in which disqualification is required applies whether or not a party files a motion to disqualify the judge. Impartiality might reasonably be questioned if a person within a third degree of relationship to the judge or the judge's domestic partner/spouse is a person with more than a de minimis interest that could be substantially affected by the proceeding.

Answer 121

The correct answer is choice D. A judge must be disqualified from any participation in a proceeding in which the judge's impartiality might reasonably be questioned. If the judge previously served as a prosecutor, and in that capacity participated substantially and personally as a lawyer regarding the proceeding, the judge's impartiality might reasonably be questioned.

Answer 122

The correct answer is choice D. A judge must make a reasonable effort to keep informed about the personal economic interests of the judge's domestic partner or spouse and minor children residing in the judge's household in order to know when the judge must be disqualified from participation in a proceeding.

Answer 123

The correct answer is choice B. A judge who is subject to disqualification, other than for bias or prejudice, may disclose the basis of the judge's disqualification and ask the parties and their lawyers to consider, outside the presence of the judge and court personnel, if they will waive disqualification.

Answer 124

The correct answer is choice C. The general rule of disqualification is subject to exceptions and may be overridden due to necessity.

Answer 125

The correct answer is choice C. Although a judge may participate in extrajudicial activities, there are some extrajudicial activities that are prohibited by law, that interfere with the proper exercise of judicial duties, that lead to frequent disqualification, and that undermine judicial independence, integrity, and impartiality, and such conduct cannot be tolerated.

Answer 126

The correct answer is choice A. When participating in extrajudicial activities, a judge may not engage in conduct that would appear to a reasonable person to be coercive.

Answer 127

The correct answer is choice B. When engaging in extrajudicial activities, a judge must not make use of court staff, premises, equipment, stationary, or other resources, except for incidental use for activities that concern the legal system, the law, or the administration of justice.

Answer 128

The correct answer is choice D. Generally, a judge must not appear voluntarily at a public hearing or otherwise consult with executive or legislative officials or bodies.

Answer 129

The correct answer is choice B. A judge must not accept appointment to a governmental committee, commission, board, or other governmental position unless the position concerns the law, the legal system, or the administration of justice.

Answer 130

The correct answer is choice C. Only if a judge is duly summoned may the judge testify as a character witness in an administrative, judicial, or other adjudicatory proceeding. Testifying as a character witness without a subpoena abuses the prestige of judicial office in order to advance someone else's interest.

Answer 131

The correct answer is choice B. A judge's membership in an organization that engages in invidious discrimination gives rise to perceptions that the judge's impartiality is impaired and the judge must immediately resign from such an organization upon learning of the same.

Answer 132

The correct answer is choice D. Generally, judges may engage in non-profit educational, religious, charitable, fraternal, or civic extrajudicial activities, even when such activities do not involve the law. The judge may solicit contributions only from family members or other judges over whom the judge lacks authority.

Answer 133

The correct answer is choice C. A judge cannot serve in a fiduciary position when a trust, estate, or ward for which the judge is responsible becomes involved in adversary proceedings in the court on which the judge serves, or another court under its appellate jurisdiction.

Answer 134

The correct answer is choice B. A judge may not act as an arbitrator or a mediator or perform other judicial functions separate from the judge's official duties. However, a judge may participate in arbitration, mediation, or settlement conferences conducted as part of assigned judicial duties.

Answer 135

The correct answer is choice C. A judge may not practice law. However, a judge may, without compensation, provide legal advice to, and draft or review documents for, a member of the judge's family.

Answer 136

The correct answer is choice A. A judge may not serve as a director, officer, manager, general partner, employee, or advisor of any business entity. However, a judge may participate or manage in a business closely held by the judge or member of the judge's family or a business entity mainly involved in investment of the judge's financial resources and those of the judge's family members.

Answer 137

The correct answer is choice D. A judge may not engage in management of business entities if their financial activities will involve the judge in frequent transactions or continuing business relationships with lawyers or other persons likely to come before the court on which the judge serves.

Answer 138

The correct answer is choice B. A judge may not accept compensation if such acceptance would appear to a reasonable person to undermine the judge's independence, integrity, or impartiality.

Answer 139

The correct answer is choice A. A judge must report accepted invitations to a judge and spouse to attend without charge an event connected with the judge's civic activities if the identical invitation is given to nonjudges who are involved in that activity in similar ways as the judge.

Answer 140

The correct answer is choice A. A judge must report accepted gifts, loans, bequests, benefits, or other things of value, if their source is a party or an attorney who has appeared, or is likely to appear before the judge in a court, or whose interests have or could come before the judge in a court.

Answer 141

The correct answer is choice B. Reimbursement of a judge's expenses for necessary food, travel, lodging, or other incidental expenses is limited to the actual costs reasonably incurred by the judge and, when suitable to the occasion, by the judge's spouse. Such reimbursement must be publicly reported.

Answer 142

The correct answer is choice D. A judge must publicly report the amount of certain permissible reimbursements and other things of value received by the judge. A judge must file reports as public documents in the court on which the judge serves or another office designated by law. If public reporting is required, the report must contain a description of the thing of value, the activity for which the judge received it, and the source of reimbursement of expenses or waiver of fees or charges.

Answer 143

The correct answer is choice B. A judge must make a required public report at least annually. However, a judge must make a required public report about reimbursement of expenses and waiver of fees or charges within 30 days after the end of the event or program for which the judge received that reimbursement and waiver.

AMERIBAR BAR REVIEW

MPRE Practice Questions

PRACTICE QUESTIONS

PRACTICE MPRE QUESTIONS

A.   Questions

QUESTION 1

An attorney has an active law practice. Many of the attorney's clients neither fully nor timely pay the attorney's bills. The attorney feels limited in the ability to withdraw from representing these clients because many non-paying clients fail to pay at an advanced stage of the representation. The attorney adds a clause to the attorney's standard representation agreement as a proactive measure to prevent this problem in the future. Any new client is required to execute the agreement before the attorney begins working for the client. The clause provides that the attorney may withdraw from representing the client based on the client's non-payment and/or late payment of the attorney's bills, provided that attorney provides reasonable warning that the attorney will withdraw unless the payment obligation is timely fulfilled. Under the agreement, the client is provided with the opportunity to consult with a different lawyer about the agreement before executing it. The clause provides that the attorney will invoke the clause if the client fails to pay legal fees.

Assuming the attorney does not represent clients in a capacity in which the approval of a judge would be required for withdrawal of legal representation, would it be proper for the attorney to invoke the clause for withdrawal if a new client does not pay the attorney's bills?

(A)   No, because withdrawal is not warranted simply because a client fails to pay the attorney's bills.

(B)   No, because the clause does not allow the client time to consult with a different lawyer about the agreement before executing it.

(C)   Yes, because the clause gives the client notice that the attorney will invoke the clause if payment is not received.

(D)   Yes, because a client expressly agrees to the withdrawal by executing the agreement.

QUESTION 2

A plaintiff hires an attorney to pursue a tort cause of action against a defendant. The plaintiff receives a satisfactory award of damages after pretrial mediation of the case. The plaintiff forwards to the attorney the entire amount due for services rendered by the attorney, up through obtaining the award.

Following that final event of their attorney-client relationship, a state agency contacts the attorney. The agency requests that the attorney complete and return a detailed financial disclosure form regarding the mediation award. When the attorney notifies the plaintiff of the agency's request, the plaintiff directs the attorney not to comply with it. State law does not require completion of the form by the attorney.

Will it be proper for the attorney to complete and return the form to the agency?

(A)   No, unless the attorney considers compliance to be in the plaintiff's best interest.

(B)   No, because the plaintiff directed the attorney not to complete and return the form.

(C)   Yes, if the form will not reveal the attorney's work product.

(D)   Yes, because the attorney's representation of the plaintiff ended a while ago.

QUESTION 3

An attorney agrees to represent a plaintiff in a discrimination action. The attorney files a civil rights complaint against a defendant in a federal district court. Before trial, Congress repeals the federal statute upon which the complaint is based. On behalf of the defendant, another lawyer files a motion alleging that existing law does not warrant the claims in the complaint due to the statute's repeal, which the motion properly documents. In less than 21 days after the motion is filed, the attorney properly amends the complaint to substitute other valid federal civil rights law for the former statute. Existing law governs the case, not the law existing when the complaint was filed.

Will the attorney be subject to a litigation sanction?

(A)   No, unless the attorney knew that the repeal of the statute was being debated at the time that the original complaint was filed.

(B)   No, because the attorney appropriately amended the complaint within 21 days after filing the motion.

(C)   Yes, unless the attorney disclosed the statute's repeal to the plaintiff before the complaint was filed.

(D)   Yes, because the attorney should have premised the original complaint upon the other valid federal civil rights law.

QUESTION 4

A state agency in charge of state employment hires an attorney to develop and implement an employee handbook for all employees of the state. The attorney is now in private practice. Three years after the attorney completed the handbook, the state discharges an employee for violating a handbook provision. The employee seeks to retain the attorney to sue the department for wrongful discharge. The attorney recalls that when developing and implementing the handbook, the state's attorney general issued an opinion (for internal use only) that authorized discharges on grounds similar to those that were used against the employee. At that time, the attorney disagreed in writing with the attorney general's opinion. Nonetheless, the attorney incorporated the attorney general's opinion on authorized grounds for discharge into the handbook.

The attorney believes that the grounds for disagreement with the opinion are still valid. The attorney believes that asserting the grounds for disagreement would improve the employee's prospect of being reinstated, or increase the potential for prevailing in a lawsuit against the department.

It would be proper for the attorney to:

(A)   Reject the employee as a client but reveal the basis for disagreement with the attorney general.

(B)   Reject the employee as a client and not reveal the basis for disagreement with the attorney general.

(C)   Accept the employee as a client only in a lawsuit against the department without revealing the basis for disagreement with the attorney general.

(D)   Accept the employee as a client and seek to have the employee reinstated by revealing the basis for disagreement with the attorney general.

QUESTION 5

An attorney and a client execute a representation agreement regarding the attorney's handling of the client's divorce action against a defendant. The client agrees that if she is awarded alimony and child custody, she would transfer title to certain real property to the attorney. The case advances to trial. The client receives alimony and child custody by judicial order. The client transfers title to the real property to the attorney.

Does the execution of the representation agreement subject the attorney to discipline?

(A)   No, because the client received alimony and child custody.

(B)   No, because the attorney and the client voluntarily executed the representation agreement.

(C)   Yes, because the attorney entered into a contingency fee agreement.

(D)   Yes, because the client's real property was improperly subject to the attorney's proprietary interest.

QUESTION 6

An attorney belongs to the state bar. She pays a corporation to broadcast a television advertisement of her services in the state. The advertisement states that she has a perfect trial win record. However, the attorney did lose a trial, although she prevailed on appeal of that case.

Will the attorney be subject to discipline?

(A)   No, because the advertisement is proper under the rules of professional conduct.

(B)   No, because the advertisement is protected by principles of constitutional freedom of speech.

(C)   Yes, because the advertisement is not protected by principles of constitutional freedom of speech.

(D)   Yes, because the advertisement is improper under the rules of professional conduct.

QUESTION 7

A builder enters into an enforceable contract with an owner to construct a home. A judge's spouse owns and operates an interior design business. The spouse enters into a valid agreement with the owner to decorate the home. While the spouse is performing services pursuant to the agreement, the owner files a breach of contract action against the builder in the court where the judge works. The owner gives a gift to the judge that is not part of the spouse's compensation under the agreement.

Will it be proper for the judge to accept the gift?

(A)   No, if the gift was incident to the spouse's business and could reasonably be perceived as intended to influence the judge in performance of judicial duties.

(B)   No, unless the owner gave the same gift to the builder.

(C)   Yes, because the owner does not have a direct business relationship with the judge.

(D)   Yes, because a judge can accept gifts from anyone.

QUESTION 8

An attorney duly commences a plaintiff's lawsuit against a defendant. A lawyer agrees to represent the defendant in that lawsuit, and timely files an initial responsive pleading. Pursuant to the jurisdiction's court rules, the lawsuit is subject to mandatory pre-trial mediation. The plaintiff's attorney prevails in her motion to adjourn the scheduled mediation for 30 days. The defendant's lawyer timely files a mediation summary in advance of the rescheduled mediation date. The plaintiff's attorney fails to either notify the plaintiff to attend the mediation or file a mediation summary. Neither the plaintiff's attorney nor the plaintiff appear as required for the mediation session. Consequently, the court clerk properly enters a default against the plaintiff and serves the attorney with a notice of default.

Although the plaintiff's attorney promises the plaintiff that she will get the default set aside, the plaintiff's attorney instead goes on a 30-day vacation and does nothing to address the default. The defendant's lawyer subsequently prevails on a motion for a default judgment against the plaintiff. After the vacation, the plaintiff's attorney files a motion to set aside the default judgment. The motion alleges that the attorney has good cause and a meritorious defense for not participating in mediation. The court denies the motion. The plaintiff does not authorize the attorney to pursue the case any further.

Will the attorney be subject to discipline?

(A)   No, if she pays the plaintiff the cause of action's fair market value.

(B)   No, because the court should have granted the motion to set aside the default judgment.

(C)   Yes, unless the court should have granted the motion to set aside the default judgment.

(D)   Yes, because she failed to make the required filing of a mediation summary or a motion to set aside the default, and she did not move to set aside the default judgment until after her vacation.

QUESTION 9

An attorney only practices transactional law. The attorney has no partners and is not associated with any other lawyers. On a monthly basis, the attorney runs radio spots. They broadcast that her "office exclusively handles transactional matters, including foreign contracts." An individual hears the attorney's radio spot, and they meet to discuss representation. The attorney conducts a typical client-screening interview with the individual. At its conclusion, the attorney states:

"Unfortunately, my case load is at its highest level ever. Your requested enforcement of a foreign contract could be rather complex. I would like to recommend a different attorney who also handles foreign contract matters and who might have time to represent you. I strongly suggest that you meet with a different attorney soon in order to preserve your right to enforce the foreign contract."

The individual declines the attorney's offer of a referral and leaves the office quite discouraged that she was unavailable. About a half year later, the individual locates a different transactional lawyer that deals with foreign contracts. At that time, this lawyer advises that the foreign country's statute of limitation for enforcing the contract expired nearly three months after the individual's meeting with the attorney.

Will the attorney be subject to civil liability?

(A)   No, because the attorney complied with the relevant rules of professional conduct and acted reasonably with respect to declining the representation.

(B)   No, because the attorney had the right to decline representation of the individual.

(C)   Yes, because the attorney's advertisement was false and misleading.

(D)   Yes, because the attorney failed to provide notice of the foreign country's statute of limitation.

QUESTION 10

A plaintiff retains an attorney to bring a negligence lawsuit against a defendant. Although the plaintiff's cause of action lacks any legal foundation, the plaintiff seeks to waste the defendant's time and funds in defending it. The attorney's complaint incorporates and is premised upon the plaintiff's misrepresentations of fact. The attorney is unaware of the plaintiff's misrepresentations.

When the case goes to trial, the plaintiff gives testimony conforming to the complaint's factual allegations. The judge renders a decision in favor of the plaintiff. Following the entry of an order of judgment, the plaintiff sends the attorney a "confidential" fax confessing that he had initially made false statements of fact and repeated them on the witness stand at trial.

The defendant submits a grievance to the professional authority alleging that the attorney used the plaintiff's trial testimony while knowing of its falsity. Consequently, the disciplinary authority commences disciplinary proceedings against the attorney.

Will it be proper for the attorney to present the plaintiff's fax as part of a defense in the disciplinary proceedings?

(A)   No, because the plaintiff revealed what he did in a confidential fax.

(B)   No, because the plaintiff could be prosecuted for perjury if the confidential fax is revealed.

(C)   Yes, because disclosure of the fax is needed for the attorney's defense.

(D)   Yes, because the plaintiff's testimony did not perpetrate a fraud on the judge.

QUESTION 11

An attorney belongs to the bar of her home state. In another state, the attorney maintains a physician's license. The attorney knowingly makes a misrepresentation of a material fact in her physician's license renewal form.

Will the attorney be subject to discipline by the bar in her home state for the misrepresentation?

(A)   No, because her conduct did not occur while serving as an attorney.

(B)   No, because her conduct did not occur in her home state.

(C)   Yes, because her false statement constituted dishonest conduct.

(D)   Yes, only if she is convicted of a crime in the other state.

QUESTION 12

A defendant hires an attorney to defend her in a criminal case. The attorney informs her that he expects the cost of representation to exceed the amount of her initial deposit. Without the defendant's knowledge, her grandfather gives the attorney a $500 check with directions to credit it against the costs of defense. The grandfather's only request is that the attorney not inform the defendant about the check because she had told him to "stay out of her life." The attorney applies the $500 towards the balance due from the defendant.

Will it be proper for the attorney to keep and use the grandfather's check?

(A)   No, because someone other than the defendant cannot fund her defense.

(B)   No, because the attorney lacks the defendant's informed consent to use the funds for her defense.

(C)   Yes, because the grandfather has not tried to affect the attorney's handling of the defense.

(D)   Yes, because the attorney has not decreased costs based on the grandfather's payment.

QUESTION 13

An attorney and a client execute a valid retainer agreement that automatically renews from year to year. It provides that the attorney will charge the client $150 per hour for the attorney's services and $75 per hour for a paralegal's services. These amounts are reasonable rates in comparison to the average hourly rates in the jurisdiction where the attorney practices law. After the first year, the attorney increases those hourly rates to $175 and $100, respectively. The attorney does not communicate this change to the client, although the attorney bases the client's bills in the second year on the new hourly rates. The client continues to use and pay for the services of the attorney and the paralegal during the second year of their agreement.

Will the attorney be subject to discipline?

(A)   No, because the $25 hourly increases were reasonable.

(B)   No, because the retainer agreement obligated the client to pay the hourly rates.

(C)   Yes, because the retainer agreement was in writing.

(D)   Yes, because the attorney failed to obtain the client's consent to the changed hourly rates.

QUESTION 14

An attorney works for a retail corporation, which is experiencing unexplained discrepancies between its sales records and cash receipts. As the corporation's counsel, the attorney seeks to determine the cause of these discrepancies. She believes that they may be attributable to theft by a cashier, who works for the corporation. The cashier handles and collects the daily cash register returns. The attorney plans to question the cashier about the situation. The attorney does not want to reveal that she considers the cashier responsible for the discrepancies. The attorney intends to falsely tell the cashier that she is not being accused of taking cash and that any answers that she provides are confidential. The attorney intends to use the answers she provides against her in any related proceedings against the cashier.

Will the attorney be subject to discipline for conducting this questioning?

(A)   No, because no impending legal proceedings existed against the cashier.

(B)   No, because the attorney failed to provide the cashier with legal advice.

(C)   Yes, because the attorney made false statements to the cashier.

(D)   Yes, unless the attorney instructs the cashier to retain a lawyer before the questioning occurs.

QUESTION 15

An attorney works for a state's law enforcement department. The attorney handles a major consumer fraud case during the last year she works for the department. As lead counsel, she works on the discovery, litigation, and appellate phases of that case concerning a telemarketing investment scheme perpetrated by a telemarketing corporation. The corporation defrauded thousands of people of substantial amounts of money including the life savings of many of the victims. Pursuant to state law, the department makes certain data that the attorney gathered when working on the case available to the public.

The final judgment in the department's favor enjoins the corporation's domestic operations, but does not enjoin the corporation's foreign operations. This judgment imposed substantial punitive fines against the corporation.

Pursuant to the controlling law, individuals can bring their own actions against the corporation for damages arising from its fraudulent activities.

The attorney opens her own law office after leaving the department. Five individuals file separate actions against the corporation alleging damages from its fraudulent activities attributable to the foreign operations. The corporation contacts the attorney seeking her representation in those actions.

Will the attorney be subject to discipline by defending the corporation in these private actions?

(A)   No, because of the attorney's particular knowledge of this type of law.

(B)   No, because certain data gathered by the attorney is now available to the public.

(C)   Yes, because the final judgment is completely dispositive of the corporation's liability.

(D)   Yes, because of the attorney's substantial responsibility in the department's case against the corporation.

QUESTION 16

An attorney enters into a valid contingency fee agreement to represent a client in a legal malpractice lawsuit. The agreement awards the attorney 15% of the recovery in a trial and 10% of the recovery from a settlement. The total legal fee cannot be greater than $75,000. The attorney does not have much trial experience. The attorney contacts a trial lawyer seeking assistance in the event that the case goes to trial. The client provides written consent to the arrangement with the trial lawyer following complete disclosure. Pursuant to the fee contract between the attorney and the trial lawyer, the trial lawyer associates with the attorney because of the trial lawyer's special competence with trial of legal malpractice matters. The attorney and the trial lawyer reasonably estimate that the attorney will provide a majority of the work if the case settles before trial, and that the trial lawyer would provide a majority of the work if the case goes to trial.

The fee contract between the attorney and the trial lawyer provides:

"This matter's entire fee is fifteen percent of the recovery in a trial and ten percent of the recovery from a settlement, with a total fee not greater than $75,000. The attorney will participate in pre-trial work and be the client's contact person. The trial lawyer will develop the case and try the case if no settlement occurs. The fee will be split as follows: (1) If the case settles - 70 percent to the attorney and 30 percent to the trial lawyer; (2) If the case goes to trial - 30 percent to the attorney and 70 percent to the trial lawyer"

Will the attorney and the lawyer be subject to discipline for their fee-splitting arrangement?

(A)   No, because the fee split between them seems proportionate to the work each will actually do.

(B)   No, because the entire fee amount is the same as in the agreement between the client and the attorney.

(C)   Yes, because the client provided written consent.

(D)   Yes, because the attorney cannot present the case at trial.

QUESTION 17

Three attorneys form a law firm. These attorneys only practice law in their home state. Unlike a neighboring state, the home state does not require mandatory continuing legal education. At the partners' monthly meeting, two attorneys vote not to include continuing legal education courses as an expense that the firm will reimburse. After casting a dissenting vote, the dissenting attorney declares that he will not participate in any optional continuing legal education courses because of the firm's policy against reimbursement. The firm maintains malpractice insurance coverage for the attorneys.

Will it be proper for the dissenting attorney not to participate in any continuing legal education courses?

(A)   No, because absent the dissenting attorney's participation in those courses, he will not maintain legal competence.

(B)   No, because the firm provides malpractice insurance coverage.

(C)   Yes, because the dissenting attorney does not practice law in the neighboring state.

(D)   Yes, if the dissenting attorney keeps abreast of changes in the law and its practice, and engages in continuing study and education.

QUESTION 18

A corporation's stock is traded on a public stock exchange. Some of the shareholders want to bring a lawsuit against the corporation because they are upset with certain conduct by the corporation's management. An attorney agrees to represent the complaining shareholders of the corporation in a derivative action. The attorney properly files the action against the corporation in a civil court. The court clerk places the action on a judge's civil docket. A trust account maintained for the judge owns some shares of publicly traded corporations. Before any pre-trial proceedings commence in the derivative action, the judge checks with the trustee about whether the trust contains any shares of the corporation. The trustee tells the judge that the trust owns a substantial number of shares of the corporation's stock. Only the trustee and the judge know of the stock ownership. The judge goes forward with pre-trial proceedings in the derivative action.

Will the judge be subject to discipline?

(A)   Yes, because the judge did not disclose the stock ownership.

(B)   Yes, because the judge did not disqualify himself from the case.

(C)   No, because the judge holds the shares in a trust, not in direct ownership.

(D)   No, because only the trustee and the judge know about the shares.

QUESTION 19

Al Attorney and Barbara Lawyer are members of the state bar. The two attorneys were friends in graduate school where Al obtained his L.L.M. and Barbara obtained her Ph.(D) After exclusively practicing bankruptcy law for 10 years at different firms, they form a partnership. The firm places an advertisement in a monthly magazine that is circulated in their home state.

The advertisement states:

Al Attorney, J.(D), L.L.M.
Barbara Lawyer, J.(D), Ph.(D)
Attorney & Lawyer, P.(C)
1 Main Ave., City, State, 11111
Phone Number (888) 888-8888.

Will the attorneys be subject to discipline?

(A)   Yes, because the appearance of L.L.M. and Ph.(D) is superfluous.

(B)   Yes, if the firm's practice is restricted to the subject matter in which the degrees of L.L.M. and Ph.(D) are needed.

(C)   No, because only law is a licensed profession.

(D)   No, because they have the degrees referenced.

QUESTION 20

A state administrative agency issues a subpoena to a witness to testify at a hearing. An attorney agrees to represent the witness at the hearing. The attorney counsels the witness that she could exercise a constitutional right not to respond to some questions that the attorney reasonably believes would be against the witness's best interest to answer. The attorney bases this incorrect advice on an overruled Supreme Court decision. The administrative law judge instructs the witness that her failure to answer constitutes a criminal offense for which she would be prosecuted, and informs the attorney of the subsequent Supreme Court decision. Nonetheless, the attorney persists in advising the witness not to testify. Relying on the attorney's repeated counsel, the witness continues to remain silent in response to the questions. As a result, the witness is convicted for not answering the question.

Will the attorney be subject to discipline?

(A)   No, because the witness followed the attorney's advice.

(B)   No, because the attorney had a reasonable belief that the witness was legally entitled not to answer the question.

(C)   Yes, because the attorney's repeatedly incorrect advice shows a lack of preparation.

(D)   Yes, because the witness violated the law by heeding the attorney's counsel.

QUESTION 21

An attorney's friend requests that the attorney complete a form provided by a jurisdiction's bar admission authority. The friend would like the attorney to provide a favorable description of her step-cousin's character and fitness to practice law. The friend only briefly sees and visits with her step-cousin once a year. The step-cousin's father, however, has described the step-cousin to the friend as possessing the character traits of truthfulness and diligence. The friend tells the attorney of this description and that the friend believes in its accuracy. The attorney met the friend's step-cousin at a social gathering and found her to appear truthful and honest. The attorney, based on the experience at the gathering, and trust of her friend's opinion, completes the form favorably.

Unbeknownst to the attorney and the friend, the step-cousin was involved in a plan to embezzle money from a former employer, for which the step-cousin entered a plea deal.

Will the attorney be subject to discipline for filling out the form?

(A)   No, because the attorney reasonably believes the friend's representations.

(B)   No, unless the attorney learns of the step-cousin's involvement in the plan and does not notify the proper authority.

(C)   Yes, because the attorney should have completed an investigation into the step-cousin's character.

(D)   Yes, because by completing the form the attorney misrepresented the facts.

QUESTION 22

A district attorney handles the prosecution of an accused for stealing a car from a dealership's inventory lot. The accused refutes the charges on the basis that she was at her boyfriend's residence when the alleged offense occurred. An employee, who works for the dealership, provides trial testimony. The employee testifies that he recognized the accused's picture in a photographic array, which a police officer showed to him. The district attorney presents a recording of the employee's 911 call reporting the event and describing the accused and the car. The judge renders a judgment of conviction and sentences the accused for the offense. After the trial, the accused's lawyer discovers additional evidence that the employee initially picked another person's photograph from the photographic array before the police officer suggested the accused's picture to him. The accused's lawyer learns that the district attorney knew of that evidence, but failed to reveal it to the lawyer. The lawyer's pretrial discovery request did not seek such evidence.

Will the district attorney be subject to discipline?

(A)   No, because the lawyer failed to make a pretrial discovery request for that type of information.

(B)   No, because the district attorney did not have to initially disclose the additional evidence that was later discovered.

(C)   Yes, because the judge could have identified the accused based on the 911 call recording.

(D)   Yes, because the subsequently discovered evidence tends to negate the accused's culpability for the offense.

QUESTION 23

A defendant is called to testify before a legislative committee. The defendant provides testimony before the committee under oath, subject to the penalty of perjury, without being represented by counsel. The defendant is subsequently charged with perjury allegedly arising from that testimony. After an attorney agrees to represent the defendant in the perjury prosecution, the defendant informs the attorney that she made fraudulent statements in her testimony before the committee.

The attorney will be subject to discipline if he:

(A)   fails to provide notice of the fraudulent statements to the police.

(B)   provides notice of the fraudulent statements to the police.

(C)   remains the defendant's counsel.

(D)   remains the defendant's counsel unless the defendant admits her fraudulent statements.

QUESTION 24

A partner attorney, a partner in a law firm, specializes in antitrust law. A conglomerated company hires the partner attorney's firm in response to receiving a government notice to cease and desist from violating antitrust law. Although the partner attorney agrees to represent the company, another existing case that she was handling unexpectedly was set for trial at an imminent time after an anticipated settlement did not occur. Because that trial would bring the firm more revenue than the company's case, the partner attorney transfers the company's case to an associate lawyer in the firm.

The associate lawyer objects to this new assignment based on an ignorance of antitrust law. He also states that he lacks reasonable time to gain sufficient legal competence to handle the company's case without the partner attorney's assistance. The partner attorney replies that her caseload prevents her from assisting him and that she believes he can handle this assignment.

Did the partner attorney properly handle this case?

(A)   No, because of the partner attorney's awareness that the associate lawyer lacked the competence to handle the case and her failure to provide adequate oversight to ensure the company's protection.

(B)   No, because the partner attorney lacked the company's consent to transfer its case to the associate lawyer.

(C)   Yes, because the associate lawyer's license to practice law qualified him to handle any type of case.

(D)   Yes, because the partner attorney could withdraw from any case if handling it would cause her substantial financial hardship.

QUESTION 25

A defendant meets with an attorney and requests representation as defense counsel against charges of being a minor in possession of controlled substances. In the state where the defendant is charged with this offense, a minor is defined as a person less than 21 years old. The defendant informs the attorney that her state identification card indicates that she is 22 years old. The defendant admits to the attorney that she has a fake identification card, but asks the attorney not to reveal her true date of birth at the trial on the charged offense. The defendant states that she would not reveal her true date of birth as a trial witness. The attorney advises that, in order to provide a valid defense, the defendant must take the witness stand at trial. When the attorney asks the defendant what is her date of birth, she gives the date on the fake identification card. The attorney does nothing in response to this answer.

Will the attorney be subject to discipline?

(A)   No, because the attorney became aware of the defendant's real date of birth through representing her.

(B)   No, because the defendant's real date of birth is not an issue in the proceeding.

(C)   Yes, because the attorney used the defendant's date of birth in defense of the case despite knowing of its falsity.

(D)   Yes, because the defendant violated the law by using a fake identification card.

QUESTION 26

An attorney and a client have a written fee contract. The client agrees to pay an hourly fee that the attorney will invoice monthly. The client must pay each invoice within one month. Each invoice states that delinquent payment or non-payment could result in withdrawal by the attorney.

Four months before the trial of the client's case, the client pays that month's invoice one month late. Three months before the trial, the client fails to pay that month's invoice. Two months before the trial, the client does not pay that month's invoice, which states:

"You made a delinquent payment of an invoice and did not pay the last invoice. If you fail to pay off your account balance pursuant to this invoice, I will move to withdraw from representing you."

One month before the trial, the attorney writes the client a letter stating that he will move to withdraw from the representation if the client does not pay the last invoice within one week. At the end of the week, when the client does not make any payment, the attorney files a motion to withdraw from representing the client with the court.

Will the attorney be subject to discipline?

(A)   Yes, because the contract is invalid.

(B)   Yes, because the conduct of the attorney and the client does not support withdrawal.

(C)   No, because the client's conduct requires withdrawal.

(D)   No, because the attorney may move to withdraw under these circumstances.

QUESTION 27

A plaintiff and an attorney enter into a contingency fee agreement regarding a legal matter. The agreement provides the attorney with 20% of the plaintiff's recovery of money damages in the matter. Pursuant to the plaintiff's request, the attorney files a trespass lawsuit against a defendant. The defendant's lawyer makes an offer of settlement that the plaintiff accepts. The settlement provides that the defendant would make five equal payments to the attorney of $1,000 over the next five months. Upon receiving the first $1,000 check, the attorney deposits it in her general account and promptly issues a $800 check to the plaintiff.

Will the attorney be subject to discipline?

(A)   No, because the attorney deposited the check in a proper account because the case is over.

(B)   No, because the attorney issued the check to the plaintiff in a correct amount.

(C)   Yes, because the attorney deposited the check in an improper account.

(D)   Yes, because the attorney issued the check to the plaintiff in an incorrect amount.

QUESTION 28

An attorney, a solo practitioner, undertakes representation of a plaintiff, an individual. The plaintiff brings a complex business law action against a major company defendant. The defendant retains a large law firm that deluges the attorney with lengthy pleadings and numerous motions. This case involves extensive discovery requiring review of voluminous documents. The plaintiff objects to the pretrial process as being far more time consuming and costly than anticipated. The attorney advises that to reduce the pretrial process would adversely affect the plaintiff's prospects of prevailing. The attorney thinks that the pretrial process must continue for several more months. The attorney believes that the plaintiff must file several motions and serve additional discovery requests, while the plaintiff wants the process to end, and to go to trial as soon as possible. The plaintiff demands that the attorney expedite the case to trial. The attorney feels that the plaintiff's persistent demands are making prosecution of the case extremely difficult. Many other lawyers are available and competent to handle this matter.

Would it be proper for the attorney to seek the trial court's approval to withdraw from representing the plaintiff?

(A)   No, because the attorney is obligated to obey the plaintiff's directions.

(B)   No, because the plaintiff has not authorized the attorney to withdraw.

(C)   Yes, because the attorney is entitled to withdraw from representing the plaintiff at any point before a trial occurs.

(D)   Yes, because the plaintiff's demands render it unreasonably difficult for the attorney to competently and effectively represent the plaintiff.

QUESTION 29

A prosecutor charges a defendant with murder. The defendant, a famous athlete, retains an attorney, a high-profile defense counsel. The defendant declines to enter a plea agreement with the prosecutor. The attorney advises the defendant that a trial will be very costly. The defendant states that:

"I could only afford to give you the initial retainer payment. But I cannot pay for any additional fees. I would like to transfer to you any present or future rights that I might have to develop any type of media entertainment from this pending trial and its related circumstances. If you accepted this offer of transfer, no further payment would be required for your legal services for the entire trial."

The attorney responds that:

"Let me think about your proposal. For now, I suggest that you consult with another attorney regarding if such an arrangement would be advantageous to you. You could do that and get back in touch with me in a few days."

The defendant does not consult with another lawyer about the proposal.

Will the defense attorney be subject to discipline?

(A)   No, because the defendant failed to consult with another lawyer.

(B)   No, because the murder case is a criminal proceeding rather than a civil proceeding.

(C)   Yes, because the attorney is not permitted to enter into an agreement giving the attorney literary or media rights of the client.

(D)   Yes, because the attorney has not completed representing the defendant.

QUESTION 30

A title company and a real estate attorney enter into a contract. The company allows the attorney free use of an office in its main office building. The company permits the attorney to use the office for a private law practice under two conditions. First, while using the office, the attorney may not represent any clients that present a conflict of interest to the company. Second, the attorney would assist with work relating to the company's clients for free.

If a company's client needs legal work with respect to a deed or contract, the company's non-lawyer employee would assist that client and determine if the client needed any legal documents. The employee would tell the client that the company's staff would develop the appropriate document or documents and later present them to the client for signature.

Pursuant to the employee's written instruction regarding the needed documents, the attorney would develop the documents and do all related legal work. The attorney neither met with the company's clients, nor billed them for work.

Will the attorney be subject to discipline?

(A)   No, because the attorney does not charge the company's clients for work.

(B)   No, because the attorney is not advising the company's clients directly.

(C)   Yes, because the agreement is restricting the attorney's right to practice law.

(D)   Yes, because the agreement is causing the attorney to assist the company in the practice of law.

QUESTION 31

A judge is up for election to the state supreme court. Recently, the judge authored a divisive opinion for the state court of appeals. The opinion interprets when the compensation clause of the state constitution allows state government to take private property for public use. That interpretation expands the scope of permissible takings beyond only those that are necessary for public use. The new scope of takings include those that are beneficial for economic development. The judge participates in a public debate with an opponent. They discuss the case about governmental takings of land. The judge says, "I correctly decided the case and I would decide the same way if I hear the case on the Supreme Court." The case is on appeal to the state supreme court.

Will the judge be subject to discipline for that statement?

(A)   No, because the judge is exercising the constitutional right of free speech.

(B)   No, because the judge has immunity.

(C)   Yes, because the statement indicates that the judge will not fairly decide the issue.

(D)   Yes, because the judge discussed the topic in public.

QUESTION 32

A company utilizes an attorney as retained outside counsel for almost a decade. A recent change in the company's business affects the company's legal status. The attorney's research discovers that the change arguably renders an existing corporate document on file with a state office misleading and fraudulent. The attorney promptly informs the company's board of directors that the company must change the filing immediately to avoid civil liability. The board rejected the attorney's request to make the change on the basis that the change did not make the filed document misleading and fraudulent. In response to the attorney's threat to cease representing the company, the board asserts that by quitting, the attorney would be indicating that the filing was flawed. The board requested that the attorney remain outside counsel. The board stated that the company's corporate counsel would handle this issue. The attorney wishes to withdraw from representing the company based on a reasonable belief that the filing is unlawful. The attorney is uncomfortable with the filing in its present form.

Will it be proper for the attorney to withdraw?

(A)   No, because the attorney's withdrawal would indicate that the filing is unlawfully flawed.

(B)   No, because the attorney's withdrawal could adversely impact the company's prospects of timely correcting the filing.

(C)   Yes, because the attorney can permissively withdraw if the company is persisting in a course of conduct that the attorney reasonably believes, but does not know, is fraudulent.

(D)   Yes, because the attorney must withdraw since the company is persisting in a course of conduct that the attorney reasonably believes, but does not know, is fraudulent.

QUESTION 33

A plaintiff's attorney is campaigning to be elected as a trial court judge. A defense lawyer is a solo practitioner in the same jurisdiction that the plaintiff's attorney seeks to serve as a trial court judge. Often they have appeared in the same courtrooms and even litigated cases as representatives of party opponents. In light of the defense lawyer's awareness of how the plaintiff's attorney conducts herself in judicial proceedings, the defense lawyer's opinion is that the plaintiff's attorney lacks a judicial temperament. Both represented opposing litigants in a high-profile local case. After a major hearing, a local television station broadcasts a press conference of the defense lawyer. In the broadcast, the defense lawyer comments on camera that: "I believe that the attorney is the worst candidate for a seat on the trial court bench. She is not qualified to be a judge."

Did the lawyer make proper comments?

(A)   No, because the comments dishonored the judiciary.

(B)   No, because lawyers cannot make public remarks about judicial candidates.

(C)   Yes, because the lawyer was not campaigning to be a trial judge.

(D)   Yes, because the lawyer reasonably believed what he said about the attorney.

QUESTION 34

A plaintiff, an individual, retains an attorney to pursue a breach of contract action against a defendant, a business. The defendant's corporate counsel files a notice of appearance in the action. Upon the plaintiff's request, the attorney contacts a freelance reporter who agrees to attempt to obtain evidence from the defendant. The freelance reporter is to be compensated for questioning the defendant's contract administrator for a purported "news story." The attorney prepares the reporter to ask about the transaction subject to litigation with the plaintiff. The reporter obtains answers that include crucial evidence supporting the plaintiff's action.

Will the attorney be subject to discipline?

(A)   Yes, because the attorney should have interviewed the contract administrator.

(B)   Yes, because the attorney prepared the reporter to ask about the transaction.

(C)   No, because the attorney fulfilled the plaintiff's request.

(D)   No, because the answers contained evidence important to the action.

QUESTION 35

The government files a complaint against a defendant in a federal court. The government alleges that the defendant violated federal tax law. The defendant files an answer presenting several complex legal issues. At the close of the case, the judge finds that the parties have not sufficiently developed or explained those issues. The judge wants further legal advice in the matter from an expert in tax law that she knows. The expert lacks any interest in the case.

Will it be proper for the expert to consult the judge?

(A)   No, unless the parties have provided advance written consent to the expert's advising of the judge.

(B)   No, unless the judge discloses who the expert is, the subject matter of the expert's advice, and provides the parties with a reasonable opportunity to respond to this advice.

(C)   Yes, because the expert lacks any interest in the case.

(D)   Yes, if the judge considers the expert's advice necessary to further the interests of justice.

QUESTION 36

An attorney holds a law license and a real estate agent license in the jurisdiction where she lives. Instead of practicing law there, the attorney works as a real estate agent. Although the attorney could have held inactive status as a member of the bar, she maintains an active bar membership status in the jurisdiction. In relation to a real estate transaction in which the attorney represents a seller, she makes misrepresentations of fact to a buyer regarding a house that is being sold. The buyer prevails in a civil action against the attorney alleging misrepresentation. The attorney loses her appeal of the judgment awarding damages to Buyer.

Will the attorney be subject to discipline?

(A)   No, because the attorney was not convicted of committing a criminal offense.

(B)   No, because the attorney acted in the seller's best interest.

(C)   Yes, because the attorney engaged in a real estate career when her bar membership remained active.

(D)   Yes, because the attorney made a misrepresentation to the buyer.

QUESTION 37

A bar admissions applicant graduates from a public law school. The applicant requests and receives a packet from the state's professional authority to apply for membership to the state bar. One of the questions that the applicant must answer to complete the application form asks if the applicant has ever been convicted of a criminal offense. The question does not indicate if it applies to either juvenile or adult offenses. Without contacting the professional authority and inquiring whether the question applies to either or both types of offenses, the applicant assumes that it only applies to adult offenses. The applicant answers "no" to the question because the applicant was not convicted of any adult criminal offenses. However, the applicant was convicted of multiple juvenile offenses.

Did the applicant properly answer the question?

(A)   No, because the applicant did not attempt to contact the professional authority to inquire whether the question applied to either or both types of offenses.

(B)   No, because the applicant failed to disclose a fact necessary to correct a misapprehension.

(C)   Yes, because the applicant reasonably believed that the question only applied to adult offenses.

(D)   Yes, because the applicant knowingly made an accurate statement of material fact.

QUESTION 38

An attorney works for a state social services office for three years. While serving in that position, other employees of the office investigate an accused for suspected child abuse and neglect. The attorney does not participate in that investigation and it is not the subject of media reporting. After leaving the office's employ, the attorney joins a law firm that handles family law matters.

Subsequently, the accused is charged with child abuse and neglect pursuant to the office's investigation. The accused seeks to retain the attorney in responding to those charges. The attorney refuses to accept the accused as a client, but indicates that a partner lawyer, another member of the law firm, might accept him as a client. The partner lawyer reviews the case and accepts the accused as a client. The attorney neither aids the partner lawyer with defending the accused, nor is the attorney compensated in any way.

Will the partner lawyer be subject to discipline for accepting the representation?

(A)   No, because the attorney did not assist the partner lawyer with handling the accused's defense or receive any compensation.

(B)   No, because the attorney lacked involvement in or awareness of the investigation of the accused.

(C)   Yes, because the attorney worked for the office during its investigation of the accused.

(D)   Yes, unless the state social services office is immediately contacted and agrees to allow the partner lawyer to accept the accused as a client.

QUESTION 39

A married couple wants to adopt a child. An attorney agrees to assist the couple with adopting a child. During the first month of representation, the couple takes various steps to facilitate the adoption that are available without requiring the attorney's involvement. The couple assumes that the attorney was also taking the needed steps to prepare for accomplishing their objective. When the couple contacts the attorney for more assistance that is necessary to facilitate the adoption, they discover that he has not done any work for them in over a month. At that time, the attorney returns the couple's retainer and acknowledges that they could select another lawyer. The couple finds and meet with a new lawyer. The couple explains the original attorney's handling of the adoption matter to the new lawyer, but asks that she keep quiet about it because they understand that it resulted from some extenuating circumstances over which the original attorney lacked control. Realizing that the original attorney no longer represents the couple and that the couple needs assistance to complete the impending adoption, the new lawyer agrees to represent the couple. The lawyer does not report the original attorney's conduct to the professional authority.

Will the new lawyer be subject to discipline?

(A)   No, because the original attorney did not commit professional misconduct.

(B)   No, because the new lawyer does not have to report the original attorney's conduct.

(C)   Yes, because the original attorney committed professional misconduct.

(D)   Yes, because the couple asked the new lawyer not to reveal what they told her.

QUESTION 40

An attorney's practice involves handling civil cases on appeal. She enters into a written retainer agreement with a client. The agreement sets forth the attorney's hourly rate of $150. It also provides for the client's payment of a $1,000 appeal bond. The state appellate court rules require posting of the bond if the court grants leave to appeal. The attorney estimates that it will take her 10 hours to prepare and file a notice of appeal and all papers seeking leave to appeal.

Accordingly, the agreement provides for a total retainer amount of $2,500, which the client provides to the attorney. Upon receiving the client's payment, the attorney places the $2,500 in a client trust account that is separate from her general account. The attorney spends 10 hours preparing the notice of appeal and the pleadings seeking leave to appeal before timely filing them. The attorney informs the client that the court of appeals declined to grant leave to appeal. The client, experiencing financial hardship, requests that the attorney return the entire amount of the retainer payment. The attorney issues a $1,000 check to the client and keeps $1,500 in the client trust account pending a determination of how to dispose of the $1,500.

Will the attorney be subject to discipline?

(A)   No, because the attorney issued a check in the correct amount, although she could have moved the other funds from the client trust account into her general account.

(B)   No, because the attorney issued a check in the correct amount, and did not move the other funds.

(C)   Yes, because the attorney should have issued a check to the client for the entire retainer amount, and brought an action to recover legal fees.

(D)   Yes, because the attorney issued a check in the wrong amount, and should have kept the other funds in the client trust account.

QUESTION 41

A father is in a permanent comatose condition. His living will designates his daughter, a federal district court judge, as his first patient advocate. The living will alternatively designates his son as his second patient advocate. The daughter believes that she is qualified to serve as the father's patient advocate. Unlike the son, who is estranged from the father, the daughter has always had a close relationship with the father. She reasonably believes that serving as a patient advocate would not impair her performance of judicial duties. The daughter's main role would involve making decisions regarding the father's health care. Although the son or another family member could challenge the living will's validity, that is improbable. Otherwise, the daughter may not need to participate in legal actions concerning her service as a patient advocate. For purposes of this question, a person designated as a patient advocate by a living will occupies a fiduciary position as a type of personal representative of the patient.

Will it be proper for the daughter to serve as patient advocate?

(A)   No, because, as a federal judge, she is prohibited from serving in a fiduciary capacity.

(B)   No, because the father's family members could challenge the living will's validity.

(C)   Yes, because she has a closer relationship to the father than his son does.

(D)   Yes, because she believes that assisting the father in this way would not interfere with her performance of judicial duties.

QUESTION 42

A prosecutor primarily handles cases involving charges of drunk driving. In a high-profile case, a defendant declines the prosecutor's plea agreement proposals and demands a jury trial. The defendant is represented by an attorney, who is well known for successfully defending alleged drunk drivers. The prosecutor seeks to gain an advantage in the pending trial of the defendant's case. The prosecutor believes that if the local media presents some negative publicity about drunk driving, it might cause prospective jurors to be more likely to convict the defendant. The prosecutor contacts some local media outlets and asks them to further investigate and report about the circumstances of the defendant's offense, as well as the negative statistics about, and tragic consequences of, drunk driving. Some of these media outlets comply with her request and publicize such stories prior to jury selection in the prosecutor's case against the defendant. The stories provide negative publicity that biases and prejudices prospective jurors against the defendant, contrary to applicable criminal law.

Will the prosecutor be subject to discipline for making this request?

(A)   No, because the media outlets informed the public.

(B)   No, because the prosecutor did not directly contact any prospective jurors.

(C)   Yes, because the media outlets' publicity did not affect the prospective jurors.

(D)   Yes, because using the media for this purpose was unethical.

QUESTION 43

A prosecutor prepares and files an information charging a defendant with homicide. The defendant retains an attorney who obtains the defendant's release from custody on bail. Based on the defendant's evidence and representations, the attorney is convinced that the defendant is innocent and that another person is guilty of the charged offense. The defendant, however, doubts that the prosecutor, the trial court, or a jury, will believe the defense. The defendant asks the attorney for advice regarding avoiding further judicial proceedings. The defendant asks the attorney where to go to escape being apprehended for an offense that the defendant did not commit. The attorney declines to answer these questions and advises the defendant to participate voluntarily in all subsequent judicial proceedings and not attempt to escape being apprehended. After the defendant left this meeting with the attorney, the defendant left the country without informing anyone of his destination. When the defendant fails to appear as scheduled for trial, the attorney explains to the prosecutor what transpired in the last discussion with the defendant.

Will the attorney be subject to discipline?

(A)   No, because the attorney cannot be disciplined as a result of a defendant's conduct.

(B)   No, because the attorney advised against the defendant's avoidance of judicial
        proceedings and escape from being apprehended.

(C)   Yes, because the defendant failed to appear as scheduled.

(D)   Yes, because the defendant failed to heed the attorney's advice.

QUESTION 44

An entertainment lawyer represents a client, who is an actor. A movie company's attorney contacts the entertainment lawyer to negotiate a contract employing the client. The company wants to include the client in a movie. The entertainment lawyer and the attorney conduct negotiations and develop a contract that the client and the company approve and execute. While shooting the movie, the client notices that the company did not furnish the specific type of refreshments that he always consumes on the set. The company informs the client that the contract does not require the company to provide the refreshments. As a result, the client makes arrangements for someone to supply them at the client's own cost. The client brings this situation to the entertainment lawyer's attention.

The entertainment lawyer admits that he should have negotiated for, and obtained for the client, a contract provision requiring the company to provide the refreshments. The entertainment lawyer offers to pay the client the value of the refreshments that should have been furnished under the contract. Although the client could have obtained a greater amount of compensation by suing the entertainment lawyer for legal malpractice, he accepts the entertainment lawyer's offer. The entertainment lawyer prepares, and they both sign, an agreement reflecting this arrangement. The entertainment lawyer does not provide the client with either written advice to obtain advice from separate legal counsel before they made that agreement or an opportunity to obtain such advice. The client does not have such counsel when discussing and signing their agreement.

Did the entertainment lawyer engage in proper conduct?

(A)   No, because the entertainment lawyer should have provided the client with a legal opinion regarding the agreement.

(B)   No, because of the entertainment lawyer's conduct with respect to the client in formation of the agreement.

(C)   Yes, because the client voluntarily entered into the agreement with the entertainment lawyer.

(D)   Yes, because of the lawyer's representation of the client in formation of the contract with the company.

QUESTION 45

An attorney works for a state agency's legal department for four years. During that time, she handles consumer protection cases. While there, she is lead counsel in an investigation of a company's deceptive advertising practices. As a result of the investigation, the department files criminal fraud charges against the company. After leaving her position with the department, the attorney goes to work for a law firm. At the firm, she discovers that the company has retained a lawyer, a partner of the firm, to assist the company's counsel in defending the client from the criminal fraud charges resulting from her investigation. Promptly, the firm implements measures to screen the attorney from the partner lawyer's representation of the company, such that the department can ensure that the attorney will not breach her duty of confidentiality. The firm also provides written notice of the screening to the agency.

Will it be proper for the firm, and the partner lawyer, to remain involved in defending the company?

(A)   No, because the attorney worked for the department prior to working for the firm.

(B)   No, because of the attorney's substantial responsibility for the investigation and consequent charges against the company.

(C)   Yes, because the firm's measures will prevent the attorney from disclosing to the lawyer any confidential information that she obtained when working for the department.

(D)   Yes, because the attorney is obligated to seasonably reveal any exculpatory evidence to the lawyer.

QUESTION 46

As a sole practitioner who recently became a bar member, an attorney has only one client, Beta, a small business. Pursuant to their retainer contract, the attorney does transactional work for the client. The attorney relocates her office. Without the client's knowledge, the attorney develops an advertisement for dissemination. In addition to her name, the advertisement states:

"Announcing the opening of my new office at 111 Office Center, phone number (777) 777-7777. I practice these types of transactional law: contracts, property, partnerships, and corporations. Based on my representation of Beta, a small business, I can draft, review, and enforce documents regarding those legal subjects. Contact me for considerate and effective legal representation at reasonable rates."

Will the attorney be subject to discipline for the advertisement?

(A)   No, because the advertisement includes the attorney's name and is truthful.

(B)   No, because the advertisement identifies the type of law that the attorney practices.

(C)   Yes, because the advertisement states that the attorney represents the client.

(D)   No, because the advertisement includes the attorney's address.

QUESTION 47

Under state court rules, each party in a criminal case is only entitled to one continuance as a matter of right. A party must make all other requests for continuances by motion with notice to the other party, which may be granted in a trial judge's discretion. A state trial court judge provides notice to all parties in any criminal proceedings before him that he will only grant a second continuance if the moving party can prove that either the party or the party's counsel will be unavailable on the originally scheduled court date due to death or a life-threatening physical condition. In the judge's opinion, no other grounds are sufficient to merit granting a second continuance. The judge believes that to liberally grant a second continuance would cause unmerited delay and risk violating an accused's constitutional right to a speedy trial. In the state's appellate courts, parties may challenge the judge's decisions made pursuant to this policy.

Is the judge's personal policy on granting second continuances proper?

(A)   No, because it is not supported by a legal requirement.

(B)   No, because it is not fair to either party when the grounds for granting a second continuance is limited to death or a life-threatening physical condition.

(C)   Yes, because the judge implements it using discretion.

(D)   Yes, because a party whose motion is denied can challenge this decision on appeal.

QUESTION 48

An attorney agrees to provide legal consultation services to a client. In January, they entered into a written retainer agreement. The agreement provides that, pursuant to the client's written instructions, the attorney could make certain legally required payments on the client's behalf using client funds. In February, the client calls the attorney and explains that she is out of the country for an indefinite period. In March, the client writes the attorney a letter requesting that the attorney use funds enclosed in the letter to pay her estimated income taxes in April. The attorney deposits the funds into the client trust account. On April 15, the attorney uses the client's tax payment funds to pay for overdue office rent payments. The attorney does that because the penalties and interest rates were more than the comparable penalties and interest for overdue income taxes. On April 30, the attorney receives a substantial bequest to him from a decedent's estate. He deposits those funds into the general account. On the same day, the attorney issues checks from that account in sufficient amounts to pay the client's income taxes with interest and penalties. The attorney sends the client's income tax payment with interest and penalties to the government. The client does not object when the attorney subsequently informs her of all of the payments.

Will the attorney be subject to discipline?

(A)   No, because the attorney's payments using the client's funds did not adversely affect the client and the attorney thought that the client would not object to the payments.

(B)   No, because the client implicitly ratified the conduct by not objecting to it.

(C)   Yes, because the attorney's actions resulted in a penalty to the client.

(D)   Yes, because the attorney improperly utilized the client's funds for office rent payments.

QUESTION 49

A foreign retail corporation that sells headlights is represented by a litigation attorney in a tort lawsuit alleging interference with contractual relations against a domestic automobile manufacturer. The foreign retail corporation alleges that the domestic automobile manufacturer has been contacting the retailer's largest commercial clients, attempting to persuade them to stop doing business with the foreign retailer. The foreign retailer and domestic automobile manufacturer are both in the automotive industry. Another lawyer, a corporate lawyer, is handling the foreign retailer's application for a certificate of authority to transact business in the state where the domestic automobile manufacturer does business. State law provides for an administrative agency to process this application. The agency's determinations are subject to judicial review by state courts.

Another competitor, a domestic headlight retailer, is also in the automotive industry. The domestic headlight retailer contacts the foreign retailer's litigation attorney requesting representation to challenge the foreign retailer's application for a certificate of authority. The domestic competitor is aware that the foreign retailer is represented by the litigation attorney in the tort lawsuit.

Will representation of the domestic competitor by the litigation attorney be proper?

(A)   No, because the foreign retail corporation is presently being represented by the litigation attorney in the tort lawsuit.

(B)   No, if both the tort lawsuit and the application to transact business case could be decided by the same appellate court.

(C)   Yes, if neither the application to transact business nor the tort action involve the same factual and legal issues.

(D)   Yes, because the application to transact business is an administrative matter, whereas the tort action is a civil action.

QUESTION 50

An attorney runs a television advertisement on the local affiliate of a nationwide television network. He appears in the commercial and says to the viewers:

"Has someone you care about, or have you, been involved in a situation resulting in harm, such as an accident? Call me for a no cost, no obligation consultation about your legal rights and remedies. My toll free number is (800)-888-8888. Let me work to protect your interests."

Will the attorney be subject to discipline for this advertisement?

(A)   No, if the attorney's entire statement in the television advertisement is truthful and not misleading.

(B)   Yes, because the television advertisement may be broadcast into other jurisdictions where the attorney does not belong to the bar.

(C)   Yes, because the attorney does not describe his credentials or similar specifics.

(D)   Yes, because the television advertisement is intended to promote more lawsuits.

QUESTION 51

An attorney would like to facilitate her client's payment of her bills for legal fees. For this purpose, the attorney drafts a client agreement whereby the attorney receives the right to publish a book about the client's case upon accepting representation of the client.

Will it be proper for the attorney to use the agreement?

(A)   No, because the agreement grants the right upon accepting representation.

(B)   No, because the agreement may not grant any right upon accepting representation.

(C)   Yes, because the attorney already has the literary right as a matter of law.

(D)   Yes, because the attorney has absolute discretion in contracting with clients.

QUESTION 52

An attorney enters into a written agreement to represent a client in pending litigation. Under the agreement's terms, the client retains the attorney pursuant to an initial retainer payment of $7,000, which is to be applied to the attorney's legal fees and costs. The attorney agrees to provide the client with any unearned remainder of the funds. The agreement requires the attorney to issue regular invoices for services rendered and deduct the amount earned from the client's initial payment. The agreement does not specify if the payment is to be placed in a client trust account or a general account. The agreement did not address when the attorney would deduct the amount earned. The attorney places the funds in a client trust account. The attorney subsequently provides the client with regular invoices stating the balance of the client's initial payment and accurately describing work that the attorney did for the client. The attorney does not deduct any of the client's payment from the client trust account until more than 18 months from when the attorney deposited it. By that time, the attorney concludes representation of the client. The attorney transfers $6,000 (the amount of the attorney's fees in representing the client) to the attorney's general account, and mails the client a check for the remaining balance of $1,000.

Did the attorney engage in proper conduct?

(A)   No, because the attorney's failure to withdraw funds as earnings accrued caused an improper commingling of funds.

(B)   No, because the attorney received the client's payment of funds for the legal fees and costs in advance.

(C)   Yes, because the attorney placed the client's funds in the client trust account.

(D)   Yes, because the attorney regularly issued invoices to the client.

QUESTION 53

An attorney mainly practices in the field of contracts law. A person selling a piece of real property hires the attorney to prepare a real estate contract for the property. The attorney and her secretary serve as attesting witnesses for the execution of the property's deed. The buyer acquires the property for use by a partnership. The seller becomes mentally incompetent two years after the execution of the deed. A conservator is appointed to handle the seller's legal and financial affairs. The secretary who witnessed the deed's execution dies.

The buyer retains a litigation lawyer, who files a lawsuit against the conservator as the legal representative of the seller's estate, alleging that the deed conveyed defective title. The complaint alleges that a defect exists in the chain of title, which is the only contested issue. The conservator asks the attorney who prepared the real estate contract to defend the estate against the lawsuit. The attorney is the sole attesting witness to the deed's execution. The litigation lawyer will call the attorney to testify at the trial of the lawsuit only to prove the deed's execution.

Will it be proper for the attorney to represent the estate against the lawsuit?

(A)   No, because it is not necessary for the attorney to represent the estate in order to prevent substantial hardship to the estate.

(B)   No, because the attorney will be called as a witness in the lawsuit about execution of the deed.

(C)   Yes, because no contested issue exists regarding the deed's execution.

(D)   Yes, because the attorney lacks any beneficial interest pursuant to the deed.

QUESTION 54

An attorney is a sole practitioner. She represents a client in a case involving a few different types of law. When working on the case, the attorney discovers a complicated legal bankruptcy matter about which she lacks legal competence. Although she exercises due diligence in gaining some competence regarding the matter, the attorney reasonably believes that associating with a bankruptcy lawyer is necessary to ensure that she properly handles the matter. The attorney contacts and explains this situation to the client. She also explains that she wants to associate with another lawyer on this matter only. The client assents to the attorney' association with a bankruptcy lawyer she knows, who has competence concerning the matter.

Will it be proper for the attorney to associate with the bankruptcy lawyer?

(A)   Yes, because no regulations apply to the association.

(B)   Yes, because the client consented to the association after the attorney explained it to the client.

(C)   No, because the attorney personally knows the bankruptcy lawyer.

(D)   No, because the attorney cannot associate with the bankruptcy lawyer under these circumstances.

QUESTION 55

Three attorneys are members of the same bar. They all work in the same office building that has an outside sign stating "Law Offices." Each of them rent separate and adjacent office suites. They represent their own clients and do not share fees earned from this representation.

Sometimes, they each refer prospective clients to one another without receiving any compensation for doing so. However, they equally pay for the costs of a secretary, paralegal, and answering service. They meet and decide to change the outside sign to read "Three Attorneys, Law Partners." That sign replaces the former one. The three attorneys have never entered into any type of formal partnership agreement or arrangement.

Are the three attorneys subject to discipline?

(A)   No, because they equally share the costs of a secretary, paralegal, and answering service.

(B)   No, because sometimes they refer prospective clients to each other.

(C)   Yes, because the three attorneys have not entered into any type of partnership agreement or arrangement.

(D)   Yes, because members of the bar can never refer to themselves as law partners.

QUESTION 56

A judge has a good reputation in the community surrounding the state court in which she serves. Her supporters respect her record as a jurist and trust her opinion on legal matters. The judge is friends with a couple who have a daughter. The daughter attends law school and wants to get a position clerking for a law firm when school is not in session. The daughter asks the judge for a letter of recommendation because she knows the judge and thinks that the letter could increase her prospects of working for a law firm. Wanting to help the daughter, the judge provides her with a general letter of recommendation addressed "to whom it may concern." Because the daughter has not worked for the judge, the letter simply refers to the daughter's character. The letter, which appears on court stationary, contains only truthful statements.

Will the judge will be subject to discipline?

(A)   Yes, because she wrote the letter on court stationary.

(B)   Yes, because she knows the daughter and is friends with her parents.

(C)   No, because she knows the daughter.

(D)   No, because the letter will afford the judge an improper advantage.

QUESTION 57

An attorney is a sole practitioner. Her general practice includes matters involving contract law, criminal law, domestic relations, property law, and torts. She does not handle legal matters involving wills, trusts, corporations, or partnerships. Late one Friday night, she receives a phone call while at her home. Her aunt informs her that her step-uncle suffered a near-fatal injury and was not expected to live much longer. Further, the aunt reveals that the step-uncle has no last will and testament. The aunt implores the attorney to meet with them as soon as possible in order to make a will for the step-uncle before he dies. The attorney replies that her law practice does not involve preparing wills, and she lacks the knowledge and skill to properly draft a will for the step-uncle. The aunt, however, insists that it is imperative that the attorney do this under the circumstances and would not accept "no" for an answer.

The attorney goes to the hospital and meets with the aunt and the step-uncle. The treating physician says that the step-uncle only has two days to live. The attorney takes detailed notes of the step-uncle's intentions about his property's disposition. The attorney tells the aunt and the step-uncle that on Saturday morning she will try to find a lawyer who specialized in wills who is available then to properly draft one. However, none of the lawyers in the phone book whose listing mentioned wills are in the office when she contacts them. Therefore, the attorney promptly drafts the step-uncle's will based on her notes and using a standard form. She delivers it to the step-uncle and has it duly executed.

Did the attorney engage in proper conduct?

(A)   No, because the attorney lacked experience in or special training about wills.

(B)   No, because the attorney lacked the legal competence to prepare the step-uncle's will.

(C)   Yes, because in this emergency situation, it was impractical for the attorney to either refer the matter to, or associate with, another lawyer.

(D)   Yes, because of the attorney's familial relationship with the aunt and the step-uncle.

QUESTION 58

A judge and her husband live in the same household. The judge is one of five trustees of a charitable trust for the local community's benefit. The husband serves as the trust's accountant. A corporation files a lawsuit against a company alleging tortious interference with a business relationship. The judge is scheduled to preside over the trial of the corporation's case against the company. Subsequently, the husband provides the trustees with a current accounting of the trust's assets. The total value of $1,000,000 includes 1 share of the company's stock, which has a current market value per share of $1. Although the judge then notices the trust's ownership of the company stock, she believes that it will not affect her handling of the corporation's case. The judge does not disqualify herself from presiding in the case.

Will the judge be subject to discipline?

(A)   No, because the judge does not personally own shares of the company's stock.

(B)   No, because the trust only possesses a *de minimis* economic interest in the company.

(C)   Yes, because the judge cannot handle the case in a fair manner.

(D)   Yes, because the results of the case will not impact the company's stock cost.

QUESTION 59

A landowner retains an attorney for the purpose of bringing a tort action against a neighbor. The attorney files the action alleging trespass and seeking injunctive relief to prevent future trespass by the neighbor upon the landowner's premises. A lawyer agrees to represent the neighbor. At the pre-trial conference in this action, the lawyer makes an offer of compromise. Acceptance of the offer would have two results. First, the neighbor would agree to stay off of the landowner's property and to pay liquidated damages to the landowner for any future instance of going on that property. Second, the attorney would be precluded from representing the landowner in any other type of legal matter involving the parties to the action. The attorney explains to the landowner that the effect of accepting the offer of compromise would be prevailing in the action without going to trial. The attorney further explains that she could not represent the landowner again in any other legal matter involving the neighbor. However, other lawyers could competently represent the landowner in such other legal matters. Moreover, the attorney considers the neighbor's offer of compromise to be in the landowner's best interest, or the best way to accomplish the goals in this case.

Would it be proper for the attorney to recommend accepting the offer of compromise?

(A)   No, because the offer would improperly prevent the attorney from representing the landowner in any other legal matter involving the neighbor.

(B)   Yes, because other lawyers could provide the landowner with competent representation in any other legal matter involving the neighbor.

(C)   Yes, because the attorney is only prevented from representing the landowner in any other legal matter involving the neighbor.

(D)   Yes, because the attorney thinks that this is the best method for the landowner to achieve her objectives in this action, or is in her best interest.

QUESTION 60

Upon becoming members of the bar, two attorney who are friends, maintain separate law practices. In order to diversify and supplement their income, the two attorneys purchase an office building as co-tenants with two other non-lawyers. The non-lawyer co-tenants manage the building. No partnership exists between the attorneys and the two non-lawyers. The two attorneys maintain separate law offices in the building for five years until the one is elected as a trial court judge. The judge retains his co-tenancy in the building during his subsequent four-years on the bench.

Three other candidates are campaigning to unseat the judge at the end of his term of office. The judge tells the attorney co-tenant that he plans to appoint a new law clerk upon his reelection. The attorney co-tenant decides to financially support the judge as an incumbent judge seeking reelection. The attorney co-tenant contributes money to the judge's campaign in order to influence the judge to consider or appoint him as the new law clerk. After winning the election, the judge appoints the attorney co-tenant as his new law clerk.

Will the attorney co-tenant be subject to discipline for accepting the appointment by the lawyer?

(A)   No, because the attorney may accept the appointment under any circumstances.

(B)   No, because the attorney and judge have an established professional and financial relationship.

(C)   Yes, because they have an established professional and financial relationship.

(D)   Yes, because the attorney made the contribution for an improper purpose.

QUESTION 61

A state prosecutor files charges against a defendant alleging that she committed armed robbery. At the defendant's first court appearance in this case, the judge appoints an attorney as her defense counsel. The judge denies the attorney's request for bail.

After the first appearance, the prosecutor presents some plea agreement proposals to the attorney. Outside of the prosecutor's presence, the attorney discusses those proposals with the defendant. The defendant rejects them. The defendant insists upon pleading not guilty and demands a trial.

The attorney then communicates the results of this discussion with the prosecutor adjacent to the defendant's holding cell. The attorney briefly steps away, leaving the prosecutor outside the defendant's cell. The defendant then asks the prosecutor if he would consider dropping the charges if the defendant turns state's evidence against someone else. Before walking away, the prosecutor tells the defendant that he cannot talk to him because the attorney represents him.

Will the prosecutor be subject to discipline?

(A)   Yes, because the prosecutor communicated with the defendant.

(B)   Yes, because the prosecutor presented the plea agreement proposals to the attorney, rather than the defendant.

(C)   No, because the prosecutor declined to talk with the defendant.

(D)   No, because the prosecutor has immunity.

QUESTION 62

A large insurance company serves its insureds in one state. The company's insurance policies protect the insureds' property. Recently, major storms and natural disasters have adversely affected the property of the state's population. In turn, the number and amount of property insurance claims have reached a historically high level. Consequently, a committee of the state legislature is conducting hearings regarding the sufficiency and improvement of property insurance.

The company employs an attorney to perform most of its regulatory compliance work. The attorney has worked in this capacity for the company for several years. The attorney handles at least half of all of the company's legal matters. The remainder is divided between in-house corporate counsel and a law firm that handles litigation.

Pursuant to the company's direction, the attorney testifies in the property insurance hearings of the state legislature's committee. The attorney's testimony reflected the position that the company wanted to convey regarding property insurance. The appearance form that the attorney filed, however, did not refer to the company. Thus, the committee was not aware of the attorney's relationship with the company. The company paid the attorney for time and expenses of providing that testimony.

Did the attorney engage in proper conduct?

(A)   No, because the attorney did not reveal that he appeared as the company's retained counsel.

(B)   No, because the company paid the attorney for testifying before the committee.

(C)   Yes, because the attorney could not reveal his relationship with the company on account of the duty of client-lawyer confidentiality.

(D)   Yes, because the attorney could not reveal his relationship with the company on account of the attorney-client evidentiary privilege.

QUESTION 63

An attorney, an associate in a law firm, practices business law. While at home one Saturday morning, a friend calls the attorney. The friend explains that the police had just taken her only child, a young boy, into protective custody based on allegations of neglect and abuse. The friend swears that the boy only suffered injuries from another child and that the boy received appropriate medical treatment. The friend asks the attorney to help regain custody of the boy immediately. The attorney replies "I have never practiced domestic relations law, but I will try to help." Finding no lawyer who specialized in protective child custody available on Saturday, the attorney goes to the police station. The attorney's efforts on the friend's behalf do not secure the boy's release.

Was it proper for the attorney to assist the friend?

(A)   No, because the attorney assisted the friend because of a prior relationship.

(B)   No, because the attorney lacked the requisite legal competence to handle the friend's matter.

(C)   Yes, because the attorney attempted to obtain the boy's release from the police station.

(D)   Yes, because the attorney tried to represent the friend in a way that was reasonably necessary under the circumstances.

QUESTION 64

In January, a plaintiff retains a litigation attorney in order to bring a defamation lawsuit against a defendant, whom a defense lawyer represents. In April, a judge appoints the litigation attorney as defense counsel for an accused in a felony criminal case. A prosecutor advises the litigation attorney that the prosecutor will be ready for trial in July. The plaintiff notifies the litigation attorney that she could participate in her civil trial throughout the summer. At a civil pretrial conference, the litigation attorney, the defense lawyer, and the judge schedule the plaintiff's trial for August. The plaintiff does not attend the conference. The litigation attorney does not ask for the plaintiff's approval of the trial date after the conference. However, the litigation attorney seasonably notifies the plaintiff of the trial date, and accurately advises that it would not adversely impact her interests. At a criminal pretrial conference, the litigation attorney, the prosecutor, and the judge set the accused's trial for July. No local criminal court rule regarding speedy trials applies.

Did the litigation attorney act properly by setting a civil trial date without the plaintiff's approval?

(A)   No, because the attorney is allowed to control the scheduling of trials in order to expedite litigation.

(B)   Yes, because no local criminal court rule regarding speedy trials applied.

(C)   Yes, because the date set for the civil trial does not prejudice the plaintiff's interests.

(D)   Yes, because criminal trial scheduling usually has priority over civil trial scheduling.

QUESTION 65

An inventor retains an attorney to assist with licensing a patented invention. The inventor accurately describes the invention, an electric vehicle battery, to the attorney as capable of powering an electric vehicle further and faster -- but not longer before recharge -- than other comparable batteries. On the inventor's behalf, the attorney contacts another lawyer, who represents a manufacturer, about licensing and producing the invention. The attorney describes the invention as capable of powering an electric vehicle the "furthest, fastest, and longest before recharge of any battery ever produced."

Will the attorney be subject to discipline?

(A)   No, because the attorney made a statement to the other lawyer rather than the manufacturer.

(B)   No, because the attorney's description of the invention constituted "puffing" for sales purposes, rather than a false statement.

(C)   Yes, because the attorney made a misrepresentation of material fact to the other lawyer.

(D)   Yes, because the attorney overstated the invention's capabilities.

QUESTION 66

A defendant, a foreign citizen, lives and works in the United States. The defendant becomes socially involved with several unsavory characters. In the defendant's dealings with them, a personal disagreement becomes heated, and one of them runs at the defendant with clenched fists raised. At the last possible moment, the defendant steps aside to avoid the attacker. The attacker rushes by the defendant and crashes through a 10-story window, plummeting to his death. The other witnesses to this incident are the attacker's friends. In order to avenge his death, they all agree to the same story that the defendant intentionally threw the attacker out the window.

The witnesses tell their story to the police. The police arrest the defendant. The defendant makes a written statement describing the events. A prosecutor files murder charges against the defendant. The court appoints an attorney as defense counsel for the defendant. The court releases the defendant into the attorney's custody subject to the requirement that the defendant not leave the metropolitan area. The attorney believes the defendant's version of events, but cannot prove them without any corroborating witness testimony. The attorney believes that the only way that the defendant will receive justice is if the case does not go to trial. The attorney tells the defendant that if he returns to his home country, he cannot be tried for the offense because the United States does not have an extradition treaty with that country. The defendant returns to his country.

Will the attorney be subject to discipline?

(A)   No, because the defendant gave a written statement indicating his innocence.

(B)   No, because the attorney believed the defendant's version of events.

(C)   Yes, because the attorney's counsel caused the defendant to flee the court's jurisdiction and United State's extradition power in order to avoid prosecution.

(D)   Yes, because the defendant violated the conditions of his release.

QUESTION 67

A plaintiff corporation brings an antitrust action against a defendant corporation in federal court. The court assigns the case to a judge. The case raises several issues of first impression arising under recently enacted federal antitrust law. After the parties complete discovery, the judge disposes of several pretrial motions and conducts a pre-trial conference. Once the judge is ready for trial based on her familiarity with the law and facts, she discovers that her husband, a stockbroker, owns a significant quantity of the defendant corporation's stock.

The judge concludes that this case's outcome could substantially affect her husband's financial interest in the defendant corporation. While the judge thinks that she would fairly adjudicate the case, she discloses the husband's interest to the parties and their counsel. After she asks them to waive disqualification, they agree to do so with her participation.

Will it be proper for the judge to preside over the case?

(A)   No, because the parties cannot waive the judge's disqualification that is mandatory due to the husband's economic interest.

(B)   No, because the parties have not effectively waived the judge's disqualification under the circumstances.

(C)   Yes, because the judge is especially prepared to be this case's presiding judge.

(D)   Yes, because the judge believes that she can be impartial despite the husband's ownership of the large corporation stock.

QUESTION 68

An attorney runs a commercial for his law practice on several local radio stations. The broadcast range of the stations is limited to the jurisdiction in which he is licensed to practice law. The entire commercial consists of the attorney's own recorded voice saying:

"If you need effective legal representation, please call me. The toll-free number for a no obligation initial consultation is 888-888-8888."

The attorney maintains a file containing the commercial's script, his recording of it, and all information from the radio stations regarding when the commercial will be run and its cost.

Is the attorney's commercial proper?

(A)   Yes, because the commercial complies with all applicable requirements.

(B)   No, because he did not pay a professional to record the commercial.

(C)   No, because the commercial does not indicate whether a fee applies to the initial consultation.

(D)   No, because the attorney did not identify himself or his office location in the commercial.

QUESTION 69

A plaintiff retains an attorney. The attorney represents the plaintiff in civil litigation against a defendant. The plaintiff prevails and receives an award of damages pursuant to the judgment. The plaintiff's retainer fee fully compensates the attorney. No balance remains for repayment to the plaintiff. The defendant sends the attorney a check for $75,000, the entire amount of damages awarded. The attorney endorses the check, which was payable to the attorney, to the plaintiff and mails it to the plaintiff. The plaintiff deposits the check without objection.

Will the attorney be subject to discipline?

(A)   No, because the plaintiff received the proper amount of damages.

(B)   No, because the plaintiff did not object to the check.

(C)   Yes, because the attorney improperly processed the check.

(D)   Yes, because the attorney failed to pay the plaintiff in cash.

QUESTION 70

An attorney opens a law office after becoming a member of the bar. The attorney registers with a trial court to be appointed as defense counsel. A prosecutor charges a defendant with unrelated felony and misdemeanor offenses. A judge of the trial court appoints the attorney to represent the defendant. The defendant demands a trial by jury on all charges. The attorney obtains all relevant information from the defendant and performs research for trial purposes. After spending several days working on the case, the attorney realizes that her legal skill and understanding are insufficient to provide effective counsel to the defendant. The attorney tells the defendant what she realized. The attorney gets the defendant's informed consent to her continued sole representation.

Will the attorney's representation of the defendant be proper?

(A)   Yes, because the trial judge appointed her as sole counsel.

(B)   Yes, because the defendant knowingly and voluntarily accepted her continued
        representation.

(C)   No, because the attorney lacks appropriate legal skill and understanding.

(D)   No, because the attorney is not a certified specialist in criminal defense.

QUESTION 71

An attorney represents a plaintiff in a breach of contract action against a defendant. The attorney secures a judgment in favor of the plaintiff. The defendant mails a check to the attorney for $15,000, the amount of damages set forth in the judgment. The attorney places the check in the attorney's client trust account. The plaintiff has previously fully paid the attorney's fees and costs of representation in the contract action.

Upon learning of the plaintiff's judgment, a creditor contacts the attorney regarding the plaintiff's past due debt. The creditor asserts that the plaintiff owes $2,400 for missing six vehicle loan payments. The creditor claims that it is entitled to a payment of that sum out of the amount of damages that the plaintiff recovered. The creditor warns the attorney that it has a lien on the damages and that it would assert its legal rights, including repossession of the vehicle, if the demanded payment of $2,400 is not made immediately. The attorney promptly communicates this information to the plaintiff, who replies:

"It does not matter what the creditor says. That vehicle is my second car, so I do not really need it. The creditor can do what it wants to. They can have that worthless piece of junk back. I have bad credit already, so whatever happens cannot make my credit any worse. Just mail me a check for $15,000."

Applicable law provides that the creditor has a lawful claim, which the attorney has a legal duty to protect, and that the claim is not frivolous.

Will the attorney be subject to discipline for doing what the plaintiff requested?

(A)   No, because the plaintiff was entitled to the damages recovered.

(B)   No, because the creditor was not entitled to the damages recovered.

(C)   Yes, because the client and the creditor both claim interests in the damages recovered.

(D)   Yes, because the attorney informed the plaintiff that the creditor would enforce its legal rights against the plaintiff.

QUESTION 72

A developer pre-sells 100 homes in a subdivision before constructing them. The standard form purchase contract states that each home will be identical to a model home's design. However, 75 of the homes are built using a different design having one less bathroom. An attorney files a breach of contract action against the developer on behalf of the 75 homeowners. The developer makes an offer of compromise providing an aggregate settlement of all of the homeowners' claims in the amount of $750,000. Based on research and consultation, the attorney determines the approximate value of each of the homeowners' claims, which constitutes their respective settlement amount. This amount is based on the estimated market value of the missing bathroom, subject to adjustment based on when the home was built.

The attorney considers this to be a reasonable and equitable method for dividing the damages among all of the homeowners. The developer makes its offer contingent upon acceptance by each and every one of the homeowners of each homeowner's settlement amount. The attorney advises each of the homeowners of the offer's total amount and the homeowner's individual settlement amount. All of the homeowners are willing to accept the offer based on the settlement amount. But the attorney has not revealed to any of the homeowners the respective value of every other one of the homeowners' settlement amount. The attorney is concerned that doing this could possibly undermine the prospects of the offer's universal acceptance if some of the homeowners believe that their settlement amount is not fair in comparison to the settlement amount of any of the other homeowners.

Will the attorney be subject to discipline if the offer is accepted without further disclosure?

(A)   No, because revealing all settlement amounts could undermine the prospects of the offer's universal acceptance.

(B)   No, because each of the homeowners will receive a fair settlement amount and they each will accept it.

(C)   Yes, because the attorney is assisting the developer in making an aggregate settlement of all of the homeowners' claims.

(D)   Yes, because none of the homeowner need to know the settlement amount that any of the other homeowners will receive.

QUESTION 73

An attorney represents a plaintiff in a tort action against a defendant company. The company sells widgets. The plaintiff's complaint makes a defective product claim seeking recovery of damages. The complaint alleges that plaintiff sustained personal injuries while using the widget as the company intended. Specifically, the complaint asserts that the company's defective design of the widget caused the plaintiff's injuries. During pre-trial discovery, the attorney makes a proper request for documents from the company about the product's design. In reviewing the documents requested, the company's in-house lawyer finds a widget designer's handwritten note stating that, due to the widget's design, the widget could cause the type of injury that plaintiff sustained. The in-house lawyer does not provide the note or refer to it in response to the request for documents or otherwise.

Will the in-house lawyer be subject to discipline?

(A)   No, because the note is confidential.

(B)   No, because the note is work product.

(C)   Yes, because he has a constitutional duty to disclose the note.

(D)   Yes, because he prevented the plaintiff from obtaining the note.

QUESTION 74

An attorney works as corporate counsel for a health maintenance organization. The attorney reviews applications for payment of medical care by the organization. The attorney provides legal advice regarding how to handle the applications. A patient applies for medical care. The attorney reviews the patient's application before leaving the organization to work in a law firm.

Pursuant to the attorney's advice, the organization denies the patient's application. A few months later, the patient goes to the attorney's office. The patient requests that the attorney accept him as a client in his proposed lawsuit against the organization to recover payment for his medical care.

Will it be proper for the attorney to accept the patient as a client?

(A)   Yes, because of the attorney's knowledge and experience.

(B)   Yes, because the attorney does not represent the organization.

(C)   No, because the attorney represented the organization.

(D)   No, because the attorney has not worked at the law firm long enough.

QUESTION 75

A watercraft insurance company employs an attorney in its legal department. The attorney examines claims made by the company's insureds for maritime losses. The attorney gives legal counsel to the company about whether to pay the claims. An insured individual makes a claim for loss of her yacht, which a hurricane destroyed. After the attorney examines the individual's claim, the company fully pays for her loss. Instead of replacing the yacht, the individual buys a kayak, which insurance does not cover.

The attorney leaves the company and opens his own law office as a general practitioner. Some years later, the company's promotional motorboat collides with the individual's kayak, causing her personal injuries. The individual goes to the attorney's office seeking representation in her potential tort lawsuit against the company.

Will it be proper for the attorney to represent her?

(A)   Yes, because of the subject matter of the representation.

(B)   Yes, because the attorney does not represent the company.

(C)   No, because the attorney represented the company.

(D)   No, because the attorney examined the individual's claim.

QUESTION 76

An attorney represents a plaintiff in a civil dispute against a defendant. To formalize the arrangement for representation, the attorney provides a standard retainer contract and a waiver form, which he typically uses with most clients. The contract includes the following terms:

The client will provide an initial retainer fee of $ _____. After this amount has been applied to legal fees earned in representing the client, the client will timely pay all of the attorney's other bills for legal fees. The attorney's hourly rate is $150.00. By signing this contract and a waiver form, the client waives any and all legal malpractice claims that the client has or acquires as a result of the attorney's representation.

A waiver form is attached to the contract. The attorney advises the client that she should have another lawyer review the retainer contract and waiver form before she signs them. The client, however, decides not to obtain the advice of another lawyer. Although the client has no other lawyer represent her when entering into the agreement, she duly signs the retainer contract and waiver. The attorney charges a reasonable hourly rate and is qualified to represent the client.

Are the lawyer's retainer contract and waiver form proper?

(A)   No, because they seek to prospectively limit the attorney's exposure to legal malpractice liability.

(B)   No, because the attorney uses the same forms with most clients.

(C)   Yes, because the attorney provided consideration by agreeing to represent the client.

(D)   Yes, because the attorney's hourly rate is reasonable and he is qualified to represent the client.

QUESTION 77

An attorney and a licensed securities dealer, execute a contract. The contract provides that the attorney will only refer to the dealer any of her clients who want to trade stocks or obtain related investment services. The contract also provides that the dealer will refer any of his customers that need legal representation only to the attorney in exchange for a small payment. The attorney mainly practices securities law. The attorney does not tell her clients about the contract. The attorney and the dealer charge their clients reasonable fees for their respective professional services. With the exception of the small payment for a referral made to the dealer, neither of them share in each others' fees paid by their clients and customers.

Will the attorney be subject to discipline based on this contract?

(A)   No, because the dealer does not share in the attorney's fees and the attorney does not share in the dealer's fees.

(B)   No, because neither the dealer nor the attorney charge unreasonable fees for their respective professional services.

(C)   Yes, because the attorney is paying the dealer for referrals.

(D)   Yes, because under this contract the attorney is essentially practicing law with the dealer, a non-lawyer.

QUESTION 78

A husband and wife are experiencing serious marital difficulties. The wife retains an attorney, who files a divorce action on behalf of the wife. Another lawyer agrees to represent the husband in the action. The extent of the parties' irreconcilable differences has caused them to become very adversarial. Moreover, the wife engaged in an extramarital affair. Feeling particularly vindictive, the husband tells his lawyer that he wants him to take an aggressive approach to litigation. The husband says: "My wife does not deserve any favors or concessions from us. We need to win this case even if it's on procedural grounds."

The husband's lawyer serves the wife's attorney with a notice of taking the wife's deposition. The wife's attorney writes the husband's lawyer with a request that he reschedule the deposition because it is set for the same date as the wife's surgery for a life-threatening condition. The husband objects to rescheduling the deposition.

Will the husband's lawyer be subject to discipline if he agrees to reschedule the deposition?

(A)   No, because the husband's rights would not be prejudiced by rescheduling the deposition.

(B)   No, because the husband has the right to determine the means and objectives of legal representation.

(C)   Yes, because the lawyer would not be following the husband's directive.

(D)   Yes, because the lawyer lacked the husband's approval to reschedule the deposition.

QUESTION 79

A client retains an attorney to represent her in estate planning matters. The client and the attorney enter into a valid retainer agreement, pursuant to which she issues a check to the attorney in the requested amount of $2,000. The attorney deposits the check in a trust account for the client. The agreement requires the client to issue another $2,000 check to the attorney upon receipt of notice from the attorney that the account balance is $100 or less. The bank that holds the account imposes a monthly service charge on all accounts for which the balance falls below $100. After the attorney completes half of the estate planning work for the client, he properly draws his earned fee against the client's trust account. At that point, its balance falls to zero and the attorney mails the client notice of that fact. However, the client does not receive that notice because it arrives the day that the police declare her a missing person. The attorney learns of the declaration in the local news. Then the bank provides the attorney with notice that it will impose a $10 service charge on the client's trust account because it has a zero balance. The attorney withdraws $10 from his general account and deposits $10 into the client's trust account.

Will the attorney be subject to discipline for commingling funds?

(A)   Yes, because the attorney made an improper deposit.

(B)   Yes, because the attorney mixed his funds with the client's funds.

(C)   No, because the attorney made a proper deposit.

(D)   No, because of the client's legal status.

QUESTION 80

An attorney is a sole practitioner in a small town. The nature of his law practice and scope of experience requires a support staff of one secretary and three paralegals. The staff all report to the attorney as their supervisor, who delegates secretarial, clerical, and paralegal work to them. For purposes of performing their work, the staff may access the files of the attorney's clients. The attorney compensates his staff with both hourly wages and a profit sharing arrangement. The profit sharing occurs every six months. The staff shares in five percent of the attorney's legal fees.

Is it proper for the attorney to pay the staff in this manner?

(A)   No, because an attorney may not share legal fees with non-lawyers.

(B)   No, because the attorney is assisting the staff as non-lawyers in practicing law.

(C)   No, because the staff have access to his clients' files.

(D)   Yes, because the staff lacks control over the attorney's professional judgment.

QUESTION 81

A girl goes to the police and reports that her dance instructor inappropriately touched her during a private dance lesson at his dance studio. The police investigate the matter and find no other evidence that corroborates the girl's accusation. The police cannot question the instructor in person because he is out of the country. The police present this information to a prosecutor, a lawyer, who is assigned to the case's investigation and prosecution. Seeking publicity to support his reelection campaign, the prosecutor holds a press conference. At the conference, the prosecutor describes the girl's accusation in detail, which the media broadcasts in full. The prosecutor promises to hold the instructor accountable. The media conduct a survey that produces results showing that a vast majority of people believe that the instructor is guilty of a crime. Upon the instructor's return to the country, he retains a defense attorney. With the instructor's permission, the defense attorney calls and holds a press conference. The defense attorney truthfully states that the instructor has never met or taught the girl, who later admits that she falsely accused the instructor.

Will the defense attorney be subject to discipline for holding the press conference?

(A)   Yes, because he called and participated in the press conference.

(B)   Yes, because he made a statement about what his client, the instructor, told him.

(C)   No, because he made a statement in order to protect the instructor.

(D)   No, because the instructor gave him permission to have the press conference.

QUESTION 82

An attorney works for a state's law enforcement department after becoming a member of the bar. While serving in that position, the attorney directly participates in several prosecutions against parties who perpetrated criminal offenses against the public interest. These offenses did not affect the attorney's personal economic interests. Following the attorney's election to the state's court of appeals, the attorney resigns his position with the department. Some of the prosecutions with which he was involved are pending as cases on the state court of appeals' docket. Upon becoming a judge on the court, the court clerk assigns one of those cases to him. The judge believes that he can make an impartial decision about the case, but does not disclose his role in the case.

Would it be proper for the judge to decide the case?

(A)   No, because the judge failed to disclose his role in the case.

(B)		No, because the judge worked for the department when the case was prosecuted.

(C)		No, because the judge directly participated in the department's prosecution of the case.

(D)		Yes, because the judge lacks any personal economic interest the criminal case.

QUESTION 83

A judge serves on the bench in a federal district court. For several years, the judge has been an uncompensated member of the state bar's board of a philanthropy. Every year the board of philanthropy hosts a fundraising dinner at which a person who is considered worthy of recognition for serving their community is honored. At this year's dinner, the state bar plans to recognize the judge for 20 years of public service.

The state bar's "public testimonial committee" has announced that it will accept special contributions from both lawyers and non-lawyers. The committee will apply these contributions towards paying for a sculpture bust of the judge, which the committee will give to the judge. The committee decides to take these steps after determining that they were lawful and ethical for the state bar, the committee, the philanthropy, contributing lawyers and non-lawyers, and the judge. The committee takes those steps and gives the bust to the judge at the dinner. After receiving the bust, the judge does not submit any regulatory paperwork that refers to it.

Will the judge be subject to discipline?

(A)		Yes, because the judge accepted the sculpted bust as a gift.

(B)		Yes, because the judge did not officially account for receiving the sculpted bust.

(C)		Yes, because the judge received the sculpted bust incident to the public testimonial.

(D)		No, because the judge has not been compensated for serving on the philanthropy's board.

QUESTION 84

A law firm primarily practices insurance defense. After enjoying several years of success, the firm falls on hard times. One of the firm's partners is a neighbor of a world-renowned insurance defense attorney. The world-renowned insurance defense attorney has a substantial roster of clients and is well-connected in the insurance industry. The firm partners believe that the new business generated by the addition of the world-renowned insurance defense attorney would breathe new life into the firm. The firm's attorneys unanimously agree to recruit the world-renowned insurance defense attorney as a new partner. The world-renowned insurance defense attorney agrees to the arrangement and becomes a new partner. The firm enters into an agreement with the new partner. The agreement obligates the firm to pay the new partner 10% of total profits each year. The firm is obligated to continue to make payments to the estate of the new partner for 100 years after the new partner's death.

Will the firm be subject to discipline for this agreement?

(A)   No, because the agreement is lawful and ethical.

(B)   No, because an attorney can enter into any agreement with the firm.

(C)   Yes, because the agreement is unlawful.

(D)   Yes, because the agreement is unreasonable.

QUESTION 85

A hunter lawfully hunts deer on state land. While there, the hunter receives a gunshot wound from an unidentifiable shooter. The state land is located near the defendant landowner's private property. A prosecutor charges the defendant with a felony for allegedly shooting the hunter. The defendant retains an attorney to defend him. The attorney calls and speaks by phone with the defendant's only potential witness. The witness says that on the day of the shooting, she was with the defendant in the state. The attorney finds no evidence contradicting what the witness said. At trial, the attorney does not present any evidence that the defendant was absent from the state when the shooting occurred. However, in closing argument, the attorney states that the defendant was out of the state when the shooting occurred.

Will the attorney be subject to discipline?

(A)   Yes, because the attorney did not present any evidence to support the statement.

(B)   Yes, because the attorney said that the defendant was out of the state at the time of the shooting.

(C)   No, because the attorney has a duty to zealously defend every client.

(D)   No, because the attorney used best efforts in representing the client.

QUESTION 86

The police arrest a defendant based on probable cause that she is involved in a reported kidnapping of a victim. The kidnappers demand that the state pay a ransom, which the state refuses to pay. At the defendant's request, an attorney represents her during custodial interrogation by the police. The defendant does not make any incriminating statements to the police. Afterwards, the defendant informs the attorney in confidence of the kidnapping victim's location. The defendant tells the attorney that the defendant's accomplice will kill the victim if the state does not pay the ransom as demanded. The attorney knows that the state will not pay the ransom. The attorney thinks that the defendant is telling the truth because he has previously defended her in other criminal matters.

Will it be proper for the attorney to reveal the defendant's statement to the police?

(A)   No, because the defendant's statement is subject to and protected by client-lawyer confidentiality.

(B)   No, because doing so would be in conflict with the defendant's best interest.

(C)   Yes, because the defendant's admission of guilt to the attorney is not protected by client-lawyer confidentiality.

(D)   Yes, because the defendant's statement is not protected by client-lawyer confidentiality because of the type of information it provides.

QUESTION 87

For several years, a small city employs an attorney on a part-time basis to handle its litigation. When not working for the city, the attorney represents clients as a sole practitioner. The local rules authorize this arrangement.

The attorney represents the city in a civil action against a citizen to recover unpaid property taxes. The city recovers a judgment against the citizen that has yet to be enforced. The citizen approaches the attorney and requests that the attorney represent the citizen in litigation against the city. The attorney's political beliefs align with the citizen's position, so the attorney agrees to represent the citizen in a lawsuit challenging the validity of the city's property tax ordinances and enforcement procedures. Before accepting the representation, the attorney formally ceases representing the city. The attorney does not request that the city consent to her representation of the citizen in this case.

Will the attorney be subject to discipline for agreeing to take the citizen's case?

(A)   No, because the attorney ceased representing the city before representing the citizen.

(B)   No, because the attorney can have clients while being employed by the city.

(C)   Yes, because the attorney failed to obtain the city's oral consent to representing the citizen.

(D)   Yes, because the attorney substantially participated in the city's civil action against the citizen.

QUESTION 88

A law firm handles civil litigation. The firm agrees to represent a client in a medical malpractice action arising from outpatient care of the client. The firm's managing partner directed an associate attorney, who recently became a member of the bar, to prosecute the client's civil action. The associate attorney's research did not discover a special service of process provision for medical malpractice actions. Consequently, the associate attorney improperly served process, which resulted in the dismissal of the client's action with prejudice. This precluded the client from recovering on her claim worth $3,000. Both the firm and the associate attorney may have civil liability exposure in the client's potential legal malpractice action.

Will the associate attorney be subject to discipline?

(A)   Yes, because the associate attorney had a duty to decline undertaking responsibility for the case.

(B)   Yes, because the associate attorney did not fulfill her duties when acting at another attorney's direction.

(C)   No, because the associate attorney acted at the managing attorney's direction.

(D)   No, because the action's minimal dollar value qualifies as de minimis.

QUESTION 89

An attorney serves as a sales company's corporate counsel. The sales company employs a large number of people, including a sales person. In January, the sales company makes an unsecured loan to the sales person of $500 for which she signs an enforceable agreement to repay the sales company. In May, the sales person resigns from the sales company. At that time, however, the sales person has not made any payment to the sales company of the balance due on the loan. The attorney does not learn of the sales person's resignation until December, when the sales company's accountant notices that the $500 debt remains unpaid. The accountant calls and speaks with the sales person about making payment arrangements to satisfy this debt. She replies that if the sales company "wants me to pay, it will have to make me pay." The accountant then explains the situation to the attorney. The attorney's research determines that the statute of limitations on the loan has not expired and that the agreement could be enforced in small claims court. He tells the sales company's president: "The sales company has a valid agreement with the sales person. It is enforceable by means of a small claims action, which I could file before the statute of limitations expires. The sales company could prevail in this action. However, the time and effort involved in pursuing this claim, which could involve my appearance in court with the accountant, might be more than it is worth. Also, enforcing this agreement might harm the sales company's business interests if the sales person were to tell others about it. How will her former co-workers here and/or our clients whose accounts she used to serve, think about the sales company? I recommend that the sales company does not enforce this agreement with the sales person."

The president decides not to enforce the loan agreement.

Was the attorney's conduct proper?

(A)   No, because the attorney's advice included both legal and economic factors.

(B)   No, because the attorney's advice not to pursue the small claim violated his duty of zealous advocacy.

(C)   Yes, because the president accepted the attorney's advice and decided against enforcing the loan agreement.

(D)   Yes, because the attorney's advice could include both legal and economic factors.

QUESTION 90

A prosecutor represents the state in a criminal trial. An attorney serves as defense counsel. The trial judge renders a judgment finding the defendant guilty of vehicular homicide. Pursuant to the defendant's informed consent, the attorney appeals the judgment of conviction. The attorney drafts the appellate brief after checking the evidence and trial testimony. In the brief, the attorney writes: "Undisputed evidence shows that the traffic light was green for the defendant when her vehicle approached it and passed under it as the deceased victim ran in front of her oncoming vehicle." However, one of the prosecutor's witnesses testified at trial that the traffic light was red for the defendant when her vehicle struck the deceased victim who was walking across the street. The attorney has both previously heard and read this testimony.

The attorney experiences a severe stroke a few days before oral arguments are scheduled before the state court of appeal. The attorney's secretary contacts a new lawyer, who is "of counsel" to the attorney's law practice. The new lawyer decides to stand in the attorney's place at oral arguments. Although the attorney cannot communicate with the new lawyer, his secretary provides him with the appellate brief and the trial transcript. Due to time constraints, the new lawyer only reads the brief and some of the transcript, but does not read the contradictory testimony of the prosecutor's witness. Presuming that the attorney's entire brief is accurate, the new lawyer's oral argument quotes its statement that undisputed evidence shows that the traffic light was green for the defendant when her vehicle drove under it and the deceased victim ran out in front of the vehicle.

Will the new lawyer be subject to discipline for quoting from the brief?

(A)   No, because the new lawyer was unaware of the quoted excerpt's falsity.

(B)   No, because the new lawyer did not make the first instance of misrepresentation.

(C)   Yes, because the quoted text involved a false statement.

(D)   Yes, because the new lawyer did not diligently research whether the quoted text was true or false.

QUESTION 91

A criminal law attorney and a probate lawyer are members of the bar in the same state. The state bar provides an assistance program for lawyers suffering from addictions. The criminal law attorney practices as a sole practitioner and serves on a state bar committee that oversees the assistance program. The probate lawyer works for a law firm and primarily handles matters involving wills, estates, and trusts. The probate lawyer serves as the trustee of several trusts containing substantial assets of high-value clients. The probate lawyer goes to the criminal law attorney and retains him because he is concerned about having some criminal liability. The probate lawyer tells the criminal law attorney that one time he took some of his client's funds and used them to support his gambling addiction. The criminal law attorney advises him not to do that again and to use the lawyer assistance program's services.

Is the criminal law attorney obligated to report the probate lawyer's misuse of clients' trust funds to the state's professional authority?

(A)   No, because the criminal law attorney obtained this information while representing the probate lawyer.

(B)   No, because a lawyer in the probate lawyer's law firm having knowledge of the lawyer's misconduct is obligated to report it.

(C)   Yes, because the criminal law attorney obtained this information while representing the lawyer.

(D)   Yes, because the criminal law attorney's failure to report the probate lawyer's conduct would help conceal the probate lawyer's breach of fiduciary duty.

QUESTION 92

A plaintiff and a defendant are litigating a complex commercial law case before a judge. The case involves some novel issues of Uniform Commercial Code (UCC) law pertaining to interstate secured transactions. An attorney, who specializes in UCC law and does not represent either party to the case, makes a telephone call to the judge. The attorney and the judge extensively discuss the case and the governing law. The judge makes detailed notes on her conversation with the attorney and keeps them with her other materials regarding the case. The judge does not then disclose the phone call or the contents of her notes to either the plaintiff or the defendant.

After the parties finish presenting their respective cases, the judge takes the case under advisement as the trier of fact and law. Along with the parties' pleadings, the judge takes the notes of the attorney's phone call and its points into consideration when preparing her written opinion.

Was it proper for the judge to utilize her notes based on the attorney's phone call?

(A)   No, because the judge did not disclose the attorney's call and her notes to the parties.

(B)   No, because the judge cannot obtain the opinion of a disinterested third-party expert.

(C)   Yes, because the attorney called the judge and the judge did not call the attorney.

(D)   Yes, because no client with interests that this case's outcome could affect was represented by the attorney.

QUESTION 93

A plaintiff's attorney agrees to represent a plaintiff in a tort action alleging claims of products liability in negligence and strict liability. The action alleges that a defective vehicle manufactured by the defendant corporations caused the plaintiff's severe and permanent injuries when its gas tank spontaneously exploded. A defense lawyer represents the defendant, which agrees with him to make an offer of compromise.

The offer is for a $1,000,000 lump sum payment in exchange for dismissal of the tort action with prejudice. The plaintiff's attorney describes the offer to the plaintiff and tells him that he probably could obtain more damages by means of a jury trial than by the compromise. The plaintiff decides to accept the recommendation that he reject the offer. The plaintiff's attorney communicates that rejection to the defense lawyer. In response, the defense lawyer sends a letter directly to the plaintiff asking him to compromise because the defense lawyer reasonably believes that the plaintiff's attorney wants a trial to get free media coverage.

Will the defense lawyer be subject to discipline?

(A)   No, if the lawyer based his request upon a reasonable belief.

(B)   No, because the communication was made in writing, not in person.

(C)   Yes, because the plaintiff was represented by an attorney.

(D)   Yes, because the plaintiff decided not to compromise.

QUESTION 94

A prosecutor charges a defendant with murder, a capital crime. The prosecutor alleges that the defendant's speeding vehicle struck and killed a victim in front of eyewitnesses. This fatal collision occurred on a clear and sunny day when the victim had the right of way in a crosswalk. The defendant retains a high-profile attorney to represent him. The attorney is widely known for representing criminal clients in publicized trials. The prosecutor offers to reduce the charge to involuntary manslaughter, a non-capital crime, if the defendant agrees to plead guilty to the charge. The attorney recommends that the defendant reject the offer because a jury possibly could acquit the defendant of the murder charge. Consequently, the defendant rejects the offer. Later, the prosecutor hears the attorney tell a friend that he recommended that the defendant reject the offer because he wants to go to trial due to its media coverage. The attorney provides effective assistance of counsel at the trial, which has media coverage. The defendant is convicted of murder and sentenced to death.

Based on the law and facts, the prosecutor reasonably believes that the attorney placed his personal desire for media coverage over the defendant's best interest in not going to trial in this case.

Will it be proper for the prosecutor to inform the relevant professional authority of his concerns about the attorney's motive for recommending rejection of the offer?

(A)   No, because the attorney provided the defendant with effective assistance of counsel at trial.

(B)   No, because the defendant could have been acquitted as a result of a trial, which could not have resulted from accepting the offer.

(C)   Yes, because the prosecutor has evidence that the defendant's rejection of the offer is attributable to the attorney's desire for media coverage.

(D)   Yes, because the trial of the case received extensive media coverage.

QUESTION 95

An attorney employs several paralegals as assistants in his law practice. These paralegals have credentials from properly accredited academic institutions. The attorney represents a client. One of the paralegals fails to make an entry in her case calendar for the critical filing deadline for the client's civil cause of action. Consequently, a filing required to prosecute the client's action does not timely occur. As a result, the client's action can neither be maintained nor reinstated.

Which of the following statements accurately describes the attorney's professional culpability?

(A)   The attorney is NOT subject to discipline unless the attorney negligently supervised the paralegal, but the attorney is subject to civil liability.

(B)   The attorney is NOT subject to either discipline or civil liability if the attorney was not personally negligent.

(C)   On the basis of vicarious liability, the attorney is subject to both discipline and civil liability.

(D)   The client may decide if the attorney is either subject to discipline or civil liability.

QUESTION 96

A physician, a medical doctor, would like to formalize a professional relationship with an attorney. The attorney's practice exclusively involves medical malpractice actions. The attorney believes that this relationship would benefit her practice because the physician is a medical malpractice expert who regularly provides testimony in these types of cases. The physician would like to be the attorney's partner and make this arrangement evident in advertisements of their firm, as well as on its letterhead. These materials would identify the professional titles and degrees of both the physician and the attorney.

Will the attorney be subject to discipline for entering into this proposed relationship?

(A)   No, because it will provide clients with the benefit of the physician's and the attorney 's combined experience and expertise.

(B)   No, if only the attorney will provide legal advice to clients.

(C)   Yes, because a partnership of the attorney and the physician would involve rendering legal services to clients.

(D)   Yes, because the attorney would receive other non-legal fees in addition to legal fees.

QUESTION 97

Two accountants, a brother and sister, decide to form an accounting partnership. They retain an attorney who assists them by preparing and filing the requisite documents. The two partners equally share profits, losses, and control of their partnership.

A year after forming the partnership, a client brings an action against the partners and the partnership. The attorney agrees to represent the partnership and both of the partners individually in a civil action that a client brought against them. The attorney provides this representation in compliance with all applicable law and ethical rules. However, during this representation, the sister fails to inform the brother of certain partnership information that would have supported their objectives of representation. The partners and partnership lost the case after a trial.

Subsequently, the brother requests that the attorney file a tort lawsuit against the sister on the basis of the sister's negligence in failing to provide the missing partnership information in the prior, proper representation. The brother reasonably believes that if his sister had provided this information, the results of litigation would have been different.

Will it be proper for the attorney to litigate the brother's tort lawsuit?

(A)   No, because the attorney represented both the brother and sister in the civil action in which the sister allegedly negligently failed to provide information to her brother.

(B)   No, because a different lawyer will represent the sister in the brother's lawsuit.

(C)   Yes, because the attorney did not receive the information during the clients' joint civil action.

(D)   Yes, if the brother reasonably believed that if the sister had provided the information, the results of litigation would have been different.

QUESTION 98

Two family law attorneys separately practice law in a jurisdiction. The attorneys decide to form a partnership and both move into a new office together. To announce their partnership and obtain new clients, they run a radio commercial in the jurisdiction. A professional announcer provides the name of the law firm, the names of the attorneys, and the firm's office address. The announcer continues to state:

"The attorneys have combined forces to provide you with effective and competent representation. The attorneys want to put their experienced in domestic relations matters to work for you.

If you call (888) 888-8888 today, they will waive their standard hourly fee for your initial consultation. This offer also applies if you mention this commercial while visiting their new office to arrange an initial consultation.

At that consultation, the attorneys can determine the fairness of your award of alimony, child custody, or visitation in a divorce, as well as similar matters."

Will the attorneys be subject to discipline?

(A)   No, if their conduct complies with the contents of their commercial.

(B)   No, because their commercial does not target people who are either represented or unrepresented by other counsel.

(C)   Yes, because they are seeking, as prospective clients, people with whom they lack any existing relationship.

(D)   Yes, because a person must mention the commercial to obtain a free initial consultation when the person visits the new office to arrange that consultation.

QUESTION 99

A prosecutor files charges against a defendant in a criminal case. An attorney serves as the defendant's defense counsel in a bench trial before a judge. The trial raises novel issues of law and fact regarding criminal liability for drug offenses involving a chemical substance that was similar to a legally prohibited controlled substance. The parties do not provide expert testimony regarding the novel issues.

At the close of the case, the judge informs the parties that he will render a judgment as soon as possible. The prosecutor becomes concerned that the judge's possible delay in rendering a decision might violate the local speedy trial rule. That rule does not authorize any *ex parte* communication during the proceeding. The prosecutor writes a letter to the judge. The letter mentions the prosecutor's concern and offers to provide additional pleadings or expert testimony if necessary to assist judge in making a decision. The prosecutor does not send a copy of this letter to the attorney. The next day the judge renders the judgment.

Was the prosecutor's letter to the judge proper?

(A)   No, because it constituted an *ex parte* communication during the proceeding.

(B)   No, because the judge rendered the judgment the day after the prosecutor wrote the letter.

(C)   Yes, because the prosecutor reasonably believed that a violation of the local speedy trial rule could have occurred.

(D)   Yes, because the prosecutor's letter did not seek to influence the judge's decision.

QUESTION 100

State law permits an attorney to maintain a law practice while serving part-time as a county commissioner in a county of the state. State law provides that if the county's commissioners authorize the construction of a new courthouse and the funding of 50% of its construction cost, the state will provide the other 50% of the funding. A contractor is a regular contributor to the attorney's campaign for the position of county commissioner. The contractor's business is being prosecuted for fraudulent charges in a case over which a judge is presiding. The judge sits on the bench in a courthouse that needs to be replaced because of its size and originally poor construction. As instructed by the contractor, the attorney writes a letter to the judge. The letter states that as a county commissioner, the attorney would be willing to support funding for a proposed new courthouse if the contractor's case is timely scheduled on the docket.

Will the attorney be subject to discipline?

(A)   No, because the attorney wrote the judge pursuant to the contractor's instructions.

(B)   No, because state law allows the attorney to maintain his part-time law practice while serving as a commissioner.

(C)   Yes, because the judge could find the contractor not guilty on all charges.

(D)   Yes, because the attorney's letter sought to influence the judge in the contractor's case.

QUESTION 101

An attorney agrees to represent a contractor as a plaintiff in a breach of contract lawsuit against a government defendant. The attorney and the plaintiff execute a retainer agreement specifying the hourly billable rate. The controlling law does not provide governmental immunity for this type of lawsuit. The attorney's litigation of the case both exhausts the plaintiff's retainer and involves additional billable hours for which the plaintiff has not paid the attorney. A jury returns a judgment awarding the plaintiff $75,000 in damages, which the defendant does not appeal. The defendant sends a check to the lawyer satisfying the judgment. The attorney places the defendant's payment of damages in the client trust account and invoices the plaintiff $10,000, the amount due for unpaid billable hours of work. The attorney calls the plaintiff and informs the plaintiff of the amounts of the damage award and the invoice. The plaintiff replies that it would only pay $7,000 because it considered that sum to be reasonable. The attorney issues a $65,000 check to the plaintiff and moves $10,000 from the client trust account into the attorney's general account.

Will the attorney be subject to discipline?

(A)   No, because the plaintiff must pay the attorney pursuant to their agreement.

(B)   No, because the attorney paid the undisputed amount to the plaintiff and invoiced the plaintiff for $10,000.

(C)   Yes, because the attorney and the plaintiff dispute the amount owed.

(D)   Yes, because the attorney must receive the amount stated by the client and bring a claim for the balance.

QUESTION 102

A family law attorney and a criminal law attorney enter into a law partnership. The lawyers properly convert the organizational status of the partnership into a professional corporation.

They designate the family law attorney's spouse, who is not an attorney, as the professional corporation's president. The family law attorney's spouse has no direction or control of the attorneys' professional judgment. The family law attorney serves as the professional corporation's vice-president and is a shareholder. The criminal defense attorney serves as the professional corporation's secretary and is a shareholder. The criminal defense attorney's sister serves as an office assistant in the firm. The family law attorney and the criminal defense attorney decide to add another attorney to the firm in order to handle a growing case load. They offer a salaried associate attorney position to a new lawyer. They do not make the new lawyer an officer, shareholder, or member of the professional corporation. When they make the offer of employment, the family law attorney and the criminal defense attorney disclose their status as officers, shareholders, or members, along with the fact that the professional corporation's president is not an attorney.

Will the new lawyer be subject to discipline for accepting this offer of employment?

(A)   No, because the lawyer is not an officer, shareholder, or member of the professional corporation and only holds the position of a salaried employee.

(B)   No, because the president neither directs nor controls the professional judgment of the family law attorney, the criminal defense attorney, or the new lawyer.

(C)   Yes, because the family law attorney's spouse is the professional corporation's president.

(D)   Yes, because the criminal defense attorney's sister serves as the firm's office assistant.

QUESTION 103

A judge is an incumbent member of the state court of appeals. The judge is up for re-election in the voting district where an attorney lives. The attorney is considering whether to be a candidate for a judicial office. If the attorney decides to be a candidate, he would run against the judge to win the seat. The attorney seeks to discover if any grievances were filed against the judge and/or if the judge has been disciplined for judicial misconduct. In response to the attorney's proper inquiry, the state judicial conduct commission provides a letter on official stationary indicating that, as a result of two grievances, the commission imposed discipline for one instance of judicial misconduct. Based in part on this letter's information, the attorney decides to run for election. During his campaign, the attorney uses this letter's information in a public speech. It is subsequently brought to his attention that the commission imposed discipline for two instances of judicial misconduct.

The existence of grievances and the commission's determinations are a matter of public record.

Will the attorney be subject to discipline for making an incorrect statement about the commission's imposition of discipline?

(A)   No, because the attorney did not knowingly misrepresent any fact concerning the judge.

(B)   No, because in a contested election the attorney can make any statement about the judge.

(C)   Yes, because the typographic error in the letter cannot excuse the attorney's false statement of a material fact.

(D)   Yes, because the judge was disciplined for two instances of judicial conduct.

QUESTION 104

An attorney usually represents clients pursuant to a retainer agreement. A plaintiff, a musician, suffers a serious loss of income when a defendant, a music company, fails to pay the plaintiff any royalties on the music he wrote and performed. In order to obtain the attorney's services without initially providing any funds, the plaintiff suggests a contingency fee arrangement. The plaintiff offers to make payments to the attorney of 10% of the royalties that the defendant pays to the plaintiff after the plaintiff prevails against the defendant in this civil action to receive royalties. The plaintiff proposes that the attorney would recover her legal fees and litigation expenses from these payments by the plaintiff. The attorney agrees to pursue a civil action for the plaintiff against the defendant pursuant to those terms.

Will the attorney be subject to discipline based on this agreement?

(A)   No, because the plaintiff requested the agreement's terms and conditions.

(B)   No, because the attorney and the plaintiff can agree to a reasonable contingency fee.

(C)   Yes, because the attorney obtained a proprietary interest in the plaintiff's civil action.

(D)   Yes, unless the attorney's total fee is not greater than that which she could have obtained by billing a reasonable hourly rate.

QUESTION 105

An attorney worked for a law firm prior to being elected to the state legislature. Once elected, the attorney resigns from the firm. He serves in the state legislature for three two-year terms and cannot run for office again due to the state's term limit law. The attorney decides to go into private practice of law at the end of his final term. The attorney composes the following notice, which contains the attorney's name at the top of the notice, and pays for its publication in a daily legal newspaper:

"Following six-years of public service in the state legislature, I am returning to the practice of law. My new office is located in the Office Plaza, at 100 Central Avenue, City, State, 99999. Please feel free to call regarding questions or with requests for legal assistance. My number is (222) 222-2222."

Will the attorney be subject to discipline for publishing this notice?

(A)   No, because the notice consisted of true statements.

(B)   No, because the notice did not include any information that was not otherwise publicly accessible.

(C)   Yes, because the notice was published to people who had not been his clients.

(D)   Yes, because the attorney's service as a legislator had no bearing upon his competence as a lawyer.

QUESTION 106

A law firm employs a supervising attorney and a subordinate attorney. The supervising attorney is responsible for oversight of the work of the subordinate attorney. The law firm represents a product manufacturer who has been sued in a products liability action. The supervising attorney instructs the subordinate attorney to review their client's documents and identify any of them having legal significance. The subordinate attorney provides copies of the legally significant documents to the supervising attorney, who reviews and returns those copies with instructions that the subordinate attorney destroy certain original versions of those documents. The subordinate attorney complies with the supervising attorney's instructions.

Will the subordinate attorney be subject to discipline for complying with the supervising attorney's instructions?

(A)   No, because the subordinate attorney had a duty to obey the supervising attorney's instructions.

(B)   No, because neither the supervising attorney nor the subordinate attorney violated any ethical rule.

(C)   Yes, because the supervising attorney violated an ethical rule.

(D)   Yes, because the subordinate attorney cannot avoid responsibility for violating an ethical rule by obeying the supervising attorney's instructions.

QUESTION 107

An attorney is an active member of a non-profit organization. The organization's purpose is to rescue, shelter, and protect victims of domestic abuse. The attorney maintains a law office as her full time occupation. Her general law practice includes criminal defense work. The attorney serves as an appointed attorney for criminal defendants in some of the local courts in the jurisdiction where she is admitted to the bar. The attorney incurs significant expense when representing criminal defendants for which a court appoints her as defense counsel in a small number of assigned cases. A court seeks to appoint the attorney to represent a defendant during his prosecution for repeated and severe instances of domestic abuse. The attorney strenuously objects to this appointment on the basis of her personal beliefs and membership in the organization. The attorney asserts that, based on the charges against the defendant, she cannot represent him.

Will the attorney be subject to discipline for seeking to avoid being appointed to represent the defendant?

(A)   Yes, because the attorney must represent everyone she is appointed to represent.

(B)   No, because representing the defendant could impose a financial burden upon the attorney.

(C)   No, because representing the defendant will probably violate an ethical rule.

(D)   No, because the defendant is so repugnant to the attorney as to probably impair their client-lawyer relationship or her ability to represent him.

QUESTION 108

A prospective client calls a criminal defense law firm. The prospective client meets with an attorney in the firm for an initial screening interview. In response to his request for representation at an arraignment in 10 days, the attorney in the firm takes the prospective client's paperwork and tells him not to be concerned about the arraignment. In the next eight days, neither the attorney nor the law firm respond to the prospective client, who does not contact them or any other defense counsel to request representation. The attorney calls the prospective client back on the ninth day and refuses to represent him. The attorney has no reason for denying the representation.

Will the attorney be subject to discipline for refusing to represent the prospective client?

(A)   No, because no client-lawyer relationship could arise from an initial screening interview.

(B)   Yes, because an attorney has a duty to represent a client who requests representation.

(C)   Yes, because a client-lawyer relationship existed between them based on detrimental reliance.

(D)   No, because the attorney can always refuse to represent any client who requests representation.

QUESTION 109

A manufacturer contacts an attorney seeking representation in a business dispute with a distributor. The attorney agrees to represent the manufacturer and they execute a valid written retainer agreement. During the attorney's representation of the client, they discover that the dispute involves a retailer. The attorney agrees to represent the manufacturer in the business dispute with respect to the retailer as well as the distributor. Because the disputing parties fail to make any compromise or settlement agreement, the manufacturer instructs the attorney to commence litigation against both the distributor and retailer. During the course of litigation, one year after they made their agreement, the attorney incurs some unexpected increases in her costs of doing business. The attorney seeks to enter into another contract modifying their agreement by increasing her hourly billable rate from $125 to $150. Initially, the manufacturer objects to the modification, but then agrees to it in order to continue the attorney's representation.

Will the attorney be subject to discipline?

(A)   Yes, because the attorney changed her billing rate during term of the representation.

(B)   Yes, because the manufacturer initially objected to the change in billing rate.

(C)   No, because the attorney experienced increases in her business costs.

(D)   No, because the attorney communicated the billing rate increase and the manufacturer agreed to it.

QUESTION 110

An attorney resides in a house on a street that has a commercial business on its corner. The attorney is personal friends with the owner of the business.

A prospective client meets with the attorney. During their initial meeting and interview, the prospective client explains that he provided certain services to the owner's business for which the owner has not compensated him. The prospective client has invoiced, called, and written the owner to request payment several times. The prospective client has received no promises or assurances of payment from the owner. The prospective client requests that the attorney represent him on a contingency fee basis whereby the attorney would recover a reasonable and legally permitted percentage of the amount of funds that the owner owes to the prospective client.

Will the attorney be subject to discipline for declining to represent the prospective client?

(A)   No, because an attorney can always refuse to represent any prospective client for any reason.

(B)   No, because the attorney's personal friendship with the owner may negatively impact his relationship with the prospective client as a client.

(C)   Yes, because the attorney has a duty to represent every prospective client.

(D)   Yes, because the attorney's personal friendship with the owner will not adversely affect his relationship with the prospective client as a client.

QUESTION 111

An attorney works in a small firm and mainly practices domestic relations law and probate law. The attorney is the granddaughter of a prospective client and they have known each other since her childhood. The prospective client visits the attorney's office because he is seeking her probate law services. He requests that she prepare his last will and testament. As her client, he wants the will to include, in addition to its usual terms and conditions, certain bequests to his family members and friends. Specifically, the client instructs the attorney to include a bequest to the attorney of a classic automobile.

Will the attorney be subject to discipline if she prepares the will as instructed?

(A)   No, because an attorney can prepare a will for a client giving a substantial gift to herself if the gift is made knowingly and voluntarily.

(B)   No, because the attorney can prepare, for the client, a will giving the attorney a substantial gift because they are relatives.

(C)   Yes, because the attorney cannot prepare for any client an instrument giving a substantial gift to herself.

(D)   Yes, because the attorney cannot prepare, for the client, a will giving a classic automobile to the attorney because they are relatives.

QUESTION 112

A mortgagee (lender) retains an attorney to represent its interests in a commercial real estate deal. A mortgagor (borrower) requests a special business loan for funds to acquire a parcel of real estate and construct a skyscraper on the parcel. The loan will be secured by a mortgage on the parcel and the skyscraper. The loan and mortgage documents will be complicated. If they are incorrectly drafted, it could prevent the mortgagee's interest from being properly secured. The mortgagee will process the loan if the attorney drafts the loan and mortgage documents and the mortgagor pays the attorney's costs for this work. This approach is common in this situation of skyscraper development where the attorney works. The attorney reasonably believes that he can provide both the mortgagee and mortgagor with competent and diligent representation. They both provide written consent to the representation after each having consulted with independent lawyers.

Is it proper for the attorney to prepare the loan and mortgage documents?

(A)   No, because the mortgagor, not the mortgagee, will pay the attorney.

(B)   No, because the interests of the mortgagor and the mortgagee are different.

(C)   Yes, because both the mortgagor and the mortgagee provided informed consent to the attorney's representation.

(D)   Yes, because this approach is common where the attorney works.

QUESTION 113

In response to an attorney's advertisement, a client stops by an attorney's office and schedules an initial consultation. After the client consults with the attorney, they execute a valid retainer agreement setting the attorney's hourly rate at $150. The attorney allows the client to mail in a $9,000 retainer check. Before the check arrives, the attorney performs 10 hours of work on the client's matter.

After receiving the check, the attorney places it in her client trust account. Next, the attorney moves $3,000 of the client's retainer into her general account. The $3,000 consists of $1,500 as her legal fees for the initial 10 hours of work, and $1,500 for work the attorney legitimately expects to perform (another 10 hours) on the client's matter on the following day. The attorney, however, only works five hours on the matter before the client calls her the next day. The client informs the attorney of a change in the situation as a result of which the attorney does not need to spend further time on the matter. Consequently, the attorney moves $750 from the general account back into the client trust account and retains the remaining $750 of the $1,500 as legal fees for services rendered.

Will the attorney be subject to discipline?

(A)   No, because the attorney moved the $750 that she did not earn from the general account back into the client trust account.

(B)   No, because the attorney legitimately expected to perform another 10 more hours of work on the client's matter the next day.

(C)   Yes, because the attorney withdrew $1,500 before completing all legal work for the client.

(D)   Yes, because the attorney moved $3,000 of the retainer into the general account when she had only earned $1,500 in legal fees.

QUESTION 114

An attorney works in a law firm that primarily represents corporate clients in business matters. The majority of the attorney's practice involves drafting, reviewing, and enforcing commercial landlord-tenant agreements. The attorney receives notice of a recent change in the law governing such leases that will affect the lease that the attorney drafted three years ago for a client, whom the attorney no longer represents. The attorney contacts the client to inform it of the change in the law and the resulting necessity of modifying the lease.

Will the attorney be subject to discipline for soliciting employment?

(A)   No, provided the attorney does not subsequently prepare a new lease for the client.

(B)   No, because the attorney formerly represented the client.

(C)   Yes, if the attorney possessed any basis to think that the client obtained other counsel.

(D)   Yes, because the attorney would be soliciting legal business from someone other than a current client.

QUESTION 115

An attorney is a high-profile criminal justice law specialist and author. The attorney testifies in a state legislative committee's fact-finding proceeding. He gives opinion testimony, both as an individual and an expert regarding state criminal justice issues. He does not, however, reveal that he is appearing on behalf of a paying client that has contracts with the state to operate state correctional facilities.

The attorney's testimony corresponds with his client's position on the issues, which the attorney personally considers to be good public policy.

Did the attorney properly give the testimony and not reveal his client's name?

(A)   No, because an attorney cannot receive compensation for attempting to affect legislative action.

(B)   No, because an attorney who testifies before a legislative body needs to disclose the role in which the attorney appears.

(C)   Yes, but only if the attorney sincerely thought that he advanced a position that served the public interest.

(D)   Yes, because the legislature is concerned with the nature of the testimony rather than the source of a witness' compensation.

QUESTION 116

An attorney is a sole practitioner whose general law practice involves a variety of issues. The attorney prepares the paperwork for the formation of a business partnership by two partners. The attorney reviews and drafts other legal documents for the partnership. Subsequently, the partners meet with the attorney and explain a business situation that concerns them. The attorney informs them that this situation could give rise to criminal liability, and that he could not assist them in the furtherance of any criminal conduct. The partners request that the attorney jointly represent them.

The attorney advises them that he would consider the request and let them know if he could assist them. The attorney sends a separate letter to each partner informing each that the partners might be better served by separate attorneys rather than the same attorney. The attorney also informs them that he would represent them both so long as they were equally involved in, and responsible for, the situation. The letter further states that he might need to withdraw from the representation if a conflict of interest develops between the partners, or if either of them does not want to continue with the dual representation. In that event, they both would need to obtain new legal representation. The attorney explains that he would be equally representing them without a preference for either partner. The attorney also makes clear that any communications by the partners would not remain confidential amongst each other. The partners execute and return the attorney's original letter and representation agreement setting forth these terms.

Did the attorney agree to this dual representation on proper terms?

(A)   No, because the attorney's dual representation was conditional upon the waiver of client-lawyer confidentiality by both partners.

(B)   No, unless the attorney provided the partners with notice that they should contact independent counsel before signing and returning their letter to him.

(C)   Yes, if the risk that the interests of either partner would be materially prejudiced by the dual representation was not significant.

(D)   Yes, because the attorney had already been representing both partners with respect to their partnership.

QUESTION 117

A contracts attorney's practice primarily consists of contracts law work. The contracts attorney drafts a sales contract for a seller, who sells recreational vehicles. The contracts attorney and her secretary witness the execution of the contract by the seller and the purchaser. Two weeks after the purchaser bought the recreational vehicle, a proper judicial proceeding resulted in a determination finding the purchaser mentally incompetent. Consequently, a conservator was appointed to manage the purchaser's legal and financial affairs. The conservator retains a litigation lawyer who files a lawsuit against the seller seeking to avoid the contract between the seller and the purchaser. The lawsuit alleges that the purchaser lacked the requisite mental capacity to enter into the contract when he executed it.

The seller asks the contracts attorney to defend him against the conservator's lawsuit. The contracts attorney's secretary and the seller died before the contracts attorney decided whether to represent the seller. Pursuant to a local rule, the seller's legal representative was substituted in his place as a proper party to this lawsuit. The seller's legal representative renewed the seller's request that the contracts attorney provide legal representation in this lawsuit. The contracts attorney remains the sole person who witnessed the contract's execution. In the contracts attorney's opinion, the purchaser was mentally competent when he executed the contract and thus possessed the mental capacity to enter into it. The contracts attorney is willing to testify about that if necessary.

Will it be proper for the contracts attorney to agree to represent the seller's legal representative?

(A)   No, because the attorney may be called to testify regarding a contested issue.

(B)   No, because the attorney drafted the contract that gave rise to the lawsuit.

(C)   Yes, because the attorney is the only attesting witness still alive.

(D)   Yes, because the attorney can testify regarding a contested issue.

QUESTION 118

An attorney represented a client for twenty years. The attorney prepared the client's will. The attorney and the attorney's receptionist acted as the two subscribing witnesses to the will's execution. The will provided 5 percent of the client's estate to her best friend, 15 percent to her daughter (who was the client's only heir), and the residue was left to a charity the client volunteered for during her lifetime. The will appointed the client's accountant to act as executor. The client died one year after the will was executed. The accountant named as executor in the will asked the attorney to represent her through the probate process. The client's daughter believed that the client suffered from mental illness during the last few years of life. The daughter informed the accountant that she planned to challenge the validity of the will on the grounds of mental incapacity. The attorney disagrees with the daughter's assertion. The attorney reasonably believes that the client was fully competent during the attorney's entire relationship with the client, leading up to the client's death. The attorney plans to testify about the client's mental capacity if called as a witness in the action. The attorney's receptionist at the time of will execution, who acted as the other subscribing witness to the will, fled the country to evade unrelated criminal charges and has not been found despite a diligent effort by law enforcement authorities.

Would it be proper for the attorney to represent the accountant for the will probate action?

(A)   No, because the attorney's testimony relates to a contested issue.

(B)   No, because the client's daughter, as surviving heir, obtains the benefit of the fiduciary duty to the client by the attorney.

(C)   Yes, because the attorney is the only available subscribing witness to the will's execution.

(D)   Yes, if the attorney makes a good faith effort to locate the receptionist.

QUESTION 119

An attorney, who is a sole practitioner, runs a general practice, but she is rapidly gaining a reputation for her work in family law matters. The attorney has just been ordered by the court to represent a criminal defendant who has been charged with embezzling thousands of dollars of state-issued funds from the orphanage where he worked. The money he allegedly stole was earmarked for providing medical treatment to several children at the orphanage with chronic illnesses. The local newspaper has published several opinion pieces denouncing the defendant since his arrest, and two television stations are providing continuing news coverage of the case.

The attorney has handled serious criminal matters before, and is confident that she could ably represent the defendant, despite her strong distaste for the crime with which he has been charged. However, she is worried that, given the extensive news coverage of the case, there is a chance that her association with a defendant who people believe stole from orphans will harm her reputation and cause potential clients with family law matters to seek out other attorneys. The attorney has not yet met with the defendant or entered an appearance on his behalf.

May the attorney decline the court's request that she represent the defendant?

(A)   Yes, because she strongly dislikes the crime the defendant is charged with committing.

(B)   Yes, because she has not yet established an attorney-client relationship with the defendant.

(C)   No, because the mere possibility that new clients will not hire her does not create an unreasonable financial burden.

(D)   No, because she has not first obtained the defendant's informed, written consent to decline the representation.

QUESTION 120

A wife in a marriage contacts a well-reputed divorce lawyer to represent her in divorce proceedings. The wife, who is unemployed, is taking care of her two children alone. She is living in a motel room because her husband refuses to leave the house or take care of the children. The wife explains that her husband has withdrawn hundreds of thousands of dollars from their bank accounts and, as a result, she cannot access any funds to pay the attorney a retainer. The wife is worried that if she does not take legal action soon, her husband will spend or hide all of their money, leaving her unable to take care of their children.

The lawyer is a seasoned divorce attorney who feels that the wife has been wronged by her husband. The lawyer wants to help the wife and agrees to represent her without a retainer. Because he is confident that he can secure a divorce, child support, and a sizeable alimony award for the wife, the attorney insists on his usual rate of $400 per hour, plus costs, to be paid at the end of the divorce proceedings. Less experienced attorneys in the city charge approximately $350 per hour for similar work. The lawyer's fee will be due regardless of whether the husband and wife actually divorce, and regardless of the ultimate division of assets. At the end of the initial consultation, the attorney puts the fee agreement in writing and both he and the wife sign it.

Is the fee agreement between the lawyer and the wife proper?

(A)   The fee agreement is proper because the lawyer's fee is reasonable.

(B)   The fee agreement is improper because the lawyer's agreement to accept payment at the end of the proceedings is a contingency fee.

(C)   The fee agreement is proper because even though the lawyer is charging a contingency fee, the agreement has been reduced to writing and the wife has provided written consent to the agreement by signing it.

(D)   The fee agreement is improper because the lawyer's $400 per hour fee is *per se* unreasonable.

QUESTION 121

A lawyer represented the owner of a local restaurant in a labor dispute with several of his waiters over unpaid wages. During the representation, the lawyer reviewed all of the owner's accounting books and business practices, and learned that the owner underpaid all of his employees. The lawyer detested working with the owner, but he did a good job and the matter was resolved in the owner's favor several months ago, thus ending the lawyer's representation of the owner. A group of busboys from the restaurant (who were not party to the suit by the waiters) are now claiming that the owner refuses to pay them overtime wages. The busboys have contacted the lawyer to represent them in a suit against the owner. To ensure that he complies with his ethical obligations, the lawyer calls the owner and explains that he has been contacted by the busboys and would like to take on the representation. The owner says that he didn't like working with the lawyer and couldn't care less if he represents the busboys. The owner then hangs up on the lawyer.

Which of the following best describes the lawyer's ability to represent the busboys?

(A)   The lawyer may not represent the busboys because the representation would involve a concurrent conflict of interest, which has not been waived by both parties.

(B)   The lawyer may not represent the busboys because he has not obtained the owner's informed, written consent.

(C)   The lawyer may represent the busboys because he is no longer representing the owner and the owner consented to the representation.

(D)   The lawyer may not represent the busboys because he obtained information during the previous representation that could be damaging to the owner in the busboys' lawsuit.

QUESTION 122

A small law firm recently hired an associate who graduated from law school the previous summer and who was just admitted to the bar. The associate, who has only been with the firm for a few weeks, has been fulfilling his duties at the firm under the supervision of the managing partner. Because the firm cannot afford much support staff, the associate has been given a number of administrative tasks, such as going through the mail and conducting firm business at the bank. The managing partner has thoroughly trained the associate to handle these tasks in compliance with the applicable rules of professional conduct.

Yesterday, the associate opened a letter that included a sizeable check made out to the firm as a settlement in one of the firm's cases. The associate immediately showed the check to the managing partner. The partner explained that he was relieved to receive the check, as business had slowed unexpectedly, and the firm needed the money to pay some outstanding bills. He instructed the associate to take the check to the bank and deposit it. The partner stated that he would prepare an accounting for the client. The associate dutifully took the check to the bank, where he deposited it in the firm's operating account so that the firm could pay its bills right away.

Which of the following best describes the extent to which the associate and managing partner are subject to professional discipline?

(A)   Neither attorney is subject to discipline.

(B)   The managing partner is subject to discipline, but the associate is not.

(C)   The associate is subject to discipline, but the managing partner is not.

(D)   Both attorneys are subject to discipline.

QUESTION 123

A local entrepreneur has developed a business idea designed to capitalize on the recent influx of immigrants into his community. He intends to open up an immigrants' resource center, which will provide various cultural services otherwise unavailable to its patrons, such as connecting them with local religious and civic organizations, as well as employment opportunities, for a nominal fee. The center will also serve as a platform for local businesses, which are struggling in the slow economy, to advertise their services – for a more substantial fee. The entrepreneur consults with a local immigration attorney to see if he would be interested in purchasing advertising space at the center. The attorney explains that he not only wants to advertise at the center, but that he would like to help finance the project. In exchange, he wants the center to exclusively refer its clients with legal issues to his practice. The entrepreneur is thrilled, as having the lawyer's financial assistance will eliminate some of his own risk in developing the business, and agrees to the attorney's proposal, provided that he will refer his clients to the resource center. The two agree to develop the resource center as partners, and they open it for business only a few weeks later.

Is the lawyer subject to discipline based on his agreement with the entrepreneur?

(A)   No, because none of the services provided by the resource center constitute the practice of law.

(B)   No, because there are no ethical restrictions on lawyers entering into lawful business relationships.

(C)   Yes, because a lawyer may not enter into a partnership with a non-lawyer.

(D)   Yes, because the referral agreement between the lawyer and entrepreneur is improper.

QUESTION 124

While driving home from work one afternoon, a personal injury attorney witnessed a car accident caused when a driver in a luxury sedan ran a red light. After running the light, the sedan swerved to avoid another vehicle and sideswiped a station wagon. Not one to miss a business opportunity, the attorney hurried over to the accident scene and approached the station wagon. The attorney recognized the injured station wagon driver as a local probate lawyer with whom she had a mutual acquaintance. An ambulance arrived and, as the paramedics helped the station wagon driver, who had suffered some minor injuries, into the ambulance, the attorney handed her his business card and, with all sincerity, explained: "I saw that guy run a red light. Let me take your case and I'll help you sue the pants off of him." Before the driver of the station wagon could respond, the paramedics shooed the attorney away as they loaded her into the ambulance and sped off to the hospital.

While at home recovering from her injuries, the station wagon driver found the personal injury attorney's business card and, remembering the attorney's crass, tasteless behavior during a moment when she was vulnerable, she became incensed. An attorney herself, the station wagon driver considered professional ethics to be of the utmost importance. Hoping to teach the personal injury attorney a lesson about professional behavior, she decided to report his conduct to the state bar.

If the station wagon driver reports the personal injury attorney to the state bar, will he be subject to discipline for soliciting her as a client?

(A)   Yes, because lawyers may not directly solicit business from individuals for pecuniary gain.

(B)   No, because the driver of the station wagon is a lawyer.

(C)   No, because he witnessed the accident and reasonably believed he could win the case.

(D)   Yes, because the driver of the station wagon did not want him to solicit her business.

QUESTION 125

One of a firm's named partners, who also helped found the firm, was elected to the state legislature, and he has been in office for the past six months. By law, a state legislator may hold private employment, provided that the private employment does not create a conflict of interest with a legislator's duties. Because the partner's firm is located in the state capital, and the legislature is regularly out of session, the partner has been able to remain involved in most of his cases, although he occasionally solicits help from other partners when his legislative duties require it. Moreover, the partner has dutifully avoided any conflict of interest between his legal practice and his official duties in the legislature. Since the partner began his duties in the state legislature, no action has been taken to remove the partner's name from the firm's name.

Given the above facts, which of the following most accurately describes the obligations of the firm and its partners under the Model Rules of Professional Conduct?

(A)   The partner may not serve as both a practicing attorney and a public official, and his name must be removed from the firm's name as long as he remains a legislator.

(B)   The partner may continue to practice with the firm while he is in the legislature, but his name must be removed from the firm's name.

(C)   The partner cannot continue to practice with the firm while he is in the legislature, but his name can remain part of the firm's name because it is his legacy.

(D)   The partner may continue to practice with the firm, and the partner's name may remain in the firm's name.

QUESTION 126

A business owner contacted an attorney about representing him in negotiations to acquire a competitor's business. The attorney, who had only been in practice for a short time, agreed to take on the representation and asked how the business owner got his name. The businessman explained that he was a friend of the attorney's neighbor, who had recommended him.

The negotiations took several weeks, earning the attorney a handsome $25,000 fee. The attorney was grateful to his neighbor for the referral and, as thanks for sending some business his way, showed up on the neighbor's doorstep with a $50 bottle of wine – paid for with money earned from the representation. The neighbor told the attorney that he didn't have to get him anything, but the attorney insisted, explaining that it was the least he could do for sending him such a lucrative job opportunity.

Is the attorney subject to discipline for giving the wine to his neighbor?

(A)   Yes, because he has split the client's fee with a non-lawyer.

(B)   No, because he gave his neighbor a reasonable gift in exchange for the referral.

(C)   Yes, because the lawyer cannot compensate his neighbor for the referral.

(D)   No, because the value of the gift was substantially less than the fee obtained from the client.

QUESTION 127

A prominent lawyer is on the board of directors of, and owns shares of stock in, his family's business: a company that produces medical devices. The other members of the board include the lawyer's parents, his wife, and his two sisters. The company, which is headquartered in a state on the east coast, is currently mired in state court litigation there (and only there), resulting from both regulatory actions by the state government and consumer suits. Although he serves on the board of directors, the lawyer's participation is minimal, requiring only a few days of his time each year. The lawyer lives in a state on the west coast, where he has just been appointed to the state judiciary.

Assuming that he will not violate any other provisions of the Model Code of Judicial Conduct, which of the following best describes the new judge's obligations under Model Code of Judicial Conduct Rule 3.11?

(A)   The judge may hold the company's stock and remain on the board of directors because the company is closely held by the judge and his family members.

(B)   The judge must resign from the board of directors and sell off his company stock because the company is frequently involved in state court litigation.

(C)   The judge may keep his company stock, but must resign from the board of directors because his participation will necessarily interfere with his judicial duties.

(D)   The judge must sell off his stock and resign from the board of directors because he may not participate in a business with non-lawyers.

QUESTION 128

A lawyer is representing a husband in divorce proceedings. The lawyer prides himself on helping divorcing couples get through the divorce process as amicably as possible and has had great success doing so in the past. The wife's divorce attorney, on the other hand, is known for aggressively representing his clients' interests to get them the largest possible award. The parties held negotiations, and the husband's lawyer was doing his best to deal with the wife's combative attorney, who has become nearly impossible to deal with. During a recent meeting with his attorney following negotiations, the husband became extremely emotional and stated that he had no interest in getting a divorce and just wanted to reconcile with his wife. The lawyer felt that this provided an opportunity to use his skills and, with his client's approval, he immediately phoned the wife at home. He explained that she should speak one-on-one with her husband, who still loved her and wanted to reconcile. Moved by the attorney's words, she agreed and told the lawyer to send her husband over to talk. The following day, the couple reconciled and the wife withdrew the petition for divorce.

Is the husband's lawyer subject to discipline for calling the wife?

(A)   The lawyer is not subject to discipline because his phone call was made in his client's best interest and with the client's approval.

(B)   The lawyer is not subject to discipline because the lawyer's conduct was reasonably calculated to advance his client's interest, and the wife assented to the phone call.

(C)   The lawyer is subject to discipline because he contacted the wife without first obtaining her lawyer's authorization.

(D)   The lawyer is subject to discipline because a lawyer may never directly contact an adverse party who is represented by counsel.

QUESTION 129

A woman was involved in a late-night car accident several months ago. Although neither she nor her 18-year-old son, who was in the car with her, was badly hurt, the driver of the other vehicle involved in the accident suffered a serious injury. The other driver then sued the woman, so she hired a lawyer to represent her. Although her son is likely to serve as a witness, he was not named as a defendant in the action. While the lawyer was interviewing the son to learn more about the accident, the son explained that he thought that the accident was his mother's fault. The son explained that he thinks his mother may have been falling asleep at the wheel. The lawyer asked the son not to volunteer that information to anyone else – especially the lawyer for the other driver – unless he is required to do so under oath.

Is the lawyer subject to professional discipline for his request to the son?

(A)   No, because the son is related to the lawyer's client.

(B)   Yes, because the son is not the lawyer's client.

(C)   Yes, because the other driver is entitled to know the truth.

(D)   No, because the son's communication is privileged.

QUESTION 130

A lawyer represents the owner of a bookstore in a contract dispute with the owner's former business partner. During the course of the proceedings, tensions have run high and the two parties, who were once close friends, have become bitter enemies. At two settlement conferences, the owner and his former partner almost engaged in fistfights, and all attempts to resolve the matter peacefully so far have failed. Because of the stress caused by the lawsuit, the owner's health and ability to manage his business have taken serious hits. Concerned for his client's health and well-being, the lawyer suggested that the owner offer his former partner an extremely generous settlement, cut his losses, and focus on fixing his business. The owner reluctantly agreed and the lawyer conveyed a substantial settlement offer to the former partner's attorney. The offer was ultimately rejected and the lawyer went to the bookstore to tell his client the bad news in person. The two spoke privately in the back office and, when the owner found out that his offer had been rejected, he became incensed. He removed a handgun from his desk drawer and said to the lawyer, "I'll show that jerk. This stays between you and me." The owner then fled the bookstore and sped off in his car.

Under the Model Rules of Professional Conduct, which of the following best describes how the owner's lawyer may proceed with regard to his client's statements and actions at the bookstore?

(A)   He may not contact the authorities.

(B)   He must contact the authorities.

(C)   He must seek permission from bar counsel before contacting the authorities.

(D)   He may contact the authorities.

QUESTION 131

The judge presiding over a civil jury trial invited the attorneys for the plaintiff and the defendant to her chambers to discuss an evidentiary issue outside of the jury's presence. While the judge and two lawyers were discussing the matter, the judge's clerk interrupted to tell the plaintiff's attorney that his client needed to speak with him urgently. When the plaintiff's attorney left (with the judge's permission), the defendant's attorney asked the judge if she would be amenable to taking a longer lunch break that day so that the attorney could appear before another judge in an unrelated matter. The judge said that she would agree, provided that it did not present a problem for the plaintiff's attorney. When the plaintiff's attorney returned to chambers, the judge told him that the defendant's attorney had asked for an extended lunch break to take care of another matter. The plaintiff's attorney objected to the request. Pursuant to state law, the court on which the judge sits permits lawyers to contact judges or their staff concerning scheduling issues without first contacting opposing counsel.

Are the defendant's attorney and/or the judge subject to discipline for having a discussion after the plaintiff's attorney left the room?

(A)   Only the attorney is subject to discipline because he initiated the ex parte communication.

(B)   Neither the attorney nor the judge is subject to discipline because their ex parte conversation was permissible.

(C)   Neither the attorney nor the judge is subject to discipline because their conversation was not actually ex parte.

(D)   Both the attorney and the judge are subject to discipline because ex parte communications are never permissible.

QUESTION 132

A lawyer represents a homeowner in an action against a neighbor. The homeowner has alleged that the resident has, for year after year, decorated his home with an inordinate number of holiday lights, causing him to lose sleep because of their brightness; the homeowner wants a court to enjoin the neighbor from continuing his garish light display, as well as damages. The homeowner's attorney called the neighbor to see about scheduling a settlement negotiation. When the neighbor answered the call, the attorney identified himself as the homeowner's representative, explained that he was hoping to set up a settlement conference and asked if the neighbor had retained a lawyer who the attorney could speak with. The neighbor explained that he had no interest in hiring an attorney, that the complaining homeowner had been harassing him for years, and that he was considering countersuing for harassment. The homeowner's attorney then advised the neighbor that he should consider obtaining a lawyer, but that, in his experience, the neighbor did not have a viable claim for harassment. Given the facts of the case, the attorney reasonably believed that the neighbor did not have a viable harassment claim.

Is the attorney subject to discipline for his interaction with the neighbor?

(A)   Yes, because he advised the neighbor about the merits of a possible harassment suit.

(B)   Yes, because he contacted the neighbor, who was not represented by counsel.

(C)   No, because the attorney reasonably believed that the neighbor's proposed countersuit lacked merit.

(D)   No, because the neighbor explained that he had no interest in hiring a lawyer.

QUESTION 133

A lawyer successfully represented a real estate developer in having a land parcel in a residential neighborhood re-zoned to accommodate the developer's proposed condominium. The re-zoning was the only matter the lawyer handled for the developer, and no other lawyer in his firm did any work for the developer. The condominium was completed several years ago, and a number of its residents have approached the lawyer about representing them in an action against the developer for defective construction.

Can the lawyer represent the condominium residents?

(A)   Yes, because the tenants' interests are not materially adverse to those of the real estate developer.

(B)   Yes, because the tenants' case is unrelated to the lawyer's work on the zoning issue.

(C)   No, because he has not obtained the developer's informed, written consent.

(D)   No, because the tenants' interests are materially adverse to those of the developer.

QUESTION 134

Following his arraignment on homicide charges, the defendant in a high-profile murder trial was released after posting a substantial bond. On the day jury selection was set to start, the defendant panicked and fled the state. When news got out that the defendant had fled, the prosecutor assigned to the case decided to hold a press conference. At the conference, the prosecutor declined to answer specific questions from members of the press. Reading a brief, pre-written statement, the prosecutor explained that police were investigating the defendant's whereabouts, that anyone with information about the defendant's location should contact the police, and that, because the defendant's flight was clear evidence of his guilt, anyone encountering the defendant should exercise caution.

Is the prosecutor subject to discipline for his press conference statement?

(A)   No, because he provided information concerning public safety.

(B)   No, because the prosecutor did not represent the defendant and had an adversarial role in the proceedings.

(C)   Yes, because he spoke publicly about an ongoing criminal proceeding.

(D)   Yes, because his statement was likely to prejudice potential jurors against the defendant.

QUESTION 135

A lawyer recently became a sole practitioner when his former partner split from their firm following a disagreement about the management of the practice. The former partner opened up his own firm, hired several associates, and had begun directly competing with the lawyer for clients. Hoping to build up his one-lawyer practice to stay competitive, the lawyer offered a job to a corporate attorney with a sizeable book of business. Still angry about the way he had been treated by his former partner, the lawyer included a provision in the corporate attorney's contract stating that, if the corporate attorney should leave the firm, she would not work for the former partner in any capacity.

Is the contract provision permissible?

(A)   Yes, because there are no restrictions on a law firm's ability to limit the professional conduct of its employees.

(B)   Yes, because the restriction on the corporate attorney's future practice is reasonably calculated to avoid an actual conflict of interest.

(C)   No, because it restricts the right of the corporate attorney to practice law.

(D)   No, because it was proposed by the employer, not the employee.

QUESTION 136

A judge is considering hiring his niece, a recent law school graduate, to serve as his clerk. His niece graduated at the top of her class, previously interned for a judge in the state in which she attended law school, and published a law review article while serving as articles editor on her school journal. Of the three hundred applications the judge has considered, she is among the three most qualified candidates.

Can the judge offer his niece the clerkship?

(A)   No, because she is a family member within the third degree of relationship.

(B)   Yes, because members of the judiciary have absolute control over administrative appointments.

(C)   Yes, because the judge's niece is an exceptionally qualified applicant.

(D)   No, because the judge could only hire her if she was the most qualified applicant.

QUESTION 137

A lawyer has decided to change the focus of his practice from family law to immigration and citizenship law. He has handled only one immigration case before, but has studied immigration and citizenship law extensively and is reasonably confident that he will be an effective immigration attorney. To drum up business, the lawyer places an advertisement in the local newspaper for his services. The ad contains the lawyer's name, office address, and phone number, and reads: "Specializes in Immigration and Citizenship Matters." No organization in the state in which the attorney practices certifies attorneys as "specialists" in legal subject matters.

Is the attorney subject to discipline for his advertisement?

(A)   Yes, because he may not indicate that he is a specialist if he has not been formally certified as a specialist.

(B)   Yes, because only attorneys practicing admiralty or patent law may identify themselves as specialists.

(C)   No, his advertisement is permissible.

(D)   Yes, because he has only handled one immigration case before.

QUESTION 138

A college fraternity wishes to recognize several of its prestigious alumni by hosting a free dinner in their honor. To ensure that there is enough space to accommodate everyone, the fraternity's president rents a dining hall at a fancy private club that opened recently. The fraternity has never conducted business with this club before. Unbeknownst to the fraternity's president, the club has an unwritten policy against African-Americans joining as members. Several members of the fraternity are African-Americans, as are some of the honorees who will be in attendance. Among the honorees invited to the dinner is a judge. The judge, who is white, is also unaware of the club's policy regarding African-Americans. He has never visited the club.

Will the judge violate the Code of Judicial Conduct by attending the dinner?

(A)	No, because the club is a private institution and it can therefore discriminate in accepting members.

(B)	No, because the dinner is an isolated event.

(C)	Yes, because the club discriminates on the basis of race.

(D)	Yes, because the judge has accepted the gift of a free dinner.

QUESTION 139

After a long, successful career, a sole practitioner passed away. His daughter was named the executrix of his estate, and the lawyer's will provided that his practice should be sold, if possible, so that the proceeds could be used to support his wife, who had always been a homemaker. The daughter, who was not a lawyer herself, arranged to sell her father's practice to a reputable local attorney. The purchasing attorney agreed not to raise the fees charged to the practice's existing clients. After all of the father's clients were properly notified of the proposed sale, the attorney paid the daughter, serving as the executrix, an agreed upon price for the practice. The daughter then gave the proceeds of the sale to her mother, as directed by the will. All of the father's clients agreed to keep their business with the purchasing attorney.

Was the sale of the deceased lawyer's practice proper?

(A)	No, because the attorney who purchased the firm entered into the transaction with the daughter, who was not an attorney.

(B)	No, because the proceeds of the sale went to a non-lawyer.

(C)	Yes, but only because all of the father's clients kept their business with the purchasing attorney.

(D)	Yes, regardless of whether the father's clients kept their business with the purchasing attorney.

QUESTION 140

A law firm in the city devotes part of its practice to the representation of corporations that own and manage rental apartments. In addition to his work with the law firm, an associate at the firm serves on the board of directors of the local legal aid organization, which provides free assistance to low-income individuals in a wide variety of civil matters, such as landlord-tenant disputes and employment discrimination suits. In fact, some of the organization's attorneys have represented clients in actions against the associate's corporate clients.

The legal aid organization has had its budget slashed recently and it cannot continue to devote its resources to a wide variety of cases. Another member of the board of directors has proposed that the organization seek to withdraw from representing its clients in current landlord-tenant disputes, which often require much of an attorney's time and which rarely have a broad impact on society. Some of the organization's clients are currently involved in landlord-tenant disputes with the associate's clients; the associate is aware of that fact. The board of directors is preparing to vote on the proposal.

Which of the following best describes the associate's obligations under the Model Rules of Professional Conduct?

(A)   The associate may continue to serve on the board of directors, but he may not participate in the vote.

(B)   The associate may continue to serve on the board of directors and he may participate in the vote.

(C)   The associate should resign from the board of directors and decline to participate in the vote.

(D)   The associate must report his participation with the legal aid organization to the state bar association because his participation violated the Rules of Professional Conduct.

QUESTION 141

One of a firm's named partners was elected to serve as the state's attorney general. By law, the attorney general may not hold private employment. The partner is a founder of the firm and has been a named partner since the firm's inception. If the firm changes its name, it will incur substantial costs in replacing all firm marketing materials, building signage, as well as a billboard in downtown.

Given the above facts, which of the following most accurately describes the obligations of the firm and its partners under the Model Rules of Professional Conduct?

(A)   The partner may not serve as a practicing attorney in any capacity while he is the attorney general, and his name must be removed from the firm's name as long as he remains a public official.

(B)   The partner may not continue to be a partner, but may serve as "of counsel" to the firm, while he is the attorney general, but his name must be removed from the firm's name.

(C)   The partner cannot continue to practice with the firm in any capacity while he is the attorney general, but his name can remain part of the firm's name because it is his legacy.

(D)   The partner may continue to practice with the firm, and the partner's name may remain in the firm's name.

QUESTION 142

An attorney represents a client, a defendant, involved in litigation concerning a construction dispute. The client is a builder with a good business reputation throughout the state. The client has been sued by a customer who alleges that the home builder defectively constructed a gazebo in the customer's backyard. The gazebo collapsed under the weight of four children. One of the children, the customer's son, was severely injured.

The attorney hires a recent graduate of a prestigious local paralegal training educational program. The paralegal graduated as the valedictorian of the most recent class. The attorney prepared an answer to the complaint and directed the paralegal to file the answer on the day it was due. The paralegal negligently failed to file the answer.

The court enters a default judgment in favor of the plaintiff as a result of the failure to timely file an answer.

Which of the following correctly states the attorney's professional responsibility?

(A)   The attorney is subject to discipline on the theory of respondeat superior.

(B)   The attorney is subject to discipline if the attorney failed to adequately supervise the legal assistant.

(C)   The attorney is not subject to discipline because an attorney is not responsible for the negligence of a non-attorney.

(D)   The attorney is not subject to discipline if the attorney personally was not negligent.

QUESTION 143

An attorney noted for her expertise in First Amendment law has been asked by a federal appellate court to represent an indigent litigant in a civil appeal presenting complicated free speech issues. The attorney, who is listed on a register of lawyers willing to accept pro bono appointments in federal criminal and civil cases, is the most qualified attorney on the list to handle the matter, though there are certainly other competent attorneys available. The appeal involves the litigant's right to publicly promote the ideas of a group that vehemently opposes religious minorities. The lawyer is a member of such a religious minority and, although she has never personally faced problems because of her religious affiliation, she grew up hearing stories of her grandmother's escape from religious persecution, and she cannot bear the thought of representing someone who would endorse the kind of suffering her grandmother endured.

Which of the following best describes the attorney's responsibilities under the Model Rules of

Professional Conduct?

(A)   She must accept the representation because she is presumed competent to handle the matter.

(B)   She may seek to decline the representation because representing an unpopular client will create an unreasonable financial burden.

(C)   She may seek to decline the representation because she strongly opposes the litigant's views.

(D)   She must accept the appointment because the court requires her expertise in the subject matter of this case.

QUESTION 144

A lawyer maintains a trust account at the local bank for one of his clients. Because the amount held in trust is fairly small, the bank imposes a monthly service charge of $1.99. To ensure that the service charge is covered, the lawyer deposits money from his operating account into the client trust account each month. Out of an abundance of caution, the lawyer makes each monthly deposit in the amount of $2.99. By doing so, the lawyer makes sure that the service charge never eats into the client funds held in trust. The lawyer always keeps detailed records related to his deposits to the client trust account.

Is the lawyer subject to discipline for the way he manages his client trust account?

(A)   Yes, because he deposits more of his money in the trust account than is needed to pay the maintenance fee.

(B)   Yes, because it is never permissible to mix a lawyer's money with client trust money.

(C)   No, because the deposits from the lawyer's own account exceed the maintenance fee, thereby protecting the client's entrusted funds.

(D)   No, because the lawyer maintains properly detailed records identifying which funds in the client trust account are his.

QUESTION 145

A lawyer is being paid by a businessman to represent the businessman's son in divorce proceedings. The son has given informed consent to his father's payment of the lawyer. The businessman is concerned that his son's estranged wife will take advantage of the son's generous nature, and he is especially concerned that the son will give up several valuable family heirlooms to secure an amicable divorce, but will ultimately regret such a decision. At the businessman's request, the lawyer agrees to terminate any settlement negotiations if it appears that the son is likely to give his wife any of the family heirlooms. The lawyer informs the son of his agreement with the businessman. The son explains that his only concern is making sure that his marriage ends as peacefully as possible.

Can the lawyer honor his agreement with the businessman?

(A)   Yes, because the businessman is paying for the attorney's services.

(B)   Yes, because the businessman's request is reasonably intended to benefit his son.

(C)   No, because the lawyer has agreed to an improper contingency fee.

(D)   No, because the agreement limits the lawyer's ability to exercise his own judgment.

QUESTION 146

A young man, down on his luck, has been charged with trying to cash bad checks, a criminal offense. Although he is financially eligible for court-appointed counsel, the young man does not believe a public defender will adequately represent him, so he contacts a private attorney. He explains to the attorney that he was recently laid off from work and that he only passed the bad checks because he was destitute and needed to find a way to keep food on his table without drawing on the small amount of money he has saved. The attorney feels bad for the young man, but she is facing tough times herself, as she has had trouble finding new clients. To achieve a balance in their interests, the attorney cuts the young man a deal: she will represent him for her usual fee, which amounts to a substantial portion of the young man's savings, but will only collect the fee if the young man is acquitted of the criminal charges.

Is the attorney's proposed fee agreement permissible?

(A)   No, because it is a contingent fee.

(B)   Yes, because the fee is reasonable under the circumstances.

(C)   Yes, because the young man will not have to pay if he is convicted.

(D)   No. The attorney must take on the young man's case *pro bono* because he is an indigent defendant.

QUESTION 147

Over the past several years, two friends – a tax attorney and an accountant – have worked out a beneficial arrangement. In exchange for the accountant referring legal matters to the tax attorney, the tax attorney refers business to the accountant. The accountant refers his clients to the tax attorney and other attorneys with whom he has a professional relationship. The tax attorney knows a number of good accountants, and he tries to distribute his referrals evenly among them. The attorney has decided that he doesn't want clients to think that he is only referring business to this particular accountant simply on the basis of their friendship, but rather because the accountant is good at his job. Accordingly, the tax attorney intentionally conceals the fact that they there are friends from clients that he refers to the accountant, though he does explain that they have a practice of referring clients to one another.

Is the tax attorney subject to discipline for his referral agreement with the accountant?

(A)   Yes, because he does not disclose his friendship with the accountant to clients he refers to the accountant.

(B)   No, even though he does not disclose his friendship with the accountant.

(C)   No, because there is no restriction on reciprocal referral agreements between lawyers and non-lawyers.

(D)   Yes, because the attorney can only enter into a reciprocal referral agreement if it is exclusive.

QUESTION 148

An attorney represents a business owner being sued by a former employee for gender discrimination. The former employee is represented by a lawyer, but is not happy with the lawyer's failure so far to make progress in the case. Frustrated, the former employee calls the business owner's attorney and informs him that she is tired of waiting for her lawyer to take action and will settle her case for $10,000 – far less than she requested in her civil complaint. The business owner's lawyer tells the former employee that he will relay her offer to his client.

Which of the following correctly states the responsibility of the business owner's lawyer under the Model Rules of Professional Conduct?

(A)   The business owner's lawyer is subject to discipline because he did not alert the former employee to the significant difference between her settlement offer and the amount requested in her complaint.

(B)   The business owner's lawyer is subject to discipline because he agreed to convey the former employee's offer to his client.

(C)   The business owner's lawyer is not subject to discipline because the former employee initiated the phone call.

(D)   The business owner's lawyer is not subject to discipline because he did not give the former employee any legal advice.

QUESTION 149

Several members of a family suffered serious injuries in a car accident due to a design flaw in their vehicle. They obtained the help of a lawyer, who has managed to make a very strong case on their behalf against the auto manufacturer. The lawyer has proven very skilled and was able to uncover information about the car's design process that, if revealed at trial, would certainly score a victory for his clients and probably expose the auto manufacturer to significant liability in other cases. To help avert a disaster, the attorneys for the auto manufacturer have presented the family with an extraordinarily high settlement offer. In exchange, the manufacturer insists that the damaging information be kept confidential and that, given his unique knowledge of the case, the family's lawyer may not thereafter represent plaintiffs alleging design defects in the car model at issue.

Which of the following best explains the obligations of the family's lawyer under the Model Rules of Professional Conduct?

(A)   The lawyer may agree to the proposed settlement because he has managed to obtain an unexpectedly high settlement offer, which is in his clients' best interests.

(B)   The lawyer may agree to the proposed settlement because it is functionally equivalent to a victory for his clients at trial.

(C)   The lawyer may not agree to the proposed settlement because it would be unethical to do so if the family is certain to win at trial.

(D)   The lawyer may not agree to the proposed settlement because it restricts his ability to represent other plaintiffs raising similar claims.

QUESTION 150

A young attorney wishes to open his own for-profit law practice, but he has substantial law school debt and cannot afford the startup costs on his own. His father, an accountant, offers to loan the attorney the money he needs. The father will not be a partner in the firm. However, the father is concerned that if the attorney takes any client who walks through the door, less scrupulous clients will fail to pay after legal services are rendered, and neither the attorney nor his father will see the money they are owed. To help insure his investment, the father insists on having veto authority over clients for the attorney's first six months of practice. If it appears to the father that a potential client is unlikely to pay agreed-upon fees after services are rendered, the attorney must decline the representation. According to the agreement, however, the father unequivocally gives up any such "veto" authority after six months have passed.

Is the attorney's agreement with his father permissible under the rules governing professional responsibility of lawyers?

(A)   Yes, because the father does not own a financial interest in the firm.

(B)   No, because the father can dictate which representation the attorney takes on.

(C)   Yes, because the father's "veto power" expires after a definite period.

(D)   No, because the father and his son have not formed a partnership.

QUESTION 151

During a contentious negotiation over a franchise agreement, the franchisor concludes that he would rather lose the potential contract than deal with the franchisee's attorney in subsequent matters. The franchisor agrees to each and every demand made by the franchisee plus offers to reduce monthly franchise payments by 15%. The franchisor makes only one non-negotiable demand on the franchisee. The franchisor demands that the franchisee never engage the same lawyer in any subsequent matter that arises between the parties. The lawyer has represented many prior franchisee's in negotiations with the company. The client wants to accept the offer.

The lawyer informs the client that the offer is better than any offer previously negotiated by the franchisee's lawyer. The lawyer concedes that the deal is in the client's best interest and recommends that the client accept the offer.

The lawyer's recommendation:

(A)   is in the client's best interest and, therefore, does not violate the Code.

(B)   violates the Code by restricting the lawyer's right to practice.

(C)   does not violate the Code because the agreement was fairly negotiated and the franchisee was adequately represented by his lawyer.

(D)   violated the Code by setting up a conflict of interest between the franchisee and his attorney.

QUESTION 152

An inventor develops a revolutionary new blender and asks a lawyer to file a patent application for it. The lawyer is very impressed by the blender. The lawyer inquires whether the inventor would be willing to share 15% of the first year's profits in exchange for legal fees and expenses. The inventor agrees and the attorney drafts a fee agreement setting forth the appropriate fee percentage. Both parties sign the writing. The lawyer, unsure of the expenses involved in filing a patent, indicates that the parties would negotiate those expenses at a later date.

The contingency fee agreement is:

(A)   allowed as it sets forth a known percentage to be paid by the inventor in exchange for legal fees.

(B)   allowed as this is neither a criminal nor domestic relations case.

(C)   not allowed as the writing fails to address the issue of how expenses will be calculated.

(D)   not allowed as the lawyer should have advised the inventor to be represented by independent counsel in negotiations with the lawyer.

QUESTION 153

A builder is excavating the sole remaining lot in a 110-house residential development when he discovers dozens of small drums labeled "hazardous chemical material" buried in the ground. The builder quickly covers the drums with the original soil and posts the site for sale.

When the builder purchased the property several year earlier, the seller provided a written disclosure statement that provided that the seller was unaware of any hazardous material on the property. The builder has attempted to locate the seller, but the seller cannot be located.

The builder retains an attorney. The builder informs the lawyer of the finding and tells the lawyer that the builder simply wants to be rid of the property. The lawyer strongly urges the builder to notify the authorities of the hazard and to take the necessary steps to clean the property. The builder refuses, citing lack of time and money to address the problem.

A local family shows interest in purchasing the lot and building their dream home. The lawyer researches the situation regarding the drums and learns that these types of drums are an imminent health hazard. The lawyer learns that buried hazardous chemical material has been implicated in hundreds of deaths nationwide.

The lawyer:

(A)   can reveal information about the hazardous material to relevant authorities to the extent the lawyer reasonably believes necessary to prevent reasonably certain death or substantial bodily harm.

(B)   can anonymously reveal information to relevant authorities about the possibility of a chemical hazard existing on the property but may not disclose anything further.

(C)   cannot reveal any information he learns from a client where such disclosure may harm the client or the client's interests.

(D)   must maintain the attorney-client confidentiality until such time as the client is charged with a criminal offense.

QUESTION 154

A recently licensed attorney wanted to open a solo firm that specialized in commercial real estate development. Hoping to create a "one stop shop" for all of the potential clients' needs, the attorney approached an architect friend, and created a partnership that offered both design and legal services. In the first three months of operation, the attorney assisted two clients in preparing the legal documents necessary to secure financing, while the architect worked only on the architectural design of the two commercial buildings. The attorney and the architect shared an office suite, but their offices and work product remained completely separate.

Is the attorney subject to discipline?

(A)   No, because the partnership entity shields the attorney from discipline.

(B)   No, because the attorney and the architect kept their work product separate.

(C)   Yes, because half of the services offered by the partnership were legal services.

(D)   Yes, because the attorney and the architect shared an office suite.

QUESTION 155

A real estate developer approached an attorney who primarily practices in State A and asked him to assist him in closing a multimillion dollar apartment complex deal in State (B) The attorney had represented the developer on a number of occasions in such transactions, and although he was licensed to practice in both states, he was not as familiar with the laws of State (B) The developer informed the attorney that he was prepared to pay $20,000 for the attorney's services. The attorney agreed to represent the developer for that fee; however, he told the developer that he was unwilling to prepare the attorney's opinion required by the lender without a local counsel opinion upon which to rely. The developer, understanding that he would have to find separate counsel to prepare the opinion, signed a written agreement for representation with the attorney.

Is the attorney subject to disciplinary action?

(A)   No, because the $20,000 fee was insufficient to cover the cost of the entire transaction.

(B)   No, because the limitation was reasonable, and the developer gave informed consent.

(C)   Yes, because the attorney cannot agree to limit the amount of fees to which he is entitled in such a complex transaction.

(D)   Yes, because refusing to write the opinion without local counsel opinion was unreasonable since the attorney was licensed in both states.

QUESTION 156

An attorney placed a series of late night television ads promoting his services as a tax attorney, specifically relating to settlements with the IRS. Two days after the first series of ads ran, a woman entered the attorney's office seeking assistance with reducing a $40,000 debt to the IRS. The attorney and the woman discussed the woman's situation for 45 minutes, after which the attorney declined to represent the woman. The attorney informed her that he did not feel that he was competent to handle such a complicated case, but he provided the woman with the names of several very qualified tax attorneys and told her that she would need to seek the advice from one of them within one year or she would be unable to challenge due to the running of the statute of limitations.

Would the attorney be subject to discipline when he declined to represent the woman once he consulted with her for 45 minutes?

(A)   Yes, because he now is in possession of confidential client information.

(B)   Yes, because his advertisements obligated him to represent potential clients who responded.

(C)   No, because the woman did not have a reasonable expectation of forming an attorney-client relationship.

(D)   No, because the attorney performed duties beyond those owed to the woman.

QUESTION 157

A long-time client entered his attorney's office and asked her to hold a sales contract in trust to be delivered to the buyer when directed by the client. The contract was for the sale of a large parcel of commercially zoned property owned by a partnership, and the client was the general partner. The attorney noticed that the signatures of the other two partners appeared to have been written by the same person, and the client admitted that he had asked his wife to sign for the other two partners. The attorney suggested that the client reprint the signature pages, have two different individuals sign for the partners, and fax the signature pages in so that it would be more difficult for someone to determine whether the signatures were genuine.

After thinking about the attorney's advice, the client decided to get the other partners to sign the document and gave the legally executed document to the attorney. When the client directed, the attorney delivered the document to the buyer.

Could any of the attorney's actions subject her to discipline?

(A)   Yes, the suggestion to use two different signatories and to fax the signature pages.

(B)   Yes, the delivery of the executed document to the buyer.

(C)   No, the attorney delivered a valid document to the buyer.

(D)   No, the attorney was merely discussing the legal consequences of the client's actions.

QUESTION 158

An attorney had been involved in a contentious contract dispute between a contractor and a subcontractor. The subcontractor, the attorney's client, claimed that it was owed $40,000 under the contract for work completed ahead of schedule, but the contractor maintained that the contract clearly stated that the subcontractor was only entitled to a flat payment, regardless of when the work was completed. The parties and their attorneys had tried several rounds of settlement negotiations but had yet to reach an agreement. On the eve of the trial, the contractor called the attorney and said that he was willing to settle the dispute for the full amount the subcontractor claimed plus attorney's fees to avoid what was sure to be a highly public and damaging trial. The attorney, who had previously received full authority from his client to settle, accepted the contractor's settlement offer and drafted a settlement agreement to present for the parties' signatures.

Was it appropriate for the attorney to accept the contractor's settlement offer?

(A)   No, because the offer was made under the imminent threat of litigation and therefore was not voluntary.

(B)   No, because the contractor's attorney was not on the phone when the offer was made.

(C)   Yes, because the contractor initiated the conversation.

(D)   Yes, because the settlement terms were in his client's best interest.

QUESTION 159

An attorney was retained by a professional football player to represent him in negotiating his upcoming contract with his current team. During the off season, the player had elective surgery on his knee to correct a nagging injury, and although he was participating in private practices, his doctor was not certain that the player would regain his full skill level or be able to play for much longer. The team was aware of the surgery, and during the negotiations, the team representatives expressed concern about the impact of the knee injury on the player's longevity. The attorney told the representatives that there was no need for concern because his client was showing in private practices that his knee had fully healed during the off season and doctors believed that he would be able to play for another five to ten years. The team, reassured by the attorney's statements, agreed to sign the player to a five year, fifty-million-dollar contract.

Was the attorney's conduct during the negotiations appropriate?

(A)   Yes, because he has a duty to obtain the best possible contract for his client.

(B)   Yes, because puffery is permitted in the course of negotiations.

(C)   No, because the attorney should have disclosed the doctor's assessment to avoid a fraudulent act by his client.

(D)   No, because the attorney lied to the team representatives about the doctor's assessment.

QUESTION 160

A client approached her attorney to help negotiate the sale of three one of a kind guitars. The client had already placed an advertisement in a trade paper and had been contacted by several prospective buyers. She told the attorney that the guitars could either be sold as a set or individually, as long as the prices met or exceeded the reserve that the client had set. After a few days of negotiations, the attorney presented the client with offers from three buyers to each buy a guitar at amounts exceeding the reserve. The client accepted the offers, instructed the attorney to proceed with the sales, and headed out for a week-long vacation without any instructions as to what to do after the sales were completed.

The first two buyers came to the attorney's office the following day and completed the sales. The attorney accepted the payments for the guitars and placed them in a trust account for the client. The attorney did not want to disturb the client's vacation and so did not call to let her know the sales were completed. After the third buyer came by a week later, the attorney contacted the client who came to retrieve the sale proceeds.

Were the attorney's actions appropriate?

(A)   Yes. The attorney communicated the offers to the client before accepting.

(B)   Yes. The attorney insured that the funds were held in a trust account for the client.

(C)   No. The client should have been present for the negotiations.

(D)   No. The attorney did not notify the client when the first two sales were complete.

QUESTION 161

An insurance defense attorney and employment law attorney practice as a professional corporation. The practice has been struggling for several years. The attorneys agree that they must place a national advertisement on television in order to obtain more clients. The national television advertisement is expensive and the attorneys do not have the money to place the ads. The employment law attorney has a wealthy parent who offers to provide the funds required for the advertisement. In order to protect the sizeable investment, the parent requires to be provided with an ownership interest in the professional corporation. The attorneys agree to the arrangement under two conditions. First, the attorneys have the right to repurchase the ownership interest from the parent on demand at a predetermined price. Second, the parent has no right to direct or control the professional judgment of the attorneys. The parent agrees.

Will the attorneys be subject to discipline for entering into this arrangement?

(A)   No, because the parent does not have the right to direct or control the professional judgment of the attorneys.

(B)   No, because the parent is not an officer of the professional corporation.

(C)   Yes, because the parent would own an interest in the professional corporation.

(D)   Yes, because the parent is related to one of the attorneys within two degrees of kinship.

QUESTION 162

A couple decided to end their marriage after twenty years, and the wife hired her best friend from law school, who was a family law attorney, to represent her in the divorce. The husband initially opted to proceed pro se in an attempt to save money. The wife's friend felt that the husband would be at a very serious disadvantage in the divorce without representation, and after disclosing that she would be working only for the wife, she advised him to seek an attorney before the proceedings moved forward. The husband heeded the advice and hired an attorney, which enabled him to reach an amicable settlement with the wife.

Would the wife's friend be subject to discipline?

(A)   No, because she disclosed to the husband that she would only be representing the wife.

(B)   No, because the husband hired an attorney and reached a positive settlement.

(C)   Yes, because she provided advice to an unrepresented party.

(D)   Yes, because the husband might misunderstand the wife's friend's role in the divorce proceedings.

QUESTION 163

A criminal defense attorney was hired to represent a defendant in a capital murder trial. The prosecution has turned over all of the relevant evidence, and without information from the defendant, the situation looked bleak. The defense attorney believes that the defendant is taking a fall for a friend, and he met with the defendant on numerous occasions where he repeatedly asked her to provide him with the name of the friend or other information that would help to clear her name. The defendant, though, has repeatedly refused to provide any information and in fact, through her random statements to others, had made it unreasonably difficult for the defense attorney to continue the representation.

In light of the difficulty he was facing, the defense attorney notified the defendant that he was going to seek the court's permission to withdraw from the representation. The court, after hearing the defense attorney's justification for the withdrawal, denied the request.

May the defense attorney nonetheless withdraw from the representation?

(A)   Yes, because the defendant's actions have made it unreasonably difficult to continue the representation.

(B)   Yes, because the defense attorney has a moral objection to the defendant covering for a friend.

(C)   No, because the defense attorney could still represent the defendant despite her obstructive behavior.

(D)   No, because the court denied the defense attorney's request to withdraw.

QUESTION 164

A new associate was working late at a midsized firm when a phone call came through from a client who was seeking to purchase a parcel of property from a landowner who was heading out of the country the next day for an extended vacation. The associate had never handled a real estate transaction. Even though one of the senior real estate partners was down the hall, the associate wanted to make a positive impression on the partners by handling the transaction by himself. Without telling the client about his lack of knowledge, the associate contacted the landowner and negotiated the sale. Both parties came into the office, and the landowner provided the client a duly executed, valid warranty deed that the associate sent for recording the following morning.

Is the associate subject to discipline?

(A)   No, because the landowner leaving the country the following day constituted an emergency.

(B)   No, because the transaction occurred without any issues.

(C)   Yes, because he did not disclose his lack of experience with real estate transactions.

(D)   Yes, because the associate could have consulted with the senior real estate partner before negotiating the sale.

QUESTION 165

Two young women were apprehended for selling narcotics to an undercover officer. The women hired the same attorney to represent each of them in the matter. The attorney met with the district attorney to discuss the case, and the district attorney suggested that the women might consider pleading guilty to receive two years' probation. If either of the women refused to plead guilty, then the plea offer would be revoked, and the women would each face 3 years in prison. The attorney relayed the offer to each of the women, but purposefully withheld the condition that both women accept the deal. One woman was willing to enter a guilty plea, but the other refused, and because of the second woman's refusal to plead guilty, the district attorney withdrew the offer.

Is the attorney subject to discipline?

(A)   No, because he conveyed the plea offer to both women.

(B)   No, because the women had the ultimate say in whether to accept the plea offer.

(C)   Yes, because the attorney was willing to accept a plea for his clients that required both clients to consent.

(D)   Yes, because the attorney did not tell the women the full conditions of the plea offer.

QUESTION 166

An attorney was representing a nursing home in a wrongful death suit. A recently deceased resident suffered serious injuries when the door to her room fell off of the hinges and knocked her down. The nursing home responded quickly to the injuries, but the resident never recovered and passed away three days later. In the suit, the resident's family alleged that the nursing home failed to properly maintain the facility and that the failure led directly to the resident's death.

The attorney learned through discussions with the head nurse that a relative of the resident's roommate witnessed the maintenance staff working on the door the day it fell. The relative said that the staff only put in two of the six screws that normally secured the door to the frame, and the two screws were not fully tightened. The head nurse said that the plaintiff's attorney did not know about the relative's story. The attorney asked the head nurse to approach the relative and request that the relative not tell the plaintiff's attorney about what he saw that day.

Is the attorney subject to discipline?

(A)   Yes, because an attorney may never request that a person withhold information from another attorney.

(B)   Yes, because the witness was not an employee of the nursing home.

(C)   No, because the witness was a relative of the roommate.

(D)   No, because the attorney did not personally approach the relative.

QUESTION 167

An attorney at a small boutique tax firm sat down with a new client prior to beginning representation and explained the process that he would take to help resolve the client's dispute with the tax authority. The attorney explained that because he worked in a small firm, it was not unusual for the attorneys to discuss cases amongst themselves in order to pool their resources; however, the attorney explained that it was up to the client to determine whether or not the attorney could do so. The client, who had previously worked with another attorney at the firm on another matter, mulled over the proposition and decided that he had no problem with the attorney disclosing the information to any of the attorneys in the firm but his former counsel. The client signed a consent form that memorialized that agreement.

As the attorney worked through the client's case, he frequently discussed the facts with other attorneys in the office. Because the client's former counsel was an expert in the area, the attorney met with her on several occasions to discuss the client's case. After building a compelling case with the assistance of the former counsel, the attorney reached a favorable outcome for his client.

Is the attorney subject to discipline?

(A)   No, because conferring with the former counsel was instrumental in the positive outcome of the case.

(B)   No, because the former counsel was a member of the attorney's firm.

(C)   Yes, because the client could not consent to disclosure of confidential information to other attorneys.

(D)   Yes, because the client expressly told the attorney to not disclose information to the former counsel.

QUESTION 168

An attorney worked for a small boutique firm that worked exclusively on family law matters. He was hired by a husband to represent the husband in a contentious divorce proceeding. The wife had hired a large firm attorney to represent her. Because of the combative nature of the parties involved, the divorce dragged on for many months, and the attorneys spent hundreds of hours in negotiations both in person and on the phone. The large firm attorney quickly realized the skill of the boutique attorney and suggested to the hiring partner that the firm could benefit from the boutique attorney's expertise. The hiring partner, respecting her colleague's opinion, contacted the boutique attorney about possibly joining the larger firm. The boutique attorney expressed an interest in the employment, and, unbeknownst to the husband, began negotiating for the lateral hire. The boutique attorney was ultimately able to negotiate for a divorce settlement that was very favorable to the husband and thereafter began working for the large firm.

Is the boutique attorney subject to discipline?

(A)   No, because the boutique attorney was able to competently represent his client.

(B)   No, because the boutique attorney was only representing the husband.

(C)   Yes, because he had a duty to the husband as a former client to refrain from working for the firm that represented the wife.

(D)   Yes, because the large firm was representing the wife in the divorce proceeding.

QUESTION 169

An attorney, who was licensed in State A, was retained as outside counsel for a corporation that was organized in State A and occasionally transacted business in surrounding states. Generally, the attorney's work consisted of negotiating contracts and representing the corporation in court in State A; however, on one occasion, he was asked to represent the corporation in court in State B because of his intimate knowledge of a particular transaction. Before appearing in court, the attorney petitioned the State B Supreme Court to permit him to represent the corporation, and his petition was granted. The attorney successfully defended the corporation.

Is the attorney subject to discipline in either state?

(A)   No, because he was providing legal services to a corporation that had business connections in more than one state.

(B)   No, because he received permission to represent the corporation from the Supreme Court.

(C)   Yes, because he was required to petition State A as well prior to commencing his representation.

(D)   Yes, because was not licensed in State B when he appeared in court.

QUESTION 170

A respected attorney in the local community was friends with an attorney who was running for district attorney. A student reporter from the high school newspaper was assigned to cover the election and asked the attorney if she could interview him about the candidates. During the course of the interview, the student reporter asked the attorney if he felt that his friend was qualified to be district attorney since the friend's only legal experience was in real estate. The attorney said that he had watched his friend during several intense negotiations and honestly felt that his friend's significant negotiation skills would translate well into litigation. The student reporter published the remarks in the school paper, and because the story was so well written, the local newspaper reprinted it.

Will the attorney be subject to discipline for his remarks?

(A)   Yes, because the attorney should not have expressed an opinion about a candidate for election.

(B)   Yes, because the story was reprinted in the local newspaper and distributed to a wider audience.

(C)   No, because the attorney expressed his honest belief based on his own observations.

(D)   No, because the statements were about his friend and not the opponent.

QUESTION 171

The chief justice of State A's Supreme Court had the power to appoint bailiffs as necessary for her court and the appellate courts. Although it was highly unusual for two different panels of judges to be in session at the same time, the chief justice appointed a full-time bailiff for each court room and each panel. These appointments resulted in several bailiffs who only worked sporadically.

Was the chief justice's decision appropriate?

(A)   No, because appointing a bailiff for each court displays favoritism for these courts over other courts.

(B)   No, because the appointments were unnecessary given the caseload for the courts.

(C)   Yes, because the chief justice had the power to appoint as she saw fit.

(D)   Yes, because the appointments assured that there would always be an available bailiff.

QUESTION 172

An elderly client hired an attorney to draft a will providing for the disposition of the client's estate. As the attorney was preparing the will, she realized that the elderly client was in need of liquidity to pay immediate expenses. She also noticed that the client owned several thousand shares of a very popular and valuable company. Quickly seeing a means to benefit both herself and her client, the attorney prepared a written offer to the client disclosing that she would be willing to purchase the shares for ninety five percent of their current market value, a reasonable offer. The written offer explained that the attorney would not be representing the client but rather would be operating as a private purchaser, and advised that it would be in the client's best interest to ask another attorney for advice. The attorney gave the client twenty-four hours to accept or decline the offer, but the time was not sufficient for the client to meet with another attorney. The next day, the client returned to the attorney's office, signed a document that reiterated the contents of the offer and provided consent to the attorney's role in the transaction, and accepted the offer.

Is the attorney subject to discipline?

(A)   No, because the attorney advised the client to seek the advice of another attorney.

(B)   No, because the offer was reasonable.

(C)   No, because the client provided signed, written informed consent.

(D)   Yes, because twenty four hours was not sufficient time to confer with another attorney.

QUESTION 173

A small business owner had recently fired an elderly employee, allegedly for repeated violations of the employment policies, and replaced her with a much younger employee at a considerably lower salary. The elderly employee believed that the true reason she was fired was her age, and she hired an attorney to represent her in an employment discrimination complaint with a federal agency. The business owner was unsophisticated and overconfident in the merits of her defenses and refused to spend money she did not have on a lawyer.

After filing the charge with the agency, the employee's attorney contacted the business owner without the agency's consent. The attorney identified himself by name and as a person interested in the employee's discrimination case. The attorney further indicated that he was conducting a routine preliminary investigation into the employee's claims and asked for a candid explanation of the business owner's side of the story. The business owner explained that she needed someone younger who could lift the products. Based on the business owner's statement, the attorney moved for summary judgment.

Is the attorney subject to discipline?

(A)   Yes, because on the face there was no basis for the employee's claim.

(B)   Yes, because the attorney did not disclose that he was representing the employee.

(C)   No, because the business owner voluntarily provided the information.

(D)   No, because the information the business owner provided would have been discovered as the case progressed.

QUESTION 174

An attorney was working on a particularly difficult intellectual property case involving a complex medicinal compound. Although the attorney had been practicing in this area of the law for over fifteen years, he found himself confounded by several aspects of the case. The attorney had a friend who was an experienced intellectual property attorney who worked at a different firm. The attorney met with the friend for dinner on several occasions throughout the course of the case, and they discussed minute details of the compound at the center of the case as well as specific information about the client's business model. The friend signed a confidentiality agreement with the attorney wherein she agreed to refrain from disclosing the information from the meetings to anyone else. The client, a large pharmaceutical corporation, was unaware of the meetings between the attorney and his friend.

Will the attorney be subject to discipline?

(A)   Yes, because the friend worked at a different firm.

(B)   No, because the meetings were for the purposes of representing the client.

(C)   No, because the friend signed a confidentiality agreement.

(D)   No, because the friend was experienced in the field and therefore competent.

QUESTION 175

Three college friends decided to open a sandwich shop. They form a member-managed LLC to own and operate the business. The LLC operating agreement, which all three friends sign, states that the profits of the LLC will be divided equally. It also provides that all disputes relating to the rights and responsibilities of the members would be decided by a court of competent jurisdiction, and that the prevailing party or parties would be entitled to recover attorney's fees from the other party or parties.

In the third year of the venture, the working member who is responsible for the daily operations of the sandwich shop asks the other two members to reconsider the profit distribution to give a larger share to him to compensate him for his efforts. The other two passive members, who are enjoying the windfall without the work, immediately refuse his suggestion.

The working member hires a solo practitioner attorney to represent him in a lawsuit to force the change. Remarkably, the court sides with the working member, and orders the LLC to amend its operating agreement.

As the prevailing party, the working member is awarded attorney's fees. The losing members dispute the amount of fees charged by the solo practitioner. The only option for establishing the validity of the fees is for the solo practitioner to testify about the work that she completed on the case. The other members do not object to the solo practitioner's testimony.

Would it be proper for the solo practitioner to continue to represent the working member?

(A)   Yes, because there were no objections to the testimony.

(B)   Yes, because the solo practitioner is testifying about legal services.

(C)   No, because the solo practitioner's testimony is necessary.

(D)   No, because the other members are disputing the amount of the fees.

QUESTION 176

A congressional committee was investigating alleged shipments of goods to a country in which such shipments were banned. The CEO of a large multinational supplier was subpoenaed to testify before the committee regarding his company's role in the shipments. Because of the serious nature of the hearing and the allegations involved, the CEO requested that the company's in-house counsel assist him in preparing for the hearing and to accompany him to the hearing. At the hearing, the CEO and the counsel both provided their names to the congressmen, and the counsel informed the committee on the record that he was there in his capacity as a representative of the CEO. During the testimony, the CEO frequently conferred with the counsel regarding his responses, and on several occasions, the counsel advised the CEO to refrain from answering the question on the ground that the answer would be self-incriminating.

Is the in-house counsel subject to discipline?

(A)   No, because he informed the committee that he was representing the CEO.

(B)   No, because the CEO acted within his rights by bringing his counsel to the hearing.

(C)   Yes, because the counsel cannot accept a fee for trying to influence a legislative committee.

(D)   Yes, because the counsel advised the CEO to refrain from answering questions from the committee.

QUESTION 177

An employee named his employer in a sexual harassment suit against his supervisor. The employee, who was the only male employee in his department, alleged that his supervisor had created a hostile work environment by making lewd comments during staff meetings. The employer vigorously denied any liability, and its general counsel prepared to represent the employer in what promised to be a difficult jury trial.

During the first day of jury selection, the judge called for a thirty-minute lunch break, and the general counsel went to a nearby café to eat. While he was standing in line, a woman in line behind him whom he recognized to be member of the jury pool introduced herself and asked him how he thought a local high school football team would fair in the Friday match-up with its rival. The general counsel responded that he thought the other team would win, and the two of them began a vigorous debate. Another prospective juror overheard the conversation, and upon returning to the courthouse, told the judge that she had seen them talking.

Is the general counsel subject to discipline?

(A)   No, because the general counsel did not begin the conversation.

(B)   No, because the conversation did not involve the facts or merits of the case at hand.

(C)   Yes, he did not leave the café when he noticed the prospective juror.

(D)   Yes, because the general counsel spoke with the prospective juror without first notifying the other attorneys.

QUESTION 178

A client approached his attorney to prepare a simple last will. The client's goal, which he expressed to the attorney, was to provide for the most favorable tax treatment for the distribution of the estate. The attorney had prepared many simple wills during his career and was fully competent to prepare the client's requested will; however the attorney told the client that he was not comfortable with tax issues.

After discussing the client's estate and wishes, but without entering into a formal written agreement, the attorney prepared the will but did not expressly address the tax concerns. Because the will was so easy to draft, the attorney orally agreed to waive his customary preparation fee.

What is the most likely ground for discipline?

(A)   The attorney prepared a will without being an expert in tax law.

(B)   The attorney did not get the client's express consent to not address the tax issues.

(C)   An attorney is not permitted to limit any duties to the client.

(D)   The attorney was not permitted to waive a client's duty to pay a fee.

QUESTION 179

A criminal defendant sought out the services of an attorney in defending against charges of burglary and assault with a deadly weapon. The defendant was cash poor, but he owned several large tracts of viable farm land that he received through inheritance. The attorney suggested that the defendant execute a deed of trust on one of the tracts in favor of the attorney that would secure the payment of the attorney's fees incurred during the course of representation. The value of the land was roughly equal to the value of the services the attorney anticipated providing, which was fair to the defendant. The attorney provided all of the details of the arrangement in a letter written in plain English. Because the attorney specialized in criminal defense, he recommended that the defendant ask another attorney to draft the deed of trust and advise him on the benefits and potential problems with the arrangement.

The defendant scraped together enough money to pay another attorney to advise him on the arrangement and draft the deed of trust, which he delivered to the defense attorney. Without obtaining any other written documents from the defendant, the attorney proceeded with the successful representation of the defendant. Unfortunately, the defendant was still cash poor at the end of the representation, and the attorney foreclosed on the deed of trust to recover the value of his services.

Is the attorney subject to discipline?

(A)   Yes, because the attorney did not secure the defendant's written consent to the transaction and the attorney's role.

(B)   Yes, because taking a deed of trust to secure the payment of attorney's fees is not fair to the defendant.

(C)   No, because the defendant received independent counsel, including advice related to the drafting of the deed of trust.

(D) No, because the attorney provided a written explanation of the transaction to the defendant.

QUESTION 180

Two experienced litigators – one who specialized in contract disputes and one who worked exclusively on tort claims – were waiting outside of a courtroom and began discussing the current legal market. Both litigators were bemoaning the fact that the downturn in the legal market coupled with the increase in recent graduates had made it difficult to secure new clients, when they decided that one way to generate clients would be to refer clients to each other.

The two litigators met with each other a week later in the tort litigator's office to finalize the details of their arrangement. They agreed to refer clients to each other with the understanding that the tough market might necessitate that either of them enter into similar arrangements with other attorneys or professionals. They also agreed to disclose to each client referred that they had entered into this arrangement and that neither attorney was receiving monetary compensation directly from the other for the referrals.

Is either of the litigators subject to discipline?

(A) Yes, because each litigator will receive something of value from the arrangement.

(B) Yes, because the litigators did not pay each other for the arrangement.

(C) No, because the litigators specialize in different areas of law.

(D) No, because the arrangement was nonexclusive, and the clients will be notified of the arrangement.

QUESTION 181

A former patient at a city hospital approached a personal injury attorney to represent him in a suit against the hospital. The former patient alleged that the unsanitary conditions at the hospital led to a moderate, persistent infection in his arm that made it impossible to use his dominant arm for more than a few minutes at a time. The personal injury attorney saw merit in the former patient's claim, and she recognized that once she had developed the case for this cause of action, she could represent subsequent clients in similar actions without a great deal of additional work.

To generate a larger client base, the personal injury attorney entered into an agreement with the former patient whereby the personal injury attorney would pay the former patient an additional $300 for each additional client the former patient referred to her with the same complaint against the hospital. The legislature had declared such agreements void as against public policy six months earlier; so when the former patient referred clients to the personal injury attorney, she refused to pay the agreed upon fee. Frustrated by the personal injury attorney's refusal, the former patient went to another lawyer to represent him in a breach of contract claim against the personal injury attorney.

Will the lawyer be subject to discipline for representing the former patient?

(A)   Yes, because the legislature had declared such agreements void as against public policy.

(B)   Yes, because the former patient was the attorney's client.

(C)   No, because there is a valid claim for a breach of contract for failing to pay the fee.

(D)   No, because the lawyer is not required to believe that the claim will be successful.

QUESTION 182

A recently licensed attorney decided to hang out her own shingle and start a solo firm specializing in elder law and estate planning. The attorney's sister owned a floral shop in the city's largest office building. Hoping to more quickly generate a client base, the attorney asked her sister to place the attorney's business cards near the register and to refer the attorney's services to customers who asked for a recommendation. In return, the attorney agreed to place brochures for her sister's floral shop in the lobby. Both sisters agreed that they could refer other attorneys and floral shops if they were approached to do so and that they would tell customers about the arrangement.

Is the attorney subject to discipline?

(A)   Yes, because her sister is a florist.

(B)   Yes, because the sister receives value from the reciprocal referrals.

(C)   No, because the attorney made the referral arrangement with her sister.

(D)   No, because the arrangement is not exclusive.

QUESTION 183

An established medium-sized firm hoped to bring in new clients through an aggressive television advertising campaign.   The advertisement, which contained the name of one of the firm's partners and the firm's principal office address, as well as the areas of law in which the firm practiced, also contained a list of awards obtained for five previous clients. All of the awards were for amounts greater than $1,000,000. At the end of the advertisement, the spokesperson stated that the listed awards were not typical and that the outcome of each client's case would depend on the facts of that particular case.

Was the firm's advertisement appropriate?

(A)   No, because the advertisement includes statements regarding prior client awards.

(B)   No, because a firm cannot state the areas of practice.

(C)   Yes, because the statements regarding the awards were truthful.

(D)   Yes, because the advertisement included a disclaimer regarding the facts of each case.

QUESTION 184

A founding senior partner at a well-established law firm passed away at the age of 70 after battling a long illness. During the years that he suffered from the illness, the senior partner met with members of the firm regarding personal estate plans. As part of this planning, the partner, a widower, and the law firm, reached an agreement that the firm would continue to pay the partner's best friend, a local shop owner, the funds the partner would have made from the earned legal fees from matters the partner was responsible for bringing to the firm. Both parties felt the arrangement was reasonable in terms of duration and amount.

Would the firm be subject to discipline?

(A)   No, because an attorney is permitted to make arrangements regarding his earnings for estate planning purposes.

(B)   No, because the duration of the payments was reasonable.

(C)   Yes, because the firm cannot make payments to a non-relative after an attorney's death.

(D)   Yes, because the firm cannot make payments of earned legal fees to a non-lawyer.

QUESTION 185

A client was discussing her income, which had increased significantly, and taxes with her attorney three years ago when she casually asked about investing in overseas bank accounts and whether they would be beneficial for tax purposes. The attorney, who had written several law review articles about the use and means of structuring overseas accounts, discussed the process of placing money in these accounts and what the benefits and risks of the accounts were. Unbeknownst to the attorney at the time, the client was looking for a means of laundering the money she was embezzling from her employer. This past year, the attorney read on the internet that the client's employer was suffering substantial financial losses, and that the employer suspected an employee was at fault. The attorney immediately remembered the conversation from three years ago and suspected the client was responsible for the financial losses.

Can the attorney reveal the conversation to the police?

(A)   No, because the conversation arose during the course of the attorney's representation of the client.

(B)   No, because the client did not consent to the disclosure to the police.

(C)   Yes, if the attorney reasonably believes doing so is necessary to prevent further financial harm to the employer.

(D)   Yes, the attorney is required to disclose the conversation to prevent charges against him.

QUESTION 186

A recently licensed attorney was hired by the state attorney general's office. During his employment, the attorney worked with a senior attorney exclusively on litigation against a nationwide tobacco company in which the state alleged that the tobacco company was marketing its product to minors. After two years with the attorney general's office and while the case was on remand from the supreme court, the attorney was hired by a boutique firm whose sole client was the defendant tobacco company. The attorney was assigned to represent the tobacco company in litigation brought by the attorney general related to advertisements claiming that smokeless tobacco was safer than cigarettes.

If the attorney represents the tobacco store in litigation with the attorney general, will he be subject to discipline?

(A)　Yes, because an attorney can never defend a client against whom he has previously brought suit.

(B)　Yes, because more than a year had passed since the initial litigation.

(C)　No, because the attorney was only an assistant to the lead attorney on the prosecution.

(D)　No, because the attorney did not participate in litigation relating to the advertising claims.

QUESTION 187

A husband suspected his wife was having an affair with one of her work associates, and in order to confirm his suspicions, he and his friend, an attorney, went to lunch at the restaurant where the husband believed his wife was meeting the associate. When the husband and the attorney arrived at the restaurant, they saw the wife and the associate in a passionate embrace in the parking lot. The husband immediately confronted the wife and demanded a divorce. The attorney, who had never represented the wife in any matter, offered to represent the husband in the divorce proceedings.

Under the circumstances, the husband asserted infidelity as the grounds for the divorce. The wife did not deny that she was having the affair. The only witness other than the husband to any behavior substantiating the affair was the attorney, though, and he was prepared to testify during the proceedings as to what he witnessed. The husband had no objections to the attorney providing the testimony and signed a statement to that effect. The wife's attorney, on the other hand, challenged the arrangement and asked the court to bar the testimony.

Should the court permit the testimony?

(A)　Yes, because the wife did not deny that she was having the affair.

(B)　Yes, because the attorney was the only available witness.

(C)　No, because the attorney is representing the husband in the case.

(D)　No, because the testimony does not relate to the attorney's services.

QUESTION 188

A nonprofit national civil rights organization maintains a list of attorneys qualified to practice in each state and territory who are willing to represent clients alleging civil rights violations. Because each of the cases referred has the potential for generating a large amount of publicity for both the referred attorneys and the nonprofit organization, the attorneys take the cases through an arrangement whereby they agree to pay the nonprofit organization one third of any attorney's fees awarded at the conclusion of the case.

An attorney at a small firm agreed to be placed on the referral list and was almost immediately provided with a promising case. The case made its way to the state's highest court, which found for the attorney's client and awarded $300,000 in attorney's fees. The attorney deposited $100,000 in the nonprofit organization's account.

Is the attorney subject to discipline?

(A)   No, because the attorney is permitted to share court awarded fees with whomever he wishes.

(B)   No, because the nonprofit referred the case to the attorney.

(C)   Yes, because he shared the fees with a non-lawyer organization.

(D)   Yes, because the amount of fees shared was not commensurate with the nonprofit organization's contribution to the case.

QUESTION 189

A judge in her first year in elected office was presiding over a case in which the defendant was indigent and needed to have appointed counsel. The town in which the court operated was fairly small, and the court did not maintain a list of attorneys who were qualified and available to represent indigent parties. Although several of the local attorneys had indicated candidly that they were available to assist the defendant, the judge decided instead to appoint an attorney from a nearby town in an effort to avoid local gossip. Shortly after the appointment, the plaintiff's attorney filed a timely motion objecting to the appointment, arguing that the appointment was inappropriate because the attorney had, unbeknownst to the judge, contributed a large amount to the judge's election campaign one year earlier. The judge dismissed the motion and continued with the trial.

Is the judge subject to discipline for appointing the defense attorney?

(A)   Yes, because he learned of the contributions via the plaintiff's counsel's timely motion.

(B)   Yes, because the judge was required to appoint an attorney from within the available pool in the town.

(C)   No, because the judge was unaware of the contribution at the time of the appointment.

(D)   No, because the court did not maintain a list of available counsel.

QUESTION 190

A husband entered a law firm and asked to speak to the lawyer with the most experience in family law. The husband told the lawyer that he was thinking about seeking a divorce, and he disclosed to the lawyer his grounds for divorce and what he hoped to achieve through the divorce settlement. After a thirty minute discussion, the lawyer outlined the fees he would charge and the anticipated hours needed to complete the work. The husband thanked the lawyer for the information, left the office, and never contacted the lawyer again.

What duty, if any, does the lawyer owe to the husband?

(A)   The lawyer must contact the husband and provide advice based on the information the husband disclosed.

(B)   The lawyer must decline to represent a customer of the husband in a negligence action against the husband.

(C)   The lawyer must not reveal the information the husband divulged about his marriage to the wife.

(D)   The lawyer owes no duty because he did not form a client-lawyer relationship.

QUESTION 191

A corporation was organized under the laws of State A, which had a 10% corporate tax rate. The CEO called the in-house counsel to discuss the prospect of setting up an affiliated company in State B, where the corporate tax rate was only 3%. The counsel informed the CEO that while the corporation could organize an affiliated company in the second state by filing the necessary corporate documents with the Secretary of State, doing so would be tantamount to tax evasion, which could subject the corporation and potentially its executive to criminal penalties. The CEO listened to the counsel's advice and took the information back to the board for discussion, and the board opted to pursue a different course of action.

Is the in-house counsel subject to discipline for his discussion with the CEO?

(A)   Yes, because he told the CEO how to form an affiliated company in a different state.

(B)   Yes, because the counsel's advice is equivalent to assisting the CEO in fraudulent activity.

(C)   No, because the counsel was merely discussing the consequences of carrying out the CEO's plans.

(D)   No, because the board of directors rejected the proposed course of action.

QUESTION 192

A husband retained an attorney to assist him in obtaining a divorce from his wife because he discovered that she had been having an affair. Before the attorney filed the petition, the husband asked that the attorney contact the wife to discuss the terms of a potential settlement. The wife admitted that she was having an affair, and told the attorney that her concern with the outcome of the divorce was that she be able to share custody of their children with the husband. She said she was not particularly concerned about the outcome of the property disposition and asked the attorney to contact her lawyer to discuss the particulars. The attorney said that he would call the wife's lawyer the next morning, but he asked the wife if she would prefer to keep the couple's primary residence or their beach-front property. The wife said that she would prefer to keep the beach property and all of the personal items in the residence, and the attorney said that he would prepare a draft settlement and send it to the wife's lawyer.

Was the attorney's conversation with the wife appropriate?

(A)   Yes, because the attorney must communicate with the wife in order to reach a settlement.

(B)   Yes, because the attorney did not know the wife had a lawyer when he began discussing the terms of the settlement.

(C)   No, because the discussion was premature since the attorney had not yet filed the petition.

(D)   No, because the attorney continued to discuss the terms of a settlement after the wife asked him to contact her lawyer.

QUESTION 193

The owner of a television channel hired an attorney to help negotiate with a cable company to carry the channel in its local package. After a week of negotiations, the parties came to a mutually beneficial contractual arrangement that would span five years. The relationship worked smoothly for three years, but then the owner's share of profits began to fall from the agreed upon amounts, and the owner again retained the attorney to represent him in a breach of contract dispute.

Several months into discovery, the attorney learned that the cable company had begun to preempt the channel's coverage to play football games. The contract provided that the cable company could preempt the programming in extraordinary circumstances, but the owner did not believe a football game qualified as such. The contract permitted the cable company to withhold payments and pocket the proceeds from any preemption broadcast.

The crux of the owner's argument was that the parties agreed on a definition of "extraordinary circumstances" that was not written in the contract, and the contract did not prohibit the parties from bringing in extraneous information. Because the owner did not attend the negotiations, the attorney was the only person who could testify on the owner's behalf as to what was said. The cable company objected to the attorney continuing to represent the owner. Neither side could have foreseen at the outset of the negotiations that the attorney would need to testify, and if the attorney were disqualified, the owner would be at a substantial disadvantage because any new attorney would need several months to get up to speed (not to mention the additional fees that he would charge).

Should the attorney be disqualified?

(A)   Yes, because his testimony is necessary for the owner's case.

(B)   Yes, because the attorney has a vested interest in the outcome of the case.

(C)   No, because the owner would suffer a substantial hardship if he had to find a new attorney.

(D)   No, because the cable company will still have an opportunity to question him.

QUESTION 194

A large internet company was preparing to purchase a small internet startup company. The larger company had determined that the smaller company's value was approximately $250 million; however, the smaller company was only asking for $100 million. The in-house counsel for the large company represented the large company during its negotiations with the CEO of the smaller company, and when the CEO offered to sell for the lower amount, the in-house counsel accepted without informing the CEO of the higher valuation. Three weeks after the deal was finalized, the CEO learned of the higher valuation and complained to the state bar.

Can the in-house counsel be subject to discipline for his actions during the negotiations?

(A)   Yes, because nondisclosure of the value is tantamount to a false statement.

(B)   Yes, because the counsel was required to provide that information for negotiations.

(C)   No, because the counsel did not have an affirmative duty to tell the CEO of the higher valuation.

(D)   No, because he did not have a court order requiring the disclosure.

QUESTION 195

An attorney was hired to represent a businesswoman in the sale of a shopping center. The parties to the sale had agreed that the buyer would purchase the center in four equal payments of $250,000 over the course of a year. Prior to beginning the negotiations, the attorney and the client entered into a written agreement, which contained a provision directing the attorney to retain the first three payments in a separate interest bearing account until the fourth payment was made. Over the course of the year, the buyer made three on-time payments, which the attorney deposited in the client trust account after promptly notifying the businesswoman that the funds had been delivered. Once the buyer delivered the fourth payment, the attorney notified the businesswoman and arranged to transfer the funds to her.

Is the attorney subject to discipline?

(A)   No, because the businesswoman consented to the withholding of funds.

(B)   No, because the funds were maintained in an interest bearing account.

(C)   Yes, because the attorney had an obligation to immediately deliver the received funds to the client.

(D)   Yes, because the businesswoman could not agree to waive a duty owed to her by the attorney.

QUESTION 196

With the constriction of the economy, an established lawyer in a medium-sized town was having difficulty maintaining a steady stream of business and decided to prepare a number of advertisements to be shown during the local nightly news. Although the lawyer was a general practitioner, he knew that the population in the town was aging and wanted to emphasize his elder law and estate planning practice. In the advertisement, the lawyer provided his name and address and stated that he had worked in the community for a number of years and that he specialized in elder law and estate planning.

Is the lawyer subject to discipline for his advertisement?

(A)   No, because the advertisement contained his name and address.

(B)   No, because the lawyer was advertising services that he hoped would meet the community's need.

(C)   Yes, because he did not include a statement that the spot was "Advertising Material."

(D)   Yes, because the lawyer does not practice exclusively in elder law and estate planning.

QUESTION 197

In a state where district court judges are elected every four years, a judge lost a heated reelection bid and returned to private practice. During her tenure as a judge, she had presided over a divorce in which the former spouses had each fought to obtain full custody of the three children. After hearing all of the evidence, the judge had ruled in favor of the husband because he was retaining the family home and had the most stable job since the wife was still completing her medical degree.

The ex-wife had since graduated from medical school, was working in a thriving family practice, and had purchased a home in a neighborhood near the ex-husband's home. Because of the change in circumstances, the ex-wife wanted to seek a modification of the custody order. Knowing that the former judge was knowledgeable about the case, the ex-wife requested that she represent her in the petition to modify the order. The former judge disclosed to the ex-spouses separately the potential conflicts that could arise if she were to represent the ex-wife, and both ex-spouses signed forms consenting to the representation. The former judge proceeded to represent the ex-wife, and she won custody.

Is the former judge subject to discipline?

(A)   No, because both spouses consented to the representation.

(B)   No, because the ex-wife's situation had improved to the point where she could reasonably care for the children.

(C)   Yes, because the former judge had presided over the initial custody hearing.

(D)   Yes, because the ex-husband lost custody because of the former judge's expertise.

QUESTION 198

An experienced lawyer left a large firm to form a venture capital LLC with a friend who was largely regarded as one of the most savvy business executives in the state. The lawyer had previous experience representing venture capital firms. The LLC would be member managed, with both the lawyer and the friend serving as managers. The friend would select the startups that the LLC would fund. The lawyer would draft any necessary legal documents and represent the LLC in any negotiations or litigation.

Is the lawyer likely to be subject to discipline?

(A)   Yes, because the lawyer is practicing law while in a business association with a non-lawyer.

(B)   Yes, because serving as a manager of an LLC of which the lawyer is a member is a conflict of interest.

(C)   Yes, because the lawyer was not competent to represent the LLC.

(D)   No, because the lawyer formed an LLC with the friend.

QUESTION 199

A general practice lawyer was at a family event with her husband. The attorney handled a wide variety of cases, but spent a large amount of time on medical malpractice cases. While at the event, she was approached by one of her cousins who had been involved in an automobile accident. The cousin said that he had been hit in an intersection by a teenager who ran a red light while texting and driving. The cousin also said that he had sustained serious injuries as a result of the collision and would like to sue the teenager to recover for his medical bills, his pain and suffering, and the value of his car. The attorney told the cousin that she would be more than happy to represent him because one of her specialties was accident litigation, and in the last two cases she'd handled, the clients had each recovered the full amount of damages sought. The two prior cases involved allegations of medical malpractice, and the attorney's statements about the award amounts were truthful. The cousin requested the attorney's office number and contacted her the following Monday.

Is the attorney subject to discipline?

(A)   Yes, because this discussion is a direct solicitation for pecuniary gain.

(B)   Yes, because the statements to the cousin were false and misleading.

(C)   No, because the conversation was with a family member.

(D)   No, because the statement about the damage awards was truthful.

QUESTION 200

A former partner at a law firm decided to run for state attorney general against a very popular incumbent. When the former partner left the firm, many of his former co-workers harbored hard feelings because they felt that he had left the firm in a bind by leaving during a difficult transitional period. A client of an associate at the firm asked the associate whether he felt that the former partner would be qualified to be attorney general. The associate replied that he felt the former partner was a sleazy individual who was likely to embezzle funds from the treasury, but the associate had not actually worked with the former partner and was basing his opinions on gossipy stories from those who had worked with him.

Were the attorney's remarks proper?

(A)   Yes, because the associate based his comments on what the former partner's former co-workers had said.

(B)   Yes, because the associate was permitted to respond to a candid question from a client.

(C)   No, because an attorney cannot make a statement about a candidate for elected legal office.

(D)   No, because the associate does not know if the statements were true.

QUESTION 201

A patient at a hospital was injured when a door that had recently been repaired fell off of its hinges and hit her on the head. Hospital records showed that the last person to repair the door was the maintenance supervisor. The patient brought negligence suits against both the maintenance supervisor and the hospital. The general counsel for the hospital met frequently with executives of the hospital and the maintenance supervisor, who the general counsel knew had not yet hired an attorney, to discuss the facts of the case and strategy. The general counsel would only represent the hospital in the case, but the maintenance supervisor believed that the general counsel would assist in his representation. Based on the context of the discussions and the questions the maintenance supervisor asked, the general counsel reasonably should have known that the maintenance supervisor believed he would receive such assistance; however, the general counsel did not advise the maintenance supervisor to seek separate counsel.

Is the general counsel subject to discipline?

(A) No, because the maintenance supervisor was a hospital employee and thus entitled to advice from the hospital's general counsel.

(B) No, because discussing the facts of the case with the employee is acceptable when preparing for litigation against the hospital.

(C) Yes, because the general counsel did not get the maintenance supervisor's written consent before entering the discussions.

(D) Yes, because the general counsel did not explain to the maintenance supervisor that he was only representing the hospital.

QUESTION 202

A doctor consulted with his attorney about a malpractice suit being brought against him by a former patient. The patient alleges that the doctor failed to prescribe the correct dosage of a particular medication, which caused the patient to irrevocably lose all of her hair. The doctor told the attorney that he does not remember writing the wrong prescription, but he admitted that at the time he was struggling with an addiction to prescription drugs. After reviewing the case, the attorney recommended settling with the patient and suggested that during negotiations they divulge that the doctor had an addiction at the time without any discussion of how doing so would impact the amount of the settlement. The doctor agreed to disclose.

Is it proper for the attorney to disclose the doctor's addiction?

(A) No, because the patient is not facing reasonably certain death or substantial harm.

(B) No, because the doctor was not fully informed of the consequences when he consented.

(C) Yes, because the disclosure is impliedly required to obtain the most favorable settlement for the doctor.

(D) Yes, because the doctor explicitly consented to the disclosure.

QUESTION 203

A judge had a large case load involving domestic issues and found that it was often difficult to obtain advocates for children in domestic violence cases. His wife's sister had a thriving family law practice, one of several in the city, and the judge approached her to see if she would be willing to be appointed as an advocate in any future cases where he could not find counsel to serve. The sister-in-law agreed, and for the following six months, the judge appointed the sister-in-law advocate in fifteen cases.

Were the judge's actions proper?

(A) Yes, because there was a real need for advocates in his court.

(B) Yes, because a judge is afforded wide latitude in making administrative appointments.

(C)   No, because the attorney appointed was the judge's wife's sister.

(D)   No, because the appointments were not necessary.

QUESTION 204

A criminal defense attorney was meeting with his client who was charged with possession with intent to distribute. Although the police had raided the client's home, they had only recently discovered that he had several different houses throughout the region where he stashed evidence of his crimes. During the course of the meeting, the client told the attorney that several of his homes were rigged with booby traps that were intended to kill or at least severely injure intruders.

Will the attorney be subject to discipline if he does not reveal this information?

(A)   No, unless another law requires him to disclose the information.

(B)   Yes, but only if the client did not give the attorney informed consent.

(C)   No, because such a disclosure would be an improper disclosure of client information.

(D)   Yes, because the attorney is required to disclose information if it will prevent reasonably certain death or substantial bodily harm.

QUESTION 205

A local attorney who specialized in civil defense was approached by a plumber who had been named as a defendant in a suit over a contract dispute. The plumber was not financially able to hire an attorney and was preparing to represent himself in the suit. The attorney agreed to sit down with the plumber and answer any questions the plumber might have about procedure or the actual substantive law. The attorney also agreed to be available after the meeting should the plumber have any additional questions. Using the information that he obtained from the attorney, the plumber appeared in court and was able to successfully defend the suit against him.

Is the attorney subject to discipline for his actions?

(A)   Yes, because he assisted an unlicensed person in the practice law.

(B)   Yes, because agreeing to be available for any of the plumber's questions was beyond any permissible assistance to an individual proceeding pro se.

(C)   No, because he was licensed in the state.

(D)   No, because he was assisting an individual in representing himself.

QUESTION 206

An attorney had a growing family law practice and had hired a May law graduate in June to assist in preparing the cases. Initially the graduate's only job duty was to draft pleadings under the attorney's supervision, but as the workload increased and the graduate became competent in the work, the graduate began conducting discovery, appearing in court without the attorney present, and sharing in the revenue generated by his work.

Is the attorney subject to discipline?

(A)   No, because the graduate has a law degree.

(B)   No, because the attorney supervised the graduate until he was capable of handling the work on his own.

(C)   Yes, because the graduate did not yet have a license.

(D)   Yes, because the graduate was only qualified to draft pleadings.

QUESTION 207

One member of a limited liability company believed that the other member had misappropriated LLC funds, and pursuant to the LLC's operating agreement, the concerned member filed a suit in district court. The judge ordered that the parties meet with a mediator in an attempt to resolve the dispute through a settlement, and a local attorney was appointed to serve as a mediator. During the negotiations, each party permitted the local counsel to share nearly all of the disclosed information with the other party. Although the parties met on several occasions over the course of three weeks, they were unable to reach a resolution, and the case proceeded to trial.

The accused member, who had not yet hired counsel, reached out to the local attorney who had served as the mediator to represent him at the trial. The concerned member was not consulted prior to the first hearing and did not learn of the representation until the parties stepped into the courtroom.

Will the local counsel be subject to discipline?

(A)   No, because each party had permitted the local counsel to share almost all of the disclosed information with the other party.

(B)   No, because a litigant is permitted to choose his or her counsel without the other party's input.

(C)   Yes, because the local counsel did not disclose the potential conflict to the court.

(D)   Yes, because the local counsel had served as the mediator prior to the trial.

QUESTION 208

An attorney was retained by a client to pursue a medical malpractice claim against a prominent local hospital. After the parties had completed discovery, the hospital recognized that the plaintiff was likely to succeed on the merits and recover a large judgment; thus, the hospital offered to settle for a sizeable but smaller sum than it anticipated the jury would award. The attorney communicated the settlement offer to his client and told the client that in his professional experience, a settlement offer at this stage of litigation generally indicated that the defendant strongly believed that it was not going to prevail. The attorney also told his client that the settlement offer was likely a mere fraction of the amount that the client could recover at a jury trial.

The client asked to sleep on the offer and the following morning informed the attorney that he would like to accept the offer. The attorney, unbeknownst to the client, told the attorney for the hospital that his client would accept no less than twice the amount originally offered (which was far closer to the amount the client could recover in court) and that if settlement was not reached for that amount, the parties would proceed to trial. The hospital's attorney was authorized to settle for anything less than four times the original offer and immediately accepted. The attorney then communicated the settlement amount to his client who was ecstatic to learn of the much larger recovery.

Is the attorney subject to discipline?

(A)   No, because he successfully negotiated a larger settlement than his client was willing to accept.

(B)   No, because the attorney outlined all of the information that his client would need to consider prior to accepting a settlement offer.

(C)   Yes, because he knew that his client could recover more through a jury trial and failed to pursue this more beneficial course of action.

(D)   Yes, because the client had instructed the attorney to accept the original settlement offer.

QUESTION 209

A driver was driving in his vehicle with his cousin, a passenger, on the way to a meeting for a large land deal when his vehicle collided with a tractor trailer on the interstate. The driver walked away from the accident with only minor injuries, but the passenger was severely injured and spent three weeks in the hospital. Once the passenger was back on his feet, he and the driver approached the attorney who was going to represent them in the land deal and asked the attorney to represent them in a negligence suit against the truck driver and the truck driver's company.

During discussions between the attorney and the passenger in preparation for the trial, the passenger tells the attorney that immediately prior to the collision, the driver was in the process of responding to an email from the seller in the land deal and did not look up in time to see the truck driver swerve unexpectedly into their lane. The passenger tells the attorney that he would like to bring a cross claim against the driver for his negligence. The law of the jurisdiction does not prohibit an attorney from representing two clients in situations like this one. The attorney informs the driver of this development and tells both the driver and the passenger that he feels he can competently represent both of them. After an hour of discussion, the driver and passenger sign a written consent to the joint representation.

Is the representation by the attorney of both the driver and the passenger appropriate?

(A) Yes, because the driver and the passenger both signed informed consents.

(B) Yes, because the law does not prohibit an attorney from representing the two clients in a negligence suit against a truck driver.

(C) No, because the passenger is asserting a claim against the driver.

(D) No, because an attorney may never represent two clients in the same litigation.

QUESTION 210

A former solo attorney accepted a job with the criminal division of the city attorney's office. While there, he participated as the lead attorney in the prosecution of individual members of an expansive drug ring. After two years of working with the city, he took a job with the public defender's office, where he was appointed to represent one of the drug ring members in his appeal of his conviction. The attorney contacted the city attorney's office, explained the nature of the representation he had been asked to undertake, and received a letter from the chief of the criminal division permitting the attorney to represent his new client.

If the attorney proceeds with the defense of the convicted member, he will:

(A) not be subject to discipline because his role as lead attorney would not be considered substantial participation.

(B) not be subject to discipline because he informed the city of his new representation and received a letter approving his participation.

(C) be subject to discipline because as lead attorney he participated substantially and personally in the prosecution of the drug ring members.

(D) be subject to discipline because an attorney cannot overcome the conflict that arises from switching sides in a representation.

QUESTION 211

The owner of several successful nursing homes retained a lawyer solely to represent him in the numerous wrongful death suits that attend ownership of residential care facilities. The lawyer had a high success rate, and the owner was quite pleased with her services. When one of the owner's facilities began to suffer financially, the owner began discussing selling the property to a business acquaintance at a steeply discounted price. The acquaintance was familiar with the owner's lawyer and approached the lawyer to negotiate the sale transaction. The lawyer called the owner and explained that the acquaintance had asked the lawyer to negotiate the sale. The lawyer truthfully believed that she could represent each client. After mulling it over, the owner told the lawyer that he had no problem with the proposed representation.

If the lawyer represents the acquaintance in the transaction, will she be subject to discipline?

(A)   Yes, because the owner's consent was not in writing.

(B)   Yes, because the owner and the acquaintance are directly adverse in this matter.

(C)   No, because the lawyer only represents the owner in litigation matters.

(D)   No, because the owner provided informed consent to the adverse representation.

QUESTION 212

An attorney represented a company in a tort action wherein the injured plaintiff alleged that the company improperly designed a highly complex machine used in the manufacturing of laser guided missiles for the military. Because of the incredibly complicated natures of both the machine and the missiles, only one expert, an employee of the company, is available who can provide testimony on both machines. While preparing for the trial, the attorney met with the expert, who agreed to testify for the company. The attorney, recognizing that there was proprietary information about the manufacturing process that could prove damaging for the company's case, requested that the expert refrain from providing the proprietary information to the plaintiff's counsel. The expert, recognizing the potential risk to the company, readily agreed to the attorney's request.

Is the attorney subject to discipline?

(A)   No, because the attorney did not offer the expert any inducement to withhold the information.

(B)   No, because the expert is an employee of the company.

(C)   Yes, because the information that the expert had would have been relevant to the plaintiff's case.

(D)   Yes, because making the request was tantamount to improperly influencing a witness.

QUESTION 213

A prominent businesswoman was on trial for attempting to hire a hit man to kill her estranged husband. The prosecution's case rested largely on circumstantial evidence; so the defense attorney was shocked when the jury unanimously convicted his client and subsequently sentenced her to twenty years in prison. Three days after the trial, the defense attorney called the jury foreman, hoping to ask her what had caused the jury to find against his client, but the jury foreman politely told the defense attorney that she had no interest in speaking with him about the trial. Frustrated, the defense attorney asked his friend to call the jury foreman and pretend to be a publisher interested in offering her a book deal. The jury foreman was much more open with the friend and when asked, volunteered the information the defense attorney was seeking. Once he received the information, neither the defense attorney nor the friend had further contact with the jury foreman.

Is the defense attorney subject to discipline?

(A)   No, because the friend, not the defense attorney, spoke with the jury foreman the second time.

(B)   No, because neither the friend nor the defense attorney contacted the jury foreman after they received the information they wanted.

(C)   Yes, because the jury foreman told the defense attorney she did not want to speak with him.

(D)   Yes, because he contacted a member of the jury after the jury was dismissed.

QUESTION 214

An attorney was approached by a woman who claimed to have received injuries from an errant jalapeño pepper in her tomato soup at an upscale restaurant. The woman was allergic to jalapeños, and she spent several days in the hospital due to the exposure. The woman wanted to sue the restaurant for negligence to recover for her medical expenses as well as for pain and suffering. The attorney did not believe that the woman would succeed on her claim because the restaurant was known for creating spicy dishes, but he believed in good faith that he could argue that the restaurant had a duty to its patrons to warn them if the dish ordered was unduly spicy and that the restaurant breached that duty.

Will the attorney be subject to discipline if he represents the woman in this case?

(A)   Yes, because the attorney does not believe that the lawsuit will be successful.

(B)   Yes, because a claim against a restaurant for selling a spicy dish is frivolous.

(C)   No, because the woman is seeking reasonable damages.

(D)   No, because he believes in good faith that he can make an argument for negligence.

QUESTION 215

An attorney began her career working for the Environmental Protection Agency, where she participated in litigation against an oil company for its off-shore drilling practices. After two years, she took a position with the Department of Justice, where she worked in the civil division representing the IRS in defensive litigation. A large law firm approached her with an offer to work in the environmental litigation section, defending the same oil company as before in suits brought by the EPA relating to its off-shore drilling.

If the attorney is subject to discipline, what will be the most likely reason?

(A)   An insufficient amount of time has passed since the attorney worked for the EPA.

(B)   The litigation is a continuation of the litigation that she worked on while at the EPA.

(C)   Her prior work as a litigator with DOJ prohibits her from representing a private company against a federal agency.

(D)   Her litigation experiences are not sufficient to make her competent to represent a private client.

QUESTION 216

A partner at a prestigious large firm had a keen interest in the local arts scene and formed a non-profit partnership with another local patron, a retired banker, that provided grants to struggling artists in hopes that the arts would flourish in the community. Because the banker had far more time to devote to the project, the banker oversaw the daily operations. However, the two partners would regularly consult regarding the selection of the grantees and the finances of the partnership.

What reason would most likely support the partner's position that he is not subject to discipline?

(A)   The partner did not provide legal services to the partnership.

(B)   The partnership was a non-profit business entity.

(C)   The banker was primarily responsible for the daily activities of the partnership.

(D)   The partner's contributions to the partnership count toward the firm's pro bono requirements.

QUESTION 217

A judge was elected in a nonpartisan judicial campaign to a state circuit court. One of the judge's duties was to appoint referees to hear cases involving changes to visitation rights of divorced parents. The court generally kept a list of five attorneys to serve as referees when necessary. The referee position was uncompensated, and serving as a referee would satisfy a pro bono requirement for the state bar association. At the time the judge was elected, the court needed two attorneys to fill vacancies, and the judge appointed a local family law attorney who was a law school classmate. The attorney was the only family law attorney in the area who was not already included in the pool of referees and was highly qualified for the position. The attorney had contributed substantially to the judge's election campaign and had hosted several fundraisers attended by the judge.

Was the appointment of the attorney as a referee appropriate?

(A)   No, because the attorney's contributions to the campaign were substantial.

(B)   No, because the judge and the attorney had been friends for many years.

(C)   Yes, because appointing a close friend does not violate the prohibition on nepotism.

(D)   Yes, because the attorney's service as a referee would be a pro bono position.

QUESTION 218

A personal injury attorney ran into an old physician friend at a social event hosted by a local charitable organization. After conversing for a few minutes about their respective careers, the physician offered to refer patients who came in with recent injuries to the personal injury attorney. The physician said that he had kept a list of local attorneys, but he would exclusively refer the personal injury attorney going forward. The personal injury attorney was thrilled with the idea, and offered to add the physician's name to the list of doctors that he provided to clients. Both the physician and the personal injury attorney agreed to place a disclaimer on the referral sheets to inform the potential clients of the arrangement.

Is the attorney subject to discipline?

(A)   No, because the physician is a non-attorney professional.

(B)   No, because both referral sheets contained a disclaimer.

(C)   Yes, because the physician agreed to refer only the personal injury attorney.

(D)   Yes, because the personal injury attorney offered something of value to the physician.

QUESTION 219

A criminal defense attorney placed an advertisement that complied with all applicable rules and read in part "We'll give you twenty minutes of consultation for twenty dollars!" A potential client responded to the advertisement. The client was charged with vehicular manslaughter and possession of narcotics with the intent to distribute. The facts indicated that the client was likely guilty of both crimes. The client had previously engaged the services of another lawyer but had decided to switch attorneys two days before the first hearing.

The client and the attorney agreed to limit the consultation to a recommendation of how to plead in response to the charge at the hearing. At the conclusion of the twenty minute consultation, the client, upon the attorney's advice, decided to plead not guilty. The attorney charged the client twenty dollars in legal fees and concluded the representation.

If the attorney is subject to discipline, the most likely reason would be because:

(A)   The limitation of twenty minutes of consultation is unreasonable under the circumstances because it is not enough time for the attorney to give sufficient, competent advice to the client on the complex issues.

(B)   An attorney and a client can never agree to limit the scope of the attorney's representation of the client because the attorney is under a duty to represent the client to the fullest extent possible.

(C)   The attorney cannot take over for another attorney with so little time remaining before a hearing.

(D)   The attorney advised a likely guilty client to plead not guilty.

QUESTION 220

The state legislature was holding hearings on whether to amend the state's landlord tenant law. The current law was formulated prior to the creation of the uniform law on which nearly half of the states had based their laws. A representative of a group that lobbied on behalf of landlords was scheduled to appear during the second day of hearings, and the representative asked the group's attorney to accompany him for support rather than to represent him.

At the hearing, the attorney was present but remained silent throughout the representative's testimony. The attorney only spoke to provide his name and that he was present at the request of the representative for moral support. The attorney did not disclose that the representative had compensated him for his appearance.

Is the attorney subject to discipline?

(A)   No, because he was not representing the representative.

(B)   No, because the representative was testifying at a hearing and not for litigation purposes.

(C)   Yes, because the representative compensated the attorney.

(D)   Yes, because the attorney did not disclose that he was the group's attorney.

QUESTION 221

An independent contractor purposefully refused to file a tax return for four years in a row and recently received a letter from the IRS identifying him as a non-filer. The letter informed the independent contractor that tax evasion and failure to file a tax return could result in five years of jail time for each year that a return was not filed. Concerned that he might be subject to jail time, he contacted his former tax attorney who advised him to immediately prepare the delinquent returns. The tax attorney promptly filed the returns on behalf of the independent contractor but without disclosing that she was the independent contractor's attorney. The tax attorney informed the independent contractor that she would represent the independent contractor in any hearings with the IRS.

Is the attorney subject to discipline?

(A)   No, because she was unaware of the independent contractor's criminal activity.

(B)   No, because filing a tax return does not involve an official hearing or meeting of the IRS.

(C)   Yes, because she did not disclose to the IRS that she was serving as the independent contractor's attorney.

(D)   Yes, because she assisted her client in criminal activity.

QUESTION 222

A powerful businesswoman was under investigation for allegedly laundering money for a criminal organization. The federal attorney assigned to the case approached an informant within the criminal organization and asked him to secretly record conversations between himself and the businesswoman relating to transfers of funds derived from the organization's criminal activities. The most helpful conversation occurred after the businesswoman met with her retained counsel to discuss a pending business transaction. Once the attorney received the recorded conversations, she proceeded to have the businesswoman arrested and indicted.

Can the federal attorney be subject to discipline for requesting the informant to record the conversation?

(A)   No, because the informant, and not the attorney, recorded the conversation.

(B)   No, because the law permitted the government attorney to have the informant record the conversation.

(C)   Yes, because the businesswoman had an attorney on retainer and the conversation related to the subject of the investigation.

(D)   Yes, because the attorney did not request a court order for the informant to communicate with the businesswoman.

QUESTION 223

A long time solo practitioner recently decided to expand his practice to include two other attorneys. The three attorneys entered into a compensation plan that included a fixed annual salary and an end-of-the-year bonus tied to the firm's overall performance. The increased business generated by the additional attorneys increased the annual revenue of the firm tremendously, but it also created a much heavier workload for the firm's only paralegal who received hourly compensation. The practitioner, recognizing the significant increase in the paralegal's workload, decided to provide the paralegal with a much higher annual salary and to allow the paralegal to participate in the bonus program.

Is the practitioner subject to discipline?

(A)   Yes, because the paralegal is receiving, as a part of compensation, a portion of the firms legal fees.

(B)   Yes, because the paralegal's bonus is computed in the same manner as the attorney bonuses.

(C)   No, because the paralegal is an employee of the firm.

(D)   No, because increased compensation is justified by the workload.

QUESTION 224

An attorney represented a woman in her divorce from her husband. As part of the settlement, the estate was divided 40/60, with the larger share going to the husband. The wife, who was the sole signatory on the checking and savings accounts, delivered a cashier's check to the attorney on a Thursday for sixty percent of the balance of the accounts. When she handed the check to the attorney, the woman asked that the attorney wait to tell the husband about the check until the following Monday because she knew that the husband was going to the casino over the weekend, and she did not want him to spend money that once belonged to her. The woman had brought a large amount of business to the attorney, and all signs indicated that she would continue to bring business; so the attorney agreed to the woman's request. The attorney deposited the funds into a trust account, and on Monday morning, the attorney called the husband and explained that the check had been deposited with the attorney the prior week and was ready for the husband. The husband thanked the attorney for the call and picked up the check the following day.

Was the attorney's conduct proper?

(A)   Yes. The attorney was complying with the client's directions as to the use of the funds.

(B)   Yes. The husband did not object to the delayed delivery.

(C)   No. The attorney should have called the husband on Thursday in spite of the woman's directions.

(D)   No. The funds were already in a cashier's check; so they should not have been deposited over the weekend.

QUESTION 225

An attorney was hired to represent a group of twelve miners who were injured during an explosion at the mine where they worked. The miners were suing the company that owned and operated the mine at the time of the explosion, alleging that the company was negligent in maintaining the safety features of the mine and that the negligence led to their injuries.

The company, recognizing that the miners' case was strong and that the jury was likely to award the miners a sizeable amount of money, met with the miner's attorney to offer a $50 million settlement to the group. The attorney believed this settlement was a good deal for each of his clients, and because some of the clients suffered more serious injuries than the others, he determined to give a greater share of the settlement to those miners who suffered the greatest injuries. Prior to accepting the settlement, the attorney sat down with each client individually and explained the terms of the settlement, including the amount that the client would receive, the amounts that the other clients would receive, and what the clients were giving up by accepting the settlement. After meeting with each client, all of the clients provided signed, written consent to the settlement.

Is the attorney subject to discipline?

(A)   Yes, because he disclosed to each client the amounts that the other clients were going to receive.

(B)   Yes, because he assisted the company in avoiding paying a larger amount at trial.

(C)   No, because he provided disclosure of the settlement terms and participation of the other clients.

(D)   No, because there was no conflict of interest in representing multiple clients against the company.

QUESTION 226

An attorney's client was involved in a serious accident, and the client's injuries were so severe that he was rushed to the emergency room. The doctors did what they could for the client, but in the end they were only able to ease his pain in his final hours. The client asked the doctor to contact the attorney and request that the attorney come up to the hospital. When the attorney arrived, the client asked her to quickly assist him in preparing his last will. The attorney, though, had never prepared a will before. Recognizing that her client was not likely to survive long enough for her to consult a probate attorney, the attorney carefully wrote out her client's last wishes and had him sign his name at the bottom. Within the hour the client passed away, and the family offered the signed writing for probate.

Is the attorney subject to discipline?

(A)   Yes, because she was not competent to prepare a will.

(B)   Yes, because the attorney did not consult with another attorney before preparing the will.

(C)   No, because the client's imminent death made it impractical for the attorney to consult with a probate attorney.

(D)   No, because the client signed the will.

QUESTION 227

An insurance company hired a skilled litigator to represent an insured client who had been involved in a serious automobile accident. The insured client had run a red light at ninety miles per hour and collided with the plaintiff's vehicle, causing severe, non-life threatening injuries to the plaintiff and totaling her vehicle. The insurance company instructed the litigator to only settle if the offer was less than $100,000, as the company felt that such an amount would be reasonable given the circumstances of the accident. Otherwise, the insurance company believed that it would receive a more favorable outcome in court because at the time of the accident the plaintiff had a blood alcohol level that was three times the legal limit.

During their initial consultation, the litigator explained the insurance company's settlement instructions and informed the insured client that these instructions could result in lengthy litigation and potentially a less favorable outcome. Despite the limitation on settlement, the litigator informed the client that he reasonably believed that he would be fully competent to represent the insured client. After asking a number of questions, the insured client agreed to the insurance company's restrictions and signed a prepared consent form (the insurance company had already signed a similar consent). The plaintiff's settlement offer was $500,000, well above the threshold set by the insurance company; so the case proceeded to trial where the plaintiff was awarded $1.5 million in damages.

Will the litigator be subject to discipline for his handling of the case?

(A)   Yes, because it would have been in the insured client's best interest to settle for $500,000.

(B)   Yes, because it is unethical for the litigator to abide by the insurance company's instructions.

(C)   No, because the insured client signed the prepared consent form.

(D)   No, because the litigator was obligated to follow the insurance company's instructions regarding settlement.

QUESTION 228

An attorney was hired by a sophisticated businessman to represent him during the acquisition of stock sufficient to receive a controlling share of a company. In the course of the representation, the attorney provided the businessman with public information that the businessman was not aware of and that would be relevant to an investor who was interested in selling the shares for a profit. Unfortunately, the information was only beneficial if the sale was to take place within the next three weeks, which would violate insider trading laws. Despite knowing that the transaction would violate the law, the businessman used the information the attorney provided to immediately sell the shares to another investor at a significant profit.

The businessman was subsequently brought into court to defend against allegations that he violated the securities laws, and the attorney requested that he be permitted to withdraw because the businessman used his advice to commit this crime. The attorney truthfully stated that the businessman would have no trouble securing adequate representation and provided a written statement that he would turn over all relevant work product to the subsequent counsel. The judge considered the attorney's request but denied it.

May the attorney nonetheless withdraw from the representation?

(A)   No, because the attorney cannot withdraw without a material adverse impact on the businessman's interests.

(B)   No, because the judge has denied the withdrawal request.

(C)   Yes, because the businessman used his services to commit a crime.

(D)   Yes, because the attorney has made arrangements to provide the work product to the businessman's next attorney.

QUESTION 229

A recent law school graduate took a position as a paralegal with the attorney general's office where she helped research and prepare attorney general opinions. One such opinion was in response to a question from a local nonprofit legal services center regarding the appropriateness of a nearby city's zoning ordinances. The opinion concluded that the zoning ordinances were inappropriate. After passing the bar, the new attorney accepted an offer to work for the nearby city as an assistant city attorney, where she was asked to participate in litigation challenging the opinion.

Can the attorney appropriately participate in this litigation?

(A)   No, unless she receives consent from the attorney general's office.

(B)   No, because she helped prepare the opinion.

(C)   Yes, because she was not an attorney when she helped prepare the opinion.

(D)   Yes, because there is no conflict when a government employee moves from one governmental office to another.

QUESTION 230

A small boy was bitten by a toy poodle that became aggressive as soon as the boy walked near it. This biting incident was the third one in a month, each involving a different toy poodle. The state had a dangerous dog statute that classified several large dog breeds as dangerous, and owners of those types of dogs were required to take extra measures to ensure that the public is safe from their dogs. An attorney who saw news coverage of the three incidents offered to represent the small boy in a suit against the dog owner using a claim under the dangerous dog statute. Toy poodles were not included in the list of dogs under the statute; so the small boy did not really have a claim under the existing statute, but the attorney believed, in good faith, that the breed was dangerous and that the statute should be extended to include it.

Is the attorney subject to discipline?

(A)   No, because the boy suffered injuries from the bite and deserves to be compensated for his injuries.

(B)   No, because the attorney had a good faith belief that the statute should be extended to include toy poodles.

(C)   Yes, because toy poodles are not classified as a dangerous breed under the statute.

(D)   Yes, because it is unlikely that the boy's claim will be successful.

QUESTION 231

A doctor was moving to a new city and was in the market to purchase a new home. The doctor shopped around for several months and finally settled on a home that was being sold by the seller without assistance from either a realtor or an attorney. One of the doctor's fellow physicians recommended an attorney to help the doctor negotiate the sale and to handle the closing. The attorney contacted the seller and said that she was going to facilitate the price negotiations as a disinterested intermediary. When the seller told the attorney his starting price, the attorney truthfully advised the doctor that the initial asking price was fair but that he might be able to negotiate a lower price. The doctor ultimately offered to purchase the house for the asking price, and the parties completed the sale to the satisfaction of everyone involved.

Is the attorney subject to discipline?

(A)   No, because the house sold for the seller's initial offering price.

(B)   No, because she advised the doctor truthfully that the price was fair.

(C)   Yes, because the doctor agreed to purchase the house for more than he could have negotiated for.

(D)   Yes, because the attorney told the seller that she was a disinterested intermediary.

QUESTION 232

For two years after being admitted to the bar, an attorney served as a law clerk to a state trial judge who frequently heard contract dispute cases. One case that came before the trial judge was a contentious case involving a dispute between a married couple and the contractor hired to build their palatial home. The couple had appealed the trial court decision, researched and written in large part by the attorney, that held in favor of the contractor, and the appellate court reversed and remanded in part.

While the appeal was pending, the attorney had taken a new job with a local law firm, where he had successfully represented three different clients in individual contract disputes. The contractor parted ways with the lawyer who represented him at the initial trial and hired the attorney to represent him. The married couple was aware of the representation and did not object.

Is the attorney subject to discipline?

(A)   No, because he was not the judge in the initial case.

(B)   No, because the married couple did not object to the representation.

(C)   Yes, because he assisted in drafting the initial opinion.

(D)   Yes, because he does not have sufficient trial experience to provide competent representation.

QUESTION 233

A wife was charged with capital murder in the death of her husband, and she retained a prominent criminal defense attorney to represent her. The defense attorney met with the wife on a number of occasions prior to the plea hearing and advised her during one meeting that, in his experience, a jury trial is generally more favorable for criminal defendants. The wife acknowledged that she understood the advice and would think about it. Immediately prior to the plea hearing, the defense attorney asked the wife whether or not she wanted a jury trial, and she told him emphatically that she would prefer to have the judge decide the case.

At the hearing, the judge asked the defense attorney how the wife wished to plead, and the defense attorney responded not guilty. The defense attorney, knowing that his client was almost certain to be found guilty by the judge, also told the judge that the wife wished to have her case tried by a jury. After a week-long trial and four hours of deliberation, the jury found the wife not guilty of capital murder, and she was acquitted of all charges.

Is the attorney subject to discipline?

(A)   Yes, because the defense attorney should have provided advice on more than one occasion about the benefits of a jury trial.

(B)   Yes, because the wife expressly told the defense attorney that she wanted to waive her right to a trial by jury.

(C)   No, because the defense attorney's experience indicated that it was in the wife's best interest to have a jury trial.

(D)   No, because the wife received a favorable verdict due to the defense attorney's decision.

QUESTION 234

An attorney was planning to get married and to go on a two-week European honeymoon. Although he had endeavored to complete any outstanding work prior to the wedding, one of the attorney's clients was involved in a protracted dispute with a former employee, and it appeared unlikely that the case would be resolved before the attorney's vacation. The attorney asked his partner, an experienced practitioner, to handle any matters that arose in the case during his absence and delivered the client's case file to the partner. Prior to leaving for the wedding, the attorney informed the client that he would be unavailable and that he had made arrangements for the partner to monitor the client's case. The client had not previously asked the attorney to refrain discussing the case with the partner, and the attorney did not ask the client to sign a consent form. He also told the client that the client was free to seek alternate representation.

Is the attorney subject to discipline?

(A)   No, because the attorney knew his partner was competent to handle the client's case.

(B)   No, because the client had not instructed the attorney to restrict the client's information to himself.

(C)   Yes, because the attorney did not get the client's written informed consent before sharing the client's file with the partner.

(D)   Yes, because a honeymoon is not sufficient justification for the attorney to disclose the client's information.

QUESTION 235

A cyclist was riding toward oncoming traffic in a bike lane on a busy road (as required by local ordinance) when she was struck by a large SUV. The cyclist was thrown from her bike and sustained severe, life-threatening injuries. A personal injury attorney happened to be drinking his morning coffee at an outdoor café at the time of the accident and witnessed the entire thing. He clearly saw that the driver of the SUV was typing a message on his mobile phone before the accident and crossed into the bike lane. Although other people in the area saw the vehicle strike the cyclist, he was the only person to witness the driver's negligent behavior with the phone. The driver maintained his innocence and claimed that he had both hands on the wheel at the time of the accident.

Three weeks after the accident, the cyclist had recovered enough from her injuries to seek the advice of counsel, and her family told her that the police officer had spoken with the attorney at the scene. Thinking that it was a stroke of luck that the attorney was there that day, the cyclist contacted the attorney and asked if he would be willing to represent her. The attorney agreed to the representation on the condition that the cyclist provide written consent to his providing testimony on her behalf. He explained that although the driver's phone records indicate that he sent a text right before the accident, the cyclist's case would be much stronger if she could use the attorney's eyewitness testimony to help establish the driver's negligence. The cyclist was more than willing to provide the consent.

Is it proper for the attorney to represent the cyclist?

(A)   Yes, because he was the only witness who saw the driver texting.

(B)   Yes, because the client provided informed consent to the attorney providing eyewitness testimony.

(C)   No, because it is improper for an attorney to represent a client when he witnessed the accident.

(D)   No, because the attorney is the only witness to the driver's texting.

QUESTION 236

An attorney's nephew had been involved in an altercation, and he was being held in the county detention center on aggravated assault charges. The nephew used his one phone call to call the attorney at 3:00 a.m., waking him up, and asked him to come to the detention center to attempt to get him out on bail. The attorney's primary practice was in elder law, and his only experience with criminal law was when he participated in the criminal clinic at his law school, nearly twenty years before. Despite this lack of skill, the attorney arrived at the detention center and, using his general understanding of the law, succeeded in getting his nephew out on bail. The next morning, the attorney contacted one of his law school friends who practiced criminal law and who agreed to represent the nephew going forward.

Is the attorney subject to discipline?

(A) No, because his nephew's arrest was an emergency situation.

(B) No, because he secured competent representation for his nephew as soon as practicable.

(C) Yes, because the attorney did not have adequate knowledge of criminal law.

(D) Yes, because the attorney's only criminal law experience was twenty years prior to the nephew's arrest.

QUESTION 237

A teenager was stopped by a city police officer while driving down a neighborhood street on a Friday evening, and during the course of the stop, the officer searched the vehicle and found an unlabeled bottle of pills. The pills were a type that was commonly abused by teenagers, and the teenager was arrested and charged with possession of a controlled substance. A public defender was assigned to represent the teenager, and she learned that the prosecutor intended to produce the teenager's pharmacist as a witness. Thus, the public defender requested that the pharmacist produce all pharmacy records relevant to the teenager's case. The public defender hoped to show that the teenager had a valid prescription for the pills. The pharmacist said that he would meet with the public defender as long as the prosecutor was present.

At the meeting, the public defender requested to see the teenager's prescription records, but as the pharmacist was reaching for the documentation, the prosecutor advised him to withhold the records for the month immediately prior to the arrest. The prosecutor told the pharmacist that withholding the documents would not adversely affect the pharmacist's interests.

Is the prosecutor subject to discipline?

(A) No, because the pharmacist's records were not relevant to the teenager's defense.

(B) No, because the prosecutor reasonably believed that withholding the documentation would not harm the pharmacist's interests.

(C) Yes, because the pharmacist is not related to the teenager.

(D) Yes, because advising the pharmacist to withhold the records was tantamount to asking the pharmacist to falsify testimony.

QUESTION 238

A prominent defense attorney was invited to a charitable event at a local country club hosted by the state bar association. He and his wife arrived fashionably late and proceeded to make the rounds, speaking with friends and colleagues, including the counsel for the plaintiff in a negligence suit that the defense attorney was handling. As they walked up to the buffet, the defense attorney noticed that the judge assigned to the negligence suit, who also happened to be a long time friend of both the defense attorney and plaintiff's counsel, was also in attendance. The defense attorney needed to request an extension for discovery and felt that approaching the judge in a casual setting might help his chances. He found the plaintiff's counsel and told him that he planned to speak to the judge, and the plaintiff's counsel did not object. The defense attorney then approached the judge while he was alone and made his request.

Is the defense attorney subject to discipline?

(A) No, because the defense attorney spoke to plaintiff's counsel about his plans prior to speaking with the judge.

(B) No, because the judge was the defense attorney's personal friend.

(C) Yes, because the plaintiff's counsel was not present when the defense attorney spoke with the judge.

(D) Yes, because it is improper to conduct business at a social function.

QUESTION 239

Two former business partners have been locked in a contentious dispute because one partner violated the partnership agreement by transferring his entire membership interest to his wife. The remaining partner retained a lawyer to represent him in settlement negotiations with the former partner, and the lawyer and the former partner's attorney had met several times in an attempt to resolve the issue. While the negotiations were ongoing, the local arts council hosted a fundraising dinner at the former partner's home, and the attorney attended. The former partner approached the attorney, asked her how she was doing, and discussed the upcoming season for the local theater group.

Was the attorney's conduct appropriate?

(A) Yes, because the attorney and the former partner discussed the local art scene.

(B) Yes, because the former partner initiated the conversation.

(C) No, because the former partner is represented in the negotiations.

(D) No, because attending the dinner has the appearance of impropriety.

QUESTION 240

A businessman was preparing to purchase a competitor's business and retained an attorney to help in negotiating the sale and preparing the documents. The attorney provided the businessman with a written estimate of his fees and the number of hours he expected to devote to the work. The businessman wrote the attorney a check for the full estimated amount, which the attorney deposited into the one interest-bearing trust account he had set up for his client's funds. After the check had cleared, the attorney used all of the available funds to pay outstanding debts incurred by his firm.

Subsequently, the attorney successfully negotiated a favorable purchase price for the business and prepared all of the necessary paperwork, but the transaction was more labor-intensive than expected, and the attorney billed the businessman for an additional thirty hours of work. The businessman promptly paid the bill.

Is the attorney subject to discipline?

(A)   No, because the attorney earned the fees that he used to pay bills.

(B)   No, because the attorney deposited the funds into a separate interest-bearing account.

(C)   Yes, because the attorney accepted a check for fees that he had not earned.

(D)   Yes, because the attorney used client funds prior to earning them.

QUESTION 241

A lawyer was hired to represent a celebrity who was accused in several hit and run accidents, one of which had resulted in the death of the other driver. The trial, as was to be expected, became a media spectacle, and the lawyer suddenly became a household name. While eating at an upscale diner one evening, the lawyer was approached by a television movie producer who was interested in producing a movie based on the facts of the trial. Seeing the offer as potentially beneficial to both his client and himself, the lawyer approached his client and asked her to give him one quarter of the media rights. The client agreed, and the lawyer negotiated a movie deal. After months of testimony, the jury found the celebrity client not guilty. The not guilty verdict generated even more interest in the film, and the lawyer and the client made millions of dollars.

Is the lawyer subject to discipline?

(A)   No, because the lawyer received only a one quarter interest in the media rights.

(B)   No, because the arrangement was beneficial to both the lawyer and the client.

(C)   Yes, because the lawyer entered into the transaction prior to the jury reaching the verdict.

(D)   No, because arranging for the movie deal did not adversely impact the lawyer's ability to
        represent the client.

QUESTION 242

A luxury home developer entered into a contract with a general contractor to oversee the construction of fifteen multimillion dollar homes in a new subdivision. The contract outlined the fees to be paid to the contractor and stipulated that the general contractor was to be paid upon the completion of each home. After the first home was completed and occupied, the general contractor submitted his invoices, and the developer mailed the general contractor a check; however, the general contractor maintained that the check should have been for a larger amount based on the wording of the contract.

The developer hired a lawyer to represent her during the contract dispute. Because the developer informed the lawyer that she did not want to settle during mediation, the case went to trial. The lawyer and developer discussed the possibility of the developer testifying on her own behalf, and the developer informed the lawyer that she wished to take the stand. During the trial, though, the lawyer felt that the case was going so well that calling the developer to testify would not help the case, so he rested without calling her to the stand. The court ultimately decided in favor of the general contractor.

Is the lawyer subject to discipline?

(A)   Yes, because the developer told the lawyer that she wished to testify.

(B)   Yes, because the case was decided against the developer.

(C)   No, because the lawyer abided by the developer's wish to not settle during mediation.

(D)   No, because the case was a civil case.

QUESTION 243

An attorney was approached separately by a husband and wife who each wanted the attorney to draft their individual wills. The wife told the attorney that she intended to leave her entire estate to her husband if she were to pass first. In the course of individual discussions, though, the husband disclosed to the attorney that he had fathered a child with a one-time fling, and he wished to provide for the child and the child's mother in his will. This gift would substantially reduce the amount that the wife would receive if she were to outlive her husband.

If the attorney tells the wife of the child and the gift, will she be subject to discipline?

(A)   No, because the attorney has implied authority to disclose the information in order to effectively represent the wife.

(B)   No, if the attorney reasonably believes the disclosure is necessary to prevent financial injury to the wife.

(C)   Yes, because the attorney can never represent a husband and wife concurrently.

(D)   Yes, because the husband has not given informed consent to the disclosure.

QUESTION 244

At a cocktail party hosted by a local arts consortium, a slightly inebriated doctor approached an attorney and began telling her about a recent surgery that had not gone well. According to the doctor, he had accidentally left a sponge in the patient after a kidney transplant, but he did not realize it until it was too late. Before he stumbled to the next guest, the doctor said that he hoped the patient would not realize the error because he no longer had medical malpractice insurance.

A month later, the patient began having health issues, and her general practitioner discovered the sponge. The patient has approached the attorney to represent her in a suit against the original doctor.

Can the attorney represent the patient against the doctor without being subject to discipline?

(A)   No, because the doctor disclosed damaging information to the attorney at the party.

(B)   No, because the doctor and attorney were discussing forming an attorney-client relationship.

(C)   Yes, because the doctor could not expect confidentiality when discussing the information outside of the attorney's office.

(D)   Yes, because the doctor was not a prospective client.

QUESTION 245

An attorney was preparing for his client's upcoming trial on battery charges. The key to his client's defense was testimony by the client who stated during deposition that the she was not in the room when the victim was struck in the back of the head by a baseball bat. The night before the client was set to take the stand, she disclosed to her attorney that she was in fact in the room when the battery occurred but was not the one wielding the bat. The attorney advised the client to keep her trial testimony consistent with the deposition testimony because otherwise the other parties would discover that her original testimony was false. At trial the client testified that she was not in the room when the battery occurred.

Is the attorney subject to discipline for her trial preparation?

(A)   Yes, because he should have asked his client prior to the deposition whether or not she was present at the scene of the crime.

(B)   Yes, because he advised the client to continue the lie that she began at the deposition.

(C)   No, because the client's testimony was consistent with her deposition.

(D)   No, because the attorney had a duty to provide the advice necessary for his client to win her case.

QUESTION 246

An attorney represented her current client, a businessman, in negotiating an agreement with a multinational manufacturing corporation to supply widgets. Two years prior to negotiating the agreement, the attorney had worked as in-house counsel for the corporation. The attorney properly disclosed the prior representation, both the businessman and corporation consented in writing to the attorney's representation of the businessman, and the attorney did not use any of the corporation's confidential information in her representation of the businessman. The final agreement, which was signed by both the client and a representative of the corporation, contained a provision that stated that the attorney was solely representing the businessman in the transaction and that the corporation waived any conflict of interest arising from the representation. The attorney signed the agreement as well, affirming that it was a complete, true, and correct statement of the parties' agreement. Unbeknownst to the businessman, the corporate representative had consulted with the attorney on the contents of the agreement, including the provision relating to her representation of the businessman, and had relied heavily on her advice to the exclusion of the advice of the corporation's current in-house counsel.

Can the attorney be subject to discipline for her actions?

(A)   Yes, because the agreement contained a false statement.

(B)   Yes, because an attorney cannot represent a new client with interests adverse to a former client.

(C)   No, because the attorney received informed written consent from the corporation to represent the new client.

(D)   No, because the attorney did not use any of the corporation's confidential information in representing the businessman.

QUESTION 247

A newly licensed attorney decided after passing the bar that she would rather hang out her own shingle than attempt to compete with other recent graduates for a job at an established firm. The new attorney had studied tax law extensively in law school and had spent two summers working for one of two tax firms in the city; so she decided to work exclusively on tax related matters as there appeared to be a need. After securing an office, the attorney placed several advertisements in online trade magazines that included the firm's name – The Tax Law Associates, LP , the attorney's name, the office address, and the statement that the attorney specialized in tax law. A prospective client noticed the advertisement and called the attorney, and the attorney was able to successfully represent the client with the IRS.

Is the attorney subject to discipline for any of her actions?

(A)   Yes, because the attorney is not permitted to state a specialty in an advertisement.

(B)   Yes, because the attorney is a solo practitioner.

(C)   No, because the advertisement provided the attorney's name and address.

(D)   No, because the attorney intended to work exclusively on tax law matters.

QUESTION 248

A judge came into the office several hours early one morning to prepare for a hearing that was scheduled for 10:00 a.m., partly because his assistant was on vacation for the week. While he was working, he received a frantic call from his daughter telling him that his wife had broken her ankle and they were heading to the emergency room. Knowing that the other judges were not expected to be in the office until well after 10:00 a.m., the judge attempted to first call plaintiff's counsel to reschedule the hearing, but was directed to voicemail. After leaving a message that the hearing would have to be rescheduled for the following week due to a personal emergency, he called the defendant's counsel, who answered the phone. The judge explained the situation and asked the defendant's counsel to decide on a new time with the plaintiff's counsel and let one of the other judges know what they decided. On his way to the hospital, the judge left another voicemail for the plaintiff's counsel explaining what he and the defendant's counsel had discussed, affording him the same opportunity to provide input on the date for the rescheduled meeting.

Is the judge subject to discipline?

(A)   No, because the assistant was not available to make the call for him.

(B)   No, because he called to reschedule a hearing and informed the other party of the details of the call.

(C)   Yes, because the plaintiff's counsel was not on the call with the defendant's counsel.

(D)   Yes, because he should have waited for another judge to make the call.

QUESTION 249

A member of the local school board recently resigned amid the fallout from a scandal, and two candidates had placed their names on the ballot for a replacement. One of the candidates, a doctor, was good friends with a local tax attorney. While leaving the supermarket, the tax attorney was approached by a television reporter who asked her what she thought of the doctor's opponent. The tax attorney, recalling that the opponent had been arrested a number of years before for driving while intoxicated, said that the opponent was a lush and was not capable of setting a good example for the community's youth.

Were the tax attorney's remarks proper?

(A)   Yes, because the candidates are running for the school board.

(B)   Yes, because the tax attorney's statements were based on her honest opinion.

(C)   No, because the tax attorney made the remarks with reckless disregard as to whether they were true.

(D)   No, because attorneys are not permitted to weigh in on elections.

QUESTION 250

A general practice attorney has been retained by a realtor to represent her in litigation involving a contract dispute with a former employee. During an informal meeting, the realtor told the attorney that she would like to better assist her seller clients in navigating a sale and asked the attorney about seller's rights under the state's law, which included the right to rescind an offer within three days of making it. The attorney had learned this information through a local bar association website. Shortly thereafter, the realtor advised a seller of his right to rescind his offer, and the seller successfully relied on that advice in making his decision.

Is the attorney subject to discipline?

(A)   Yes, because the realtor provided advice to her client on his rights under state law.

(B)   Yes, because the attorney was not competent to provide advice on real estate law.

(C)   No, because information on the seller's right to rescind was available on the internet.

(D)   No, because there was privity between the seller and the attorney through the realtor.

QUESTION 251

An attorney with a solo practice was in a terrible car accident, and despite the best efforts of the medical staff, the brain injuries that the attorney suffered left the attorney with severely diminished mental capacity. Recognizing that the attorney would never be able to practice law again, the attorney's spouse, a college professor, made arrangements, with another solo practitioner, to sell the firm for a reasonable purchase price over the course of three years. Payment for the practice was to be made from the legal fees earned by the solo practitioner from the attorney's existing clients. The purchasing solo practitioner agreed not to increase the client's fees. The attorney's spouse sent notices to each of the clients including the required disclosures (all in compliance with the rule for the sale of a law practice).

Is the purchasing solo practitioner subject to discipline?

(A)   Yes, because the purchase price is being paid from earned legal fees to a non-attorney.

(B)   Yes, because she did not purchase the practice from a deceased attorney.

(C)   No, because the purchase price is reasonable.

(D)   No, because the attorney was disabled and unable to continue practicing law.

QUESTION 252

A partnership was formed by two friends to develop shopping malls in small towns across the country. During construction of one of the malls, a concrete wall collapsed on a construction worker, causing permanent paralysis. The worker brought suit against the partners to recover for his injuries and for other amounts, and the partners hired an attorney to represent them in the case. The partners acknowledged that they would likely fare better if they were to settle with the worker prior to trial, so they authorized the attorney to discuss a potential settlement of up to $5 million with the worker. At pre-trial discussions, the worker's lawyer offered to settle for $4 million, and the partners' attorney decided that it would be best for the wealthier of the partners to bear the larger share of the settlement.

When the attorney met with the wealthier partner, he told the partner that the worker had offered to settle and that the partner's share would be $3.5 million. When he met with the other partner, he told that partner that his share of the settlement would be $500,000. Concerned that the partners would not agree to the settlement if they knew what the other was paying, the attorney did not disclose the amount of each payment to the other partner. After the discussions, each partner signed a written consent form, agreeing to the settlement.

Is the attorney subject to discipline?

(A)   Yes, because the partners might have succeeded in owing a smaller amount if the case had proceeded to trial.

(B)   Yes, because he did not tell each partner what the other would be paying in the settlement.

(C)   No, because the partners acknowledged that a settlement might be more beneficial than the risk of losing at trial.

(D)   No, because the partners provided written consent to the settlement.

QUESTION 253

A businessman seeking to open a local franchise of a nationwide restaurant contacted his attorney to see if he would be interested in investing in the venture. The attorney, who had extensive experience in drafting organizational documents for various business entities, suggested that they form a partnership and offered to draft the organizational documents.

The businessman agreed to the arrangement, and the attorney prepared the partnership agreement. The agreement was nearly fifty pages long and included a small provision stating that as compensation for preparing the agreement, the attorney would receive double the return on his investment before any creditors were paid if the business failed. The attorney signed the agreement and sent it to the businessman with a note on the cover that the businessman should review the agreement and sign it if he had no objections. The businessman signed the agreement without reading it. When the restaurant closed down three years later, the attorney demanded the double return provided for in the agreement.

Was the attorney's conduct proper?

(A)   Yes, because the attorney provided a service in exchange for the return on his investment.

(B)   Yes, because the attorney advised the businessman to review the agreement before signing it.

(C)   No, because the attorney did not follow the requirements for entering into a business arrangement with his client.

(D)   No, because the attorney used his expertise in drafting business documents to the detriment of his client.

QUESTION 254

An attorney was approached by a college student who had been arrested for selling a controlled substance and who was seeking representation for the criminal trial. The attorney, who had handled hundreds of similar cases, informed the college student that his normal fee was $5,000, and the two parties agreed that the fee could be paid in twelve monthly installments. The agreement presented to and signed by the college student clearly stated that the attorney would withdraw from representation upon 30 days' notice if any monthly installment was more than five days late. Once the agreement was reached, the attorney began appearing at hearings for the college student and conducting other business on his behalf.

The college student failed to pay the fourth month's installment, and six days after the due date the attorney mailed him a written notification that his services would terminate in thirty days. At the scheduled hearing the next week, the attorney entered a request with the court - as required by the law in the jurisdiction -- to withdraw from his representation. The attorney presented the agreement and a copy of the mailed notice as evidence that the college student was on notice of the imminent withdrawal. The judge ruled that the attorney could withdraw and appointed a public defender to represent the college student going forward.

May the attorney withdraw at the end of the thirty days?

(A)		Yes, because the judge permitted the withdrawal.

(B)		Yes, because the fee agreement permitted the attorney to withdraw when the fee was not paid.

(C)		No, because the withdrawal will have a material adverse impact on the college student's interests.

(D)		No, because an attorney may not withdraw from representation for mere nonpayment of fees.

MPRE ANSWERS

MPRE Practice Questions

ANSWERS AND EXPLANATIONS

B.   Answers and Explanations

ANSWER 1

THE CLIENT-LAWYER RELATIONSHIP

C is the correct answer in this permissive withdrawal situation. Under MRPC 1.16(b)(5), an attorney may withdraw from representation if the attorney's client fails substantially to satisfy an obligation to the attorney regarding the attorney's services and has been given reasonable notice that the attorney will withdraw unless the obligation is satisfied. Although the agreement gives the client notice of the possibility of withdrawal, the attorney would still need to give the client notice that the attorney is going to invoke the clause because the client would need time to seek new counsel. Keep in mind that, in some cases, the attorney may need to obtain permission of a court. In any event, the attorney must take steps to protect the client's interests.

A is a wrong answer because it is too categorical, and failure to pay for services is an explicitly listed reason for permissive withdrawal. Likewise, B is wrong because, although attorneys should afford their clients the opportunity to execute certain types of agreements between them after consulting with some other lawyer, this is not the question's dispositive issue. Answer D is wrong because it does not cover all of the requirements for withdrawal, particularly that the attorney warned the client that the attorney intended to withdraw unless the obligation was fulfilled.

ANSWER 2

CLIENT CONFIDENTIALITY

B is the correct answer in this client-lawyer confidentiality situation. MRPC 1.6 provides that the attorney may not reveal information relating to the representation of a client unless (1) the client gives consent, (2) disclosure is required in order to carry out the representation, or (3) the disclosure falls within six specific categories. Here, the client specifically ordered the attorney not to fill out the form, and because the dispute is settled, disclosure is not required to carry out the litigation. Therefore, because the state's law does not require attorneys to complete the form, no basis exists for the attorney's disclosure here.

C is a wrong answer because disclosure would not be proper even if the attorney's work product is not revealed. A is an incorrect answer because disclosure of this information is not subject to a best interest standard, and the client's best interest is not one of the six situations where an attorney must reveal confidential information. D is a wrong answer because the duty of confidentiality continues even after the attorney ceases representing the plaintiff.

ANSWER 3

LITIGATION AND OTHER FORMS OF ADVOCACY

B is the correct answer to this question regarding the filing of baseless or frivolous pleadings. Both Federal Rule of Civil Procedure 11 and MRPC 3.1, the Rule requiring meritorious claims and contentions, require that an attorney base a pleading's claims on existing law. Here, the repeal of the federal statute caused the attorney's complaint to lose its support by existing law. But the attorney's timely compliance with Rule 11 by means of filing a valid amended complaint cured that violation. A is a wrong answer because it is not based on those legal provisions. C and D are incorrect because they do not state valid grounds for a litigation sanction.

ANSWER 4

CONFLICTS OF INTEREST

B is the correct answer in this conflict of interest situation. The attorney cannot accept the employee as a client because his former employment by the department disqualifies him from representing her after his involvement in the handbook's development and disagreement with the attorney general. No facts indicate that the attorney sought or the department provided consent to his representation of the employee in a manner that would be directly adverse to the department. Accordingly, C and D are incorrect. A is wrong because the attorney cannot reveal to the employee the confidential information about the disagreement because the department is his former client.

ANSWER 5

THE CLIENT-LAWYER RELATIONSHIP

C is the correct answer because it accurately states the dispositive reason that would subject the attorney to discipline. Contingency fee agreements are prohibited in both criminal cases and domestic relations matters. Here, the attorney improperly entered into such an agreement that would transfer real property to him if he achieved the client's objectives in her divorce action. D is a wrong answer because it is not the dispositive issue based on these facts. A and B incorrectly answer "yes" based on irrelevant reasons.

ANSWER 6

COMMUNICATION ABOUT LEGAL SERVICES

D is the correct answer because the advertisement will subject the attorney to discipline because it is misleading or false. MRPC 7.1 provides that attorneys may not make false or misleading communications about their legal services. A communication is false or misleading if it contains a material misrepresentation of fact. Here, the advertisement stated that attorney had a perfect trial win record when she actually lost one trial. Although she won on appeal of the case, her advertisement made a material misrepresentation of fact -- that she had a perfect trial win record -- because she lost one trial. A communication is false or misleading if it omits a fact necessary to make the statement considered as a whole not materially misleading. Here, the attorney's advertisement left out the fact that she lost one trial, which is required to make her statement about her trial win record, considered as a whole, not materially misleading. Because the attorney's advertisement made a false communication about her services, it was improper under MRPC 7.1. As such, A is a wrong answer because it states the opposite as D. B is not correct because principles of constitutional freedom of speech do not protect attorney advertisements that are false or misleading. Thus, C is incorrect because it is not the most on-point answer, although it is accurate with respect to the attorney's false or misleading advertisement.

ANSWER 7

JUDICIAL CONDUCT

A is the correct answer because it accurately applies the relevant rule to these facts. The gift could arguably be incident to the spouse's business and could reasonably be perceived as intended to influence the judge in terms of the owner's action against the builder. B is wrong because the owner's giving of the same gift to the builder would not mitigate the fact that the judge should not accept the gift under the Rule. C is incorrect because a business relationship is not required to prohibit the receipt of a gift by the judge. D is incorrect because judges can only accept gifts under limited circumstances.

ANSWER 8

COMPETENCE, MALPRACTICE, AND OTHER CIVIL LIABILITY

D is the correct answer because the attorney's conduct violated MRPC 1.3, which requires the attorney to act with reasonable diligence and promptness in representing the plaintiff. The attorney's failure to file a mediation summary or motion to set aside the default, and her vacation before filing the motion to set aside the default judgment, shows a lack of diligence and promptness in prosecuting the plaintiff's case against the defendant. Thus, the attorney lacked a good cause for and meritorious defense to the default. Consequently, the court properly denied her motion to set aside the default. Accordingly, answers B and C are incorrect. A is a wrong answer because the dispositive issue is the attorney's lack of diligence and promptness and she cannot affect her liability by paying the plaintiff the cause of action's fair market value.

ANSWER 9

COMPETENCE, MALPRACTICE, AND OTHER CIVIL LIABILITY

A is the correct answer because the attorney did not violate any pertinent rule of professional conduct and acted reasonably in declining the representation. MPRE 1.1 requires that an attorney provide competent representation to clients, which requires thoroughness and preparation reasonably necessary for the representation. Here, the attorney knew that she would not have the time to properly prepare for the individual's case, so she recommended that he meet with another lawyer. She also indicated that the individual needed to meet with other counsel quickly in order to preserve his enforcement right. Although factually accurate, B is a wrong answer because the attorney must still act reasonably in declining the representation. Thus, A is a more dispositive and definitive response. C and D are incorrect because no civil liability arises from these facts. With regard to C, the facts do not indicate that the attorney's advertisement was either false or misleading as she engages in transactional work, and she is only recommending that the individual seek different counsel because she does not have time to competently work, not because she did not perform that kind of work. With respect to D, the attorney had no duty to give the individual notice of the statute of limitations, and she performed all of her duties when she suggested that he needed to meet with another lawyer quickly.

ANSWER 10

CLIENT CONFIDENTIALITY

C is the correct answer because it follows the Rule permitting the attorney to disclose the otherwise confidential fax in order to address the defendant's allegations in the disciplinary proceeding regarding the attorney's representation of the plaintiff. Generally, MRPC 1.6(a) prohibits an attorney from revealing information obtained while representing a client. MRPC 1.6(b) permits such revelation under certain conditions. These conditions include revealing the information "to respond to allegations in any proceeding concerning the lawyer's representation of the client." Although it relates to a valid Rule, D is a wrong answer because arguably the plaintiff's testimony perpetrated a fraud on the judge. A is an incorrect answer because the general rule of client-lawyer confidentiality is subject to an exception that is controlling under these facts. B is a wrong answer for the same reason, regardless of whether the plaintiff could be prosecuted for perjury. Under these facts, it is likely that he could be prosecuted for perjury.

ANSWER 11

REGULATION OF THE LEGAL PROFESSION

C is the correct answer for two reasons. First, the Rule describing what constitutes professional misconduct, MRPC 8.4, includes instances of dishonesty such as misrepresentation. Second, MRPC 8.5 provides that regardless of where the attorney's misconduct occurs, she is subject to the disciplinary authority of state one. Indeed, she is subject to the disciplinary authority of both state one and state two. Thus, B is an incorrect answer because she is subject to discipline in both states. D is an incorrect answer because the Rules do not require that the attorney be convicted of a crime in the other state in order for her to be subject to discipline in her home state. A is a wrong answer because the attorney was licensed as an attorney when her misconduct occurred, and the Rules contemplate that misconduct that may lead to discipline may occur while an attorney is not serving in that capacity.

ANSWER 12

CONFLICTS OF INTEREST

B is the correct answer because the Rules require that the attorney inform the defendant of the grandfather's payment offer before getting the defendant's consent to keep and use the grandfather's check. Specifically, MRPC 1.8(f) permits an attorney to accept compensation from someone other than the client if (1) the client consents, (2) the third party does not interfere with the attorney's independent use of her professional judgment, and (3) the attorney does not reveal confidential client information to the third party. A is a wrong answer because the Rules do not prohibit the grandfather from paying the attorney for representing the defendant. C is an incorrect answer because, although factually accurate, the Rules do not allow the attorney's defense of the defendant to be influenced by the grandfather. Moreover, that is a less dispositive provision of the Rules than their "informed consent" requirement. D is a wrong answer because it is factually inaccurate.

ANSWER 13

THE CLIENT-LAWYER RELATIONSHIP

D is the correct answer because the client only consented to the original hourly rates in the retainer agreement, which the parties had not modified. Moreover, the attorney failed to communicate the changed hourly rates to the client, and MRPC 1.5(b) requires the attorney to communicate any changes in the fees to the client. C is a wrong answer because the fact that the retainer agreement was in writing does not subject the attorney to discipline when the Rules require that agreement to be written. Additionally, the parties may modify a written retainer agreement if the attorney communicates the change to the client. A is an incorrect answer because the client's lack of consent, not reasonableness of the hourly rate increases, is the dispositive issue. B is a wrong answer because the retainer agreement's requirement that the client pay hourly rates does not necessarily apply to the increased hourly rates.

ANSWER 14

REGULATION OF THE LEGAL PROFESSION

C is the correct answer because by making false statements to the cashier, the lawyer violates the MRPC 8.4, which makes dishonesty and misrepresentation professional misconduct. Additionally, these statements are false partly because the attorney represents that the communications will be confidential when in fact the cashier's interests are adverse to those of the corporation. In that situation, under Comment [10] of MRPC 1.13, the discussions may not be privileged. D and B are incorrect answers because the dispositive issue is the attorney's false statements, not her dealing with the cashier as an unrepresented person. However, the attorney likely should have advised the cashier of the advisability of retaining counsel. A is a wrong answer because the lack of potential legal proceedings is not the controlling issue. Note that if the attorney obtained any incriminating statements from the cashier, she might have done that in a way that violated the cashier's rights.

ANSWER 15

CONFLICTS OF INTEREST

D is the correct answer because the attorney cannot represent the individuals after her substantial participation in representing the department for one year, particularly here when no facts indicate that she has sought or received the department's written informed consent to this new representation. MRPC 1.11 mandates that a former government attorney may not, without first obtaining the consent of his former government agency, represent a client in connection with a cause of action with which the attorney "personally and substantially" participated while employed by the government. C is a wrong answer because the facts show that the final judgment was not completely dispositive of the corporation's liability, and that fact is not dispositive in this case. A is an incorrect answer because, regardless of the attorney's competence in this legal subject matter, she must obtain the department's informed consent to represent the individuals as clients. For the same reason, B is an incorrect answer even if there is no issue of confidentiality to the extent that the department made its data available to the public.

ANSWER 16

THE CLIENT-LAWYER RELATIONSHIP

A is the correct answer because it provides the best option in terms of the facts and Rules. Pursuant to MRPC 1.5(e), the attorney and the lawyer could only make a proper division of the fee between them in proportion to the services that each performs. Also, MRPC 1.5(e) requires that the client agree to the share that each lawyer will receive and that the fee be reasonable, but neither of these is a problem in this situation. Although factually correct, B is a wrong answer because the controlling part of MRPC 1.5 does not mention that the amount must be the same, although presumably that would be the case here. C is a wrong answer because the client provided written consent as the Rules require. D is an incorrect answer because the fact that only the lawyer would try the case is not a relevant consideration under the Rules.

ANSWER 17

COMPETENCE, MALPRACTICE, AND OTHER CIVIL LIABILITY

D is the correct answer. Comment [6] to MRPC 1.1 on Competence states: "To maintain the requisite knowledge and skill, a lawyer should keep abreast of changes in the law and its practice, engage in continuing study and education and comply with all continuing legal education requirements to which the lawyer is subject." In a jurisdiction such as the home state, which does not require continuing legal education, an attorney can decline to participate in such courses. Still, an attorney has a duty of providing competent representation. As the comment above contemplates, that duty may only be satisfied by maintaining sufficient competence to handle legal matters, which can be accomplished by self-guided continuing legal education. C is a wrong answer because, although factually accurate, it does not address the dispositive issue of competence to practice law in the home state, where the dissenting attorney practices law. A is an incorrect answer because, as described earlier, the dissenting attorney could maintain legal competence without participating in the courses. B is a wrong answer because, although factually accurate, the firm's provision of malpractice insurance coverage does not make proper non-participation in the courses by the dissenting attorney.

ANSWER 18

JUDICIAL CONDUCT

B is the correct answer because the judge's failure to disqualify himself from presiding over the derivative action violates MCJC R 2.11(A). The Rule **requires disqualification in a proceeding in which the judge's impartiality might reasonably be questioned. Here, the judge should know that the parties would reasonably question his impartiality if they knew that he owned many of the corporation's shares because a judgment could affect the value of the corporation and its shares.** Under MCJC R 2.11(A)(2)-(3), a judge's impartiality might reasonably be questioned, such that the judge must disqualify himself, when (1) the judge knows that he has more than a *de minimus* interest that could be substantially affected by the proceeding; or (2) the judge knows that he has an economic interest in the subject matter in dispute or a party to a proceeding before the judge. Here, based on what the trustee told him, the judge knows that he has more than a *de minimus* interest in his many shares of the corporation's stock, the value of which could be substantially affected. Therefore, the judge knows that he has an economic interest in the derivative action and the corporation it involves. Yet, the judge went forward with pre-trial proceedings despite knowing about his economic interest in the corporation, the defendant in the case.

A is an incorrect answer because disclosure of the interest is insufficient. Although C and D are factually accurate, they do not provide reasons why the judge would not be subject to discipline.

ANSWER 19

COMMUNICATION ABOUT LEGAL SERVICES

D is the correct answer. MRPC 7.1 requires that any advertisement for an attorney or lawyer must not contain "false or misleading communications about the lawyer or the lawyer's services" and defines "false or misleading" as a communication that "contains a material misrepresentation of fact or law, or [that] omits a fact necessary to make the statement considered as a whole not materially misleading." If the attorney and the lawyer both possess those referenced degrees, then their advertisement is truthful. If they did not possess those degrees, then their advertisement would be false and misleading in violation of the Rules. C is a wrong answer because whether only law is a licensed profession is irrelevant. A is an incorrect answer because whether the appearance of L.L.M. and Ph.(D) in the advertisement is superfluous is irrelevant. B is a wrong answer because the permissibility of the advertisement's reference to L.L.M. and Ph.(D) does not depend upon restriction of the firm's practice to the subject matter for which those degrees are needed.

ANSWER 20

COMPETENCE, MALPRACTICE, AND OTHER CIVIL LIABILITY

C is the correct answer. MRPC 1.1 imposes on an attorney the mandatory duty of competence to a client, which requires "the legal knowledge, skill, thoroughness and preparation reasonably necessary for the representation." An attorney who is incompetent in his or her representation may be subject to discipline. Here, the attorney did not know about, and failed to take heed of, the judge's information about the criminal penalties to which the witness would be subject if she refused to testify. Therefore, the attorney continued to incorrectly advise her against testifying. This behavior shows a lack of the attorney's competence. B is an incorrect answer because the attorney's belief that the witness had a legal right not to respond to the question would likely not protect the attorney from discipline. The judge made such a belief unreasonable by informing the attorney of the law. A is a wrong answer because the fact that the witness followed the attorney's advice does not preclude the attorney's liability for discipline. Conversely, D is a wrong answer because the witness's violation of the law by following the attorney's counsel does not necessarily subject the attorney to discipline.

ANSWER 21

COMMUNICATIONS WITH PERSONS OTHER THAN CLIENTS

B is the best answer. MPRC 8.1 provides that an attorney may not knowingly make a false statement of material fact on an application or "fail to disclose a fact necessary to correct a misapprehension known by the person to have arisen in the matter." Because the attorney did not know of the information when he completed the form, he would not have violated the Rules unless he learns of the information and fails to correct the mistake. A is not the best answer because it does not take into account that negative information that comes to light may need to be revealed. C is incorrect because the attorney may rely on representations if he reasonably believes the information. Finally, D is incorrect because at the time the attorney did not know that the statements he was making were false.

ANSWER 22

DIFFERENT ROLES OF THE LAWYER

D is the correct answer because MRPC 3.8 requires that the district attorney, a prosecutor, timely provide the accused's lawyer with all "exculpatory" evidence that the district attorney knows either tends to either negate guilt or mitigate the offense. Here, the district attorney failed to provide that information. Thus, B is an incorrect answer because the district attorney had a duty to initially disclose the additional evidence that was later discovered.

A is a wrong answer because the district attorney's duty to provide all exculpatory evidence is not contingent upon the lawyer's making an appropriate pretrial discovery request. C is an incorrect answer because, even if it describes a likely result, it is a less optimal response than D's reference to the controlling Rule.

ANSWER 23

CLIENT CONFIDENTIALITY

B is the correct answer because the defendant's admission to the attorney about her fraudulent statements is a confidential communication, which is protected by the Rule of client-lawyer confidentiality. MRPC 1.6(a) makes it mandatory for an attorney to keep information relating to the representation of a client confidential unless the client gives informed consent. MRPC 1.6(b) provides six exceptions to the mandatory rule, under which, although not required to do so, the attorney may reveal confidential information. Under these facts, the communication does not fall under any exception to this Rule, and the defendant has not consented to its disclosure. Thus, A is a wrong answer because the attorney would be maintaining the confidentiality of that communication by not providing notice of the fraudulent statements to the police. C and D are incorrect answers because the communication is not a basis for the attorney's withdrawal from representing the defendant. Note that because the attorney did not represent the defendant when she made the fraudulent statements, the attorney is not obligated to take reasonable remedial measures such as disclosure of those statements to the legislative committee.

ANSWER 24

COMPETENCE, MALPRACTICE, AND OTHER CIVIL LIABILITY

A is the correct answer because the partner attorney recognizes that the associate lawyer does not possess the competence to handle the company's case and she does not intend to sufficiently supervise him to protect the company's interest. MRPC 1.1 requires an attorney to provide competent representation to a client. Additionally, MRPC 1.16(d) states that upon terminating representation, an attorney must do what is "reasonably practicable" to protect the client's interest. Arguably, this principle applies here to the partner attorney's transfer of the case to the associate lawyer. B is a wrong answer because it provides a less dispositive reason, even if the attorney needs the company's consent to transfer the case to the lawyer. C is an incorrect answer because the associate lawyer's law license does not qualify him as having the legal competence to handle any type of case. Instead, the associate lawyer would need to gain sufficient competence to handle an antitrust law case through sufficient study and education. D is a wrong answer because the partner attorney cannot withdraw from any case solely on the basis that handling it would cause her substantial financial hardship. Further, the facts do not indicate either a withdrawal (but rather a transfer) or any financial hardship existed.

ANSWER 25

LITIGATION AND OTHER FORMS OF ADVOCACY

C is the correct answer because the attorney knows that the defendant gave false testimony regarding her date of birth and the attorney failed to take reasonable remedial measures such as disclosure of that falsity to the tribunal. MRPC 3.3(b) imposes a duty upon an attorney in this situation to take appropriate remedial measures including, if necessary, the disclosure of any known perjury. The defendant engaged in perjury by providing testimony under oath stating her false date of birth, instead of her true date of birth.

D is a wrong answer because whether the defendant violated the law by using a fake identification card is not the dispositive issue. A is a wrong answer because it would incorrectly allow the attorney to conceal the defendant's true date of birth on the basis of client-lawyer confidentiality. Here, however, the attorney is obligated to disclose that true date because he knows that the defendant engaged in fraudulent conduct by falsely stating the date in testimony. B is an incorrect answer because the defendant's real date of birth was an issue in the proceeding.

ANSWER 26

THE CLIENT-LAWYER RELATIONSHIP

D is the correct answer because, under these circumstances, the attorney could make a permissive withdrawal from representing the client if the attorney complies with MRPC 1.16. Pursuant to MRPC 1.16(b), an attorney may withdraw if (1) the client fails substantially to fulfill an obligation to the lawyer regarding the lawyer's services; and (2) the lawyer provides reasonable warning that the lawyer will withdraw unless the client fulfills the obligation. Here, the client substantially failed to fulfill the contractual obligation to pay the attorney for services rendered as invoiced. The attorney's invoices and letters provided the client with notice of this obligation, an opportunity to fulfill the obligation, and the possibility of the attorney's withdrawal for non-payment. Thus, B is a wrong answer because the conduct of the attorney and the client does support withdrawal.

C is an incorrect answer because the client's failure to pay the invoices does not require the attorney's withdrawal. Under these facts, the withdrawal is optional or permissive, rather than required or mandatory. A is wrong because the facts do not indicate that the contract is invalid.

ANSWER 27

SAFEKEEPING FUNDS AND OTHER PROPERTY

C is the correct answer because the attorney should have deposited the check in a client trust account for the plaintiff, rather than her general account. Under MRPC 1.15, when an attorney receives funds belonging to a client, she should deposit those funds in a separate trust account for the client. Here, the check represented funds that belonged to the plaintiff because the defendant paid them in settlement of the trespass lawsuit. Thus, the attorney should have deposited the check in a separate trust account for the plaintiff before paying the plaintiff the $800 pursuant to their contingency fee agreement. Accordingly, A is not correct because the attorney deposited the check in the improper account. The fact that the case is over does not eliminate this requirement. For the same reason, B is a wrong answer even though it is factually correct.

Because the facts do not indicate that the plaintiff is disputing the amount due to the attorney, she properly deducted 20% from the $1,000 when issuing the check to the plaintiff. Alternatively, the attorney could have issued a $1,000 check to the plaintiff and then billed the plaintiff for $200. D is a wrong answer because the attorney deducted the correct amount of $200 and, as a practical matter, a 20% contingency fee is reasonable.

ANSWER 28

THE CLIENT-LAWYER RELATIONSHIP

D is the correct answer because it applies a controlling Rule to these facts. MRPC 1.2 provides that the client has sole discretion for determining the objectives of the litigation. The Rule, though, places primary responsibility for the means of representation with the attorney. The attorney must, though, reasonably consult with the client regarding the means. The Rules are not clear as to how the parties should proceed if there is a conflict regarding how the attorney should represent the client, but MRPC 1.16 permits an attorney to withdraw, among other reasons, if the client has made representation unreasonably difficult, and the client is always entitled to fire the attorney. The attorney may need to provide notice or receive permission from the court to withdraw.

Thus, A is an incorrect answer because the attorney is not obligated to follow the plaintiff's directions regarding how he will represent the plaintiff. If, as here, the plaintiff is making it unreasonably difficult for the attorney to achieve those objectives, then withdrawal may occur upon motion, notice, and court approval. B is a wrong answer because, although factually accurate, the court can authorize the attorney's withdrawal even over the plaintiff's objections. C is an incorrect answer because there are limits on when the attorney may withdraw before trial. The Rules provide for either mandatory or permissive withdrawal under certain circumstances.

ANSWER 29

CONFLICTS OF INTEREST

D is the correct answer because it accurately applies the controlling Rule to these facts. MRPC 1.8(d) prohibits an attorney from making or negotiating an agreement with a client for media or literary rights "to a portrayal or account based in substantial part on information relating to the representation" prior to the resolution of the case. The Comment to MRPC 1.8 states that the Rule is intended to prevent the possibility that the marketability or lack thereof of a certain outcome might inappropriately influence the attorney's decisions to the client's detriment. Accordingly, C is a wrong answer because an attorney may obtain such rights only after the representation's conclusion.

A is a wrong answer because application of MRPC 1.8(d) does not turn upon whether the defendant consults with another lawyer about making an agreement with the attorney regarding media or literary rights. Even if the defendant consults with another lawyer, the attorney could not make such an agreement with the defendant until after the case's conclusion. B is an incorrect answer because application of MRPC 1.8(d) is not limited to a lawyer's representation of a client in either a criminal or civil matter.

ANSWER 30

REGULATION OF THE LEGAL PROFESSION

D is the correct answer because the attorney is improperly assisting the company in practicing law when the company lacks authority to do so. MRPC 5.5 governs when an attorney may practice law, and although it provides that the attorney may delegate some work to paraprofessionals under appropriate supervision, the Comments to MRPC 5.5 make clear that it is intended to protect the public from receiving legal advice or services from an unqualified individual. C is a wrong answer because the agreement's limitation on the attorney's representation to only his own clients -- who do not present a conflict of interest to the company -- is different from a restriction on the right to practice prohibited under the Rules. The Rules are concerned with such a restriction that applies after a representation relationship ends.

A is a wrong answer because the attorney's provision of "free" service to the company's clients is not the dispositive issue, and he does not have to pay rent for using the company's office space. B is an incorrect answer because the attorney's lack of advising the company's clients does not negate his involvement in the company's unauthorized practice of law.

ANSWER 31

JUDICIAL CONDUCT

C is the correct answer because the statement is impermissible in this situation. MCJC R 2.10(B) prohibits a judge from making promises that are inconsistent with the judge's impartial performance of his adjudicative duties. The judge's statement improperly makes a promise about the issue of takings that may come before him if he is elected to the state supreme court. The statement is not consistent with the judge's impartial performance of official duties because the statement shows that he would not impartially adjudicate the issue.

Thus, D is incorrect because the judge may publicly discuss the topic, provided that the judge does this in compliance with the MCJC. A is wrong because, although a judge has a constitutional right of free speech, the MCJC limits the right under certain circumstances. B is not correct because, although immunity or privilege affords a defense to defamation claims against judicial officers, the defense does not apply here to shield the judge from discipline.

Note that the judge could have made some other proper statements on the topic during the debate. The MCJC permits judicial candidates to make general statements of opinion without being subject to discipline for making such statements. For example, in the context of this question's facts, the judge could have said: "It is my opinion that the state government is constitutionally authorized to take land if doing that is beneficial for economic development." Alternatively, the judge could have said: "I consider the issue of governmental takings to be a legitimate issue for the judiciary to resolve in its decisions."

ANSWER 32

THE CLIENT-LAWYER RELATIONSHIP

C is the correct answer because it accurately applies the permissive withdrawal provision of the Rules to these facts. MRPC 1.16(b) permits an attorney to withdraw if the client insists on continuing with a course of action that the attorney reasonably believes is fraudulent or illegal. D is an incorrect answer because the mandatory withdrawal provision of these rules does not apply unless the attorney's continued representation of the company "will result in a violation of the Rules or other law." Here, the company's continuation of the potentially fraudulent activity is not dependent upon the attorney's continued representation. A is a wrong answer because it is irrelevant that, as the company asserts, the attorney's withdrawal would indicate that the filing is unlawfully flawed because the attorney's withdrawal is permitted in this situation. Although the Rule prohibits the attorney from withdrawing if doing so would have a "material adverse effect on the interests of the client, B is a wrong answer because the company's corporate counsel would still be able to correct the filing.

ANSWER 33

LAWYERS' DUTIES TO THE PUBLIC AND THE LEGAL SYSTEM

D is the correct answer because the lawyer can make comments about the attorney's temperament and qualifications as a potential judge if they are based on his reasonable belief. Conversely, MRPC 8.2(a) prohibits the lawyer from making such statements about the qualifications or integrity of the candidate that he knows to be false or with reckless disregard as to their truth or falsity. Thus, A is a wrong answer because even if the lawyer's comments dishonored the judiciary, that alone does not render them improper. B is an incorrect answer because the Rule does not completely prohibit the lawyer from making public remarks regarding judicial candidates. C is a wrong answer because the Rule applies although the lawyer was not campaigning for judicial office.

ANSWER 34

REGULATION OF THE LEGAL PROFESSION

B is the correct answer because the attorney violated the Rules by preparing the reporter to ask about the transaction. MRPC 5.3(c) states that an attorney will be responsible for any conduct of a non-lawyer employed by the attorney that would violate the rules if the attorney engaged in it. The reporter served as the attorney's agent in contacting the contract administrator. The corporate counsel represented the contract administrator as the company's employee. Because MRPC 4.2 prohibits the attorney from communicating with a represented person about the subject matter of the representation without the person's attorney's consent, the attorney -- through the reporter's actions -- engaged in unauthorized communication with a represented person without the corporate counsel's consent. A is an incorrect answer because the attorney could not have interviewed the contract administrator without the corporate counsel's consent. C is a wrong answer because the fact that the attorney fulfilled the plaintiff's request does not bring the attorney's conduct into compliance with the Rules. D is an incorrect answer because the fact that the answers obtained by the reporter contained evidence important to the plaintiff's action does not bring the attorney's conduct into compliance with the Rules.

ANSWER 35

JUDICIAL CONDUCT

B is the correct answer because it complies with MCJC R 2.9(A)(2), which states when the judge may obtain disinterested advice from an expert. The judge may obtain disinterested expert advice if (1) there is full disclosure to the parties regarding the person the judge consulted and what the advice is; and (2) the judge gives the parties reasonable opportunity to respond. A is a wrong answer because the parties' advance written consent to the expert's advising of the judge does not fulfill the MCJC's controlling provisions. C is an incorrect answer because, although factually accurate, it only describes one of the provisions required for a judge to talk to a disinterested expert. D is a wrong answer because, although it states a practical reason to obtain the expert's advice, it is not a provision of the MCJC.

ANSWER 36

REGULATION OF THE LEGAL PROFESSION

D is the correct answer because misrepresentation is one type of misconduct that MRPC 8.4 prohibits. Although C is a factually correct statement, it is a wrong answer because it lacks the dispositive fact of the attorney's civil liability for misrepresentation. That fact may give rise to subjecting the attorney to discipline for professional misconduct. A is an incorrect answer because the Rules' description of misrepresentation as misconduct is not limited to either civil or criminal culpability for such misconduct. B is a wrong answer because no exception to the Rule against misrepresentation exists for allegedly doing that in the best interest of the seller as the attorney's client.

ANSWER 37

REGULATION OF THE LEGAL PROFESSION

B is the correct answer because the question was not qualified or limited to any type of offense. MRPC 8.1 specifically prohibits a bar applicant from knowingly making a false statement of material fact. The applicant knowingly made a false statement of material fact by answering the question in the negative with respect to adult offenses when he knew that he had committed juvenile offenses. Thus, the question should have been answered in the affirmative despite the lack of adult offenses. A is a wrong answer, although it accurately states that the applicant did not contact the professional authority about the scope of the question's application. The applicant could have inquired of the authority about this to possibly avoid knowingly making a false statement of material fact, but this is not the reason he is subject to discipline. In other words, attempting to contact the authority would not relieve him of acting improperly. However, B is a better answer because it is the direct reason why the applicant is subject to discipline. C is an incorrect answer because the dispositive issue is whether the applicant knowingly made a false statement of material fact, not if he had a reasonable belief about the question's scope. The controlling Rule does not provide that a reasonable belief will excuse or justify making a false statement of material fact. D is a wrong answer because even if the applicant considered his answer to be an accurate statement of material fact regarding adult offenses, it was an inaccurate statement of material fact regarding juvenile offenses that he failed to disclose.

ANSWER 38

CONFLICTS OF INTEREST

B is the correct answer because the attorney neither participated in nor knew about the office's investigation of the accused. MRPC 1.11 is clear in that a former government employee will only be disqualified from representing a client if he or she substantially and personally participated in representation of the same matter while working for the government. The former government employee's new firm will not be disqualified from undertaking the representation unless the employee is disqualified under the above provision. Accordingly, a conflict of interest would not exist with respect to the attorney and the accused that could be imputed to the lawyer to prevent him from accepting the accused as a client. A is a wrong answer because, although factually accurate, it states a less dispositive reason than answer B does for why the lawyer will not be subject to discipline. Although C is factually accurate, it is an incorrect answer because the attorney did not participate personally and substantially in the investigation of the accused. D is a wrong answer because it describes a provision of MRPC 1.11 that would apply only when a conflict of interest exists.

ANSWER 39

REGULATION OF THE LEGAL PROFESSION

B is the correct answer because it provides the best option under the Rules and facts. Generally, MRPC 8.3(a) requires the lawyer to inform the professional authority of the attorney's violation of the Rules that raise a substantial question as to the attorney's honesty, trustworthiness, and fitness to act as a lawyer. Even if the attorney arguably violated MRPC 1.3 by his one-month delay in the couple's adoption matter, that does not necessarily raise a *substantial* question as to the attorney's honesty, trustworthiness, and fitness to act as a lawyer. Here, the attorney returned the retainer and the couple accepted his explanation for the relatively reasonable delay. Accordingly A and C are incorrect answers because they are too categorical in terms of whether or not the attorney violated the Rules such that the lawyer had to report that violation.

Moreover, pursuant to MRPC 8.3(c), a lawyer does not have to disclose information protected by MRPC 1.6, the Rule of confidentiality. Here, the couple wanted to keep confidential what they told the lawyer about the attorney's conduct. Thus, D is a wrong answer because arguably the lawyer properly complied with the couple's request and the Rules by not reporting the attorney's conduct.

ANSWER 40

SAFEKEEPING FUNDS AND OTHER PROPERTY

B is the correct answer for two reasons in this legal fee dispute situation. First, the client is entitled to receive from the attorney that part of the retainer that was not needed for an appeal bond, and there is no dispute as to who is entitled to those funds. Second, the client's request for a refund of the entire amount constitutes a dispute regarding the $1,500 in fees that the attorney earned (10 hours X $150). MRPC 1.15(d) requires that the attorney keep this disputed amount separate from other funds until the dispute is resolved. Thus, the attorney cannot move the $1,500 from the client trust account into her general account until that occurs.

A is a wrong answer because the attorney would violate the Rule by moving the other funds ($1,500) from the client trust account to her general account.

C is an incorrect answer because the attorney is not required to return the full retainer amount. The attorney may keep the funds in the client trust account subject to resolution of the dispute.

D is not a correct answer for two reasons. First, as explained earlier, the attorney issued the check in the correct amount because the attorney must return the unearned portion of the retainer, the $1,000 for an appeal bond, to the client. Second, the attorney correctly kept the remaining funds in the client trust account because moving $1,500 to her general account would violate MRPC 1.15(d).

ANSWER 41

JUDICIAL CONDUCT

D is the correct answer because it properly applies the relevant MCJC provision to these facts. MCJC R 3.8(A) prohibits judges from serving as a fiduciary except for members of their families when doing so will not interfere with their proper performance of judicial duties. A is a wrong answer because, of itself, the fact that the daughter is a federal judge does not prohibit her from serving as a fiduciary for her father, a family member. However, those facts could preclude her from serving in that capacity when additional facts show that doing so would interfere with her proper performance of judicial duties. B is a wrong answer because, although the father's family members could challenge the living will's validity, the facts state that their doing that is improbable. Moreover, their doing that would not necessarily interfere with the daughter's proper performance of her judicial duties. C is a wrong answer because, although the daughter is closer to the father than the son, that fact does not make the daughter's service as a patient advocate proper.

ANSWER 42

LITIGATION AND OTHER FORMS OF ADVOCACY

D is the correct answer because the prosecutor violated MRPC 3.5(a), which prohibits an attorney from seeking to influence prospective jurors by any means prohibited by law. The Comment to this Rule indicates that such violations will be defined by either criminal law or the MCJC. Here, the facts state that the publicity resulted in biasing and prejudicing prospective jurors, contrary to applicable criminal law. C is a wrong answer because it is factually inaccurate. A is an incorrect answer because, even if it were factually accurate, it does not excuse the prosecutor's misconduct. Although it is factually true, B is a wrong answer because the prosecutor can violate the Rule by either directly or indirectly seeking to influence a prospective juror.

ANSWER 43

THE CLIENT-LAWYER RELATIONSHIP

B is the correct answer because the attorney's advice (1) attempted to prevent the defendant from violating the law by avoiding judicial proceedings and escape being apprehended; and (2) did not assist the defendant in doing that. MRPC 1.2(d) prohibits an attorney from helping a client in conduct that the attorney knows is criminal or fraudulent, but that prohibition does not extend to counseling a client as to the consequences that might flow from such action. Here, the attorney's conduct conformed to that Rule. A is incorrect because an attorney can be subject to discipline if the attorney assists a client in engaging in illegal or fraudulent conduct or advises the client to engage in such conduct. C and D are incorrect answers because the attorney will not be subject to discipline for the defendant's failure to appear when the attorney advised the defendant to appear as required and the defendant did not follow that advice.

ANSWER 44

COMPETENCE, MALPRACTICE, AND OTHER CIVIL LIABILITY

B is the correct answer. MRPC 1.8(h)(2) prohibits attorneys from settling potential malpractice claims with an unrepresented client unless the client is advised in writing to seek independent legal counsel before making the agreement and is given reasonable time to do so. Here, the facts show that the lawyer failed to take those required steps before formation of his agreement with the client. Thus, A is an incorrect answer. C is not a correct answer because, although factually accurate, the client might not have voluntarily entered into the agreement with the lawyer if the lawyer had properly advised the client to seek independent legal counsel and had provided enough time for the client to do that. D is a wrong answer because the lawyer did not engage in proper conduct when the lawyer admittedly failed to include a provision about refreshments in the contract with the company.

ANSWER 45

CONFLICTS OF INTEREST

C is the correct answer. MRPC 1.11, which governs conduct for attorneys transitioning between government employment and private practice, prohibits a former public officer or government employee from representing a client in connection with a matter in which the attorney "participated personally and substantially" while employed by the government. The Rule provides an exception, however, if the government gives written consent. Additionally, if an attorney is disqualified by reason of her participation, then the new firm is also disqualified unless the attorney is screened in a timely manner and the agency is given notice of the screening to ascertain compliance with the rule. Here, the firm and the lawyer can remain involved in the representation because the attorney was promptly screened from the representation, such that the department can ensure compliance with MRPC 1.6, the Rule concerning confidentiality.

B is incorrect because, although factually accurate, MRPC 1.11's prohibition is not absolute, as C indicates and is explained above. For the same reasons, A is an incorrect answer because it broadly states the controlling Rule's effect without considering other facts referenced in the correct answer. D is a wrong answer because it describes a different Rule that does not apply here after the attorney ceased working for the department.

ANSWER 46

COMMUNICATION ABOUT LEGAL SERVICES

C is the correct answer because the attorney did not comply with MRPC 7.2. This Rule concerns information about legal services contained within advertising by attorneys. One of the Rule's comments provides that an attorney's advertisement may state the name of a regularly represented client, only with the client's consent. Here, the attorney regularly represents the client, Beta, pursuant to their contract. However, the attorney did not even inform the client of the brochure. Thus, the attorney lacks the client's consent to name the client in the brochure. Thus, she violated the Rule by stating in the advertisement that she represents the client. Accordingly, the attorney will be subject to discipline.

MRPC 7.2(c) requires that an attorney's advertisement, which communicates information about the attorney's services, must state the name and address of the attorney responsible for the advertisement. Here, the attorney complied with these requirements.

MRPC 7.4(a) permits an attorney to communicate the fact that the attorney practices particular types of law. Answers A, B, and D are not correct because the attorney identified the client without consent.

ANSWER 47

JUDICIAL CONDUCT

This is a very difficult question. B is the correct answer because the judge's personal policy is not fair to either party because the only grounds for granting a second continuance are either the death of, or a life-threatening physical condition of, a party or the party's counsel. MCJC R 2.2 requires the judge to dispose of all judicial matters fairly. The judge's personal policy is not fair because of its extreme limitation on when the judge can grant a second continuance. A is a wrong answer because the facts state, and the call of the question indicates, that the judge is following his personal policy, not any legal requirement limiting the granting of a second continuance, and the law specifies that the granting of a continuance is at the judge's discretion.

C is an incorrect answer because, as a result of the judge's personal policy, he has limited the scope of his discretion. Although it is factually accurate, D is a wrong answer because whether a party whose motion is denied can appeal is not the dispositive issue.

ANSWER 48

SAFEKEEPING FUNDS AND OTHER PROPERTY

D is the correct answer because the attorney improperly utilized the client's funds. MRPC 1.15 requires attorneys to keep client funds separate from their own funds and to use client funds only to pay client expenses. Here, the attorney commingled personal and client funds and used client funds to pay his own personal expenses. Although factually accurate, C is a wrong answer because the fact that the client was assessed a penalty is less dispositive than the fact that the attorney utilized the client's funds. A is a wrong answer because the attorney's payments using the client's funds adversely affected the client because she was assessed a penalty. It is irrelevant that the attorney thought that the client would not object to those payments. B is an incorrect answer because even if the client implicitly ratified the payments that the attorney made, that does not preclude the attorney from being subject to discipline for violating the controlling Rule.

ANSWER 49

CONFLICTS OF INTEREST

A is the correct answer in this concurrent conflict of interest situation. A lawyer cannot generally represent two clients who have a concurrent conflict of interest. MRPC 1.7 states that a "concurrent conflict of interest exists if (1) the representation of one client will be directly adverse to another client; or (2) there is a significant risk that the representation of one or more clients will be materially limited by the lawyer's responsibilities to another client, a former client or a third person or by a personal interest of the lawyer." The litigation attorney's representation of the domestic headlight retailer would be improper because she is already currently representing the retailer, and the domestic headlight retailer's action is directly adverse to the interests of the retailer. There is an exception to this Rule prohibiting representation of clients with a concurrent conflict of interest, but it can only apply if the lawyer reasonably believes that the lawyer will be able to provide competent and diligent representation to each client. Because the domestic headlight retailer is challenging the retailer's application, the litigation attorney can have no such reasonable belief. B is a wrong answer because whether the tort lawsuit and the application to transact business case could be decided by the same appellate court is not the dispositive consideration as to whether the litigation attorney can properly represent the domestic headlight retailer. C is an incorrect answer because whether either the application to transact business or the tort action involves the same factual and legal issues is not the dispositive consideration as to whether the litigation attorney can properly represent the domestic headlight retailer because the action is still directly adverse. D is an incorrect answer because the distinction between the application to transact business being an administrative matter and the tort action being a civil action is not the dispositive consideration as to whether the litigation attorney can properly represent the domestic headlight retailer.

ANSWER 50

COMMUNICATION ABOUT LEGAL SERVICES

A is the correct answer because the Rules allow advertisements unless they are false or misleading. B is a wrong answer, although it raises a valid issue that if the advertisement is broadcast in other jurisdictions where the attorney is not licensed, the Rule against the unauthorized practice of law could apply. C is an incorrect answer because the Rules do not require that advertisements state a lawyer's credentials. D is a wrong answer because the attorney's advertisement is intended to offer legal services to people, rather than promote more lawsuits.

ANSWER 51

CONFLICTS OF INTEREST

A is the correct answer because MRPC 1.8(d) prohibits an attorney from, before the conclusion of representation of a client, negotiating or making an agreement with the client giving the attorney literary or media rights to an account or portrayal based in substantial part on information regarding the representation. Here, the attorney is trying to make such an agreement before the conclusion of representation of the client by means of the provision that would improperly grant the rights to the attorney upon accepting representation. The attorney would make such an improper agreement if he and the client signed it upon the start of representation. However, the attorney may not make such an agreement until *after* the attorney finishes representation of the client.

B is not correct because it states a blanket prohibition upon an agreement granting any right to an attorney upon accepting representation of a client. That categorical prohibition goes far beyond the scope of MRPC 1.8(d). As a practical matter, that prohibition could conflict with an attorney's ability to enter into such contracts granting rights, provided that they are lawful and do not violate the Rules.

C is a wrong answer because the law does not grant an attorney the right to publish a book about her client's case, and MRPC 1.8(d) governs this matter. D is incorrect because an attorney's discretion in contracting with clients is subject to the Rules and the law.

Incidentally, in order for the attorney to facilitate her clients' payment of her bills for legal fees, the attorney could (1) enable clients to get loans from creditors with which to pay the legal fees; or (2) process payment of the legal fees by debit and credit cards along with checks.

ANSWER 52

SAFEKEEPING FUNDS AND OTHER PROPERTY

A is the correct answer because it accurately applies the controlling Rule to the facts. MRPC 1.15 requires that an attorney withdraw funds from a client's trust account as they are earned, and may only place his personal funds in the client's trust account for the purpose of paying bank service charges. By failing to withdraw funds from the client trust account when earned, the attorney's funds became commingled with the client trust account's funds. B is a wrong answer because, although factually accurate, the attorney failed to properly withdraw his earnings from the client's funds as the earnings accrued. Although the attorney did not engage in improper conduct by receiving the client's payment in advance, the attorney engaged in improper conduct by not withdrawing funds upon earning them. C and D are incorrect answers because, although the attorney's placement of the funds in the account and regular issuance of invoices complied with the Rules to some extent, this compliance did not obviate the attorney from the obligation to withdraw the funds from the client trust account as earnings accrued. A provides the best answer because it addresses this improper handling of the funds by the attorney when the other answers refer to his proper handling of them.

ANSWER 53

LITIGATION AND OTHER FORMS OF ADVOCACY

C is the correct answer because the attorney can represent the estate even though he is likely to be a necessary witness because the attorney's testimony would relate to the uncontested issue of the deed's execution. MRPC 3.7(a) provides that an attorney may serve as an advocate and a necessary witness who testifies in the same trial if "(1) the testimony relates to an uncontested issue; (2) the testimony relates to the nature and value of legal services rendered in the case; or (3) disqualification of the" attorney would result in substantial hardship to the client. If the testimony, however, would have concerned a contested issue such as the deed's defective title, then the attorney could not represent the estate pursuant to MRPC 3.7(a)(1). Although it is factually accurate, D is an incorrect answer because the attorney's lack of a beneficial interest pursuant to the deed is not one of the exceptions to the Rule's prohibition on an attorney serving as both an advocate and a necessary witness in the same trial. A is a wrong answer because it refers to another exception to MRPC 3.7 that is not applicable under these facts. The facts do not indicate that the disqualification of the attorney would work a substantial hardship to the estate. B is an incorrect answer because the fact that the lawyer will call the attorney as a witness in the lawsuit does not automatically and completely prohibit the attorney from representing the estate.

ANSWER 54

COMPETENCE, MALPRACTICE, AND OTHER CIVIL LIABILITY

B is the correct answer because it accurately reflects that, as required by the Rules, the client consented to the attorney's to association with the bankruptcy lawyer after the attorney explained it to the client. MRPC 1.1 requires a lawyer to provide competent representation to all clients. The Comment to that rule states that "[c]ompetent representation can also be provided through the association of a lawyer of established competence in the field in question." In order to associate with another lawyer, though, an attorney would have to reveal confidential information to the lawyer, which, according to MRPC 1.6(a), requires the client's informed consent. A is a wrong answer because, as addressed earlier, the Rules regulate the attorney's association with the bankruptcy lawyer. C and D are incorrect answers because the attorney and the bankruptcy lawyer can associate under certain circumstances, such as here, when the client consents to the association after receiving information about it (even if they know each other personally).

ANSWER 55

COMMUNICATION ABOUT LEGAL SERVICES

C is the correct answer because MRPC 7.5(d) provides that members of the bar can only state or imply that they practice law as partners if that is true. Here, the replacement sign indicates that the attorney, the lawyer, and the counselor are practicing law in a partnership, and the facts do not support that representation. A is a wrong answer because a partnership does not result from them equally paying the costs of a secretary, paralegal, and answering service. D is an incorrect answer because members of the bar can refer to themselves as law partners if they are in fact members of the same partnership in a law firm. B is a wrong answer because the fact that the attorney, the lawyer, and the counselor refer prospective clients to each other does not make them law partners.

ANSWER 56

JUDICIAL CONDUCT

C is the correct answer because Comment 2 of MCJC R 1.3 allows the judge to provide the letter because she knows the daughter and the facts do not indicate that the judge violated any Rule. Rather, the facts state that the letter contains only truthful statements, which are permissible. The judge did not write the letter for an improper purpose that would subject her for discipline for violating the controlling Rule, such as using her position to get special treatment or gain some personal advantage. Accordingly, D is wrong because no facts indicate that the letter will afford the judge an improper advantage when it could benefit the daughter and is not addressed to any particular recipient. B is an incorrect answer because, as mentioned earlier, the fact that the judge knows the daughter provides a reason why the judge will not be subject to discipline for providing the letter of recommendation. The fact that the judge is friends with the daughter's parents implicitly tends to support the fact that the judge personally knows the daughter.

A is not a correct answer because the fact that the judge wrote the letter on court stationary does not violate the Rule unless the judge had used her official letterhead in order to get some advantage in her personal business affairs. Here, the judge used such paper to write the letter for the daughter's benefit, not her own.

ANSWER 57

COMPETENCE, MALPRACTICE, AND OTHER CIVIL LIABILITY

C is the correct answer because the attorney faced an emergency situation making it impractical to refer the matter to, or associate with, another lawyer in order to draft the will. The Comment to MRPC 1.1 states that in an emergency situation where it would be impractical to consult with or refer a case to another lawyer, an attorney may give legal advice or assistance even when the attorney is not competent in the matter at issue. On the next day after becoming aware of the case, the attorney unsuccessfully attempted to refer the case to another lawyer. Given the nature of the situation, it would have been prudent for her to draft the will before the step-uncle's imminent death. D is a wrong answer because a familial relationship is not an exception to the requirement of competence in a lawyer's representation of a client. Although factually accurate, both A and B are incorrect because their descriptions of the requirement of competence in representation are subject to the emergency exception that applies here.

ANSWER 58

JUDICIAL CONDUCT

B is the correct answer because the judge is not required to disqualify herself. Thus, her presiding over the case does not subject her to discipline for violating any rule. MCJC R 2.11 requires disqualification in a proceeding in which the judge's impartiality might reasonably be questioned. Here, the corporation may not reasonably question the judge's impartiality in the case based on the facts that she is one of five trustees of a trust that holds one millionth of its value in the company's stock. Under MCJC R 2.11(A)(3) a judge's impartiality might reasonably be questioned, such that the judge must disqualify herself, when the judge knows that she, as a fiduciary, has an economic interest in the subject matter in dispute or a party to a proceeding before the judge. As the trust's trustee, the judge occupies a fiduciary position. Generally, an economic interest means ownership of more than a *de minimus* interest.

Here, the judge does not have to disqualify herself because she knows that, as a fiduciary of the trust, she does not have more than a *de minimus* interest in the case or the company. Moreover, the judge knows that, as a fiduciary, her economic interest in the case or the company is *de minimus* because the trust only contains one millionth of its value in the company's stock.

Accordingly, A is a wrong answer because, although factually accurate, even if the company stock ownership were attributed to her personally rather than as the trustee, she would still hold such a minimal interest as to not affect her impartiality. Therefore, C is an incorrect answer because it is likely that the judge could impartially handle the case. D is a wrong answer because the results of the case could impact the company stock's cost.

ANSWER 59

REGULATION OF THE LEGAL PROFESSION

A is the correct answer because MRPC 5.6(b) prohibits the provision of this offer of compromise that restricts the attorney's right to practice law. Specifically, an attorney may not participate in offering or making an agreement in which a limitation on the attorney's "right to practice is part of the settlement of a client controversy." If this offer lacked the aforementioned type of prohibited provision, then it would not violate this Rule and would be a valid means of settling the case. C is a wrong answer because the Rule prohibits any restriction on the attorney's right to practice law, regardless of how minimal the impact of the restriction might be. B is an incorrect answer because the Rule does not provide an exception for the fact that another lawyer could provide the landowner competent representation in any other legal matter involving the neighbor. D is a wrong answer because the Rule is not conditional upon, and lacks an exception for, when an attorney believes that a settlement that limits the attorney's right to practice is the best method for a client to achieve its objectives, or is in the client's best interest.

ANSWER 60

LAWYERS' DUTIES TO THE PUBLIC AND THE LEGAL SYSTEM

D is the correct answer because, although the attorney can make a contribution to the lawyer's reelection committee, the attorney may not accept the appointment because he made the contribution for the purpose of obtaining or being considered for the appointment. Thus, A is not a correct answer because it makes an inaccurate statement that is too categorical.

B and C are incorrect answers because the propriety of the attorney's acceptance of the appointment is not contingent upon his established professional and financial relationship with the lawyer. Subject to certain limitations, MCJC R 3.11(A) permits the lawyer as a judge to hold and manage investments such as real estate.

ANSWER 61

COMMUNICATIONS WITH PERSONS OTHER THAN CLIENTS

C is the correct answer because, by telling the defendant why he cannot talk, the prosecutor complied with MRPC 4.2. Generally, this Rule prohibits the prosecutor from talking with the defendant because the attorney represents the defendant. The Rule applies even when the attorney is not present or the defendant tries to initiate the discussion. Thus, the prosecutor cannot speak with the defendant without the attorney being present. Pursuant to the Rule, the prosecutor immediately terminated the conversation that the defendant attempted to initiate. Therefore, A is wrong because prosecutor limited the communication with the defendant to only ending the defendant's attempted conversation. B is incorrect because the prosecutor complied with the Rule by presenting the plea agreement proposals to the attorney, rather than the defendant.

In the factual context of this question, the prosecutor would be subject to discipline for violating the Rule by replying to the defendant's statement with either of the following statements: (1) "That is an interesting development that we should discuss further." or (2) "I will consider doing that and let you know when my decision is made." By making either of these statements, the prosecutor would be speaking to the defendant in furtherance of the defendant's attempt to negotiate with the prosecutor directly, instead of through his attorney, when the prosecutor knows that the attorney represents the defendant. In that event, the prosecutor would be subject to discipline.

D is not a correct answer because (1) the prosecutor has no need for immunity from discipline for what occurred here; and (2) immunity does not exist for what could have occurred here in violation of the Rule. Federal constitutional law may provide the President of the United States with absolute immunity for civil actions seeking money damages arising from the President's conduct while in office. Although the prosecutor represents an executive branch, it is part of the state's government. For those reasons, that legal principle does not apply here.

ANSWER 62

DIFFERENT ROLES OF THE LAWYER

A is the correct answer because MRPC 3.9 requires the attorney to disclose that he appeared before the committee as the company's representative. B is a wrong answer because the company's payment to the attorney for testifying did not violate the Rule. C is an incorrect answer because the duty of client-lawyer confidentiality does not apply when the Rule required the attorney to reveal his relationship with the company. D is a wrong answer because the attorney-client evidentiary privilege does not apply when the Rule required the attorney to reveal his relationship with the company.

ANSWER 63

COMPETENCE, MALPRACTICE, AND OTHER CIVIL LIABILITY

D is the correct answer because in this emergency situation, the scope of the attorney's representation of the friend is limited to what is reasonably necessary under the circumstances. Generally, MRPC 1.1 requires that an attorney provide competent representation to clients. But in an emergency situation, when the attorney cannot reasonably consult with or refer a case to another, more competent lawyer, the attorney may give advice or assistance. Even in this situation, though, the advice or assistance is limited to what is reasonably necessary under the circumstances. A is a wrong answer because the fact that the attorney assisted the friend because of their relationship does not make the attorney's conduct improper. B is an incorrect answer because, although the attorney lacked the requisite legal competence to handle the friend's matter, under these circumstances, it was proper to assist the friend. C is not a correct answer because the fact that the attorney attempted to obtain the boy's release from the police station does not make the attorney's conduct proper.

ANSWER 64

THE CLIENT-LAWYER RELATIONSHIP

C is the correct answer because, prior to the civil pretrial conference, the attorney obtained the plaintiff's informed consent to go to trial during the summer. MRPC 1.4 requires an attorney to keep his client reasonably informed about the status of the case and explain situations arising during representation so that the client may make informed decisions. Here, the attorney timely informed the plaintiff of the trial date, and correctly counseled her that it would not negatively affect her interests. A is a wrong answer because the attorney acted appropriately. B is an incorrect answer because it is not relevant when the facts do not indicate a speedy trial issue. Even if D describes a valid general principle, it is a wrong answer because that principle is not the dispositive consideration for answering this question

ANSWER 65

COMMUNICATIONS WITH PERSONS OTHER THAN CLIENTS

C is the correct answer because the attorney improperly made a false statement of material fact to a third party, which MRPC 4.1(a) prohibits in the course of representation. This false statement is that the battery operated the "longest before recharge of any battery ever produced." The attorney said this despite the inventor's prior statement to the contrary. This third factor about the invention's novelty could have been decisive in either the lawyer's or the manufacturer's decision-making process regarding whether to agree to license the invention. Accordingly, D is a wrong answer because the attorney did not simply "overstate" the invention's capabilities. A is an incorrect answer because the attorney's statement violated the Rule, whether he made his statement to the lawyer, the manufacturer, or any other third party. B is a wrong answer because the attorney's description of the invention did not merely constitute harmless "puffing" for sales purposes.

ANSWER 66

THE CLIENT-LAWYER RELATIONSHIP

C is the correct answer because the attorney violated MRPC 1.2(d), which prohibits him from assisting the defendant in conduct that the attorney knows is criminal. Moreover, attorneys may not counsel clients to engage in conduct that the attorney knows is criminal or fraudulent. While the Rule permits attorneys to discuss the legal consequences of a course of action, here the attorney overstepped that limit. The attorney's statement to the defendant that he could avoid trial by going back to the country, and any research necessary to make that statement accurate, assisted the defendant in breaking the law in terms of disobeying the terms of his pretrial release and applicable laws against fleeing and eluding the police. D is a wrong answer because it is implicitly contained within the more dispositive answer (C) Although factually correct, A and B are incorrect answers because the Rule lacks exceptions applicable in those circumstances.

ANSWER 67

JUDICIAL CONDUCT

B is the correct answer because in this situation the judge's disqualification is mandatory and a proper waiver of disqualification did not occur. Under MCJC R 2.11(A), a judge is required to disqualify herself from a proceeding in which her impartiality might reasonably be questioned. Under MCJC R 2.11(A)(2), a judge's impartiality might be reasonably questioned, such that the judge must disqualify herself, when she knows that she or her spouse has more than a *de minimis* economic interest that could be substantially affected by the proceeding. This provision applies because the husband owns a significant quantity of the large corporation's stock. However, MCJC R 2.11(C) allows the parties and attorneys to waive disqualification if the judge discloses the basis of her disqualification and asks the parties and their attorneys to consider waiving disqualification. If they agree, without the judge's participation, that the judge should not be disqualified, then she may participate in the proceeding. Answer B reflects that the waiver did not conform to the Rule's requirement that the agreement of the parties and their attorneys to waive disqualification occur without the judge's participation. A is a wrong answer because it inaccurately indicates that the Rules do not provide for waiver of disqualification, which can occur under certain circumstances. Although it is factually accurate, C is an incorrect answer because the disqualification that must occur here is not subject to an exception on the basis that a judge is particularly well prepared to preside over the case. D is wrong because, even if the judge would be impartial notwithstanding the husband's ownership of large corporation stock, that is not an exception to the disqualification requirement.

ANSWER 68

COMMUNICATION ABOUT LEGAL SERVICES

D is the correct answer because the commercial does not include the information required by MRPC 7.2. Specifically, subject to other requirements within the Rules, an attorney may advertise his services through public media, but any advertisement must include the attorney's name and office address. However, the attorney's commercial complies with all of the other requirements, including that the advertisement not be false or misleading with regard to his services. MRPC 7.1. A, then, is incorrect because the advertisement does not comply with all of the Rules' requirements. C is a wrong answer because the commercial need not indicate whether a fee will be charged for the initial consultation. B is an incorrect answer because the Rules do not require or prohibit the use of a professional to record a commercial.

ANSWER 69

SAFEKEEPING FUNDS AND OTHER PROPERTY

C is correct because the attorney did not handle the check as required by MRPC 1.15(d). Pursuant to that Rule, the attorney should have processed the check by depositing it in a client trust account for the plaintiff, notifying the plaintiff of its receipt, and mailing the plaintiff a $75,000 check issued from the client trust account.

The attorney did not follow that proper approach by endorsing the defendant's check and forwarding it to the plaintiff. Alternatively, note that the attorney would have followed an improper approach by depositing the defendant's check in the attorney's general account for the plaintiff, notifying the plaintiff of its receipt, and mailing the plaintiff a $75,000 check issued from the general account. In that event, the attorney would have used the wrong type of account, rather than a proper, client trust account.

Because the attorney improperly processed the check in violation of the Rule, A, B, and D are not correct because their factually accurate reasons all lead to wrong conclusions.

ANSWER 70

COMPETENCE, MALPRACTICE, AND OTHER CIVIL LIABILITY

C is the correct answer because the dispositive issue is competent representation, not whether the defendant provides informed consent to the attorney's continued sole representation. Thus, B is an incorrect answer because, although based on informed consent, the defendant's decision to accept the attorney's continued sole representation does not relieve the attorney of the duty to provide competent representation.

MRPC 1.1 requires an attorney to provide competent representation to clients. In order to do that, the attorney may need to learn enough to become competent or associate with an attorney having competence. D is the wrong answer because the attorney does not have to be or become a certified specialist in criminal defense in order to satisfy the Rule's requirement of competence.

A is wrong because the attorney's representation of the defendant is not automatically or necessarily proper simply because the trial judge appointed her as sole counsel. Again, the attorney's competence is a key prerequisite to proper representation.

In response to her realization, the attorney could have taken a couple of steps to properly address the competence requirement. The attorney could have informed the judge that she lacks the legal competence to try the case and wants to make a permissive withdrawal from being the defendant's counsel. Alternatively, the attorney could have informed the judge that he needs to appoint a co-counsel with legal competence in this subject matter and grant a postponement of the trial in order for both defense counsels to properly prepare for it.

ANSWER 71

SAFEKEEPING FUNDS AND OTHER PROPERTY

C is the correct answer because the creditor and the plaintiff both claim interests in the damages recovered, which are disputed property. MRPC 1.15(e) requires an attorney to keep disputed property received by him separate until the dispute is resolved when two or more people claim an interest in that property. The attorney must immediately distribute any portion of that property that is not in dispute. The Comment to MRPC 1.15(e) provides that applicable law can obligate the attorney to protect a third-party's lawful claims upon a client's funds, which the lawyer possesses, from a client's wrongful interference. In that event, if the third-party's claim is not frivolous, the lawyer may not release the funds or property to the client until resolution of the competing claims occurs. The facts state that applicable law provides that the creditor has a lawful claim, which the attorney has a legal duty to protect, and that the claim is not frivolous.

Thus, the attorney may not disburse the disputed $2,400 until resolution of the dispute occurs. However, the attorney must promptly disburse the other $12,600 to the client.

Accordingly, A is a wrong answer because, although the plaintiff recovered the damages, a portion of them is subject to the creditor's claim of lien and in dispute. B is an incorrect answer because it is factually inaccurate when the facts indicate that the creditor is entitled to some of those funds. D is a wrong answer because the fact that the attorney informed the plaintiff that the creditor would enforce its legal rights against the plaintiff does not subject the attorney to discipline because the attorney has a duty to communicate with the plaintiff.

ANSWER 72

CONFLICTS OF INTEREST

C is the correct answer because MRPC 1.8 only permits an aggregate settlement based on each of the homeowner's informed written consent if they are also informed about every other homeowner's participation in the settlement. Comment 13 to the Rule contemplates that an attorney must inform all clients in an aggregate group of the material terms of the settlement including the amounts awarded to each client. Here, the attorney did not inform each of the homeowners about every other homeowner's participation in the settlement in terms of their respective settlement amounts. Accordingly, A is a wrong answer because the Rule requires the attorney to reveal all settlement amounts, even if doing that could undermine the prospects of the offer's universal acceptance. B is an incorrect answer because the attorney will not have fully complied with the Rule simply because each of the homeowners will receive a fair settlement amount and each of them will accept it. D is a wrong answer because it inaccurately reflects the above described Rule.

ANSWER 73

LITIGATION AND OTHER FORMS OF ADVOCACY

D is the correct answer because MRPC 3.4 prohibits an attorney from unlawfully obstructing another party's access to evidence or concealing something with potential evidentiary value. Here, the lawyer violated the Rule by neither providing the note nor referring to it at all, when the lawyer did not have any lawful basis for preventing the plaintiff's discovery of the note. Generally, the attorney may discover any evidence that is relevant to the controversy, provided that the evidence is neither privileged nor work product. Here, the lawyer cannot contend that the law of either attorney-client privilege nor work product protection make lawful his obstruction of the attorney's access to the note and concealment of it. Thus, answers A and B are not correct. C is an incorrect answer because the lawyer does not have any constitutional duty to disclose the note as would a prosecutor have a duty to disclose exculpatory evidence to a criminal defendant. However, the Rule prohibits the lawyer's unlawful obstruction of the attorney's access to the note and his concealment of it.

ANSWER 74

CONFLICTS OF INTEREST

C is the correct answer because the attorney cannot represent the patient after having represented the organization because doing so would involve a conflict of interest. As a general rule, MPRC 1.9(b) prohibits a lawyer from knowingly representing "a person in the same or a substantially related manner in which a firm with which the lawyer formerly was associated had previously represented a client (1) whose interests are materially adverse to that person; and (2) about whom the lawyer had acquired [confidential information] that is material to the matter." The organization qualifies as a type of law firm.

Here, the attorney worked for the organization and represented it in all of its legal dealings, including the matter giving rise to the patient's proposed lawsuit. The attorney was privy to confidential information pertinent to the patient's application, so unless the organization gives informed, written consent to this proposed representation pursuant to MPRC 1.9(a), the attorney may not represent the patient. Therefore, answer B is incorrect because, even though the attorney no longer represents the organization, representing the patient would violate the Rule unless the organization provides informed consent. As a practical matter, that is not likely to occur.

Note that the attorney may not permit another member of the firm to assist the patient without the attorney receiving any share of the fee in that matter. Under MRPC 1.10(a), that situation would also involve an improper conflict of interest, which would be imputed to the firm's other members.

A is a wrong answer because, although factually accurate regarding the attorney's apparent competence to handle the patient's case, the Rule against conflicts of interest controls this situation and trumps application of the Rule regarding competence.

Answer D is not correct because the amount of time that the attorney has worked at the law firm is not a relevant factor relating to the rule against conflict of interest. In other words, the rule lacks any factor that takes into account how much time has passed between when the attorney represented one client whose interests conflict with the attorney's other, prospective client.

In this situation, the attorney could provide the patient with a list of recommended lawyers who are qualified to assist him, or decline to speak with the patient about the proposed lawsuit.

ANSWER 75

CONFLICTS OF INTEREST

A is the correct answer because it is most related to MRPC 1.9 as it applies here regarding conflicts of interest. Generally, a lawyer may not knowingly represent "a person in the same or a substantially related manner in which a firm with which the lawyer formerly was associated had previously represented a client (1) whose interests are materially adverse to that person; and (2) about whom the lawyer had acquired [confidential information] that is material to the matter." The company qualifies as a type of law firm.

Here, the Rule does not prohibit the attorney from representing the individual, a new client, because this representation against the company, a former client, would not involve the same or substantially related matter as the one in which he previously represented the company. A tort lawsuit is the subject matter of the attorney's new representation of the individual against the company. An unrelated insurance claim was the subject matter of the attorney's former representation of the company in relation to the individual. These two separate matters are neither identical nor substantially related, such that it is proper for the attorney to represent the individual.

B is not a correct answer because it is less related to MRPC 1.9 than answer A is, when the fact that the attorney no longer represents the company does not necessarily mean that the attorney's later representation of the individual would be proper. Rather, answer A refers to the dispositive fact that the attorney's present representation of the individual would not concern the same or a substantially related manner as the attorney's former representation of the company. Accordingly, answer C is incorrect because the attorney may represent the individual now although he previously represented the company. Answer D is wrong because the fact that the attorney examined the individual's claim is not dispositive in light of the foregoing explanation.

ANSWER 76

COMPETENCE, MALPRACTICE, AND OTHER CIVIL LIABILITY

A is the correct answer because MRPC 1.8(h) provides that an attorney may not make an agreement, such as the retainer contract and waiver form, that prospectively limits the attorney's exposure to legal malpractice liability to a client unless the client is independently represented by another lawyer when making the agreement. Although the attorney offered the client an opportunity to have another lawyer review the retainer contract and waiver form, the attorney made the offer after he gave them to her. Moreover, the client lacked independent representation when making the agreement. B is a wrong answer because the attorney may use the same form when representing most clients. C is an incorrect answer because the attorney violated the Rule, even though he provided consideration by agreeing to represent the client. D is a wrong answer because the attorney violated the Rule, regardless of whether he thinks that his hourly rate is reasonable and he is qualified to represent the client.

ANSWER 77

COMMUNICATION ABOUT LEGAL SERVICES

C is the correct answer because MRPC 7.2(b)(4) generally provides that an attorney cannot pay a non-lawyer professional such as the dealer for referrals except in certain situations. The arrangement here, however, does not qualify as one of those situations for two reasons. First, this reciprocal referral contract is exclusive, which MRPC 7.2(b)(4)(i) does not permit, because both the dealer and the attorney must only refer "any" of their respective customers or clients to each other. Second, the facts indicate that the attorney does not inform the clients of the contract's existence and nature, as required by MRPC 7.2(b)(4)(ii). A is a wrong answer because the contract here is not a fee sharing arrangement that is generally prohibited under another governing Rule. B is an incorrect answer because the contract is invalid because it improperly provides for referrals. B's issue of the reasonableness of the fees charged by the dealer and the attorney is not dispositive. D is a wrong answer because the contract does not provide for the attorney's practice of law with the dealer.

ANSWER 78

THE CLIENT-LAWYER RELATIONSHIP

A is the correct answer for two reasons, despite the husband's directive that the lawyer must take an aggressive approach to litigation. First, the lawyer can exercise reasonable discretion in the conduct of litigation by agreeing to reschedule the deposition. MRPC 1.2 provides that a client determines the objectives of the representation, but the means of accomplishing those objectives is generally within an attorney's discretion. Second, the lawyer will not be subject to discipline because such an agreement would not prejudice the husband's rights. According to the first reason above, C is a wrong answer because the lawyer is not required to follow the husband's directive. Similarly, D is an incorrect answer because the lawyer did not need the husband's approval to reschedule the deposition. B is a wrong answer because, although the attorney has the right to determine the means of the representation, the client has the right to determine the objectives of the representation.

ANSWER 79

SAFEKEEPING FUNDS AND OTHER PROPERTY

C is the correct answer because MRPC 1.15(b) allows an attorney to deposit the attorney's own funds in a client trust account for the sole purpose of paying bank service charges on that account, but only in an amount necessary for that purpose. Here, the attorney's conduct complied with the Rule. However, if the attorney had deposited more than was required to pay bank service charges, then the attorney would have made an improper deposit, which would make A correct. However, A is not correct because the attorney only deposited the amount necessary to pay the bank service charge. Thus, B is a wrong answer because the attorney could not improperly commingle his funds with the client's when the attorney followed the Rule. As a factual matter, B is an incorrect answer because the attorney's funds could not commingle with the client's funds because the client trust account had a zero balance. D is not correct because the fact that the client had a legal status of a missing person does not affect the Rule's application to these facts.

ANSWER 80

REGULATION OF THE LEGAL PROFESSION

D is the correct answer. Ordinarily, MRPC 5.4(a) does not allow attorneys to share legal fees with non-lawyers, but there are exceptions to that general rule. The rule serves to protect an attorney's independent professional judgment. D is the correct answer for two reasons. First, the facts indicate that the staff cannot control the attorney's judgment because he supervises them and delegates work to them, which is subject to his review. Second, MRPC 5.4(a)(3) allows the attorney to include non-lawyer employees in his compensation plan, which is partially based on a profit-sharing arrangement. Accordingly, A is a wrong answer. B is an incorrect answer because the facts do not indicate that the staff is practicing law by doing secretarial, clerical, and paralegal work. Thus, the attorney is not improperly assisting them in unauthorized practice of law in violation of the Rules. C is a wrong answer because in the attorney's office his staff's access to client files may be necessary and unavoidable for purposes of performing their work.

ANSWER 81

LITIGATION AND OTHER FORMS OF ADVOCACY

C is the correct answer because MRPC 3.6(c) allows an attorney to make a statement that a reasonable attorney would consider necessary to protect a client from the substantial undue prejudicial effect of recent publicity not initiated by the attorney or the attorney's client. Here, the attorney reasonably considered his truthful statement necessary to protect the instructor from the substantial undue prejudicial effect of the prosecutor's press conference that neither the attorney nor the instructor initiated. That press conference appears to have had such an impact based on the media survey results showing that most people believed that the instructor is guilty. A is a wrong answer because the attorney complied with the Rule when he called and participated in the press conference. Likewise, B is an incorrect answer because the instructor permitted the attorney to call and hold the press conference, such that the instructor allowed the attorney to state information provided to him by the instructor.

D is not a correct answer because the fact that the instructor permitted the attorney to call and hold the press conference does not satisfy the above Rule's terms for when the attorney may make the statement that the attorney did. Although client consent is one exception to the Rule of confidentiality that seems satisfied by the instructor's permission, the question tests the main issue of whether the Rule allows the attorney to make the statement that he did.

The prosecutor might have violated MRPC 3.6(a) by making his extrajudicial statement about the instructor that he reasonably should have known would have been disseminated by means of a public communication and would have a substantial likelihood of materially prejudicing an adjudicative proceeding, i.e. a potential trial of the instructor, in the matter of the girl's accusation.

ANSWER 82

JUDICIAL CONDUCT

C is the correct answer because it would be improper for the judge to decide the case because one could reasonably question his impartiality about it. Generally, MCJC R 2.11(A)(2) requires a judge to disqualify himself in a proceeding in which the judge's impartiality might reasonably be questioned. Here, one could reasonably question the judge's impartiality in deciding the case on appeal after he directly participated in the department's prosecution of it at trial. Under MCJC R 2.11(A)(6)(b), a judge's impartiality might reasonably be questioned, such that the judge must disqualify himself, when the judge served in governmental employment, and in this capacity participated substantially and personally as a public official or lawyer regarding the proceeding. Here, this provision requires disqualification of the judge from deciding the case on appeal because, while employed by the department, he worked substantially and personally as the state's attorney in the same case. Thus, B is a wrong answer because, although comparable to C, it does not refer to the controlling Rule as clearly as C does.

D is an incorrect answer because, although factually correct, the judge's lack of personal economic interest in the case does not affect his mandatory disqualification as explained earlier. However, note that mandatory disqualification can result when a judge has a sufficient economic interest in a case before the judge.

A is a wrong answer because the judge's disclosure of his role the case would be insufficient to make it proper for him to participate in deciding it. Moreover, the judge's failure to disclose his role in the case is not a basis for mandatory disqualification.

ANSWER 83

JUDICIAL CONDUCT

B is the correct answer. Generally, MCJC R 3.13(A) provides that a judge must not accept a gift if "acceptance is prohibited by law or would appear to a reasonable person to undermine the judge's independence, integrity, or impartiality." Here, the facts indicate that the judge's acceptance of the gift is neither prohibited by law nor otherwise unethical. Accordingly, A is an incorrect answer because the judge's acceptance of the sculpted bust as a gift, of itself, will not subject the judge to discipline.

MCJC R 3.13(C)(1) provides that, unless otherwise prohibited (which is not the case here as explained above), a judge may accept certain types of items, but must publicly report accepted "gifts incident to a public testimonial." Here, the judge received the bust as a gift from the state bar's committee pursuant to a public testimonial that occurred at the philanthropy's dinner. Accordingly, C is not a correct answer because that Rule allows for the judge's receipt of that gift incident to a public testimonial. In other words, of itself, that fact does not subject the judge to discipline. However, the judge failed to submit any regulatory paperwork about the gift as required by the foregoing Rule. Moreover, MCJC R 3.15(D) states that, generally, the judge must file such a report as a public document in the court on which the judge serves or another office designated by law. Thus, B is the correct answer because the judge failed to officially account for receiving the sculpted bust by not filing a public report about receiving it.

D is a wrong answer because the judge's uncompensated service on the board does not qualify as an exception or defense to application of the Rule requiring the judge to make a public report of receiving the sculpted bust as a gift.

ANSWER 84

REGULATION OF THE LEGAL PROFESSION

The correct answer is D because, although the facts provide no reason to consider the agreement unlawful, its 100-year duration is not reasonable as a practical matter. Because the new partner and firm entered into an agreement of an unreasonable duration, they have violated MRPC 5.4(a)(1). Generally, this Rule provides that a law firm must not share legal fees with a non-attorney. However, one of the Rule's exceptions states in part that an agreement by an attorney with the attorney's firm may provide for the payment of money to the attorney's estate for a reasonable time period after the attorney's death. Here, the new partner made such an agreement with the firm. However, the agreement improperly obligates the firm to make the payments for 100 years, which is not a reasonable duration. Thus, answer A is not correct because, although the agreement apparently is lawful, it is not ethical. Answer C is incorrect because the agreement apparently is lawful. Answer B is wrong because, as explained earlier, the applicable Rule limits agreements between the firm and its attorneys regarding the sharing or division of legal fees with a non-lawyer.

ANSWER 85

LITIGATION AND OTHER FORMS OF ADVOCACY

Answer B is correct because (1) before the trial, the witness told the attorney that the defendant was in the state with her; and (2) at the trial, no evidence supported the attorney's statement that the defendant was in another state. MRPC 3.3(a)(1) provides that an attorney is prohibited from making a false statement of material fact or law to the court. Here, it is a material fact as to whether the defendant was in the state when the hunter was shot because the defendant could not have shot the hunter if the defendant was absent from the state then. The attorney made a false statement of material fact by saying that the defendant was out of the state when the witness had told the attorney otherwise and no evidence at trial supported the attorney's statement. Thus, the attorney improperly misled the court by stating as fact what the witness contradicted and the attorney knew lacked an evidentiary basis.

Answer A is wrong because, although factually correct, the attorney's false statement of material fact violated the Rule, not the fact that no evidence supported the statement. In other words, answer A states a reason why the attorney's statement was false, not that the false statement subjects the attorney to discipline. Answer C is not correct because the attorney's duty to zealously represent a client does not excuse the attorney from the duty to be truthful to the court. Answer D is incorrect because even assuming that the attorney used best efforts, that does not spare the attorney from discipline for making the false statement.

ANSWER 86

CLIENT CONFIDENTIALITY

D is the correct answer because it accurately applies MRPC 1.6 to these facts. The Rule states that an attorney may not reveal confidential information provided by a client unless certain situations arise. Under MRPC 1.6(b)(1), one such situation exists when revealing the information will "prevent reasonably certain death or substantial bodily harm." Here, the attorney would prevent the victim's reasonably certain death by disclosing the victim's location to the police because the defendant's accomplice will kill the victim due to the state's refusal to pay the ransom. Thus, A is an incorrect answer because, although the defendant's statement is subject to the Rule, the Rule does not protect it from disclosure under these circumstances. C is not a correct answer because the admission of guilt is protected by client-lawyer confidentiality. B is a wrong answer because the Rule (and its relevant exception) applies regardless of whether its application would conflict with the defendant's best interest.

ANSWER 87

CONFLICTS OF INTEREST

D is the correct answer because MRPC 1.11(a)(2) generally prohibits the attorney's representation of the citizen following her personal and substantial involvement in the city's action against the citizen. In order to undertake such representation, the attorney must obtain the former client's informed written consent. C is a wrong answer because the Rule's exception requires written rather than oral consent. Thus, the exception could apply if the attorney had obtained the city's informed consent, confirmed in writing, to representing the client. A is a wrong answer because merely ceasing to represent the city would not permit the attorney to accept representation against the city in a matter in which she substantially participated. B is an incorrect answer because, although the attorney can have clients while employed by the city, the Model Rules limits who she may represent. Here, the attorney did not comply with the Rule requiring the city's informed written consent prior to representing the citizen.

ANSWER 88

COMPETENCE, MALPRACTICE, AND OTHER CIVIL LIABILITY

The correct answer is B because (1) the attorney did not satisfy the requirement of MRPC 1.1, which imposes the duty of competence upon an attorney representing a client; and (2) pursuant to MRPC 5.2(a), the attorney had to comply with MRPC 1.1 when acting at the managing partner's direction. MRPC 5.2(a) provides that all of the Rules bind an attorney even when the attorney acted at another person's direction. Thus, an attorney may not escape responsibility for violating a Rule -- such as MRPC 1.1 here -- simply because the associate attorney acted at the other person's direction. Therefore, answer C incorrectly indicates that the associate attorney will not be subject to discipline because she acted at the managing partner's direction.

Generally, among other things, under the duty of competence the attorney must apply the diligence (i.e., thoroughness and preparation), learning, and skill reasonably necessary for the performance of the legal service requested. Here, the attorney did not act competently in her legal representation of the client because she did not sufficiently apply those attributes in order to find and comply with the provision requiring special service of process for the client's medical malpractice action.

A is not correct because it is not clear from the facts whether the associate attorney should have declined undertaking the case. Moreover, the associate attorney could have sought assistance from another more experienced attorney.

Answer D is wrong because, as addressed earlier, the associate attorney will be subject to disciplinary action regardless of the action's dollar value.

ANSWER 89

DIFFERENT ROLES OF THE LAWYER

D is the correct answer because the attorney properly gave advice that included both legal and economic factors. MRPC 2.1 allows the attorney to refer to both the law and other non-legal considerations, "such as moral, economic, social and political factors." Thus, A is a wrong answer because the attorney complied with the Rule by providing advice including both legal and economic factors. B is an incorrect answer because the attorney's advice not to pursue the small claim complied with the Rule. The attorney should fulfill the duty of zealous advocacy of the sales company's interests subject to other controlling Rules. C is a wrong answer because the determination of whether the attorney engaged in proper conduct should not depend upon whether the president accepted the attorney's advice or not. That determination should depend upon whether the attorney complied with the Rule.

ANSWER 90

LITIGATION AND OTHER FORMS OF ADVOCACY

A is the correct answer. MRPC 3.3(a)(1) prohibits an attorney from knowingly making a false statement of fact. Here, the false statement of fact was that the evidence was undisputed about the traffic light's color when the accident occurred. Although the new lawyer did make a false statement of fact to the court, he was unaware of the statement's falsity. Once he becomes aware of the falsity, he is obligated to correct the error. Until then, however, he is not subject to discipline. Thus, C is incorrect because it does not address the fact that the new lawyer did not know of the falsity of the statement. Although factually accurate, B is a wrong answer because the new lawyer will be subject to discipline for a known misrepresentation even if it is not the first instance of the misrepresentation. D is an incorrect answer because this situation may qualify under the emergency exception to the competence Rule given the suddenness of the attorney's stroke and the time constraints on the new lawyer.

ANSWER 91

REGULATION OF THE LEGAL PROFESSION

A is the correct answer because, although MRPC 8.3(a) imposes upon the attorney a general duty to report the lawyer's violation of the Rules that raises a substantial question as to the lawyer's honesty, trustworthiness, and fitness to act as an attorney, the criminal law attorney does not have to so when doing that would violate MRPC 1.6, which governs client-lawyer confidentiality. In other words, MRPC 8.3(c) and its second comment do not require a report of misconduct that would violate the Rule of confidentiality by disclosing information it protects. Here, the probate lawyer apparently violated the Rules by his misconduct under MPRC 8.4(b) of misusing his client funds, which arguably constitutes a crime that reflects adversely upon his honesty, trustworthiness, and fitness as an attorney. However, the probate lawyer disclosed that violation during the attorney's representation of him as a client. Generally, this prevents the criminal law attorney from disclosing the probate lawyer's statements to him. Usually, MRPC 1.6(a) provides that a criminal law attorney may not reveal confidential information without informed consent or because he must do so to represent the client. The facts do not support application of either of these grounds for the attorney to reveal confidential information about the probate lawyer. The Rule provides several exceptions, one of which allows an attorney to reveal confidential information in order to prevent substantial injury to the financial interests of a third party, but only when the client is using the attorney's services in furtherance of the actions causing the injury. MRPC 1.6(b)(2)-(3). Here, although the probate lawyer's clients may have sustained injury to their financial interests due to his misuse of their funds, the facts do not indicate that the probate lawyer is now using the criminal law attorney's services in order to do that. Rather, the criminal law attorney advised the probate lawyer not to do that again and directed him to obtain assistance with his gambling addiction. Note that MRPC 8.3(c) does not require the criminal law attorney to disclose information that he obtained from the probate lawyer while the criminal law attorney is participating in the lawyer assistance program. Arguably, this could apply because the criminal law attorney served on the state bar committee that oversees the assistance program when the probate lawyer retained him.

B is a wrong answer because, although it relates to a provision of MRPC 8.3 governing reporting professional misconduct, the facts do not indicate that any lawyer in the probate lawyer's law firm has knowledge of the probate lawyer's misconduct. C is a wrong answer because the criminal law attorney's duty of confidentiality to the lawyer existed once the probate lawyer made his statement to the attorney. D is an incorrect answer because the criminal law attorney's duty of confidentiality trumps the concern that he will help conceal the probate lawyer's breach of fiduciary duty.

ANSWER 92

JUDICIAL CONDUCT

A is the correct answer in this *ex parte* communication situation. MCJC R 2.9(A) provides that, subject to certain exceptions, a judge must not initiate, permit, or consider *ex parte* communications, or consider other communications made to the judge outside the presence of the parties, regarding an impending or pending matter. MCJC R 2.9(A)(2) provides one exception that applies to the advice of a disinterested expert on the law applicable to a case before a judge. The judge is permitted to obtain the written advice of a disinterested expert if she gives the parties notice and sufficient time to respond. Here, the exception does not apply because, even assuming that the attorney qualifies as a disinterested expert on the law, the judge did not obtain written advice from the attorney. Moreover, the judge did not provide the parties with any notice or time to respond. Thus, the judge permitted and considered improper communications with the attorney about the case outside the parties' presence. B is an incorrect answer because a judge can obtain the opinion of a disinterested third party expert under the circumstances described above. D is a wrong answer because, although the attorney may have been disinterested in terms of not representing a client involved in the case, it was not proper for the judge to consult with the attorney in this situation. C is an incorrect answer because the fact that the attorney called the judge and the judge did not call the attorney is irrelevant.

ANSWER 93

REGULATION OF THE LEGAL PROFESSION

Answer choice C is correct. This question tests Model Rule 4.2, which prohibits a lawyer from communicating about the subject of the representation with another party in a matter if (1) the other party is represented by counsel, and (2) the lawyer has not first obtained consent to the communication from the other party's lawyer. The lawyer need not get consent from the other

party's lawyer if the communication is authorized under the law or by court order. Here, the defendant's attorney has not obtained the consent of the plaintiff's attorney, and the facts do not indicate that the law or a court order permits contact regarding the matter.

Answer choice A is incorrect because the attorney's subjective belief regarding the motive of opposing counsel is irrelevant.

Answer choice B is incorrect. Any communication with a represented person, whether written or oral, is prohibited.

Answer choice D is incorrect because the ultimate disposition of the communication or the case does not justify the communication. The prohibited conduct is the communication itself.

ANSWER 94

REGULATION OF THE LEGAL PROFESSION

C is the correct answer because it is the best option. MRPC 8.4 provides that an attorney commits misconduct by engaging in behavior that involves dishonesty, fraud, deceit, or misrepresentation. Under MRPC 8.3, an attorney who knows of another attorney's violation of the Rules that raises questions regarding the other attorney's honesty, trustworthiness, and fitness to act as an attorney must report such behavior.

Answer C refers to evidence that the prosecutor has that arguably could support him in reporting his concerns about the attorney's motive. Such evidence could show that the attorney engaged in misconduct under MRPC 8.4, such that the prosecutor must report that misconduct pursuant to MRPC 8.3. Primarily, this evidence consists of what the prosecutor heard the attorney say to his friend about recommending rejection of the offer to the defendant. Additionally, the facts contain other circumstantial evidence including the defendant's rejection of the offer and the media coverage of the trial. Arguably, further evidence could exist if the attorney's recommendation misled the defendant or included any other false or untruthful statements. Although the attorney's recommendation truthfully states what could happen, the prosecutor has a reasonable belief about the attorney's improper motive based on the circumstantial evidence and rather unlikely possibility of acquittal at the trial. Moreover, the attorney might have misled, or not been truthful toward, the defendant by (1) not qualifying the likelihood of an acquittal; and (2) not explaining the likelihood of a conviction in light of the facts. The latter possibility is significant because conviction of a capital crime may result in the death penalty. The defendant could have avoided that result by accepting the offer, and he might have wanted to accept the offer if the attorney had more fully advised him about these scenarios. The attorney should have done that in the defendant's best interest.

A is a wrong answer because if the attorney violated the Rule, the prosecutor would still have to report the attorney despite his providing the defendant with effective assistance of counsel at the trial. B is an incorrect answer because the fact that a defendant could get an acquittal as a result of a trial, which he could not have received by accepting the offer, does not necessarily indicate that the attorney violated the Rule. Rather, it could show that the attorney's motive for recommending that the defendant reject the offer was to seek an acquittal. D is a wrong answer because, although the trial of the case received media coverage, that does not necessarily indicate that the attorney violated the Rule.

ANSWER 95

REGULATION OF THE LEGAL PROFESSION

A is the correct answer because the attorney may be subject to civil liability because the paralegal negligently failed to make an entry in her case calendar while working for the attorney on the client's case. The civil liability may come in the form of vicarious liability, which the attorney would be liable for even if the attorney was not negligent. A is also correct because the attorney could be in violation of MRPC 5.3(b)-(c), and thus subject to discipline, if he failed to properly supervise the paralegal. B is a wrong answer because it incorrectly states that the attorney will avoid either discipline or civil liability based on his lack of negligence, when the attorney may have civil liability for the paralegal's negligence pursuant to the doctrine of vicarious liability. C is an incorrect answer because vicarious liability is not a basis for finding the attorney subject to both discipline and civil liability for the assistance's negligence, although it is a basis for finding the attorney subject to civil liability. D is a wrong answer because the client cannot make the decision of whether the attorney is subject to discipline or civil liability. The determination of whether the attorney is subject to discipline must be made by the jurisdiction's disciplinary authority. The determination of the attorney's civil liability for the paralegal's negligence must be made by the relevant court of competent jurisdiction.

ANSWER 96

REGULATION OF THE LEGAL PROFESSION

C is the correct answer because it reflects MRPC 5.4(b), which prohibits the attorney from forming a partnership with a non-lawyer that involves any activities of practicing law. D is a wrong answer because the dispositive issue is whether the attorney formed a partnership that involves his practice of law in this relationship with the physician, a non-lawyer. C directly involves that issue and implicates the controlling Rule. D indirectly involves that issue and implicates the Rule, which the attorney would violate as a result of practicing law in a partnership formed with the physician, a non-lawyer. If the attorney did not practice law in their partnership, then there would be no legal fees to possibly divide or share. In addition, implicitly D refers to this issue of fee-sharing among the attorney and the physician, a non-lawyer. MRPC 5.4(a) prohibits the attorney from sharing legal fees with a non-lawyer such as the physician. Although it may be factually accurate, A is an incorrect answer because the relationship of the attorney and the physician will violate MRPC 5.4(b). B is a wrong answer because a violation of MRPC 5.4(b) would occur even if the physician did not provide clients with legal advice.

ANSWER 97

CONFLICTS OF INTEREST

A is the correct answer in this former clients conflict of interest situation that is governed by the Rules. The attorney should not represent the brother in his lawsuit against his sister because the attorney concurrently represented both of the partners in a substantially related case in which the brother's interests are materially adverse to the sister's interests. B is a wrong answer because the Rule still applies as stated in the foregoing sentence even if a different lawyer will represent the sister in the brother's lawsuit. C is an incorrect answer because the fact that the attorney did not receive the missing partnership information in the client's civil action does not fall under any exception to the conflict of interest Rules. D is a wrong answer because the reasonableness of the brother's belief that if the sister had provided the information, the results of litigation would have been different, is not dispositive

ANSWER 98

COMMUNICATION ABOUT LEGAL SERVICES

A is the correct answer because the commercial's contents would only be improper under MRPC 7.1 if the attorneys' conduct did not comply with the commercial. In other words, the commercial would violate the Rules by being false and misleading if the attorneys failed to abide by the terms of their offer by either charging people for the initial consultation or by failing to determine the fairness of the awards in domestic relations matters. B is a wrong answer because the commercial, by its terms, does not target people who are either represented or unrepresented by other counsel. C is an incorrect answer because MRPC 7.3(a) only prohibits the attorneys from directly contacting prospective clients by the following means: in-person, live telephone, or real-time electronic contact. Their radio commercial does not involve such direct solicitation of employment for economic gain. D is a wrong answer because the attorneys do not violate the Rules by requiring one to mention the commercial when arranging for an initial consultation in person while visiting their new office.

ANSWER 99

LITIGATION AND OTHER FORMS OF ADVOCACY

A is the correct answer because MRPC 3.5 prohibits the prosecutor, a lawyer, from communicating *ex parte* with a judge by her letter during this criminal proceeding. Although the trial had occurred, the proceeding was not finished because neither a judgment nor a potential sentencing had occurred. The facts do not indicate that either the law or a court order applied as an exception to authorize the prosecutor's letter. B is a wrong answer because the timing of the judge's issuance of the opinion is irrelevant to determining the letter's propriety. C is an incorrect answer because neither the facts nor MRPC 3.5 provides an exception on the basis that the prosecutor reasonably believed that a violation of the local speedy trial rule could have occurred. Although factually accurate, D is a wrong answer because the letter is improper regardless of whether the prosecutor sought to influence the judge.

ANSWER 100

LITIGATION AND OTHER FORMS OF ADVOCACY

D is the correct answer because the attorney violated MRPC 3.5, which prohibits him from seeking to influence the judge by legally prohibited means. A is a wrong answer because the attorney would be subject to discipline for violating that Rule even though he wrote the judge pursuant to the contractor's instructions. Although factually accurate, B is an incorrect answer because the facts do not indicate that state law either authorizes the attorney's letter to the judge or has any impact on the Rule's applicability. C is a wrong answer because the attorney's letter to the judge violated the Rule, regardless of the outcome of the prosecution of the contractor.

ANSWER 101

SAFEKEEPING FUNDS AND OTHER PROPERTY

C is the correct answer because MRPC 1.15(e) requires the attorney to keep any disputed funds separate until the dispute is resolved. Here, the attorney and the plaintiff dispute whether the plaintiff owes $3,000 in addition to the undisputed $7,000. But, the attorney failed to keep $3,000 separate by including it with the undisputed $7,000 when the attorney moved the $10,000 from the plaintiff's client trust account into his general account. In order to comply with the Rule, the attorney should have moved only $7,000 into the general account and kept $3,000 in the client trust account until resolution of this dispute with the plaintiff occurred.

Note that the attorney would have violated another part of the Rule by not distributing to the plaintiff or himself any of the $75,000 until resolution of their dispute occurred. Specifically, in the event of a disputed claim, MRPC 1.15(e) requires that the attorney promptly distribute the remaining, undisputed portion of the property. Here, the attorney partially complied with that Rule by issuing the $65,000 check to the plaintiff and moving up to $7,000 into his general account. The attorney partially violated the Rule by moving the disputed $3,000 into his general account. In other words, the attorney could have fully complied with the Rule by moving only the undisputed $7,000 into his general account and leaving the disputed $3,000 in the plaintiff's client trust account until they resolved their dispute.

Although answers A and B are factually accurate, they are incorrect because they do not take into account the aforementioned effects of the Rule. Answer D is not correct because neither the parties agreement nor the Rule provides that the attorney must receive the amount stated by the client.

ANSWER 102

REGULATION OF THE LEGAL PROFESSION

C is the correct answer. This question tests MRPC 5.4(d). Pursuant to that rule the lawyer cannot practice with the other attorneys in a professional corporation because the family law attorney's spouse, a non-lawyer, is its president. A is a wrong answer because the rule applies even if the lawyer is not an officer, shareholder, or member of the professional corporation and ,only holds the status of a salaried employee. B is an incorrect answer because the Rule also applies even though the family law attorney's spouse neither directs nor controls the professional judgment of any of the attorneys. D is a wrong answer because the Rule does not preclude the criminal defense attorney's sister from working as the firm's office assistant. Note that an exception to the rule allows a fiduciary representative of a lawyer's estate to hold the lawyer's stock or interest for a reasonable time during administration.

ANSWER 103

LAWYERS' DUTIES TO THE PUBLIC AND THE LEGAL SYSTEM

A is the correct answer because it applies MRPC 8.2 (and 8.4(c)) to these facts. The attorney did not knowingly misrepresent any fact concerning the judge because he reasonably relied on the accuracy of the commission's letter. B is a wrong answer because it contradicts those provisions' prohibition against a candidate or opponent from knowingly making any misrepresentation about a candidate or opponent. C is an incorrect answer because its reason leads to the wrong conclusion and answer A provides the dispositive reason and correct conclusion. Although factually accurate, D is a wrong answer because the fact that the judge was actually disciplined for two instances of judicial conduct instead of one does not subject the attorney to discipline because he publicly stated the false information that the commission gave him.

ANSWER 104

THE CLIENT-LAWYER RELATIONSHIP

B is the correct answer because it reflects MRPC 1.5. An attorney and client may enter into a reasonable contingency fee in most actions. A is a wrong answer because the plaintiff could properly request or suggest the terms and conditions of a contingency fee agreement. C is an incorrect answer, although at first glance, it is a tempting answer. Under the comments to MRPC 1.8, a prohibited proprietary interest is treated differently from a contingency fee agreement. A contingency fee arrangement is permissible but the receipt of a property interest in the litigation is impermissible. In this case, therefore, the question turns on whether the attorney received a property interest in the litigation or entered into a contingency fee arrangement. The facts clearly state that the client suggested a "contingency fee arrangement" and agreed to pay 10% of the proceeds. It does not indicate that the attorney received a property interest. Therefore, because the plaintiff did not grant the attorney a proprietary interest in the civil action, the attorney's interest is a permissible contingency fee. This agreement is a classic example of a contingency fee arrangement permitted under MRPC 1.5. D is a wrong answer because the reasonableness of a contingency fee is not necessarily determined by comparing it to how much the attorney would have received by billing the plaintiff at a reasonable hourly rate.

ANSWER 105

COMMUNICATION ABOUT LEGAL SERVICES

A is the correct answer because MRPC 7.1 allows the attorney to publish the notice if it is true and does not contain any false or misleading statements. B is a wrong answer because, even if factually accurate, this answer is less than optimal. An attorney would be subject to discipline for publishing false information that is publicly available. C is an incorrect answer because the fact that the publication was made to people who had not been the attorney's clients does not violate the Rule. D is a wrong answer because the attorney's service as a legislator could have improved or increased his competence as an attorney. Nonetheless, it does not violate the rules to disclose service in the state legislature unless the disclosure implies the ability to unduly influence the legislative body.

ANSWER 106

REGULATION OF THE LEGAL PROFESSION

D is the correct answer because the subordinate attorney cannot escape liability for violating an ethical rule simply as a result of following the directions of a supervisory attorney. C is a wrong answer because, although it accurately states that the supervising attorney's instructions to the subordinate attorney violated the ethical rules, the subordinate attorney is not liable simply because of the supervising attorney's violation of those rules. Rather, the subordinate attorney is liable because his conduct of destroying the documents violated those rules. A is an incorrect answer because the subordinate attorney's obedience to the supervising attorney's instructions does not enable the subordinate attorney to escape responsibility for violating the rules on the basis of a duty to obey the supervising attorney. This type of defense will not protect the subordinate attorney from his own conduct in violation of the ethical rules. Only if the subordinate attorney had destroyed the documents pursuant to the supervising attorney's reasonable resolution of a question of professional duty could A be a correct answer. However, the facts do not indicate that that occurred here. B is an incorrect answer because both the supervising attorney and the subordinate attorney violated an ethical rule.

ANSWER 107

THE CLIENT-LAWYER RELATIONSHIP

Pursuant to MRPC 6.2(c), D is the correct answer because it describes a good cause for the attorney to avoid being appointed to represent the defendant based on her membership in the organization that assists domestic violence victims. C is a wrong answer because, although supported by MRPC 6.2(a), it is less dispositive than D and the attorney's representation of the defendant will not necessarily result in violating an ethical rule based on these facts. A is an incorrect answer because an attorney is not required to represent every person that the lawyer is appointed to represent. Although answer B describes a basis for the attorney not to represent the defendant, it is a wrong answer for two reasons. The first reason is that B states that representing the defendant *could impose* a financial burden upon the attorney, but MRPC 6.2(b) applies when representation *is likely to result* in an unreasonable financial burden on a lawyer. Second, the facts do not support this reason because, although the attorney incurs significant expense from her criminal defense work, she is not likely to suffer an unreasonable financial burden if either the court and/or the defendant must reimburse her for the costs of his legal defense. That can occur when a court appoints an attorney to represent a criminal defendant.

ANSWER 108

THE CLIENT-LAWYER RELATIONSHIP

C is the correct answer because under these circumstances a court could find that a client-lawyer relationship existed for two reasons. First, the attorney took the prospective client's paperwork and told him not to be concerned about the arraignment. Second, the attorney made a delayed or "last minute" expression of an absence of intent to be retained by the prospective client. D is a wrong answer because an attorney s not always required to represent any client who requests representation. Rather, an attorney may decline to represent a client under certain circumstances. A is an incorrect answer because, as explained earlier, the facts give rise to a client-lawyer relationship between the prospective client and the attorney. B is a wrong answer because under certain situations, such as appointment of an attorney by a court, an attorney may not refuse to represent a client without showing good cause for that refusal.

ANSWER 109

THE CLIENT-LAWYER RELATIONSHIP

The correct answer is D because the attorney complied with MRPC 1.5(b) by communicating the change to the manufacturer, which agreed to it. Thus, although answer B is factually accurate, it is a wrong answer because the manufacturer agreed to the change after initially opposing it. Even though answer A is factually accurate, the Rule recognizes that the attorney could change her billing rate during the representation, provided that she communicate that change to the manufacturer as happened here. Thus, C is incorrect because the fact that the attorney's business costs increased does not protect her from discipline for violating the Rule. Rather, that fact simply provides her reason for increasing her billing rate.

ANSWER 110

CONFLICTS OF INTEREST

B is the correct answer because it accurately applies the dispositive ethical rule to the facts. The attorney, a lawyer whose personal friendship with the owner, a potential party litigant, could negatively impact his client relationship with the prospective client, can decline to represent the prospective client in litigation against the owner. This is a type of conflict of interest that could adversely affect the attorney's ability to provide proper representation. A is a wrong answer because it is too categorical when under certain circumstances, such as when a court appoints an attorney to represent a defendant, the attorney generally cannot avoid that representation without having good cause to do so. C is an incorrect answer because it is too categorical when, as here, an attorney is not required to represent every prospective client. D is a wrong answer because, even if it was factually accurate, B is more responsive to the question and directly applies the controlling ethical rule.

ANSWER 111

CONFLICTS OF INTEREST

B is the correct answer because it accurately describes an exception to MRPC 1.8(c), which applies to these facts to allow the attorney to follow the client's instructions. A is a wrong answer because it is too categorical and contrary to the ethical rules, which only provide an exception for when, as here, the client is related to the lawyer. C is an incorrect answer because it is too categorical and does not provide for the exception for when, as here, the instrument makes a substantial gift to a lawyer related to the client. D is a wrong answer because the ethical rules permit the attorney to prepare this will, including its gift to her, because she is the client's relative.

ANSWER 112

CONFLICTS OF INTEREST

C is the correct answer in this conflict of interest situation. The parties have followed the governing rule pursuant to which the attorney can render legal services to both the mortgagor and mortgagee. D is a wrong answer because the dispositive issue is whether the arrangement at issue complies with the rule, not whether it is common where the attorney works. Although it is factually accurate, A is an incorrect answer because the mortgagor's payment to the attorney does not render the attorney's preparation of the documents improper. B is a wrong answer because the fact that the interests of the mortgagor and mortgagee are different does not render their arrangement improper.

ANSWER 113

SAFEKEEPING FUNDS AND OTHER PROPERTY

D is the correct answer because the attorney should have only moved $1,500 from the client trust account into the general account after she had earned $1,500 in legal fees. The controlling rule provides that an attorney can only move any of a client's retainer from the general account to the client trust account as fees are earned. Here, the attorney moved more of the retainer into the general account than she had earned and had to return $750 that she had not earned. The attorney should have only moved $1,500, rather than $3,000 initially, and only $750 after performing the other five hours of work.

A is a wrong answer because the attorney should have initially only moved $1,500 and she should have only moved $750 after having earned it by working another 5 hours. By taking that approach, the attorney would not have needed to return $750 to the client trust account. B is an incorrect answer because under the rule it does not matter if the attorney legitimately expected to perform another 10 hours of work on the client's matter the next day. An attorney can only move funds from the client trust account to the general account after they are earned. C is a wrong answer because the attorney properly withdrew $1,500 from the general account that she had placed there after completing the first 10 hours of legal work for the client.

ANSWER 114

COMMUNICATION ABOUT LEGAL SERVICES

B is the correct answer because it would be permissible for the attorney to contact the client when the attorney previously represented the client and the contact concerned the subject matter of the representation. A is an incorrect answer because the attorney is not precluded from subsequently preparing a new lease for the client after having prepared the original lease. C is a wrong answer because, even if a basis existed for the attorney to think that the client obtained other counsel, the attorney would be contacting the client regarding the subject matter of the previous representation. D is an incorrect answer because the attorney would be contacting the client to provide information regarding the change in the law, not necessarily to solicit legal business.

ANSWER 115

DIFFERENT ROLES OF THE LAWYER

B is the correct answer because an attorney representing a client before a legislative body or administrative agency in a non-adjudicative proceeding must disclose that the appearance is in a representative capacity. A is a wrong answer because an attorney can receive compensation for attempting to affect legislative action. C is an incorrect answer because whether the attorney sincerely thought that he advanced a position that served the public interest is not dispositive here or relevant under the rule. D is a wrong answer because, even if the legislature was only concerned with the nature of the testimony instead of the source of a witness's compensation, the rule requires that the attorney disclose that the appearance is in a representative capacity.

ANSWER 116

CLIENT CONFIDENTIALITY

C is the correct answer because it reflects the governing rule allowing for dual representation that would not result in a significant risk that the interests of either partner would be materially prejudiced. D is a wrong answer because the fact that the attorney had already been representing both partners with respect to their partnership is not a valid basis under the rule for their dual representation in terms of criminal liability. A is an incorrect answer because the permissibility of the attorney's dual representation is not conditional upon the waiver of client-lawyer confidentiality by both partners. B is a wrong answer because the rule does not require the attorney to notify the partners that they should contact independent counsel before they signed and returned his letter to them.

ANSWER 117

LITIGATION AND OTHER FORMS OF ADVOCACY

A is the correct answer because the controlling rule prohibits the contracts attorney from representing the seller's legal representative when it is likely that the contracts attorney will be a necessary witness whose testimony would relate to the contested issue of the purchaser's mental competency. D is a wrong answer because it states the opposite of an exception that would only allow the contracts attorney to testify if his testimony related to an uncontested issue. B is an incorrect answer because the rule does not provide that the mere fact that the contracts attorney drafted the contract precludes the contracts attorney from representing the seller. The rule applies if the contracts attorney is likely to be a necessary witness, but the rule is subject to exceptions, the application of which depends upon the factual situation in question. C is a wrong answer because the fact that the contracts attorney is the only witness still alive is not an exception to the rule.

ANSWER 118

LITIGATION AND OTHER FORMS OF ADVOCACY

A is the correct answer because the attorney cannot represent the accountant in an action in which the attorney will testify, and the testimony will relate to a contested issue in the case. MRPC 3.7(a) provides that an attorney may serve as an advocate and a necessary witness who testifies in the same trial if "(1) the testimony relates to an uncontested issue; (2) the testimony relates to the nature and value of legal services rendered in the case; or (3) disqualification of the" attorney would result in substantial hardship to the client. In this case, the mental competence of the client will be the pivotal contested issue in the will contest. Although it is factually accurate, C is an incorrect answer because the attorney's status as the only available subscribing witness is of no legal consequence to the attorney's ability to be a witness. D is incorrect because there is no rule providing that the attorney could be a witness, or avoid being a witness, even if the receptionist was found and made available to testify. B is incorrect because there is no such law.

ANSWER 119

THE CLIENT-LAWYER RELATIONSHIP

Answer choice C is correct. This question tests Model Rule 6.2, which addresses the circumstances in which an attorney may seek to avoid a representation directed by a court or other tribunal. Under Rule 6.2, a lawyer *must not* seek to avoid appointment by a tribunal to represent a person except for good cause. Good cause exists if (1) representing the client is likely to result in violation of the Rules or other law; (2) representing the client is likely to result in an unreasonable financial burden on the lawyer; or (3) the client or the cause is so repugnant to the lawyer as to be likely to impair the client-lawyer relationship or the lawyer's ability to represent the client. Thus, unless there is a real likelihood that the appointment will present an unreasonable financial burden on the attorney – for example, because the case will require all of her attention for a substantial period of time, thus preventing her from working on any income-producing cases – the mere possibility that potential clients may not seek out the attorney's services is insufficient to justify seeking to decline the appointment.

Answer choice A is incorrect because it is not enough that the attorney strongly dislikes the crime with which the defendant has been charged. Under Model Rule 6.2(c), the attorney cannot seek to avoid the appointment unless her distaste for the client or his cause is so strong as to impair the client-lawyer relationship or the attorney's ability to represent the client. Here, the facts indicate that although the attorney has strong feelings about the client's case, she is confident that she can ably represent him.

Answer choice B is incorrect because the fact that she has not established an attorney-client relationship with the defendant is irrelevant. The attorney is obliged to accept the representation unless good cause exists to avoid the appointment. Model Rule 6.2; Restatement of the Law Governing Lawyers, Third, § 14(2).

Answer choice D is incorrect because the Model Rules do not require the attorney to obtain the defendant's informed, written consent to decline the appointment.

ANSWER 120

THE CLIENT-LAWYER RELATIONSHIP

Answer choice A is correct. Under Model Rule 1.5(a), a lawyer may not charge an unreasonable fee. In evaluating whether a fee is unreasonable, several factors are to be considered, including: (1) the time and labor required, the difficulty of the issues involved, and the skill required to perform the legal service; (2) the likelihood that taking on the case will preclude other employment by the lawyer; (3) the fee customarily charged in the locality for similar legal services; (4) the amount involved and the results obtained; (5) the time limitations imposed by the circumstances or the client; (6) the nature and length of the professional relationship with the client; (7) the experience, reputation, and ability of the lawyer; and (8) whether the fee is contingent. *Id.* A lawyer's fee agreement should be communicated to the client, preferably in writing. Rule 1.5(b). Although contingent fees are acceptable in some cases, Rule 1.5(c), in no circumstance may a lawyer charge a fee in any domestic relations matter where the fee is contingent on the securing of a divorce or the amount of alimony or support awarded or settlement agreement reached. Rule 1.5(d)(1).

Under these facts, the lawyer's fee appears reasonable, given his reputation, and the fact that the fee is not substantially higher than fees charged by less experienced lawyers in the area. Although the lawyer has agreed to defer receipt of his fee until after the case is over, neither the amount of his fee, nor its receipt, is contingent on securing a divorce or obtaining any amount of money or property for the wife.

Answer choice B is incorrect because the lawyer's fee is not contingent upon the securing of a divorce or upon the amount of alimony or support, or property settlement. Model Rule 1.5(d)(1).

Answer choice C is incorrect because, as explained above, the lawyer is not charging a contingency fee. Even if he were charging a contingency fee, the fact that the agreement has been reduced to writing and that the wife has signed it is irrelevant. Model Rule 1.5(d) strictly prohibits contingency fees in divorce proceedings.

Answer choice D is incorrect because the facts do not suggest that his fee is *per se* unreasonable. Model Rule 1.5(a) presents several factors to consider when determining whether a fee is unreasonably high. As explained above, the lawyer in this case is experienced and has a good reputation, and his hourly fee does not appear substantially higher than the fees charged by less experienced lawyers in the area for similar legal work.

ANSWER 121

CONFLICTS OF INTEREST

Answer choice B is correct. This question tests Model Rule 1.9(a), which governs when an attorney may represent a client whose interests are materially adverse to those of a former client in the same or a substantially related matter. Under Rule 1.9(a), such a representation is impermissible unless the former client gives informed, written consent. Answer choice B reflects the fact that the owner has provided oral consent to the representation, not written consent.

Answer choice A is incorrect because the representation would not involve a concurrent conflict of interest, since the lawyer's representation of the owner concluded when the labor dispute was resolved.

Answer choice C is incorrect because the owner's oral consent to the representation is insufficient. Rule 1.9(a) requires the former client to give informed, *written* consent.

Answer choice D is incorrect because the lawyer's acquisition of information during the previous lawsuit that could hurt the owner in the busboys' suit does not preclude him from taking on the busboys as clients. However, the lawyer is still subject to the provisions of Model Rule 1.9(c), which govern his ability to use the damaging information against the owner.

ANSWER 122

REGULATION OF THE LEGAL PROFESSION

Answer choice C is correct. This question tests Model Rule 5.1, which explains when a lawyer will be subject to discipline for a subordinate lawyer's misconduct, and Model Rule 1.15 which sets forth an attorney's duty to safeguard a client's property. Under Rule 1.15(a), a lawyer must keep a client's property separate from the lawyer's own property, such as in a client trust account. Money earned by a lawyer must then be paid from the client trust account. Under Model Rule 5.1(c), a supervising attorney is subject to discipline for a subordinate attorney's misconduct if the supervising lawyer: (1) orders or, with knowledge of the specific conduct, ratifies the conduct involved; or (2) knows of the conduct at a time when its consequences can be avoided or mitigated but fails to take reasonable remedial action. Here, the associate has violated Rule 1.15 because he did not deposit all of the client's funds in the trust account before deducting the fees owed to the firm. However, the managing partner is not subject to discipline for the associate's conduct because, as the facts indicate, he properly trained the associate to handle client funds and did not know that the associate failed to deposit the settlement check in the client trust account.

Answer choice A is incorrect because, as explained above, the associate is subject to discipline for violating Rule 1.15.

Answer choice B is incorrect on both points, as explained above.

Answer choice D is incorrect because the managing partner did not violate Rule 5.1(c).

ANSWER 123

COMMUNICATION ABOUT LEGAL SERVICES

Answer choice D is correct. This question tests Model Rules 5.4 and 7.2. Under Rule 7.2(b)(4), a lawyer may enter into a reciprocal referral agreement provided that (i) the agreement is not exclusive; and (ii) the referred client is informed of the existence and nature of the agreement. Here, the attorney and entrepreneur have entered into an exclusive reciprocal referral agreement, thus violating Rule 7.2.

Answer choice A is incorrect. Under Model Rule 5.4(b), a lawyer may not form a partnership with a non-lawyer if any of the activities of the partnership consist of the practice of law. This choice correctly notes that none of the resource center's services amounts to the practice of law, but it overlooks the fact that, as explained above, the attorney has violated Model Rule 7.2.

Answer choice B is incorrect. Rule 5.4(b) limits a lawyer's ability to form a partnership with non-lawyers so as to preserve a lawyer's professional independence.

Answer choice C is incorrect because it overstates the applicable rule: Model Rule 5.4(b) allows an attorney to enter into a partnership with a non-lawyer, provided that the partnership does not practice law in any way.

ANSWER 124

COMMUNICATION ABOUT LEGAL SERVICES

Answer choice B is correct. Under Model Rule 7.3(a), a lawyer may not "solicit professional employment from a prospective client when a significant motive for the lawyer's doing so is the lawyer's pecuniary gain . . . ." An exception to Rule 7.3(a) exists if the prospective client is a lawyer, Model Rule 7.3(a)(1), provided that the prospective client has not made known to the lawyer a desire not to be solicited and that the solicitation does not involve coercion, duress, or harassment. Model Rule 7.3(b). Here, the lawyer solicited business from a lawyer, and nothing in the facts suggests that he coerced her or harassed her, or that she was under duress.

Answer choice A is incorrect because it overstates the applicable rule. Model Rule 7.3(a) allows a lawyer to solicit business for pecuniary gain from a lawyer or someone with whom the soliciting attorney has a family, close personal, or prior professional relationship, provided that the restrictions of Rule 7.3(b) are not violated.

Answer choice C is incorrect. Although the lawyer should not *take on the representation* because he is a potential witness, Model Rule 3.7(a), Rule 7.3 does not prohibit his solicitation on that basis. Nor does the attorney's reasonable belief about the merits of the case impact the propriety of his solicitation.

Answer choice D is incorrect. Model Rule 7.3(b) prohibits an attorney from soliciting business from a prospective client – even if the solicitation is not barred by Rule 7.3(a) – if the prospective client has made known to the lawyer that he or she does not want to receive solicitations. Although the facts here indicate that the driver of the station wagon disapproved of the solicitation in hindsight, nothing in the fact pattern suggests that she gave the personal injury attorney any indication that she did not want to be solicited.

ANSWER 125

CONFLICTS OF INTEREST

Answer choice D is correct. This question tests Model Rules 1.11 and 7.5. Under Model Rule 1.11, a lawyer serving as a public official may practice law, provided that he does not violate Rule 1.7 or Rule 1.9, which govern conflicts of interest. Under Rule 7.5(c), if an attorney practicing in a firm takes public office, the firm may continue to use the public official's name in the firm name, provided that the attorney/public official continues to actively and regularly practice with the firm. Here, the lawyer has avoided any conflict of interest between his role as a legislator and his role as an attorney, and thus has not violated any of the Model Rules in that regard. Because the facts indicate that he continues to practice with the firm actively and regularly (albeit with some additional help from his partners), the firm has not violated Rule 7.5(c) by continuing to use his name.

Answer choice A is incorrect on both accounts. As explained above, the partner/legislator may practice law as long as he complies with the rules governing conflicts of interest. And the firm may continue to use the partner's name during his term in the legislature as long as he actively and regularly practices with the firm.

Answer choice B is incorrect because, as discussed above, the partner's name does not need to be removed from the firm's name.

Answer choice C is incorrect because the partner/legislator may continue to practice in the firm, subject to Rules 1.7, 1.9, and 1.11. Moreover, if the partner ceased working at the firm because of his role in the legislature, the firm would violate Rule 7.5(c) by retaining his name in the firm's name.

ANSWER 126

COMMUNICATION ABOUT LEGAL SERVICES

Answer choice C is correct. This question tests Model Rule 7.2. Under that Rule, a lawyer generally "shall not give anything of value to a person for recommending the lawyer's services . . . ." Rule 7.2(b). Exceptions to this Rule exist if the lawyer (1) pays the reasonable costs of otherwise permissible advertisements or communications; (2) pays the charges of a legal service plan, non-profit, or qualified lawyer referral service; (3) is purchasing a law practice; or (4) is making a referral pursuant to a permissible reciprocal referral agreement. *Id.*

Answer choice A is incorrect. Model Rule 5.4 does prohibit a lawyer from sharing legal fees with a non-lawyer. However, that is not the case here. The lawyer has given his neighbor – a non-lawyer – the gift of a bottle of wine, which is distinct from a portion of the client's fees.

Answer choice B is incorrect because, under Model Rule 7.2(b), a lawyer may not give *anything* of value to a person in exchange for a referral unless the lawyer does so in compliance with one of four exceptions in Rule 7.2(b). Here, none of those exceptions has been satisfied, and the per se rule applies regardless of how reasonable the gift may seem.

Answer choice D is incorrect for the same reason as answer choice B: The value of the item given in exchange for a referral is irrelevant. The lawyer violates Rule 7.2(b) unless his conduct falls into one of the Rule's four exceptions.

ANSWER 127

JUDICIAL CONDUCT

Answer choice A is correct. Under Code of Judicial Conduct ("CJC") Rule 3.11(A), a judge may hold investments. Under Rule 3.11(B), a judge may participate in a business closely held by the judge or members of his family. A judge's ability to participate in these financial activities is limited, however, by Rule 3.11(C), which prevents a judge from doing so if his involvement will (1) interfere with his judicial duties; (2) lead to frequent disqualification of the judge; (3) involve the judge in frequent transactions or continuing business relationships with lawyers or other persons likely to come before the court on which the judge serves; or (4) result in other violations of the Code of Judicial Conduct. Here, the facts do not indicate that any of the restrictions in Rule 3.11(C) have been violated. Thus, the judge may continue to hold company stock and serve on the board of directors.

Answer choice B is incorrect because, although the company is mired in state court litigation, such litigation does not occur in the judge's state, let alone before his court. Thus, there is no chance that he will be disqualified, and it is unlikely that other persons involved with the business will appear frequently before the judge's court.

Answer choice C is incorrect. Although CJC Rule 3.11(C)(1) requires a judge to cease financial activities that interfere with the performance of his or her judicial duties, the facts here indicate that the judge's involvement with the company will not interfere with his judicial duties. His involvement requires only a few days per year, and no conflicts of interest appear likely to arise.

Answer choice D is incorrect because CJC Rule 3.11 allows a judge to participate in running a business with his family members, provided certain conditions are met. Nothing in Rule 3.11 requires that the other participants in the business be lawyers.

ANSWER 128

COMMUNICATIONS WITH PERSONS OTHER THAN CLIENTS

Answer choice C is correct. This question tests Model Rule 4.2, which prohibits a lawyer from communicating about the subject of the representation with another party in a matter if (1) the other party is represented by counsel, and (2) the lawyer has not first obtained consent to the communication from the other party's lawyer. The lawyer need not get consent from the other party's lawyer if the communication is authorized under the law or by court order. Here, the lawyer has not obtained the consent of the wife's lawyer, and the facts do not indicate that the law or a court order allow him to contact the wife regarding the divorce proceedings.

Answer choice A is incorrect because the client's interest and approval are irrelevant to the attorney's duty to abide by Rule 4.2.

Answer choice B is incorrect for similar reasons: the wife's consent, like the lawyer's intent, is irrelevant under Rule 4.2, which is designed to prevent attorneys from interfering with the interests of a represented party.

Answer choice D is incorrect because it overstates the limitations in Rule 4.2. Although a lawyer generally may not contact a represented party in a matter about the subject of the representation without first getting consent from that party's lawyer, the Comments to Rule 4.2 indicate that this prohibition does not apply to communications concerning a matter outside of the representation.

ANSWER 129

LITIGATION AND OTHER FORMS OF ADVOCACY

Answer choice A is correct. This question tests Model Rule of Professional Conduct 3.4, which requires a lawyer to demonstrate fairness towards an opposing party and opposing counsel. Under Rule 3.4(f), a lawyer may not request of a person who is not his client that the person refrain from voluntarily giving relevant information to another party unless (1) the person is a relative, employee, or other agent of the client; and (2) the lawyer reasonably believes that the person's interests will not be adversely affected by refraining from giving such information. Here, the lawyer has requested that the son not volunteer information that relates to his mother's lawsuit, and there is nothing in the fact pattern that suggests the son's interests would be adversely affected by withholding such information, provided he does not do so in violation of the law.

Answer choice B is incorrect because Rule 3.4(f) allows a lawyer to make such a request of a non-client in certain circumstances.

Answer choice C is incorrect because it overlooks the permissive nature of Rule 3.4(f). Although certain circumstances may arise in which the opposing party can demand access to relevant information, such as during discovery and at trial, the attorney may request that his client's son not volunteer relevant information unless and until such an obligation arises.

Answer choice D is a red herring. The son is not the lawyer's client, so he is not entitled to the protections of Model Rule 1.6. Since the interview in which the son told the lawyer about his mother was not a consultation about the possibility of forming a client-lawyer relationship, the son's communications to the lawyer are not privileged under Model Rule 1.18. Since no attorney-client relationship was formed with the son, the lawyer could be subject to discipline for his request unless the request fell under the exception set forth in Rule 3.4(f).

ANSWER 130

CLIENT CONFIDENTIALITY

Answer choice D is correct. This question tests Model Rule 1.6. Under Rule 1.6(a), a lawyer generally must keep confidential information given by a client relating to the representation. There are several exceptions to this Rule that allow a lawyer to disclose confidential information at the lawyer's discretion. Under Rule 1.6(b)(1), a lawyer may -- but does not have to -- reveal confidential information to the extent that the lawyer reasonably believes necessary "to prevent reasonably certain death or substantial bodily harm[.]" The facts in this question indicate that the client has a history of aggression toward his former partner and is especially angry. Although the owner has made a statement to his attorney in confidence, the facts suggest that he is likely to harm his former partner with a gun. Under the circumstances, Rule 1.6(b) would permit the attorney to disclose his client's statement and actions to prevent the death of or substantial injury to the former partner.

Answer choices A and B are incorrect because the circumstances indicate that an exception to Rule 1.6(a) exists, but the exception makes the attorney's disclosure permissible, not mandatory.

Answer choice C is incorrect because the Model Rules do not require that an attorney consult with bar counsel before making a disclosure permitted by Rule 1.6(b). Of course, the attorney *may* first seek advice from bar counsel concerning his obligations under the Rules of Professional Conduct. Model Rule 1.6(b)(4).

ANSWER 131

LITIGATION AND OTHER FORMS OF ADVOCACY

Answer choice B is correct. This question tests Model Rule of Professional Conduct ("MRPC") 3.5 and Model Code of Judicial Conduct ("CJC") Rule 2.9. Under MRPC 3.5, a lawyer is prohibited from making an ex parte communication, which is a communication made to a judge for or by one party outside the presence of the other party, unless the communication is authorized by law or court order. MRPC 3.5(b). Judges are similarly barred from initiating, permitting, or considering ex parte communications concerning a pending matter under CJC Rule 2.9. However, CJC Rule 2.9(A)(1) allows a judge to participate in an ex parte communication for scheduling, administrative, or emergency purposes, provided that "(a) the judge reasonably believes that no party will gain a procedural, substantive, or tactical advantage as a result of the ex parte communication; and (b) the judge makes provision promptly to notify all other parties of the substance of the ex parte communication, and gives the parties an opportunity to respond." Here, the defense attorney's request to adjust the day's schedule, though made ex parte, did not violate MRPC Rule 3.5 because the facts indicate that such a request is permissible under the state's laws. Likewise, the judge's ex parte discussion with the defense attorney does not appear to violate CJC Rule 2.9. It concerned a scheduling matter that did not appear to give one party an advantage over the other, and the judge immediately notified the plaintiff's attorney of the request and allowed him to respond.

Answer choice A is incorrect. The MRPC prohibits ex parte communications by lawyers, regardless of who initiates them. Likewise, the CJC prohibits judges from any involvement in an impermissible ex parte communication. CJC Rule 2.9(A) ("A judge shall not initiate, permit, or consider ex parte communications . . . ."). However, as explained above, the lawyer's ex parte communication with the judge was permissible under state law, and the judge did not violate the CJ(C)

Answer choice C is incorrect. The conversation between the defendant's attorney and the judge was clearly ex parte. However, the ex parte conversation did not violate the MRPC or CJC.

Answer choice D is incorrect because, as explained above, some ex parte communications are permitted under the MRCP and CJC. MRPC 3.5; CJC Rule 2.9(A)(1)-(5).

ANSWER 132

COMMUNICATIONS WITH PERSONS OTHER THAN CLIENTS

Answer choice A is correct. This question tests Model Rule 4.3, which regulates an attorney's communications with unrepresented persons. Under Rule 4.3, an attorney for one party may not give legal advice, other than the advice to secure counsel, to an unrepresented person if the lawyer knows or reasonably should know that the unrepresented person's interests are in conflict with, or have a reasonable possibility of being in conflict with, the interests of the attorney's client. Here, the attorney advised the neighbor, who he knew to be unrepresented, and whose interests were clearly adverse to those of the attorney's client, that (1) he should consider obtaining a lawyer and (2) that his proposed countersuit was meritless. Although the attorney acted properly in advising the neighbor to consider getting a lawyer, it was impermissible for the attorney to advise him on the proposed countersuit.

Answer choice B is incorrect because an attorney is not per se barred from contacting an unrepresented person. As explained above, however, certain communications by an attorney to an unrepresented person are impermissible under Rule 4.3.

Answer choice C is incorrect because the attorney's belief about the merits of his legal advice, reasonable or not, is irrelevant. Rule 4.3 prohibits an attorney, in dealing with an unrepresented person, from implying that he is disinterested in a matter. This Rule becomes particularly important when the interests of the attorney's client are adverse to those of the unrepresented person. As Comment [2] to Rule 4.3 notes, the danger that a lawyer will compromise the interests of an unrepresented party whose interests are adverse to those of the lawyer's client is so high that the lawyer may not provide any advice on the matter whatsoever, save for the advice that the unrepresented party should obtain counsel.

Answer choice D is incorrect for similar reasons. Even if the neighbor genuinely intended to proceed without a lawyer, the homeowner's attorney violated Rule 4.3 by giving the neighbor any legal advice beyond the advice that he obtain counsel.

ANSWER 133

CONFLICTS OF INTEREST

Answer choice B is correct. This question tests Model Rule 1.9, which governs an attorney's duties to former clients. Under Rule 1.9(a), an attorney who formerly represented one party may not then represent a second party "in the same or a substantially related matter in which that person's interests are materially adverse to the interests of the former client unless the former client gives informed consent, confirmed in writing." The key issue in this question is whether the tenants' case is the same or a substantially related matter. As Comment [3] to Rule 1.9 explains, matters are "'substantially related . . . if they involve the same transaction or legal dispute or if there otherwise is a substantial risk that confidential factual information as would normally have been obtained in the prior representation would materially advance the client's position in the matter." Given the facts in this question, it does not appear that the tenants' case and the lawyer's original representation are substantially related. They are separate legal actions, the lawyer's involvement in the re-zoning matter ended before the condos were constructed, and there is no indication that he had any knowledge about the way the condos would be built. Thus, there is no conflict of interest and the lawyer may take the tenants' case.

Answer choice A is incorrect because the tenants' interests are plainly adverse to those of the lawyer's former client. Thus, the lawyer may not represent the tenants unless their case is not a "substantially related matter" or, if it is, he obtains the developer's informed, written consent.

Answer choice C is incorrect because the lawyer would only need the developer's informed, written consent if the lawyer was representing the tenants against the developer in a matter substantially related to the original representation.

Answer choice D is incorrect because, although the tenants' interests are materially adverse to those of the lawyer's former client, that is not enough to preclude the lawyer from representing the tenants. Under Rule 1.9, he may do so if the tenants' case is not the same or a substantially related matter. Moreover, he could still represent the tenants against the developer in the same or a substantially related matter if the developer provided informed, written consent.

ANSWER 134

LITIGATION AND OTHER FORMS OF ADVOCACY

Answer choice D is correct. This question tests Model Rule of Professional Conduct 3.6. Under Rule 3.6(a), an attorney participating in the investigation or litigation of a matter may not make an out-of-court statement that he knows or reasonably should know is likely to be disseminated publicly and is substantially likely to materially prejudice an adjudicative proceeding in the matter. The Rule contains several exceptions, such as statements that an investigation of a matter is in progress; requests for assistance in obtaining evidence and information necessary to the matter; and warnings of danger concerning the person involved, if there is reason to believe that there exists a likelihood of substantial harm to an individual or the public interest. Rule 3.6(b)(3, 5-6). In addition, an attorney participating in a criminal case may also make public statements requesting information necessary to aid in the apprehension of an accused individual. Rule 3.6(b)(7)(ii). Here, most of the prosecutor's statements are permitted under Rule 3.6(b). However, the prosecutor also commented that the defendant's flight was clear evidence of his guilt, a statement which is likely to prejudice the potential jury pool against the defendant. Indeed, Comment [5(4)] to Rule 3.6 specifically identifies "any opinion as to the guilt or innocence of a defendant . . . in a criminal case" as a statement that is more likely than not to have a material prejudicial effect on the proceeding.

Answer choice A is incorrect. Although Model Rule 3.6(b)(6) indicates that a lawyer participating in a matter may make a public statement about a defendant's behavior that relates to public safety if a substantial likelihood of danger exists, a lawyer must balance such statements to avoid prejudice. In this case, the prosecutor may not be subject to discipline for alerting the public to a danger posed by the defendant, if there existed a reason to believe that the defendant likely posed such a danger. Even so, the prosecutor should not have used his warning as an opportunity to comment on his belief in the defendant's guilt. Comment [5(4)] to Rule 3.6.

Answer choice B is incorrect because the prosecutor's *adversarial* role is irrelevant. Under Rule 3.6, no attorney participating in a proceeding, including the prosecutor, may make any public statement that would materially prejudice the defendant. As explained above, the prosecutor's public statement concerning the defendant's guilt was prohibited by Rule 3.6.

Answer choice C is incorrect because it overstates Rule 3.6. Although an attorney participating a matter may not make statements that would materially prejudice the matter, Rule 3.6(b) provides a list of statements that an attorney may make regarding a proceeding, including statements related to criminal proceedings. Moreover, this list is not exhaustive. Comment [4] to Rule 3.6.

ANSWER 135

REGULATION OF THE LEGAL PROFESSION

Answer choice C is correct. This question tests Model Rule 5.6, under which a lawyer may not offer or make an employment agreement limiting the right of a lawyer to practice law after termination of the relationship. An exception to this Rule exists with respect to agreements concerning benefits upon retirement. Here, the proposed contract provision runs afoul of Rule 5.6 because, in preventing the corporate attorney from working for the lawyer's former partner in any capacity, the restriction necessarily limits the corporate attorney's ability to practice law upon termination of the employment relationship with the lawyer.

Answer choice A is incorrect because it overlooks the prohibition in Rule 5.6, which exists to protect a lawyer's professional independence.

Answer choice B is incorrect because a conflict of interest is not created simply because a lawyer leaves one firm for a competitor's law firm. And there is nothing in the facts suggesting that an actual or potential conflict of interest would arise if the corporate attorney joined the former partner's firm.

Answer choice D is incorrect because a restriction on an attorney's future ability to practice law is impermissible whether the restriction is proposed by the employer or the employee. Model Rule 5.6 ("A lawyer shall not participate in *offering or making*" an agreement limiting the lawyer's future ability to practice law.) (emphasis added).

ANSWER 136

JUDICIAL CONDUCT

Answer choice A is correct. This question tests CJC Rule 2.13 and, to a lesser extent, Rule 1.2. Rule 1.2 requires a judge to "act at all times in a manner that promotes public confidence in the independence, integrity, and impartiality of the judiciary, and . . . avoid impropriety and the appearance of impropriety." This requirement extends to the manner in which a judge makes administrative appointments, including the selection of a judge's personnel, such as clerks, secretaries, and bailiffs. CJC Rule 2.13(A), and Comment [1] thereto. Accordingly, Rule 2.13(A) requires a judge to avoid nepotism, favoritism, and unnecessary appointments.

Comment [2] to Rule 2.3 defines nepotism as "the appointment or hiring of any relative within the third degree of either the judge or the judge's spouse or domestic partner, or the spouse or domestic partner of such relative." As explained in the Terminology section of the CJC, the "third degree of relationship" includes "great-grandparent, grandparent, uncle, aunt, brother, sister, child, grandchild, great-grandchild, nephew, and niece." Here, the judge would violate CJC Rule 2.13(A) if he hires his niece as a clerk.

Answer choice B is incorrect because, although a judge may exercise considerable control when making administrative appointments, the judge must do so impartially and on the basis of merit, CJC Rule 2.13(A)(1), and avoid nepotism, favoritism and unnecessary appointments. Rule 2.13(A)(2).

Answer choice C is incorrect. A judge must exercise the power of appointment based on merit, Rule 2.13(A)(1), and the facts indicate that the judge's niece is highly qualified for the clerkship position. However, a judge must also avoid nepotism. Rule 2.13(A)(2). Thus, notwithstanding his niece's qualifications, the judge would violate the Code of Judicial Conduct if he hires her.

Answer choice D is incorrect for two reasons. First, the Code of Judicial Conduct has no requirement that a judge hire the "most qualified" applicant for a position. Indeed, it would be difficult to define what characteristics make any applicant the "most qualified." Rule 2.13(A) simply requires that personnel be hired based on merit. More fundamentally, whether a job applicant is the most qualified person or not, a judge may not hire an applicant if he or she is within the third degree of relationship, as the niece is in this fact pattern.

ANSWER 137

COMMUNICATION ABOUT LEGAL SERVICES

Answer choice C is correct. This question tests Model Rule 7.4, which governs a lawyer's communications regarding his fields of practice and specialization. A lawyer may communicate that he does or does not practice a particular field of law, Rule 7.4(a), and may generally state that he is a "specialist," "specializes in," or "practices a specialty" in a particular field or fields, provided that such statement is not false or misleading. Comment [1] to Rule 7.4. Here, the lawyer has decided to limit his practice to immigration and citizenship matters, and he appears to have a sufficient background studying immigration and citizenship law such that his decision to advertise as "specializing" in that field is not false or materially misleading, even if he has previously handled only one immigration case.

Answer choice A is incorrect. Rule 7.4 and its comments distinguish between an indication that an attorney specializes in a particular field of law, and an indication that an attorney has been *certified* by an organization as a specialist in a field of law. Under Rule 7.4(d), the latter is impermissible unless the certifying organization has been approved by proper authorities and is identified in the lawyer's communication. Comment [3] to Rule 7.4 highlights the difference: unlike the general statement that a lawyer specializes in a particular field, "[c]ertification signifies that an objective entity has recognized an advanced degree of knowledge and experience in the specialty area greater than is suggested by general licensure to practice law."

Answer choice B is incorrect because it misstates Rule 7.4. As explained above, Rule 7.4

generally permits lawyers to communicate the fact that they do or do not practice in particular fields of law, and they may do so by stating that they "specialize" in a particular field, provided that the statement is not false or misleading. Rule 7.4 contains special provisions for patent lawyers and admiralty lawyers, allowing such lawyers to use special designations other than "specialist." Rule 7.4(b), (c).

Answer choice D is incorrect. The fact that this attorney has only handled one immigration case before is arguably relevant to the question whether his use of the term "specializes" is false or misleading. However, the facts indicate that he has studied immigration and citizenship law extensively and that he is reasonably confident in his ability to practice that field of law. Thus, the facts above do not give rise to the conclusion that the lawyer's advertisement is false or misleading.

ANSWER 138

JUDICIAL CONDUCT

Answer choice B is correct. This question tests CJC Rule 3.6, which prohibits judges from affiliating with discriminatory organizations. Under Rule 3.6(B), a judge may "not use the benefits or facilities of an organization if the judge knows or should know that the organization practices invidious discrimination on one or more grounds," including race. However, a judge's attendance at an event in a facility of such an organization does not violate Rule 3.6 if the attendance (1) is an isolated event that (2) could not reasonably be perceived as an endorsement of the organization's discriminatory practices. The facts in this question indicate that this is an isolated event – a single dinner – at a club that the fraternity has not been involved with before, and which discriminates based on an "unwritten policy" of which neither the fraternity member who made the reservation nor the judge are aware. Moreover, the guests in attendance at the dinner, including some of the honorees, are African-American, suggesting that the fraternity is inclusive and that neither its current members nor its alumni endorse the club's practices. Thus, the judge's attendance would not appear to violate Rule 3.6.

Answer choice A is incorrect because, even if the club is private and cannot constitutionally be prohibited from discriminating in its membership, the judge could violate the CJC if his attendance in the club's facilities could be viewed as an endorsement of the club's invidious discrimination against African-Americans. CJC Rule 3.6(B).

Answer choice C is incorrect. That the club discriminates on the basis of race is not enough, on its own, to render the judge's attendance at an event in the club a violation of the CJC. Rather, his attendance must reasonably suggest that he endorses the club's discriminatory practices. Rule 3.6(B).

Answer choice D is incorrect because the judge is not prohibited from accepting the dinner. CJC Rule 3.13 prohibits a judge from accepting any gift that is unlawful or "would appear to a reasonable person to undermine the judge's independence, integrity, or impartiality." Rule 3.13(A). However, a judge may accept an invitation to an event related to an extrajudicial activity the judge is involved in – such as a fraternal organization – "if the same invitation is offered to non-judges who are engaged in similar ways in the activity as is the judge," provided that the judge complies with the gift reporting requirements in CJC Rule 3.15. Rule 3.13(C)(2)(b). The dinner in this fact pattern falls within the ambit of Rule 3.13(C), and the judge therefore would not violate the Code of Judicial Conduct by attending the dinner.

ANSWER 139

THE CLIENT-LAWYER RELATIONSHIP

Answer choice D is correct. This question tests Model Rules 1.17 and 5.4. Under Rule 1.17, which governs the sale of a law practice, a lawyer may purchase a practice (and, in turn, a lawyer may sell a practice) if the seller ceases to engage in the practice of law; the practice is sold, in whole or in part, to a lawyer, lawyers, or law firms; the seller notifies all of the practice's existing clients of the sale, that they may take possession of their files or retain other counsel, and that their consent to transfer the files will be presumed if no answer is received within 90 days; and the fees charged to clients are not increased by reason of the sale. As Comment [13] to Rule 1.17 explains, the Rule contemplates the sale of a practice by a non-lawyer representing a deceased attorney's estate, and such a practice is permissible because the purchasing lawyer will ensure compliance with the applicable Rules. And as Model Rule 5.4 explains, a lawyer who purchases the law practice of a deceased lawyer may pay the agreed-upon purchase price to the deceased lawyer's estate, provided that the purchasing lawyer otherwise complies with Rule 1.17.

Answer choice A is incorrect because, as Comment [13] to Rule 1.17 explains, a lawyer may purchase a law practice from a non-lawyer who represents the estate of a deceased lawyer.

Answer choice B is incorrect because the ultimate beneficiary of the sale of a law practice is irrelevant. A lawyer may purchase a law practice from a deceased lawyer's estate, and nothing in the Model Rules prohibits the proceeds of such a sale from being distributed by the estate in accordance with the deceased lawyer's wishes.

Answer choice C is incorrect because the practice's clients need not agree to keep their business with the purchasing attorney in order to validate the sale of the practice. Indeed, Rule 1.17(c) ensures that the clients of a law practice maintain the freedom to do business with that practice (or take their business elsewhere) if it is sold.

ANSWER 140

LAWYERS' DUTIES TO THE PUBLIC AND THE LEGAL SYSTEM

Answer choice A is correct. This question tests Model Rule 6.3, under which a lawyer may serve as an officer of a legal services organization. Rule 6.3 permits a lawyer to maintain a leadership role in such an organization, even if the organization serves clients whose interests are adverse to the lawyer's clients. However, a lawyer serving in a leadership role in a legal services organization may not knowingly participate in a decision or action of the organization "(a) if participating in the decision or action would be incompatible with the lawyer's obligations to a client under Rule 1.7 [governing conflicts of interest with a lawyer's current clients]; or (b) where the decision or action could have a material adverse effect on the representation of a client of the organization whose interests are adverse to a client of the lawyer." Under the facts of this question, the associate may remain on the board of directors, even though the organization represents clients whose interests are adverse to those of the associate's clients. However, the associate may not participate in the vote. If the organization is permitted to withdraw from representing its landlord-tenant clients, there is a substantial risk that those clients will be unable to get other representation and that their cases may be adversely affected. Because at least some of the organization's clients have interests adverse to those of the associate's clients, the associate should not participate in making this particular decision.

Answer choice B is incorrect because the associate may not knowingly participate in the decision if it will materially and adversely affect clients of the organization who have interests adverse to those of the associate's clients.

Answer choice C is incorrect because, as explained above, the attorney may serve on the organization's board of directors. For the same reason, answer choice D is incorrect; the associate has not violated any Rule of Professional Conduct simply by participating on the organization's board of directors.

ANSWER 141

COMMUNICATION ABOUT LEGAL SERVICES

Answer choice A is correct. This question tests Model Rules 7.5. Under Rule 7.5(c), if an attorney practicing in a firm takes public office, the firm may continue to use the public official's name in the firm name, provided that the attorney/public official continues to actively and regularly practice with the firm. Here, under state law, the lawyer cannot hold private employment. Therefore, the lawyer cannot continue to practice with the firm and consequently, he cannot be a named partner. Because the facts indicate that he cannot legally continue to practice with the firm, the firm must remove him as a named partner in order to comply with Rule 7.5(c).

Answer choice B is incorrect. As explained above, the partner may not practice law as long as he serves as the attorney general. Practicing as "of counsel" does not alter that requirement.

Answer choice C is incorrect because, although the partner cannot continue practicing law with the firm, his name must be removed from the firm name as set forth above.

Answer choice D is incorrect because, as explained above, the partner may not practice law as long as he serves as the attorney general.

ANSWER 142

REGULATION OF THE LEGAL PROFESSION

Answer choice B is correct. The attorney would be subject to discipline if the attorney failed to adequately supervise the legal assistant. This question tests Model Rule 5.3. Rule 5.3 addresses when an attorney may be subject to professional discipline for the conduct of a non-attorney assistant. Under Rule 5.3, a supervising lawyer must make reasonable efforts to ensure that the non-lawyer's conduct is compatible with the professional obligations of the lawyer. A lawyer will be responsible for conduct of such a person that would be a violation of the Rules if engaged in by a lawyer if one of the following two circumstances are present: (1) the lawyer orders or, with the knowledge of the specific conduct, ratifies the conduct involved; or (2) the lawyer is a partner or has comparable managerial authority in the law firm in which the person is employed, or has direct supervisory authority over the person and knows of the conduct at a time when its consequences can be avoided or mitigated but fails to take reasonable remedial action. Thus, if the attorney failed to adequately supervise the legal assistant, the attorney would have violated the second prong of the test, and would be subject to discipline.

Answer choice A is incorrect because the theory of respondeat superior does not apply to professional discipline for the wrongful acts of a non-lawyer assistant. However, respondeat superior could apply to whether the attorney is subject to *civil liability* for the actions of the assistant.

Answer choice C is incorrect. Under rule 5.3, an attorney may be responsible for the negligence of a non-attorney if one of the two circumstances set forth above exist.

Answer choice D is incorrect because the negligence of the attorney is not *required* under the first prong of the test set forth above.

ANSWER 143

THE CLIENT-LAWYER RELATIONSHIP

Answer choice C is correct. This question tests Model Rule of Professional Conduct ("MRPC") 6.2(c). Under Rule 6.2, a lawyer who has been asked to represent an indigent or unpopular person generally may not seek to avoid the representation unless good cause exists. Under Rule 6.2(c), good cause exists if "the client or the cause is so repugnant to the lawyer as to be likely to impair the client-lawyer relationship or the lawyer's ability to represent the client." Here, the facts indicate that, notwithstanding the lawyer's expertise in First Amendment matters, she finds the litigant's views so repugnant that she cannot bear the thought of representing him. In such a circumstance, good cause appears to exist for the lawyer to decline the representation.

Answer choice A is incorrect. Although a lawyer must generally accept an appointment by a tribunal, the lawyer may seek to avoid the appointment if good cause exists. MRPC 6.2, and its Comments, identify several circumstances creating good cause to decline a representation.

Answer choice B is incorrect because it is not supported by the facts in this question. Rule 6.2(b) notes that good cause to avoid a representation exists if "representing the client is likely to result in an unreasonable financial burden on the lawyer . . . ." Comment [2] to Rule 6.2 indicates that such a situation involves "a financial sacrifice so great as to be unjust." Although the lawyer in this question could seek to avoid the representation if it would create an unreasonable financial burden, nothing in the facts indicates that representing this particular litigant would create such a substantial burden.

Answer choice D is incorrect because although the lawyer's expertise may be relevant to whether the court ultimately permits her to decline the representation, she may nevertheless seek to decline the representation given her strong opposition to the litigant's views. MRPC 6.2(c).

ANSWER 144

SAFEKEEPING FUNDS AND OTHER PROPERTY

Answer choice A is correct. A lawyer is required to hold a client's money as a fiduciary, and he must keep such money separate from his own. MRPC 1.15(a); Comment [1] to Rule 1.15. However, Rule 1.15(b) provides that it is permissible for a lawyer to pay bank service charges on a client trust account from the lawyer's own funds, "but only in an amount necessary for that purpose." Under the facts of this question, the lawyer has acted impermissibly by depositing more of his own money in the client trust account than is required to pay the bank's service charge.

Answer choice B is incorrect. Although it is generally impermissible to commingle a lawyer's funds with client funds, the Model Rules create an exception so that attorneys may pay bank service charges on client trust accounts. MRPC 1.15(b). As Comment [2] to Rule 1.15 notes, a lawyer depositing his own funds into a client trust account to pay service charges must keep accurate records regarding which part of the funds belong to the lawyer.

Answer choice C is incorrect. That answer recognizes that a lawyer may commingle his funds with those of a client in very limited circumstances. MRPC 1.15(b). However, Rule 1.15(b) limits the amount of funds a lawyer may commingle with client funds to the amount necessary to pay bank service charges; any further commingling is impermissible.

For the same reason, answer choice D is incorrect. A lawyer commingling his own funds with client funds to pay bank service charges is required to maintain accurate records identifying which portion of the funds belong to the lawyer. Comment [2] to MRPC 1.15. However, the fact that such records are kept is irrelevant to whether a lawyer has impermissibly commingled funds by depositing more of his money in a client trust account than is needed to cover bank service charges.

ANSWER 145

CONFLICTS OF INTEREST

Answer choice D is correct. This question tests Model Rule 5.4(c), which prohibits a lawyer from allowing a non-client who pays for the lawyer to represent a client to influence the lawyer's professional judgment with regard to the representation. Here, the lawyer has agreed to proceed in a manner that may be at odds with his client's – that is, the son's – stated interest. Thus, his agreement with the businessman runs afoul of Rule 5.4.

Answer choice A is incorrect. Regardless of whether the businessman is responsible for paying the lawyer, the lawyer is responsible for maintaining his professional independence in rendering services for his client – the son. Rule 5.4(c).

Answer choice B is incorrect because the businessman's intent is irrelevant. Because the businessman's instruction to the lawyer has the effect of limiting the lawyer's ability to exercise his professional judgment, the lawyer may not agree to the instruction. Rule 5.4(c).

Answer choice C is incorrect because the answer is not supported by the facts. Under Model Rule of Professional Conduct 1.5(d)(1), a lawyer may not charge a "fee in a domestic relations matter, the payment or amount of which is contingent upon the securing of a divorce or upon the amount of alimony or support, or property settlement in lieu thereof . . . ." However, nothing in the facts of this question indicates that the amount or payment of the lawyer's fee is contingent upon obtaining a certain outcome in the son's divorce proceedings.

ANSWER 146

THE CLIENT-LAWYER RELATIONSHIP

Answer choice A is correct. Model Rule 1.5(d)(2) prohibits an attorney from charging a contingent fee for representing a defendant in a criminal case.

Answer choice B is incorrect. Even if the amount the attorney intends to charge the defendant for successfully representing him is reasonable under Model Rule 1.5(a), the agreement nevertheless runs afoul of the contingency fee prohibition in Rule 1.5(d)(2).

Answer choice C is incorrect because it overlooks the Rule 1.5(d)(2) prohibition against contingency fees for representing criminal defendants.

Answer choice D is incorrect. Although "[e]very lawyer has a professional responsibility to provide legal services to those unable to pay," Model Rule of Professional Conduct 6.1, the *pro bono publico* service requirement does not impose upon a lawyer the duty to represent at no charge every client of limited means who seeks representation. *But see* Model Rule 6.2 (governing a lawyer's responsibility to accept court-appointed cases). Indeed, Rule 6.1(b)(2) contemplates that a lawyer may take on a case "at a substantially reduced fee to persons of limited means." Here, the lawyer is not required to take on the young man's case *pro bono*. Nor, however, is she permitted to accept the representation on a contingency basis. MRPC 1.5(d)(2).

ANSWER 147

COMMUNICATION ABOUT LEGAL SERVICES

Answer choice B is correct. This question tests Model Rule 7.2(b)(4), under which a lawyer may enter into a reciprocal referral agreement with a lawyer or non-lawyer, provided that (i) the reciprocal referral agreement is not exclusive, and (ii) the client is informed of the existence and nature of the agreement. Under this agreement, the tax attorney and accountant refer clients to one another, but the agreement is not exclusive, and the attorney informs his clients of the referral agreement, even if he does not inform the clients of his personal friendship with the accountant. Thus, the agreement complies with Rule 7.2(b)(4).

Answer choice A is incorrect. Under Rule 7.2(b)(4), a reciprocal referral agreement is improper if the attorney involved does not inform clients of the existence and nature of the agreement. Although the attorney must tell clients that he and the accountant have an arrangement to refer clients to one another, nothing in Rule 7.2 requires the attorney to disclose his friendship with the accountant to his clients.

Answer choice C is incorrect. As noted above, Rule 7.2(b)(4) refers to agreements between lawyers as well as between a lawyer and a non-lawyer. However, as already noted, the reciprocal referral agreement between the tax attorney and the accountant is permissible under the Model Rules.

Answer choice D is incorrect. This answer reverses one of the requirements of Rule 7.2(b)(4) – that the referral agreement *not* be exclusive. As the facts of this question indicate, the tax attorney refers clients to several different accountants, so his agreement with his friend does not rule afoul of the Rules.

ANSWER 148

COMMUNICATIONS WITH PERSONS OTHER THAN CLIENTS

Answer choice B is correct. This question tests Model Rule 4.2, which governs an attorney's communications with other parties to a matter who are represented by counsel. Under that Rule, an attorney is prohibited from communicating about the subject of a case with a person he knows to be represented by another lawyer in the matter. As Comment [3] to Rule 4.2 notes, the Rule applies even though the represented person initiates the communication. Under the facts of this question, the business owner's attorney has been informed that the former employee is represented, and she has contacted him regarding the subject of the representation. Thus, the business owner's lawyer was required to immediately terminate the communication. Comment [3] to Rule 4.2.

Answer choice A is incorrect. Under Rule 4.2 and its comments, the business owner's lawyer is prohibited from communicating with the former employee in any way regarding her case against the business owner. This includes even helpful advice. Comments [2] and [3] to Rule 4.2.

Answer choice C is incorrect. As noted above, Rule 4.2 applies even if the represented person, not the lawyer, initiates the communication. Comment [3] to Rule 4.2. Thus, the business owner's lawyer is still subject to discipline for communicating with the represented former employee, notwithstanding the fact that the former employee initiated the communication.

Answer choice D is incorrect. The fact that the business owner's lawyer did not give any legal advice to the former employee is irrelevant. Under Rule 4.2, he is still subject to discipline because he discussed the case with the former employee.

ANSWER 149

REGULATION OF THE LEGAL PROFESSION

Answer choice D is correct. This question tests Model Rule 5.6, which generally prohibits a lawyer from agreeing to restrict his or her right to practice as part of the settlement of a case for a client. Because the proposed settlement in this case would require the family's lawyer to refrain from representing potential clients, it runs afoul of Rule 5.6. *See also* Comment [2] to Rule 5.6.

Answer choice A is incorrect because the value of the settlement to the lawyer's clients, though important, does not obviate the requirement that he not restrict his ability to represent potential clients. MRPC 5.6. Answer choice B is incorrect for the same reason.

Answer choice C is incorrect, as it is not clearly dictated by any of the rules governing attorney conduct. Indeed, there may often be good reasons to settle rather than proceed to trial in a given case, notwithstanding the likelihood of a victory. The pertinent problem here, as discussed above, is the requirement that the family's lawyer not represent other plaintiffs in related litigation.

ANSWER 150

REGULATION OF THE LEGAL PROFESSION

Answer choice B is correct. This question tests Model Rule 5.4 which governs a lawyer's professional independence. Under that Rule, a lawyer may not practice in the form of a professional corporation or association authorized to practice law for profit if "a nonlawyer is a corporate director or officer thereof or occupies the position of similar responsibility in any form of association other than a corporation," Rule 5.4(d)(2), or "a nonlawyer has the right to direct or control the professional judgment of a lawyer." Rule 5.4(d)(3). At a minimum, the attorney's agreement with his father violates Rule 5.4(d)(3) because the father, who is an accountant, not a lawyer, has the right to control the attorney's professional judgment as to whether to take the case. Further, it seems that the arrangement also violates Rule 5.4(d)(2), as the father's role is akin to that of a manager or officer.

Answer choice A is incorrect. Although this answer choice recognizes that, pursuant to Rule 5.4(d)(1), a non-lawyer may not own an interest in a firm – a condition distinguishable from the father holding a financial debt owed by the firm – it ignores those aspects of the agreement between the attorney and his father that violate Rules 5.4(d)(2) and (3).

Answer choice C is incorrect because the duration of the father's veto power is irrelevant. Rule 5.4(d)(3) speaks in absolute terms - a lawyer must not give a non-lawyer the right to control his professional judgment.

Answer choice D is incorrect. Although this answer choice recognizes that a lawyer and non-lawyer may not form a partnership if the partnership practices law in any way, Rule 5.4(b), and that the arrangement between the attorney and his father does not violate that Rule, it ignores those aspects of the agreement between the attorney and his father that violate Rules 5.4(d)(2) and (3).

ANSWER 151

REGULATION OF THE LEGAL PROFESSION

B is the correct answer. A lawyer must not participate in offering or making an agreement in which a restriction on the lawyer's right to practice is part of the settlement of a client controversy.

ANSWER 152

THE CLIENT-LAWYER RELATIONSHIP

C is the correct answer. A contingent fee agreement must be in writing and signed by the client. The agreement must state the method by which the fee is determined, including the percentage accruing to the lawyer, the expenses to be deducted, and whether the expenses are to be deducted before or after the contingent fee is calculated.

ANSWER 153

CLIENT CONFIDENTIALITY

A is the correct answer. A lawyer may reveal information relating to the representation of a client to the extent the lawyer reasonably believes necessary to prevent reasonably certain death or substantial bodily harm. In this case, the lawyer has learned that hazardous chemical material has been implicated in the death of many people nationwide. Therefore, the lawyer may reveal the existence of the drums.

ANSWER 154

REGULATION OF THE LEGAL PROFESSION

Answer choice C is correct. The attorney would be subject to discipline because the attorney practiced law as part of the partnership's business. This question tests Rule 5.4(b). Rule 5.4(b) prohibits a lawyer from forming a partnership with a non-lawyer if any of the activities of the partnership consist of the practice of law. In this fact pattern, the attorney formed a partnership with an architect with the express intention of providing legal services. Because the partnership offered legal services, the attorney would be subject to discipline.

Answer choice A is incorrect because the formation of a partnership with a non-lawyer is the basis of the violation of Rule 5.4(b) and would not shield the attorney from discipline.

Answer choice B is incorrect because keeping the work product separate will not prevent a violation of Rule 5.4(b).

Answer choice D is incorrect because lawyers and non-lawyers are permitted to share physical office spaces. It is the formation of a partnership that triggers a violation of Rule 5.4(b).

ANSWER 155

THE CLIENT-LAWYER RELATIONSHIP

Answer choice B is correct. This question tests the right of an attorney to limit the scope of representation. Restatement §19(1) provides that a client and attorney may agree to reasonably limit a duty that the attorney would otherwise owe to the client if (1) the client is adequately informed and consents, and (2) the terms of the limitation are reasonable given the circumstances. Here, the attorney told the developer prior to beginning representation that he would not write the opinion without an opinion of local counsel upon which to rely, and the developer consented to the arrangement with the full knowledge that a separate opinion would be required. Although the attorney is licensed in both states, he was not comfortable with the law of State B, and under those circumstances it was reasonable to rely upon an opinion from an attorney who was.

Answer choice A is incorrect. An attorney can, within reason, determine the fee to which he or she is entitled for a particular transaction, but whether the fee is reasonable is not determinative of whether the limitation on the scope of duties is reasonable.

Answer choice C is incorrect. An attorney is entitled to limit the amount of fees owed by the client or to waive the duty to pay a fee entirely.

Answer choice D is incorrect. Although whether the limitation is reasonable is fact specific, the facts in this case indicate that the attorney was licensed in State B but not very comfortable with the laws of the state. In that instance, it is likely reasonable for him to request an opinion upon which he can rely from an attorney who is familiar with the laws.

ANSWER 156

CLIENT CONFIDENTIALITY

Answer choice D is correct. Pursuant to Rule 1.18(a), a person who discusses with a lawyer the possibility of forming a client-lawyer relationship with respect to a matter is a prospective client. Furthermore, as set forth in Rule 1.18(b), if, after consultation, no client-lawyer relationship forms, a lawyer who has had discussions with a prospective client must not use or reveal information learned during the consultation, except as otherwise permitted by the Rules. Here, based on the advertisement, the woman had a reasonable expectation that a client-lawyer relationship could form, and consulted with the attorney based on that expectation; thus, she would be considered a prospective client. When the attorney declined representation, the only duty he owed the woman was to keep confidential the information he obtained during the course of that representation. By advising her that she had a specific time frame in which to pursue alternative legal advice and providing her with the names of other competent attorneys, the attorney performed duties beyond those required by the rules, and, therefore, would not be subject to discipline.

Answer choice A is incorrect. It is anticipated that attorneys who meet with prospective clients will likely obtain confidential information, and the Rules provide some protections to prospective clients with regard to the information that they disclose. The attorney, though, would not be subject to discipline for declining to represent the woman once he came into possession of that information.

Answer choice B is incorrect. Although the attorney advertised that he represented clients in settlement negotiations with the IRS, he was not obligated by those advertisements to accept any potential client who consulted with him.

Answer choice C is incorrect. The Comment to Rule 1.18 states that a person who unilaterally communicates information to an attorney, without reasonable expectation that the attorney will be willing to discuss forming a client-lawyer relationship, is not a prospective client within the meaning of the Rule, and is, therefore, not entitled to the protection afforded by it. Here, based on the advertisement and the consultation, the woman reasonably expected that the attorney would be willing to discuss forming a relationship, and, thus, would be afforded the protections of Rule 1.18.

ANSWER 157

THE CLIENT-LAWYER RELATIONSHIP

Answer choice A is correct. The question tests Rule 1.2(d), which provides that a lawyer shall not counsel a client to engage, or assist a client, in conduct that the lawyer knows is criminal or fraudulent, but a lawyer may discuss the legal consequences of any proposed course of conduct with a client and may counsel or assist a client to make a good faith effort to determine the validity, scope, meaning, or application of the law. Here, the attorney knew that her client was engaged in fraudulent conduct and advised him on how he might pass the documents off as legitimate. By counseling the client on how to engage in fraudulent conduct, the attorney could be subject to discipline.

Answer choice B is incorrect. The document that was delivered was legal; so delivery of that document would not subject the attorney to liability.

Answer choice C is incorrect. Although the attorney eventually delivered a legal document, she can still be subject to discipline for counseling the client on how to accomplish a fraudulent task.

Answer choice D is incorrect. While the Rules permit an attorney to discuss the legal consequences of a course of action, the attorney cannot counsel a client on how to accomplish an illegal task.

ANSWER 158

COMMUNICATIONS WITH PERSONS OTHER THAN CLIENTS

Answer choice B is correct. This question tests Rule 4.2. Under Rule 4.2, in the course of representing a client, a lawyer must not communicate about the subject of the representation with a person the lawyer knows to be represented by another lawyer in the matter, unless the lawyer has the other lawyer's consent or is authorized to do so by law or a court order. This Rule applies even if the represented person is the one who initiates the communication. Here, the attorney knew that the contractor was represented by counsel because the parties and their counsel had been involved in extensive settlement negotiations. Although the attorney did not initiate the communication, he should have immediately terminated it because it was about the subject of the representation and with a person represented by counsel.

Answer choice A is incorrect. It is not uncommon for settlements to be reached on the eve of trial, and the threat of litigation will not invalidate a settlement offer.

Answer choice C is incorrect. Rule 4.2's prohibition on communicating with a represented person about the subject of the representation applies even if the represented person initiates the communication.

Answer choice D is incorrect. Regardless of whether the settlement terms were favorable for his client, the attorney had an affirmative duty to discontinue the communication because the contractor was represented by counsel.

ANSWER 159

COMMUNICATIONS WITH PERSONS OTHER THAN CLIENTS

Answer choice D is correct. This question tests Rule 4.1. Rule 4.1 provides that in the course of representing a client, a lawyer must not knowingly (1) make a false statement of material fact or law to a third person or (2) fail to disclose a material fact when disclosure is necessary to avoid assisting a criminal or fraudulent act by a client, unless disclosure is prohibited by the Rule of Confidentiality. Here, the attorney was representing his client in negotiations with the team representatives, and he lied about the doctor's assessment of his client's projected longevity. Because that fact was material to the negotiations, and the attorney lied about it, his conduct violated Rule 4.1.

Answer choice A is incorrect. Although an attorney has a duty to zealously represent his client, the Rules prohibit an attorney from lying about material facts in the course of the representation.

Answer choice B is incorrect. The Comment to the Rule permits certain types of statements that are not ordinarily taken as statements of material fact, such as puffery, in the course of negotiations. The false statement here, though, is material to the negotiations and would not fall within the exception outlined in the Comment.

Answer choice C is incorrect. The facts do not indicate that the client was preparing to commit a fraudulent act; so the attorney did not have an obligation to disclose under that prong of the Rule.

ANSWER 160

SAFEKEEPING FUNDS AND OTHER PROPERTY

Answer choice D is correct. This question tests Rule 1.15(d). This Rule requires that an attorney promptly notify a client or third person upon receipt of funds or other property in which the client or third person has an interest. Additionally, except as permitted by the Rules, the law or by agreement with the client, the Rule also requires that the attorney promptly deliver to the client or third person any funds or other property that the client or third person is entitled to receive and, upon request by the client or third person, shall promptly render a full accounting regarding such property. Here, the attorney received the sale proceeds from two of the guitars, but the attorney did not notify the client of the receipt of the funds. Therefore, the attorney violated Rule 1.15(d).

Answer choice A is incorrect. While the attorney appropriately notified the client of the offer, the attorney is still subject to discipline for failing to notify the client that the funds had been received.

Answer choice B is incorrect. The attorney followed the Rules by segregating the client's funds (see Rule 1.15(a)), but the client should have been notified when the funds were received.

Answer choice C is incorrect. The client had given her attorney the authority to negotiate for her; so her presence was not necessary.

ANSWER 161

REGULATION OF THE LEGAL PROFESSION

The correct answer is C. This question tests Rule 5.4(d). The rule provides that a lawyer cannot practice in a professional corporation if a nonlawyer possesses an ownership interest in the professional corporation.

Answer choice A is incorrect because not having the right to direct or control the professional judgment of the attorneys is irrelevant if a nonlawyer possesses an ownership interest in the organization.

Answer choice B is incorrect because not being an officer is also irrelevant if a nonlawyer possesses an ownership interest in the organization.

Answer choice D is incorrect. Ownership of a portion of the professional corporation by a nonlawyer is prohibited regardless of whether a family relationship exists between the nonlawyer and one of the attorneys.

ANSWER 162

COMMUNICATIONS WITH PERSONS OTHER THAN CLIENTS

The correct answer is A. This question tests Rule 4.3. Under this Rule, when a lawyer is dealing on behalf of a client with a person who is not represented by counsel, a lawyer must not state or imply that the lawyer is disinterested. Additionally, the lawyer must not give legal advice to an unrepresented person, other than the advice to secure counsel, if the lawyer knows or reasonably should know that the interests of such person are, or have a reasonable possibility of becoming, in conflict with the interests of the client. Here, the wife's friend knew that her client's interests would be adverse to those of the husband, and she disclosed that she would only be representing the wife. Moreover, the only advice she provided to the husband was to secure representation. Because her actions complied with the Rule, the attorney would not be subject to discipline.

Answer choice B is incorrect. The wife's friend was not subject to discipline because her actions complied with the Rule.

Answer choice C is incorrect. The Rule permits attorneys to advise unrepresented persons to secure counsel.

Answer choice D is incorrect. It is unlikely that the husband would misunderstand the wife's friend's role in the proceedings because she was representing the wife, and she disclosed that she would be acting only on the wife's behalf.

ANSWER 163

THE CLIENT-LAWYER RELATIONSHIP

The correct answer is D. This question tests Rule 1.16(c). Under this Rule, a lawyer must comply with applicable law requiring notice to or permission of a tribunal when terminating representation. When ordered to do so by a tribunal, a lawyer must continue representation notwithstanding good cause for terminating the representation. Here, the defense attorney was justified in withdrawing from representation because the defendant had rendered the representation unreasonably difficult (see Rule 1.16(b)); however, the court ruled that the defense attorney could not withdraw. Because the court did not permit the withdrawal, the defense attorney would not be permitted to withdraw.

Answer choice A is incorrect. Although the defense attorney would have grounds for withdrawal under Rule 1.16(b), that right is subject to Rule 1.16(c), which requires that an attorney continue the representation of a client, notwithstanding good cause to withdraw from representation, if the court refuses to permit the withdrawal.

Answer choice B is incorrect. The facts do not indicate that the attorney had a moral objection to the defendant's course of action.

Answer choice C is incorrect. The facts indicate that the defendant's behavior had rendered the representation unreasonably difficult. In any event, the court ruled that the defense attorney could not withdraw from representation of the defendant.

ANSWER 164

COMPETENCE, MALPRACTICE, AND OTHER CIVIL LIABILITY

The correct answer is D. This question tests Rule 1.1. Under the Rule, a lawyer is required to provide competent representation to a client, which requires knowledge and skill reasonably necessary for the representation. Comment [3] to the Rule provides an exception for emergency situations, during which a lawyer may give advice or assistance in a matter in which the attorney does not possess the skill ordinarily required, where referral to or consultation or association with another lawyer would be impractical. In such situations, the attorney should limit the assistance to what is reasonably necessary in the circumstances to avoid doing something that could place a client's interest at risk. Here, although the situation could have been an emergency because the landowner was leaving the country for an extended vacation, the associate could and should have asked the senior real estate partner for assistance in the representation. Because the associate could have sought the assistance, Comment [3] to the Rule would not protect him from discipline.

Answer choice A is incorrect. Although this situation might be considered an emergency, the associate had time to consult the senior real estate partner who was in the office at the time the associate received the call.

Answer choice B is incorrect. Although the transaction was successful, the associate would still be subject to discipline for providing representation without the appropriate knowledge.

Answer choice C is incorrect. The Rule does not require an attorney to disclose his lack of competence; the Rule requires an attorney to provide competent representation.

ANSWER 165

CONFLICTS OF INTEREST

The correct answer is D. This question tests Rule 1.8(g). Under this Rule, an attorney who represents two or more co-clients must not participate in making an aggregate settlement of the civil claims of or against the clients, or in a criminal case an aggregated agreement as to guilty or nolo contendere pleas, unless each client gives informed consent, in writing signed by the client. According to the Comment to the Rule, the attorney's disclosure must include all material terms of the settlement, including what the other clients will receive or pay if the settlement or plea offer is accepted. Here, the attorney failed to tell each woman that the plea offer was contingent on both women pleading guilty. Because the attorney did not make this disclosure, the women could not provide informed consent to the offer, and the attorney would, thus, be subject to discipline.

Answer choice A is incorrect. Although the attorney conveyed a portion of the offer to the women, he did not disclose all of the material terms, and, therefore, he violated the Rule.

Answer choice B is incorrect. While it is true that the attorney had to abide by his clients' wishes regarding accepting a plea offer, the attorney was obligated to disclose all of the material terms of the plea offer to the client.

Answer choice C is incorrect. The attorney was only required to disclose the material terms of the offer and to abide by his clients' wishes. He could counsel them as to the benefits and risks of the offer, but he was not required to argue for a change of the terms.

ANSWER 166

LITIGATION AND OTHER FORMS OF ADVOCACY

Answer choice B is correct. This question tests Rules 3.4(f) and 8.4(a). Rule 3.4(f) provides that a lawyer must not request a person other than a client to refrain from voluntarily giving relevant information to another party unless (1) the person is a relative, employee, or other agent of a client; and (2) the lawyer reasonably believes that the person's interests will not be adversely affected by refraining from giving such information. Rule 8.4(a) provides that a lawyer must not violate or attempt to violate the Rules, knowingly assist or induce another to do so, or do so through the acts of another. Here, the relative was not an employee of the nursing home; so the exception in Rule 3.4(f) did not apply to him. Additionally, the attorney used the head nurse to make the prohibited request, thus violating Rule 8.4(a) as well.

Answer choice A is incorrect. Although requesting that a non-party withhold relevant information is generally prohibited, the Rules provide limited exceptions for relatives, employees, or other agents of the represented person or entity.

Answer choice C is incorrect. The exception in Rule 3.4(f) applies to relatives of the client, not to relatives of other parties.

Answer choice D is incorrect. Attorneys are not permitted to circumvent the Rules by asking a non-attorney to perform the prohibited act; so the fact that the attorney in this case asked the head nurse to approach the relative will not shield him from discipline.

ANSWER 167

CLIENT CONFIDENTIALITY

The correct answer is D. This question tests Rule 1.6(a). Under this Rule, a lawyer must never reveal information relating to the representation of a client unless (1) the client gives informed consent, (2) the disclosure is impliedly authorized in order to carry out the representation, or (3) the disclosure is permitted under the Rules. According to Comment [5] to the Rule, unless a client instructs his or her lawyer to restrict information to specific lawyers in the firm, a lawyer may reveal confidential information to other lawyers in the firm in the course of the firm's practice. Here, the client told the attorney that he did not want the attorney to disclose confidential information to the client's former counsel, but the attorney disclosed the information anyway. Because the attorney disclosed against the express wishes of his client, he would be subject to discipline.

Answer choice A is incorrect. Although the discussions with the client's former counsel benefitted the client, the attorney was not permitted under the Rules to disclose the information to the former counsel because his client had expressly instructed him to not do so.

Answer choice B is incorrect. While Comment [5] to the Rule does provide an exception for disclosure to members of an attorney's firm, that permission is conditioned on the client not providing instructions to keep the information confidential.

Answer choice C is incorrect. The Rules explicitly permit a client to provide informed consent to disclosure of confidential information.

ANSWER 168

CONFLICTS OF INTEREST

Answer choice D is correct. This question tests Rule 1.7. Under this Rule, a lawyer is generally prohibited from representing a client if the representation involves a concurrent conflict of interest. A concurrent conflict of interest exists if (1) the representation of one client will be directly adverse to another client or (2) there is a significant risk that the representation of one or more clients will be materially limited by the lawyer's responsibilities to another client, a former client or a third person, or by a personal interest of the lawyer. Notwithstanding a concurrent conflict of interest, a lawyer may represent a client if (1) the lawyer reasonably believes that the lawyer will be able to provide competent and diligent representation to each affected client; (2) the representation is not prohibited by law; (3) the representation does not involve the assertion of a claim by one client against another client represented by the lawyer in the same litigation or other proceeding before a tribunal; and (4) each affected client gives informed consent, confirmed in writing. Here, the boutique attorney was discussing potential employment with the large firm that was representing the opponent in the divorce proceeding, which discussions were within the attorney's personal interest. The employment negotiations raise a significant risk that the attorney will be limited in his ability to competently represent the husband, and, thus, a concurrent conflict of interest exists. Moreover, the foregoing exception that allows a lawyer to represent a client notwithstanding a concurrent conflict of interest does not apply.

Answer choice A is incorrect. Even though the boutique attorney was able to competently represent the husband and secure a favorable outcome, the attorney would still be subject to discipline because a concurrent conflict of interest exists, and the foregoing exception that allows a lawyer to represent a client notwithstanding a concurrent conflict of interest does not apply..

Answer choice B is incorrect. Although the boutique attorney was not representing a directly adverse party, he was engaging in negotiations with the firm that was representing his client's opponent, and therefore a concurrent conflict of interest existed.

Answer choice C is incorrect. Although the Rules provide for duties to former clients, the Rules do not contain a prohibition on working for a firm that represented a former adversary. There will, however, be obligations on the part of both the attorney and the firm to avoid former and current client conflicts going forward.

ANSWER 169

REGULATION OF THE LEGAL PROFESSION

Answer choice B is correct. This question tests Rule 5.5(a), which provides that a lawyer must not practice law in a jurisdiction in violation of the regulation of the legal profession in that jurisdiction, or assist another in doing so. An exception to this prohibition applies in limited circumstances such as when a lawyer who is admitted to the bar in a state seeks to temporarily provide legal services in a second state in which he or she is not admitted. Here, the attorney was admitted to practice in State A, but the representation in question occurred in State B. The attorney took the appropriate step of petitioning the court to provide temporary legal services in State B and was granted permission. Because the attorney was admitted on a temporary basis, he is not subject to discipline in either state.

Answer choice A is incorrect. Although the attorney's client conducts business in more than one state, the attorney is not permitted to do the same unless (1) he is licensed in the other states or (2) he obtains permission to represent his client on a temporary or limited basis in such states.

Answer choice C is incorrect. The attorney is licensed to practice in State A; so he would not need to seek permission from State A to represent his client in State B. The appropriate state to petition was State B.

Answer choice D is incorrect. Although the attorney was not licensed in State B when he represented his client, he had successfully petitioned the Supreme Court in State B to represent his client on a temporary basis and, thus, would not be in violation of Rule 5.5(a).

ANSWER 170

LAWYERS' DUTIES TO THE PUBLIC AND THE LEGAL SYSTEM

Answer choice C is correct. This question tests Rule 8.2(a). This Rule states that a lawyer must not make a statement that the lawyer knows to be false or with reckless disregard as to its truth or falsity concerning the qualifications or integrity of a judge, adjudicatory officer, or candidate for election or appointment to judicial or legal office. A lawyer may express an honest and candid opinion on the professional or personal fitness of a person being considered for election or appointment to a public legal office. Here, the attorney is personally acquainted with the candidate, and his statements were his honest opinions about his friend's capabilities. The Rules explicitly permit these types of comments; so the attorney should not be subject to discipline.

Answer choice A is incorrect. The Rules explicitly permit attorneys to express their honest, candid opinions about candidates for judicial or elected legal positions.

Answer choice B is incorrect. If the attorney were subject to discipline, it would be due to the falsity, or the reckless disregard as to the truth or falsity, of the statements, not the breadth of distribution.

Answer choice D is incorrect. Even if the statements were made about a friend, the attorney would still be subject to discipline if the statements were false or made with reckless disregard as to their truth or falsity.

ANSWER 171

JUDICIAL CONDUCT

Answer choice B is correct. This question tests Code Rule 2.13(A)(2). Under this Code Rule, a judge must avoid favoritism, nepotism, and unnecessary appointments when exercising the power to make administrative appointments. Here, the chief justice appointed more bailiffs than was necessary for the caseload of the courts, which resulted in the unnecessary appointment of several bailiffs who did not have sufficient work.

Answer choice A is incorrect. The chief justice's actions did not amount to favoritism. She appointed a bailiff for each court, and the facts do not indicate that she favored one candidate or court over another in the selection process.

Answer choice C is incorrect. Although a judge may have a power of appointment, he or she must exercise that power within the rules.

Answer choice D is incorrect. While the appointments did in fact ensure that a bailiff would always be available, the caseload for the courts did not warrant appointing that many bailiffs.

ANSWER 172

CONFLICTS OF INTEREST

The correct answer is D. This question tests Rule 1.8(a). Under this Rule, an attorney cannot enter into a business transaction with a client or knowingly acquire an ownership, possessory, security, or other pecuniary interest adverse to a client, unless (1) the transaction and the terms on which the attorney acquires the interest are fair and reasonable to the client, fully disclosed, and transmitted in writing to the client in a manner that can be reasonably understood; (2) the client is advised in writing of the desirability of seeking, and is given a reasonable opportunity to seek, the advice of independent counsel in the transaction; and (3) the client provides informed consent, in a writing signed by the client, to the transaction and the lawyer's role in the transaction, including whether the lawyer is representing the client in the transaction. Here, the attorney complied with all of the requirements set forth in the Rule, except the one requiring the attorney to give the client a reasonable opportunity to confer with another attorney. Because the client was not given sufficient time to receive advice, the attorney would be subject to discipline.

Answer choice A is incorrect. Although the attorney advised the client to seek the counsel of another attorney, he did not provide the client with enough time to seek the advice.

Answer choice B is incorrect. Although the facts indicate that the offer was reasonable, the attorney did not give the client enough time to seek the advice of independent counsel.

Answer choice C is incorrect. The client provided signed, written informed consent to the transaction, but there was not sufficient time to seek the advice of independent counsel.

ANSWER 173

COMMUNICATIONS WITH PERSONS OTHER THAN CLIENTS

The correct answer is B. This question tests Rule 4.3. Under this Rule, when a lawyer is dealing on behalf of a client with a person who is not represented by counsel, a lawyer must not state or imply that the lawyer is disinterested. Here, the attorney did not disclose to the business owner that he was representing the employee and implied that he was conducting the investigation as a disinterested person. Because the business owner was unrepresented, the attorney would be subject to discipline.

Answer choice A is incorrect. The business owner had replaced the employee with a younger worker; so the attorney had a reasonable basis in law or facts for filing the charge.

Answer choice C is incorrect. Although the attorney cannot be subject to discipline for simply utilizing information voluntarily provided by the opposing party, he can be disciplined for implying that he was impartial in order to secure the information.

Answer choice D is incorrect. The attorney can be subject to discipline for his actions even if the information would have been revealed during routine discovery.

ANSWER 174

CLIENT CONFIDENTIALITY

The correct answer is A. This question tests Rule 1.6(a). Under this Rule, a lawyer must never reveal information relating to the representation of a client unless (1) the client gives informed consent, (2) the disclosure is impliedly authorized in order to carry out the representation, or (3) the disclosure is permitted under the Rules. According to Comment [5] to the Rule, unless a client instructs his or her lawyer to restrict information to specific lawyers in the firm, a lawyer may reveal confidential information to other lawyers in the firm in the course of the firm's practice. This exception for disclosure to other attorneys does not extend to those outside the lawyer's firm. Here, the attorney disclosed confidential client information to an attorney at another firm. The client was unaware of the disclosure, and, thus, did not give informed consent. Because the attorney had neither implied nor informed consent to disclose the information to the friend, the attorney would be subject to discipline.

Answer choice B is incorrect. Although the attorney felt the need to confer with another attorney to understand the particulars of the case, this situation is not the type contemplated by the Rules as eligible for implied disclosure. The attorney would have needed to get informed consent from the client.

Answer choice C is incorrect. The confidentiality agreement is an extra measure of protection for the client and the attorney, but the attorney was still obligated to get the client's informed consent prior to disclosure.

Answer choice D is incorrect. The friend's competency has no relevance to whether the attorney would be subject to discipline.

ANSWER 175

LITIGATION AND OTHER FORMS OF ADVOCACY

The correct answer is B. This question tests Rule 3.7(a), which provides that a lawyer cannot act as an advocate at a trial in which the lawyer is likely to be a necessary witness unless (a) the testimony relates to an uncontested issue; (b) the testimony relates to the nature and value of legal services provided; or (c) the lawyer's disqualification would be a substantial hardship to the client. Here, the solo practitioner's testimony relates specifically to the services that she provided and the value of those services; so it falls within one of the exceptions set forth in the Rule.

Answer choice A is incorrect. The Rule does not require the opposing party to object to an attorney simultaneously acting as advocate and necessary witness; rather, it provides that an attorney cannot act in both capacities unless one of the three exceptions set forth in the Rule applies.

Answer choice C is incorrect. While the Rule generally prohibits an attorney from simultaneously acting as advocate and necessary witness, there is an exception for the provision of testimony relating to the value and nature of legal services provided.

Answer choice D is incorrect. While the Rule usually prohibits an attorney from providing testimony about a contested issue, the testimony, here, falls within one of the exceptions set forth in the Rule.

ANSWER 176

DIFFERENT ROLES OF THE LAWYER

The correct answer is A. This question tests Rule 3.9, which provides that a lawyer who is representing a client before a legislative body or administrative agency in a nonadjudicative proceeding shall disclose that the appearance is in a representative capacity, and shall conform to the Rules governing candor toward the tribunal (Rule 3.3(a)-(c)), fairness to opposing party and counsel (Rule 3.4(a)-(c)), and impartiality and decorum of the tribunal (Rule 3.5). Here, the counsel informed the committee that he was appearing as the CEO's representative; so he abided by the Rule, and would not be subject to discipline.

Answer choice B is incorrect. Although the CEO had the right to have his counsel present at the hearing, the counsel had an affirmative duty to disclose the capacity in which he was appearing.

Answer choice C is incorrect. The counsel did not accept a fee for attempting to influence a legislative committee; instead, the fee was for his provision of counsel to the CEO.

Answer choice D is incorrect. The counsel was merely advising his client, which was the purpose of his appearance.

ANSWER 177

LITIGATION AND OTHER FORMS OF ADVOCACY

The correct answer is D. This question tests Rule 3.5(b). Under this Rule, a lawyer must not communicate *ex parte* with a judge, juror, prospective juror, or other official during the proceeding, unless authorized to do so by law or court order. Here, the general counsel spoke with a prospective juror without first notifying the other attorneys and is, therefore, subject to discipline. The prohibition is absolute; so it is irrelevant that the general counsel did not initiate the conversation or that the conversation did not touch on the merits or facts of the case.

Answer choice A is incorrect. Because the prohibition on *ex parte* communication is absolute, it is irrelevant that the general counsel did not initiate the conversation.

Answer choice B is incorrect. Because the prohibition on *ex parte* communication is absolute, it is irrelevant that the conversation did not involve a discussion of the facts or merits of the case.

Answer choice C is incorrect. The Rule only prohibits *ex parte* communication with judges, jurors, prospective jurors, or other officials; there is no prohibition on being in the same room, as long as there is no communication.

ANSWER 178

THE CLIENT-LAWYER RELATIONSHIP

Answer choice B is correct. This question tests the right of an attorney to limit the scope of representation. Restatement §19(1) provides that a client and attorney may agree to reasonably limit a duty that the attorney would otherwise owe to the client if (1) the client is adequately informed and consents, and (2) the terms of the limitation are reasonable given the circumstances. In this fact pattern, although the attorney informed the client that he was not comfortable with addressing tax issues, the attorney did not receive the client's written consent to limit the attorney's duties. Because the attorney did not receive the written consent, he would be subject to discipline.

Answer choice A is incorrect. Although the attorney has a duty to be competent in his representation, he is not obligated to become competent in areas of law that he is not utilizing.

Answer choice C is incorrect because attorneys are permitted to limit their representation under the circumstances outlined above.

Answer choice D is incorrect because an attorney may agree to waive a client's duty to pay a fee Restatement §19(2).

ANSWER 179

CONFLICTS OF INTEREST

The correct answer is A. This question tests Rule 1.8(a). Under this Rule, an attorney cannot enter into a business transaction with a client or knowingly acquire an ownership, possessory, security, or other pecuniary interest adverse to a client, unless (1) the transaction and the terms on which the lawyer acquires the interest are fair and reasonable to the client, fully disclosed, and transmitted in writing to the client in a manner that can be reasonably understood; (2) the client is advised in writing of the desirability of seeking, and is given a reasonable opportunity to seek, the advice of independent counsel in the transaction; and (3) the client provides informed consent, in a writing signed by the client, to the transaction and the lawyer's role in the transaction, including whether the lawyer is representing the client in the transaction. Here, the transaction was fair, the attorney disclosed in writing the details of the transaction to the defendant, and the defendant received advice from an independent attorney. Unfortunately, the attorney did not secure the defendant's written, signed, informed consent to the transaction and the attorney's role in the transaction, as required by the Rule. Because he did not secure such consent, the attorney would be subject to discipline.

Answer choice B is incorrect. The facts indicate that the transaction was fair to the defendant, and the Rules do not prohibit an attorney from entering into such an arrangement with a client as long as the attorney takes the protective measures set forth in Rule 1.8(a).

Answer choice C is incorrect. While the Rule requires the attorney to advise the client of the desirability of seeking the advice of independent counsel, satisfying that requirement is not sufficient to protect the attorney from discipline if he does not comply with the other requirements of the Rule.

Answer choice D is incorrect. Again, while the Rule requires the attorney to provide such an explanation, the provision of the explanation is not sufficient to protect the attorney from discipline if he does not comply with the other requirements of the Rule.

ANSWER 180

COMMUNICATION ABOUT LEGAL SERVICES

The correct answer is D. This question tests Rule 7.2(b)(4). Under this Rule, an attorney can refer clients to another attorney or a non-attorney professional pursuant to an agreement (not otherwise prohibited by the Rules) providing for the other person to refer clients or customers to the attorney if (1) the reciprocal referral agreement is not exclusive, and (2) the clients are informed of the agreement's existence and nature. Here, the arrangement is between two attorneys, the arrangement is nonexclusive, and both attorneys agreed to disclose the arrangement to prospective clients. The arrangement meets all of the prerequisites of the Rule; so neither attorney would be subject to discipline.

Answer choice A is incorrect. Although there is a general prohibition against an attorney giving anything of value to another person in exchange for referrals, Rule 7.2(b)(4) contains an exception for reciprocal referral agreements if certain prerequisites are met.

Answer choice B is incorrect. Although the Rules permit attorneys to pay the reasonable costs of advertising, there is no requirement that they do so Rule 7.2(b)(1).

Answer choice C is incorrect. The area of specialization does not impact whether the arrangement is appropriate under the Rules.

ANSWER 181

LITIGATION AND OTHER FORMS OF ADVOCACY

Answer choice A is correct. This question tests Rule 3.1. Under this Rule, an attorney must not bring or defend a proceeding, or assert or controvert an issue therein, unless there is a basis in law or fact for doing so that is not frivolous. Here, the legislature had declared the agreement at issue void as against public policy prior to the personal injury attorney entering into the agreement with the former patient. Because the agreement was void prior to the parties entering into it, there is no basis in law that is not frivolous for bringing a breach of contract claim, and the lawyer would be subject to discipline for bringing the claim.

Answer choice B is incorrect. It is not unreasonable for one lawyer to represent a client against the client's former attorney if a dispute arises between the original parties, and the second attorney will not be subject to discipline if there is a non-frivolous basis in law or fact for bringing the claim.

Answer choice C is incorrect. There is no valid claim for breach of contract because the agreement was void as against public policy.

Answer choice D is incorrect. Although the Comment to the Rule indicates that a lawyer will not be subject to discipline for bringing a frivolous claim just because he does not believe that the claim will be successful, there must be a non-frivolous basis in law or fact for bringing the claim.

ANSWER 182

COMMUNICATION ABOUT LEGAL SERVICES

Answer choice A is correct. This question tests Rule 7.2(b)(4). Under this Rule, an attorney can refer clients to another attorney or a non-attorney professional pursuant to an agreement (not otherwise prohibited by the Rules) providing for the other person to refer clients or customers to the attorney if (1) the reciprocal referral agreement is not exclusive, and (2) the clients are informed of the agreement's existence and nature. Here, the agreement was not exclusive, and both the attorney and her sister agreed to disclose the arrangement to prospective customers. However, the sister is not a non-attorney professional, and, thus, the prerequisites of the Rule are not met, and the attorney would be subject to discipline.

Answer choice B is incorrect. Although there is a general prohibition against an attorney giving anything of value to another person in exchange for referrals, Rule 7.2(b)(4) contains an exception for reciprocal referral agreements if certain prerequisites are met.

Answer choice C is incorrect. The familial relationship between the parties to the reciprocal referral agreement is irrelevant in determining whether such agreement is permitted.

Answer choice D is incorrect. Although a reciprocal referral agreement must be nonexclusive, the nonexclusivity of the arrangement is not sufficient to make the arrangement acceptable in this case since the sister is not a non-attorney professional.

ANSWER 183

COMMUNICATION ABOUT LEGAL SERVICES

The correct answer is D. This question tests Rule 7.1. Under this Rule, a lawyer cannot make false or misleading communications about the lawyer or the lawyer's services. A communication is false or misleading if it contains a material misrepresentation of fact or law, or omits a fact necessary to make the statement considered as a whole not materially misleading. The Comment to the Rule states that an advertisement that truthfully reports a lawyer's achievements can still be misleading if it creates an unjustified expectation that the prospective client will obtain the same results; however, the Comment further states that including a disclaimer can preclude a finding that a statement is misleading. Here, although the firm included the list of awards, which alone could be misleading, the advertisement also included an appropriate disclaimer. Therefore, the advertisement was not misleading.

Answer choice A is incorrect. While advertisements may be misleading if they contain truthful statements regarding a lawyer's achievements, the conclusion that the advertisement is misleading can be overcome by including an appropriate disclaimer, as was done in this case.

Answer choice B is incorrect. An attorney or firm may include his, her or its areas of practice in an advertisement. Rule 7.4.

Answer choice C is incorrect. The Comment to Rule 7.1 states that even truthful statements can be misleading if they lead to unjustified expectations of success.

ANSWER 184

REGULATION OF THE LEGAL PROFESSION

The correct answer is B. This question tests Rule 5.4(a)(1). Under this Rule, a lawyer or law firm is not permitted to share legal fees with a non-lawyer except that an agreement by a lawyer with the lawyer's firm, partner, or associate may provide for the payment of money, over a reasonable period of time after the lawyer's death, to the lawyer's estate or to one or more specified persons. Here, the partner and the firm reached an arrangement to provide for the payment of earned legal fees after the partner's death to the partner's best friend, and the facts indicate that the payment was reasonable in both amount and duration. Thus, the Rule would permit this arrangement.

Answer choice A is incorrect. Although an attorney is permitted to make arrangements regarding earnings for estate planning purposes, a firm is only permitted to make payments if the duration is reasonable.

Answer choice C is incorrect. The Rule explicitly permits a law firm to make payments to a non-relative after an attorney's death.

Answer choice D is incorrect. Although there is a general prohibition on making payments of legal fees to non-lawyers, there are four exceptions set forth in the Rule.

ANSWER 185

CLIENT CONFIDENTIALITY

Answer choice C is correct. This question tests permissive disclosure of confidential client information. Rule 1.6(a) provides that an attorney may not disclose information relating to the representation of a client unless (1) the client gives informed consent, (2) the disclosure is impliedly authorized in order to carry out the representation, or (3) the disclosure is permitted by any of the enumerated exceptions in Rule 1.6(b). Rule 1.6(b)permits an attorney to disclose confidential information if he reasonably believes that doing so is necessary (1) to prevent reasonably certain death or substantial bodily harm; (2) to prevent the client from committing a crime or fraud that is reasonably certain to result in substantial injury to the financial interests or property of another and in furtherance of which the client has used or is using the attorney's services; (3) to prevent substantial injury to the financial interests or property of another that is reasonably certain to result or has resulted from the client's commission of a crime or fraud in furtherance of which the client has used the attorney's services; (4) to secure legal advice about the attorney's compliance with the Rules; (5) to establish a claim or defense on behalf of the attorney in a controversy between the attorney and the client, to establish a defense to a criminal charge or civil claim against the attorney based upon conduct in which the client was involved, or to respond to allegations in any proceeding concerning the attorney's representation of the client; (6) to comply with other law or a court order; or (7)to detect and resolve conflicts of interest arising from the attorney's change of employment or from changes in the composition or ownership of a firm, but only if the revealed information would not compromise the attorney-client privilege or otherwise prejudice the client. Here, the client has used the attorney's advice about overseas accounts to launder embezzled money, and if the attorney reasonably believes that disclosure will prevent further harm, he may disclose the information in accordance with Rule 1.6(b)(3).

Answer choice A is incorrect. The Rules provide several situations where an attorney may disclose confidential client information.

Answer choice B is incorrect because Rule 1.6(b) provides several situations where the attorney may disclose confidential client information without client consent.

Answer choice D is incorrect because the Rule permits, rather than requires, an attorney to disclose confidential client information if he reasonably believes it is necessary as set forth above.

ANSWER 186

CONFLICTS OF INTEREST

Answer choice D is correct. Under Rule 1.11(a), (1) a lawyer who has formerly represented a client in a matter or whose present or former firm has formerly represented a client in a matter shall not thereafter (a) use information relating to the representation to the disadvantage of the former client except as the Rules would permit or require with respect to a client, or when the information has become generally known; or (b) reveal information relating to the representation except as the Rules would permit or require with respect to a client; and (2) a lawyer who has formerly served as a public officer or employee of the government shall not otherwise represent a client in connection with a matter in which the lawyer participated personally and substantially as a government officer or employee, unless the appropriate government agency gives its informed consent, confirmed in writing, to the representation. Although the attorney in this fact pattern participated in litigation against the tobacco company while at the state attorney general's office, he worked solely on the suit alleging that the tobacco company marketed to minors. Because he did not participate personally and substantially in the litigation involving misleading advertising claims, he is permitted to represent the tobacco company in this matter at the boutique firm.

Answer choice A is incorrect. Subject to the restrictions of the Rules, such as those regarding conflicts and client confidentiality, an attorney may represent a client against whom he or she previously brought suit. For example, a former government employee may represent a client against whom he or she previously brought suit while working as a government employee in connection with a matter in which he or she participated personally and substantially, provided that he or she obtains the informed written consent of the appropriate government agency.

Answer choice B is incorrect. Regardless of the amount of time that has passed, a former government employee cannot represent a client in a matter in which he or she personally and substantially participated while working as a government employee, unless he or she obtains the informed written consent of the former government employer.

Answer choice C is incorrect. Although the attorney served in a subordinate capacity to the lead attorney, the suit was his sole work assignment, and he participated personally and substantially in the matter.

ANSWER 187

LITIGATION AND OTHER FORMS OF ADVOCACY

The correct answer is A. This question tests Rule 3.7(a), which provides that a lawyer cannot act as an advocate at a trial in which the lawyer is likely to be a necessary witness unless (a) the testimony relates to an uncontested issue; (b) the testimony relates to the nature and value of legal services provided; or (c) the lawyer's disqualification would be a substantial hardship to the client. Here, the wife did not deny the affair; so the issue is uncontested. Therefore, the attorney would be permitted to testify despite being the husband's advocate.

Answer choice B is incorrect. Although the attorney is the only witness, other than the husband, barring the attorney's testimony would not result in a substantial hardship because the issue is uncontested.

Answer choice C is incorrect. Representation by an attorney who is likely to be a necessary witness is generally prohibited, but the testimony here falls under one of the exceptions set forth in the Rule.

Answer choice D is incorrect. The exception for testimony relating to an attorney's services is just one of three possible exceptions under which the testimony could qualify.

ANSWER 188

REGULATION OF THE LEGAL PROFESSION

The correct answer is B. This question tests Rule 5.4(a)(4). Under this Rule, a lawyer or law firm is not permitted to share legal fees with a non-lawyer except that an attorney may share court-awarded legal fees with a nonprofit organization that employed, retained, or recommended employment of the attorney in the matter. Here, the nonprofit organization referred the case to the attorney, and the attorney shared the awarded legal fees with the nonprofit. Therefore, the attorney would not be subject to discipline.

Answer choice A is incorrect. The Rule restricts the sharing of fees with non-attorneys except in four limited circumstances.

Answer choice C is incorrect. The Rule specifically permits an attorney to share court-awarded legal fees with a nonprofit organization that referred the case to him.

Answer choice D is incorrect. The Rule does not specify how the fees are to be divided.

ANSWER 189

JUDICIAL CONDUCT

Answer choice A is correct. This question tests Code Rule 2.13(B). Under this Code Rule, a judge must not appoint a lawyer to a position if the judge either knows that the lawyer, or the lawyer's domestic partner or spouse, has contributed more than a specified dollar amount within the specified number of years prior to the judge's election campaign, or learns of such a contribution on account of a timely motion by a party or other person properly interested in the matter. Here, the appointed attorney had contributed a large amount to the judge's election campaign a year before, and the judge was put on notice by the timely motion by plaintiff's counsel; so the judge should have removed the attorney and appointed another in his place. By not doing so, the judge is subject to discipline for violating the Rule.

Answer choice B is incorrect. As long as the judge makes the appointment impartially and on the basis of merit, avoiding favoritism, nepotism, and unnecessary appointments, he or she will not be subject to discipline for appointing an attorney from another town when a local attorney is available.

Answer choice C is incorrect. Although the judge was unaware of the contribution when she made the appointment, she was put on notice by plaintiff's counsel and therefore was required to rectify the situation.

Answer choice D is incorrect. The violation stems from appointing a campaign contributor, not from appointing an attorney from another town.

ANSWER 190

CLIENT CONFIDENTIALITY

Answer choice C is correct. Pursuant to Rule 1.18(a), a person who discusses with a lawyer the possibility of forming a client-lawyer relationship with respect to a matter is a prospective client. Furthermore, as set forth in Rule 1.18(b), if, after consultation, no client-lawyer relationship forms, a lawyer who has had discussions with a prospective client must not use or reveal information learned during the consultation, except as otherwise permitted by the Rules. Here, the husband approached the lawyer, seeking an attorney to represent him in a divorce, and he disclosed information about his reasons for seeking the divorce. The lawyer told the husband what the fees would be and how many hours the representation was likely to take. These facts suggest that the husband was discussing the possibility of forming a client-lawyer relationship, thus making him a prospective client, and, after the consultation, the lawyer owed the husband a duty of confidentiality with respect to the disclosed information.

Answer choice A is incorrect. The Rules do not require a lawyer to contact a prospective client to provide advice if the prospective client has declined representation.

Answer choice B is incorrect. Rule 1.18(c) prohibits a lawyer from representing a client with interests materially adverse to those of a prospective client in the same or a substantially related matter if the lawyer received information from the prospective client that could be significantly harmful to the client in the matter, unless otherwise permitted by the Rules. However, a negligence action by a customer of the husband is not the same as, or substantially related to, a divorce.

Answer choice D is incorrect. Even though no client-lawyer relationship formed, the husband was a prospective client and, thus, the lawyer must not use or reveal information learned during the consultation, except as permitted by the Rules.

ANSWER 191

THE CLIENT-LAWYER RELATIONSHIP

Answer choice C is correct. The question tests Rule 1.2(d), which provides that a lawyer shall not counsel a client to engage, or assist a client, in conduct that the lawyer knows is criminal or fraudulent, but a lawyer may discuss the legal consequences of any proposed course of conduct with a client and may counsel or assist a client to make a good faith effort to determine the validity, scope, meaning, or application of the law. Here, the CEO and counsel are discussing a potentially criminal course of action, and counsel is providing his client with a realistic assessment of the legal consequences of the plan, which is permitted by the Rules.

Answer choice A is incorrect. Telling the CEO how to form an affiliated corporation is not necessarily assisting a client in committing a criminal act, particularly when the counsel is providing this information as he advises the client of the potential ramifications of pursuing the course of action.

Answer choice B is incorrect. The counsel is advising the client of the legal consequences of the action, which is permitted by the Rules.

Answer choice D is incorrect. Regardless of whether a client heeds the advice of counsel, the counsel can be subject to discipline for advising a client on how to commit a crime.

ANSWER 192

COMMUNICATIONS WITH PERSONS OTHER THAN CLIENTS

Answer choice D is correct. This question tests Rule 4.2. Under Rule 4.2, in the course of representing a client, a lawyer must not communicate about the subject of the representation with a person the lawyer knows to be represented by another lawyer in the matter, unless the lawyer has the other lawyer's consent or is authorized to do so by law or a court order. Here, the attorney contacted his client's wife to discuss the terms of a potential divorce settlement. The contact was not inappropriate when it began, because the attorney did not know the wife was represented; however, once the attorney became aware that the wife was represented, he should have discontinued the discussion until he could obtain the other lawyer's consent.

Answer choice A is incorrect. While the attorney would clearly need to discuss any potential settlement with the wife or the wife's attorney, he would need to obtain the consent of the wife's lawyer to communicate directly with the wife.

Answer choice B is incorrect. Although the attorney did not know that the wife was represented by counsel when he initially contacted her, he had an obligation to stop the discussions once he learned of that fact.

Answer choice C is incorrect. Regardless of the stage of representation, an attorney is not permitted to discuss the subject of the representation with a person the attorney knows to be represented by another attorney, unless the attorney has the other attorney's consent.

ANSWER 193

LITIGATION AND OTHER FORMS OF ADVOCACY

The correct answer is C. This question tests Rule 3.7(a), which provides that a lawyer cannot act as an advocate at a trial in which the lawyer is likely to be a necessary witness unless (a) the testimony relates to an uncontested issue; (b) the testimony relates to the nature and value of legal services provided; or (c) the lawyer's disqualification would be a substantial hardship to the client. Here, neither party could have foreseen the need for the attorney's testimony, and preparations for the trial were well under way when the necessity for his testimony became apparent. Given that the owner would suffer hardship because of the delay and fees involved, the attorney should not be disqualified.

Answer choice A is incorrect. While the Rule would ordinarily prohibit an attorney from representing a client if his or her testimony were likely to be necessary, there is an exception for situations where there would be a substantial hardship on the client.

Answer choice B is incorrect. The attorney would be permitted to provide testimony under the substantial hardship exception set forth in the Rule.

Answer choice D is incorrect. Presumably the other side would always have the right to question the attorney if he were to testify; so the Rule does not provide an exception when there is such an opportunity.

ANSWER 194

COMMUNICATIONS WITH PERSONS OTHER THAN CLIENTS

Answer choice C is correct. This question tests Rule 4.1. Rule 4.1 provides that in the course of representing a client, a lawyer must not knowingly (1) make a false statement of material fact or law to a third person or (2) fail to disclose a material fact when disclosure is necessary to avoid assisting a criminal or fraudulent act by a client, unless disclosure is prohibited by the Rule of Confidentiality. This Rule does not impose an affirmative duty on an attorney to disclose relevant facts, and the Comment to the Rule provides that estimates of price and value placed on the subject of a transaction are generally not considered material facts. Here, the in-house counsel did not disclose the larger company's valuation of the smaller company to the CEO during negotiations. Although the CEO would have liked to have this information, the attorney was under no obligation to disclose it and would not be subject to discipline for nondisclosure.

Answer choice A is incorrect. While there are instances where an omission can rise to the level of a false statement, failing to disclose the estimated value of the subject of a negotiation does not fall within that category.

Answer choice B is incorrect. Rule 4.1 does not place an affirmative duty upon an attorney to disclose relevant facts.

Answer choice D is incorrect. There are several instances where an attorney may disclose confidential information, including when there is a court order; however, in this case, the in-house counsel did not have an affirmative duty to disclose the higher valuation, and failing to disclose is not equivalent, under these facts, to a false statement.

ANSWER 195

SAFEKEEPING FUNDS AND OTHER PROPERTY

Answer choice A is correct. This question tests Rule 1.15(d). This Rule requires that an attorney promptly notify a client or a third person upon receipt of funds in which the client or third person has an interest. Additionally, except as permitted by the Rules, the law or by agreement with the client, the Rule also requires that the attorney promptly deliver to the client or third person any funds or other property that the client or third person is entitled to receive and, upon request by the client or third person, shall promptly render a full accounting regarding such property. Here, the attorney and the client agreed in writing that the attorney would retain the first three payments in a separate interest-bearing account until the fourth payment was received. Because the agreement overrides the obligation under the Rule, the attorney would not be subject to discipline.

Answer choice B is incorrect. While Rule 1.15(a) requires an attorney to keep client funds segregated in a client trust account, there is no requirement that the account be interest bearing.

Answer choice C is incorrect. Although Rule 1.15(d) places a duty on the attorney to promptly deliver the funds, that duty can be waived through an agreement with the client.

Answer choice D is incorrect. The Rule explicitly allows the client to waive the duty to notify.

ANSWER 196

COMMUNICATION ABOUT LEGAL SERVICES

Answer choice D is correct. This question tests Rule 7.1. Under this Rule, a lawyer cannot make false or misleading communications about the lawyer or the lawyer's services. A communication is false or misleading if it contains a material misrepresentation of fact or law, or omits a fact necessary to make the statement considered as a whole not materially misleading. According to the Comment to Rule 7.4, a statement that the lawyer "specializes in" a particular field is subject to the "false and misleading" standard applied in Rule 7.1 to communications concerning a lawyer's services. Here, the lawyer stated in his advertisement that he specialized in elder law and estate planning, but he was actually a general practitioner and did not practice only in the "specialized" fields. Because the statement was false and/or misleading, the lawyer could be subject to discipline for violating Rule 7.1.

Answer choice A is incorrect. The attorney is required to include the name and office address of at least one lawyer or law firm responsible for its content (Rule 7.2), but that alone does not keep the attorney from violating Rule 7.1.

Answer choice B is incorrect. Although the attorney may want to emphasize his elder law and estate planning services, stating that he specializes in them is misleading when he is a general practitioner.

Answer choice C is incorrect. Such a statement is only required when the communication is directly to a prospective client known to be in need of legal services in a particular matter (see

Rule 7.3).

ANSWER 197

CONFLICTS OF INTEREST

The correct answer is A. This question tests Rule 1.12(a). Under this Rule, a lawyer generally must not represent anyone in connection with a matter in which the lawyer participated personally and substantially (1) as a judge or other adjudicative officer or law clerk to such a person or (2) as an arbitrator, mediator, or other third-party neutral, *unless* all parties to the proceeding give informed consent, confirmed in writing. Here, the former judge had participated in the original custody hearings and so had participated personally and substantially in the matter in which she was preparing to represent the ex-wife. Because of that connection, the former judge was required to get the signed, written informed consent from each of the parties involved, which she did; so she would not be subject to discipline for representing the ex-wife.

Answer choice B is incorrect. The focus of this question is on the potential conflict of interest that arose when the judge who presided over the initial custody hearing began representing the ex-wife.

Answer choice C is incorrect. Although a former judge is typically prohibited from representing a client in a matter in which she participated personally and substantially as a judge, she may do so if, as was the case here, she has the signed, written informed consent of all parties involved.

Answer choice D is incorrect. While it is possible that the ex-wife received a benefit from the former judge's representation, the former judge disclosed the potential conflicts of interest to both ex-spouses, and they provided signed, written informed consent.

ANSWER 198

REGULATION OF THE LEGAL PROFESSION

Answer choice D is correct. Rule 5.4(b) prohibits a lawyer from forming a partnership with a non-lawyer if any of the activities of the partnership consist of the practice of law. In this case, the LLC is not in the business of providing legal services for a fee. Therefore, the lawyer is not violating the Rule.

Answer choice A is incorrect. Rule 5.4(b) prohibits a lawyer from forming a partnership with a non-lawyer if any of the activities of the partnership consist of the practice of law. While the lawyer may be engaged in the practice of law through the representation, the practice of law cannot be considered one of the activities of the LLC. Therefore, the lawyer is not likely to be subject to discipline for participating in the venture.

Answer choice B is incorrect. The Model Rules (the "Rules") do not prohibit a lawyer from being a manager of an LLC of which the lawyer is a member.

Answer choice C is incorrect. The facts indicate that the lawyer had experience in representing venture capital firms from prior employment, so the lawyer likely is fully competent to represent the new LLC.

ANSWER 199

COMMUNICATION ABOUT LEGAL SERVICES

Answer choice B is correct. This question tests Rule 7.1. Under this Rule, a lawyer cannot make false or misleading communications about the lawyer or the lawyer's services. A communication is false or misleading if it contains a material misrepresentation of fact or law, or omits a fact necessary to make the statement considered as a whole not materially misleading. The Rule applies to any communications, including advertisements. Here, the attorney was communicating to her cousin about her services. The statement about her specialties is false because she does not restrict her practice to that area, and the statement about the damage awards is misleading, per the Comment to Rule 7.1, because it can lead to unjustified expectations on the part of the prospective client and is not accompanied by the appropriate disclaimer. Therefore, the attorney can be subject to discipline.

Answer choice A is incorrect. Direct solicitation is prohibited when a significant motive for doing so is pecuniary gain; however, there is an exception that allows attorneys to solicit employment from family members Rule 7.3.

Answer choice C is incorrect. While an attorney may directly solicit employment from a family member, the Rules do not provide an exception to the requirement that the communication not be false or misleading. Here, the attorney's statements to her cousin regarding the damage awards and the specialization in automobile litigation were false and/or misleading.

Answer choice D is incorrect. While the statement about the awards was truthful, it can be misleading if it leads to unreasonable expectations and is not accompanied by an appropriate disclaimer. Additionally, the statement about specializing in automobile litigation is false.

ANSWER 200

LAWYERS' DUTIES TO THE PUBLIC AND THE LEGAL SYSTEM

Answer choice D is correct. This question tests Rule 8.2(a). This Rule states that a lawyer must not make a statement that the lawyer knows to be false or with reckless disregard as to its truth or falsity concerning the qualifications or integrity of a judge, adjudicatory officer, or candidate for election or appointment to judicial or legal office. A lawyer may express an honest and candid opinion. Here, the associate did not work with the former partner, and he based his opinion on the gossip of others in the firm. His statements were detrimental to the former partner, and the associate made them with reckless disregard as to their truth or falsity. Therefore, the statements were not proper.

Answer choice A is incorrect. The associate did not know if the comments were true because he based them on gossip from co-workers who had bad feelings toward the former partner.

Answer choice B is incorrect. Although the Comment to the Rule permits a lawyer to express his or her honest and candid opinions on the professional or personal fitness of persons being considered for election, the statement must be honest or not made with reckless disregard as to the truth or falsity of the statement.

Answer choice C is incorrect. The Rules expressly permit an attorney to make statements about candidates if they are true or are not made with reckless disregard as to their truth or falsity.

ANSWER 201

COMMUNICATIONS WITH PERSONS OTHER THAN CLIENTS

The correct answer is D. This question tests Rule 4.3. Under this Rule, when a lawyer is dealing on behalf of a client with a person who is not represented by counsel, a lawyer must not state or imply that the lawyer is disinterested. When the lawyer knows or reasonably should know that the unrepresented person misunderstands the lawyer's role in the matter, the lawyer must make reasonable efforts to correct the misunderstanding. Here, the general counsel knew that the maintenance supervisor was unrepresented. The facts also indicate that he reasonably should have known that the maintenance supervisor believed that the general counsel would provide him with representation at trial. Because the general counsel should have known of the misunderstanding, he was required to make reasonable efforts to correct the misunderstanding.

Answer choice A is incorrect. Although the Rules permit an attorney for an entity to represent employees of that entity (subject to the Rules regarding conflicts of interest), there is no affirmative obligation for an attorney to do so.

Answer choice B is incorrect. Such discussions would likely only be acceptable if the maintenance supervisor was aware of the limited role of the general counsel, and provided informed written consent.

Answer choice C is incorrect. Although the general counsel would need to get signed, written informed consent prior to representing both the hospital and the maintenance supervisor, the requirement did not apply in this case because the general counsel was only to represent the hospital.

ANSWER 202

CLIENT CONFIDENTIALITY

Answer choice B is correct. This question tests Rule 1.6 regarding the disclosure of confidential client information. Generally, an attorney may not disclose information relating to the representation of a client unless (1) the client gives express informed consent, (2) the disclosure is impliedly authorized in order to carry out the representation, or (3) the disclosure is permitted by any of the enumerated exceptions in Rule 1.6(b). In particular, Rule 1.6(b) permits an attorney to disclose confidential information if he reasonably believes that doing so is necessary (1) to prevent reasonably certain death or substantial bodily harm; (2) to prevent the client from committing a crime or fraud that is reasonably certain to result in substantial injury to the financial interests or property of another and in furtherance of which the client has used or is using the attorney's services; (3) to prevent substantial injury to the financial interests or property of another that is reasonably certain to result or has resulted from the client's commission of a crime or fraud in furtherance of which the client has used the attorney's services; (4) to secure legal advice about the attorney's compliance with the Rules; (5) to establish a claim or defense on behalf of the attorney in a controversy between the attorney and the client, to establish a defense to a criminal charge or civil claim against the attorney based upon conduct in which the client was involved, or to respond to allegations in any proceeding concerning the attorney's representation of the client; (6) to comply with other law or a court order; or (7) to detect and resolve conflicts of interest arising from the attorney's change of employment or from changes in the composition or ownership of a firm, but only if the revealed information would not compromise the attorney-client privilege or otherwise prejudice the client. Express informed consent exists after a lawyer provides the client with sufficient information to enable the client to recognize the impact of the lawyer's disclosure of the client's confidential information, and the client approves of the disclosure. In this case, the doctor consented to the disclosure of his confidential information, but the attorney did not provide any information relating to how the disclosure would impact the settlement of the case. Without that information, the client's consent was not sufficient to overcome the attorney's duty to keep information relating to the representation of the client confidential.

Answer choice A is incorrect. It is true that the patient is not facing reasonably certain death or substantial bodily harm, as the harm here was in the past, and the proposed disclosure would not prevent any future harm. However, the analysis does not end there. As noted above, there are several other factors to consider when determining whether the disclosure of client confidential information is proper, one of which relates to whether the client gives express informed consent. In this case, the doctor did no such thing, and that is why it would be improper for the attorney to disclose the doctor's addiction (note that the disclosure is not impliedly authorized in order to carry out the representation, and none of the exceptions that permit disclosure are applicable).

Answer choice C is incorrect. An attorney can disclose confidential information if the disclosure is impliedly authorized in order to carry out the representation of the client. Disclosing that the doctor was under the influence of prescription medication at the time he wrote the prescription is not necessary to carry out the representation of the client and, in fact, will most likely harm the doctor's chances of reaching a favorable settlement.

Answer choice D is incorrect. Although the doctor did consent to the disclosure, he did not have all of the information necessary to make an informed decision regarding whether or not to permit the disclosure.

ANSWER 203

JUDICIAL CONDUCT

Answer choice C is correct. This question tests Code Rule 2.13(A)(2). Under this Code Rule, a judge must avoid favoritism, nepotism, and unnecessary appointments when exercising the power to make administrative appointments. Here, the judge appointed his wife's sister advocate even though there were several other family law firms that he could have approached. Because he appointed a relative within the third degree of relationship of his wife, he engaged in nepotism, and his actions were not proper.

Answer choice A is incorrect. Although there was a need for attorneys to serve as advocates, the existence of need does not permit a judge to appoint his or her relatives to the position, provided that such relatives are within the third degree of relationship of either the judge or the judge's spouse or domestic partner, or the spouse or domestic partner of such relative.

Answer choice B is incorrect. Although judges are given wide latitude in exercising their appointment powers, they must still abide by the restrictions in the Rules regarding such things as merit, nepotism, and pay.

Answer choice D is incorrect. The facts suggest that there was a real need for attorneys who were willing to serve as advocates in these types of cases; nevertheless, this does not address the issue. The judge's actions were not proper because, by appointing his wife's sister advocate, he engaged in nepotism, which is prohibited by the Code.

ANSWER 204

CLIENT CONFIDENTIALITY

Answer choice A is correct. This question tests Rule 1.6 regarding the disclosure of confidential client information. Generally, an attorney may not disclose information relating to the representation of a client unless (1) the client gives informed consent, (2) the disclosure is impliedly authorized in order to carry out the representation, or (3) the disclosure is permitted by any of the enumerated exceptions in Rule 1.6(b). In particular, Rule 1.6(b) permits an attorney to disclose confidential information if he reasonably believes that doing so is necessary (1) to prevent reasonably certain death or substantial bodily harm; (2) to prevent the client from committing a crime or fraud that is reasonably certain to result in substantial injury to the financial interests or property of another and in furtherance of which the client has used or is using the attorney's services; (3) to prevent substantial injury to the financial interests or property of another that is reasonably certain to result or has resulted from the client's commission of a crime or fraud in furtherance of which the client has used the attorney's services; (4) to secure legal advice about the attorney's compliance with the Rules; (5) to establish a claim or defense on behalf of the attorney in a controversy between the attorney and the client, to establish a defense to a criminal charge or civil claim against the attorney based upon conduct in which the client was involved, or to respond to allegations in any proceeding concerning the attorney's representation of the client; (6) to comply with other law or a court order; or (7) to detect and resolve conflicts of interest arising from the attorney's change of employment or from changes in the composition or ownership of a firm, but only if the revealed information would not compromise the attorney-client privilege or otherwise prejudice the client. The facts here do not indicate that the client consented, nor is disclosure of this information impliedly authorized to carry out the representation, as disclosure would potentially damage the client's position. One of the exceptions permitting disclosure is Rule 1.6(b)(6), which permits disclosure to comply with other law. If there is a law that requires the attorney to disclose the information, and he does not disclose it, he may be subject to discipline for failing to disclose.

Answer choice B is incorrect. Regardless of whether the client gave informed consent, the attorney would still be permitted, not mandated, to disclose the information under the exception in Rule 1.6(b)(1), which permits disclosure to prevent reasonably certain death or substantial bodily harm.

Answer choice C is incorrect. As noted above, the attorney is permitted, but not required, to disclose this information to prevent reasonably certain death or substantial bodily harm.

Answer choice D is incorrect. The exception in Rule 1.6(b)(1) is permissive, not mandatory.

ANSWER 205

REGULATION OF THE LEGAL PROFESSION

Answer choice D is correct. This question tests Rule 5.5(a), which provides that a lawyer must not practice law in a jurisdiction in violation of the regulation of the legal profession in that jurisdiction, or assist another in doing so. One exception to this Rule, as set forth in the related Comment, involves counseling non-lawyers who wish to proceed pro se. Model Rules of Prof'l Conduct R. 5.5 cmt. [3] (2009). Here, the attorney provided assistance to an unlicensed individual who was practicing law by representing himself. Moreover, because a person is generally permitted to represent himself, the attorney, by assisting the person in doing so, was not assisting in the unauthorized practice of law.

Answer choice A is incorrect. It is true that the attorney assisted an unlicensed person in the practice of law, but because a person is generally entitled to represent himself, the attorney, by assisting the person in doing so, did not assist in the unauthorized practice of law.

Answer choice B is incorrect. The Rules do not impose a restriction on how much assistance an attorney can provide to a pro se defendant.

Answer choice C is incorrect. Even if an attorney is licensed in a state, he or she can still be liable for providing assistance to a person who is engaging in the unauthorized practice of law.

ANSWER 206

REGULATION OF THE LEGAL PROFESSION

Answer choice C is correct. This question tests Rule 5.5(a), which provides that a lawyer must not practice law in a jurisdiction in violation of the regulation of the legal profession in that jurisdiction, or assist another in doing so. Here, the attorney hired a law graduate the month after graduation; so the graduate did not yet have a license to practice in the state. While an attorney may hire a law graduate to perform work, the attorney must supervise the graduate and cannot rely on the graduate to perform the work on his or her own. Here, by permitting the graduate to draft pleadings, conduct discovery, appear in court, and share in fees, the attorney assisted the graduate in the unauthorized practice of law.

Answer choice A is incorrect. Although the graduate has a law degree, it is too soon for the graduate to have a license; so the attorney assisted the graduate in the unauthorized practice of law.

Answer choice B is incorrect. The attorney was required to continue supervising the graduate and to ensure that the graduate was not engaging in the unauthorized practice of law.

Answer choice D is incorrect. Regardless of whether the graduate was only qualified to draft pleadings, he was not licensed in the state, and the attorney, by permitting the graduate to engage in the activities in which he engaged, assisted the graduate in the unauthorized practice of law.

ANSWER 207

CONFLICTS OF INTEREST

The correct answer is D. This question tests Rule 1.12(a). Under this Rule, a lawyer generally must not represent anyone in connection with a matter in which the lawyer participated personally and substantially (1) as a judge or other adjudicative officer or law clerk to such a person or (2) as an arbitrator, mediator, or other third-party neutral, *unless* all parties to the proceeding give informed consent, confirmed in writing. Here, the local counsel participated personally and substantially as a mediator for the parties in the dispute, and he was privy to the information disclosed by both parties. If both parties had provided informed written consent to the local counsel representing the accused member, then he would not have been subject to discipline; however, the facts do not indicate that he obtained such consent. Therefore, he would be subject to discipline.

Answer choice A is incorrect. Although the parties had permitted the local counsel to communicate much of the information they disclosed, the local counsel would not be permitted to represent one member against the other without the informed written consent of both parties.

Answer choice B is incorrect. While a party is generally permitted to choose his or her counsel, the counsel may not be permitted to serve if there is a conflict of interest with the other party or parties.

Answer choice C is incorrect. The Rules do not impose an obligation on counsel to disclose the potential conflict to the court, but they do impose an obligation on the counsel to obtain the informed written consent of the parties involved.

ANSWER 208

THE CLIENT-LAWYER RELATIONSHIP

Answer choice D is correct. This question tests Rule 1.2(a). Under this Rule, the lawyer, within the limits imposed by law and his or her professional obligations, is required to abide by a client's decision concerning the objectives of the representation and shall consult with the client as to the means by which they are to be pursued; a lawyer may take such action on behalf of the client as is impliedly authorized to carry out the representation; a lawyer shall abide by a client's decision whether to settle a matter; and in a criminal case, a lawyer shall abide by the client's decision, after consultation with the lawyer, as to a plea to be entered, whether to waive jury trial and whether the client will testify. Here, the client told the attorney to accept the hospital's original settlement offer. The attorney disregarded his client's instructions to settle and instead jeopardized his client's possible recovery by telling opposing counsel that the settlement would be rejected if the amount was not doubled. By disregarding his client's instruction to settle, the attorney violated Rule 1.2(a).

Answer choice A is incorrect. While the outcome was far better for the client than what the client would have recovered under the original offer, the attorney still violated the Rule by disregarding his client's instruction to settle.

Answer choice B is incorrect. The attorney provided competent legal advice by providing all of the information necessary to reach an informed decision concerning the settlement offer, but the attorney was ultimately obligated to abide by his client's wish to settle.

Answer choice C is incorrect. An attorney is required to abide by his or her client's wish to settle even if the attorney has reason to believe that a different course of action might be more beneficial to his or her client.

ANSWER 209

CONFLICTS OF INTEREST

Answer choice C is correct. This question tests Rule 1.7. Under this Rule, a lawyer is generally prohibited from representing a client if the representation involves a concurrent conflict of interest. Notwithstanding a concurrent conflict of interest, a lawyer may represent a client if (1) the lawyer reasonably believes that the lawyer will be able to provide competent and diligent representation to each affected client; (2) the representation is not prohibited by law; (3) the representation does not involve the assertion of a claim by one client against another client represented by the lawyer in the same litigation or other proceeding before a tribunal; and (4) each affected client gives informed consent, confirmed in writing. Here, although the attorney stated that he felt competent to represent both parties, and both parties provided informed written consent, the passenger asserted a claim against the driver. Because one client asserted a claim against the other, the attorney is not permitted to represent both clients at the same time, even with informed written consent.

Answer choice A is incorrect. Even with informed written consent, the attorney may not represent both the driver and the passenger because the passenger is asserting a claim against the driver.

Answer choice B is incorrect. Although the law of the jurisdiction does not prohibit the attorney from representing both clients, the Rules do prohibit an attorney from representing two clients when one client is asserting a claim against the other in the same litigation.

Answer choice D is incorrect. While there are some situations where an attorney is completely prohibited from representing two clients, the prohibition does not extend to every possible situation.

ANSWER 210

CONFLICTS OF INTEREST

Answer choice B is correct. Under Rule 1.11(a), (1) a lawyer who has formerly represented a client in a matter or whose present or former firm has formerly represented a client in a matter shall not thereafter (a) use information relating to the representation to the disadvantage of the former client except as the Rules would permit or require with respect to a client, or when the information has become generally known; or (b) reveal information relating to the representation except as the Rules would permit or require with respect to a client; and (2) a lawyer who has formerly served as a public officer or employee of the government shall not otherwise represent a client in connection with a matter in which the lawyer participated personally and substantially as a government officer or employee, unless the appropriate government agency gives its informed consent, confirmed in writing, to the representation. Here, the attorney's participation in the litigation matter while employed at the city attorney's office was certainly both personal and substantial, as he was the lead prosecuting attorney and would have been intimately knowledgeable about the case. He will not be subject to discipline, though, because he received the city's informed written consent to the new representation when he received the letter from the chief of the criminal division after providing the city with the information relating to the representation.

Answer choice A is incorrect. As lead attorney, his participation would be considered both personal and substantial.

Answer choice C is incorrect. Although his participation was both substantial and personal, he received informed written consent to undertake the new representation.

Answer choice D is incorrect. As Rule 1.11(a) states, a former government attorney can overcome the conflict that arises from switching sides in a representation by obtaining the informed written consent of his or her former government employer.

ANSWER 211

CONFLICTS OF INTEREST

Answer choice A is correct. This question tests Rule 1.7. Under this Rule, a lawyer is generally prohibited from representing a client if the representation involves a concurrent conflict of interest. Notwithstanding a concurrent conflict of interest, a lawyer may represent a client if (1) the lawyer reasonably believes that the lawyer will be able to provide competent and diligent representation to each affected client; (2) the representation is not prohibited by law; (3) the representation does not involve the assertion of a claim by one client against another client represented by the lawyer in the same litigation or other proceeding before a tribunal; and (4) each affected client gives informed consent, confirmed in writing. Here, the clients are directly adverse because the owner is selling a facility to the acquaintance. The lawyer indicated that she felt competent to represent both, the representation is not prohibited by law, and the representation does not involve the assertion of a claim by one client against another client represented by the lawyer in the same litigation. While the owner provided informed consent, the consent was verbal and not confirmed in writing. Because the Rule requires the consent to be confirmed in writing, the consent is not sufficient, and the lawyer will be subject to discipline.

Answer choice B is incorrect. A lawyer may represent two directly adverse clients if all of the conditions set forth in the exception above are met. Here, though, the informed consent was not confirmed in writing.

Answer choice C is incorrect. The Comment to the Rule states that "absent consent, a lawyer may not act as an advocate in one matter against a person the lawyer represents in some other matter, even when the matters are wholly unrelated." Model Rules of Prof'l Conduct R. 1.7 cmt. [6] (2009).

Answer choice D is incorrect. The Rule requires that the informed consent be confirmed in writing.

ANSWER 212

LITIGATION AND OTHER FORMS OF ADVOCACY

Answer choice B is correct. This question tests Rule 3.4(f). This Rule provides that a lawyer must not request a person other than a client to refrain from voluntarily giving relevant information to another party unless (1) the person is a relative, employee, or other agent of a client; and (2) the lawyer reasonably believes that the person's interests will not be adversely affected by refraining from giving such information. Here, the attorney has requested that the expert refrain from voluntarily disclosing the potentially damaging proprietary information to the plaintiff's counsel. The request will not subject the attorney to discipline because (1) the expert is an employee of the client company and (2) there is no indication that the expert's interests will be adversely affected by refraining from the disclosure.

Answer choice A is incorrect. The Rule does not condition discipline on whether the attorney offers an inducement for not disclosing the information. The relevant issues are the relationship (or lack thereof) between the person and the client and the risk to the person's interests.

Answer choice C is incorrect. Although an attorney generally has an obligation to be fair to opposing parties and counsel by not attempting to obstruct access to relevant information, the Rules carve out exceptions for relatives, employees and other agents of the client.

Answer choice D is incorrect. While the Rules prohibit an attorney from improperly influencing a witness, an attorney is permitted to request that a person refrain from voluntarily giving relevant information to the other party if that person is an employee of the client.

ANSWER 213

LITIGATION AND OTHER FORMS OF ADVOCACY

The correct answer is C. This question tests Rule 3.5(c). Under this Rule, a lawyer must not communicate with a juror or prospective juror after discharge of the jury if (1) the communication is prohibited by law or court order; (2) the juror has made known to the lawyer a desire not to communicate; or (3) the communication involves misrepresentation, coercion, duress, or harassment. Here, the jury foreman told the defense attorney that she did not wish to speak with him; so the defense attorney was prohibited by the Rule from attempting to contact her. Additionally, Rule 8.4(a) provides that a lawyer cannot use another person to help him or her violate the Rules, and the defense attorney, here, used the friend to contact the jury foreman after the defense attorney had knowledge that the jury foreman did not want to speak with him. Therefore, the defense attorney violated the Rules and is subject to discipline.

Answer choice A is incorrect. Rule 8.4(a) prohibits an attorney from using another person to violate the Rules.

Answer choice B is incorrect. The defense attorney violated the Rules when he had the friend contact the jury foreman after the jury foreman indicated that she did not want to communicate with the defense attorney. The fact that the defense attorney refrained from further contact will not absolve him of the violation.

Answer choice D is incorrect. The Rules do not absolutely prohibit an attorney from contacting a member of the jury after the jury is dismissed, but the defense attorney violated the Rules when he had the friend contact the jury foreman after the jury foreman said that she did not wish to communicate with the defense attorney.

ANSWER 214

LITIGATION AND OTHER FORMS OF ADVOCACY

Answer choice D is correct. This question tests Rule 3.1. Under this Rule, an attorney must not bring or defend a proceeding, or assert or controvert an issue therein, unless there is a basis in law or fact for doing so that is not frivolous. The Comment to the Rule makes it clear that if an attorney informs himself about the facts of his client's case and the applicable law and determines that he can make a good faith argument in support of his client's position, then such action is not frivolous, even if the attorney believes that the client will not ultimately win the case. Here, the attorney does not believe that the woman will be successful in suing the restaurant; however, he believes he can make a good faith argument on her behalf that the restaurant breached its duty to warn. Because he believes he can make the argument, the attorney will not be subject to discipline for representing the woman.

Answer choice A is incorrect. An attorney will not be subject to discipline for bringing a frivolous lawsuit just because he does not think the claim will be successful, so long as he can make a good faith argument on his client's behalf.

Answer choice B is incorrect. As noted above, a claim is not frivolous just because it might not be successful.

Answer choice C is incorrect. The measure of the damages alone does not determine whether a claim is frivolous.

ANSWER 215

CONFLICTS OF INTEREST

Answer choice B is correct. Under Rule 1.11(a), (1) a lawyer who has formerly represented a client in a matter or whose present or former firm has formerly represented a client in a matter shall not thereafter (a) use information relating to the representation to the disadvantage of the former client except as the Rules would permit or require with respect to a client, or when the information has become generally known; or (b) reveal information relating to the representation except as the Rules would permit or require with respect to a client; and (2) a lawyer who has formerly served as a public officer or employee of the government shall not otherwise represent a client in connection with a matter in which the lawyer participated personally and substantially as a government officer or employee, unless the appropriate government agency gives its informed consent, confirmed in writing, to the representation. In this fact pattern, the attorney's work at the EPA involved litigation against the same oil company that she is now defending, and the litigation is a continuation of the litigation in which she participated personally and substantially while working for the EPA. Moreover, the attorney did not obtain the informed written consent of her former agency to participate in the matter.

Answer choice A is incorrect. The time that has passed since the initial representation is irrelevant in determining whether the attorney may participate in the subsequent representation. The key determining factor is whether the attorney has the informed written consent of the former government employer.

Answer choice C is incorrect. The conflict in this pattern does not arise from the attorney's work with the Department of Justice because the work there was for the IRS.

Answer choice D is incorrect. It is likely that the attorney's litigation work at the EPA in particular fully prepared her for her work at the large law firm defending the oil company. It is precisely the attorney's work at the EPA, though, that disqualifies her from representing the oil company at the large law firm without the informed written consent of the EPA.

ANSWER 216

REGULATION OF THE LEGAL PROFESSION

Answer choice A is correct. Rule 5.4(b) prohibits a lawyer from forming a partnership with a non-lawyer if any of the activities of the partnership consist of the practice of law. The partnership in this fact pattern provides grants to artists, and there is no indication that the partner provided any legal services. As long as none of the activities of the partnership consist of the practice of law, the partner is not likely to be subject to discipline.

Answer choice B is incorrect. A lawyer can be subject to discipline for practicing law in a partnership with a non-lawyer, even if the partnership is a non-profit organization.

Answer choice C is incorrect. Regardless of the division of responsibility in the partnership, if any of the activities consist of the practice of law, the lawyer could be subject to discipline.

Answer choice D is incorrect. Even if the lawyer were attempting to provide pro bono services, Rule 5.4(b) would still subject him to discipline for forming the partnership with the non-lawyer if any of the activities of the partnership consisted of the practice of law.

ANSWER 217

JUDICIAL CONDUCT

Answer choice D is correct. This question tests Code Rule 2.13(B). Under this Code Rule, a judge must not appoint a lawyer to a position if the judge either knows that the lawyer, or the lawyer's domestic partner or spouse, has contributed more than a specified dollar amount within the specified number of years prior to the judge's election campaign, or learns of such a contribution on account of a timely motion by a party or other person properly interested in the matter. One exception to this Rule is if the position to which the lawyer is appointed is substantially uncompensated. Here, the attorney contributed a substantial amount of funding to the judge's campaign and hosted fundraisers, and the judge was aware of both the contributions and the fundraisers. The position, though, is unpaid; so the appointment falls under the exception for uncompensated positions, and the judge's conduct would be excused.

Answer choice A is incorrect. Generally the judge's knowledge of the substantial campaign contributions would result in discipline for appointing the attorney, but the appointment is acceptable because the position is uncompensated.

Answer choice B is incorrect. While appointing a close friend might result in a finding of favoritism, the facts here indicate that the attorney was the only local family law attorney not currently in the pool of referees and was highly qualified to serve in that capacity.

Answer choice C is incorrect. Although it is correct that appointing a close friend does not violate the prohibition on nepotism, this does not address the issue. The judge's actions were not inappropriate because the attorney was to serve in an unpaid position.

ANSWER 218

COMMUNICATION ABOUT LEGAL SERVICES

The correct answer is C. This question tests Rule 7.2(b)(4). Under this Rule, an attorney can refer clients to another attorney or a non-attorney professional pursuant to an agreement (not otherwise prohibited by the Rules) providing for the other person to refer clients or customers to the attorney if (1) the reciprocal referral agreement is not exclusive, and (2) the clients are informed of the agreement's existence and nature. Here, the physician agreed to refer only the personal injury attorney. This arrangement is exclusive; so it does not meet the prerequisites of the Rule.

Answer choice A is incorrect. While the other party to the reciprocal referral agreement must be either another attorney or a non-attorney professional, the other prerequisites of the Rule must be satisfied in order for the attorney to not be subject to discipline.

Answer choice B is incorrect. While the client must be informed of the arrangement's existence and nature, the other prerequisites of the Rule must be satisfied in order for the attorney to not be subject to discipline.

Answer choice D is incorrect. Although there is a general prohibition against an attorney giving anything of value to another person in exchange for referrals, Rule 7.2(b)(4) contains an exception for reciprocal referral agreements if certain prerequisites are met.

ANSWER 219

THE CLIENT-LAWYER RELATIONSHIP

Answer choice A is correct. This question tests the right of an attorney to limit the scope of representation. Restatement §19(1) provides that a client and attorney may agree to reasonably limit a duty that the attorney would otherwise owe to the client if (1) the client is adequately informed and consents, and (2) the terms of the limitation are reasonable given the circumstances. In this fact pattern, the client brought a fairly complex case to the attorney, and they agreed to a limit of twenty minutes of consultation. Given the complexity of the case and the impending hearing, the limitation of twenty minutes of consultation was unreasonable under the circumstances.

Answer choice B is incorrect. As explained above, a client and an attorney may agree to limit the scope of representation if there is informed consent and the limitation is reasonable.

Answer choice C is incorrect. A client may terminate representation, although the client may be liable for quasi-contract damages.

Answer choice D is incorrect. Although the client may in fact be guilty, the attorney's advice to plead not guilty is not frivolous because a defendant is entitled to a fair trial on the merits.

ANSWER 220

DIFFERENT ROLES OF THE LAWYER

The correct answer is A. This question tests Rule 3.9, which provides that a lawyer who is representing a client before a legislative body or administrative agency in a nonadjudicative proceeding shall disclose that the appearance is in a representative capacity and shall conform to the Rules governing candor toward the tribunal (Rule 3.3(a)-(c)), fairness to opposing party and counsel (Rule 3.4(a)-(c)), and impartiality and decorum of the tribunal (Rule 3.5). Here, the attorney was asked to accompany the representative purely for support and not to represent the representative; so the attorney was not required by the Rules to make any additional disclosure.

Answer choice B is incorrect. Although the Rules recognize that an attorney does not have an exclusive right to represent non-pro se clients at legislative hearings, the Rules also acknowledge that, in those situations, an attorney has an affirmative duty to disclose his or her role to the body conducting the hearing.

Answer choice C is incorrect. The Rules do not prohibit an attorney from being compensated for attending a hearing when not acting in a representative capacity.

Answer choice D is incorrect. The attorney was not required to make any additional disclosure because he was not serving in a representative capacity.

ANSWER 221

DIFFERENT ROLES OF THE LAWYER

The correct answer is B. This question tests Rule 3.9, which provides that a lawyer who is representing a client before a legislative body or administrative agency in a nonadjudicative proceeding shall disclose that the appearance is in a representative capacity, and shall conform to the Rules governing candor toward the tribunal (Rule 3.3(a)-(c)), fairness to opposing party and counsel (Rule 3.4(a)-(c)), and impartiality and decorum of the tribunal (Rule 3.5). The Comment to the Rule indicates that filing a tax return on behalf of a client does not fall within the scope of the Rule. Here, the tax attorney merely filed a tax return for the independent contractor. Because this activity does not fall within the scope of Rule 3.9, the tax attorney would not be subject to discipline.

Answer choice A is incorrect. While the attorney would not be subject to discipline for assisting the client in criminal activity since she was not aware of the activity, this issue is not the one being tested by the question.

Answer choice C is incorrect. Because filing a tax return does not fall within the scope of Rule 3.9, the attorney would not be obligated to disclose her representation to the IRS.

Answer choice D is incorrect. The attorney did not assist the client in refusing to file the tax return. In fact, she assisted the client in complying with the law.

ANSWER 222

COMMUNICATIONS WITH PERSONS OTHER THAN CLIENTS

Answer choice B is correct. This question tests Rule 4.2. Under Rule 4.2, in the course of representing a client, a lawyer must not communicate about the subject of the representation with a person the lawyer knows to be represented by another lawyer in the matter, unless the lawyer has the other lawyer's consent or is authorized to do so by law or a court order. The Comment to the Rule indicates that communications authorized by law may include investigative activities of lawyers representing governmental entities, directly or through investigative agents, prior to the commencement of criminal or civil enforcement proceedings. Model Rules of Prof'l Conduct R. 4.2 cmt. [4] (2009). Here, the businesswoman had an attorney on retainer, and the recorded conversation concerned the subject of the representation. Such communication would violate the Rule absent the exception for the government attorney who communicates with a represented \ person through an investigative agent prior to commencing criminal proceedings. Therefore, the attorney will not be subject to discipline.

Answer choice A is incorrect. If the exception permitted by the Rule had not applied, the attorney would still be subject to discipline if an investigative agent communicated with a represented person about the subject of the representation.

Answer choice C is incorrect. Although an attorney would normally be subject to discipline for communicating, directly or through an agent, with a represented person about the subject of the representation, a government attorney is permitted by law to communicate with a represented person in the course of investigations through an investigative agent prior to commencing criminal proceedings.

Answer choice D is incorrect. Although obtaining a court order would have allowed the attorney or her informant to communicate with the businesswoman, such an order was not necessary since the attorney was already permitted by law to do so, as explained above.

ANSWER 223

REGULATION OF THE LEGAL PROFESSION

Answer choice C is correct. This question tests Rule 5.4(a)(3). Under this Rule, a lawyer or law firm is not permitted to share legal fees with a non-lawyer except that a lawyer or law firm may include non-lawyer employees in a compensation or retirement plan even though the plan is based in whole or in part on a profit-sharing arrangement. Here, the paralegal is a non-lawyer, but she is also an employee of the firm; so it was appropriate to include her in the compensation plan, including the bonus structure.

Answer choice A is incorrect. As noted above, a law firm may include a non-lawyer employee in the firm's compensation plan.

Answer choice B is incorrect. A law firm is not prohibited from computing a non-lawyer employee's compensation in the same manner as that of the attorneys.

Answer choice D is incorrect. Although the compensation is likely justified based on the increased workload, the increase is permitted based on the employee's status, and not her workload.

ANSWER 224

SAFEKEEPING FUNDS AND OTHER PROPERTY

The correct answer is C. This question tests Rule 1.15(d). Under this Rule, upon receiving funds or other property in which a client or third person has an interest, an attorney must promptly notify the client or third person. Additionally, except as permitted by the Rules, the law or by agreement with the client, the Rule also requires that the attorney promptly deliver to the client or third person any funds or other property that the client or third person is entitled to receive and, upon request by the client or third person, shall promptly render a full accounting regarding such property. Here, the woman delivered funds to the attorney on a Thursday; given the husband's interest in the funds, the attorney had an obligation under the Rule to promptly notify the husband that the funds were available and to deliver the funds to him if he so desired. Waiting over the weekend before notifying the husband does not constitute prompt notification; so the attorney's conduct was not appropriate.

Answer choice A is incorrect. An attorney should not follow the client's directions if the directions are in opposition to the attorney's duties under the Rules.

Answer choice B is incorrect. The fact that the person entitled to receive the funds or to be notified of the funds does not object to the delay does not relieve the attorney of the responsibility to notify the individual.

Answer choice D is incorrect. An attorney does not have an obligation to keep funds in the same form, as long as he or she keeps the funds separate from his own.

ANSWER 225

CONFLICTS OF INTEREST

Answer choice C is correct. This question tests Rule 1.8(g). Under this Rule, an attorney who represents two or more co-clients must not participate in making an aggregate settlement of the civil claims of or against the clients, or in a criminal case an aggregated agreement as to guilty or nolo contendere pleas, unless each client gives informed consent, in writing signed by the client. According to the Comment to the Rule, the attorney's disclosure must include all material terms of the settlement, including what the other clients will receive or pay if the settlement or plea offer is accepted. Here, the attorney was representing twelve clients, and the company offered to settle with all twelve clients. The attorney provided full disclosure to all twelve clients, including the amounts that the other clients were to receive under the settlement. After the disclosure, the clients all provided signed, written informed consent. Therefore, the attorney would not be subject to discipline.

Answer choice A is incorrect. Although the attorney has a duty to keep client information confidential, the Rule explicitly requires the attorney to disclose the amount each person will receive in the settlement.

Answer choice B is incorrect. An attorney has an obligation to communicate settlement offers and to abide by the client's wishes regarding settlement; so he would not be subject to discipline for communicating the offer to the clients.

Answer choice D is incorrect. There are potential conflicts of interest in representing multiple clients, but the key issue here is whether the attorney provided enough information to the clients for them to provide signed, written informed consent to the settlement.

ANSWER 226

COMPETENCE, MALPRACTICE, AND OTHER CIVIL LIABILITY

Answer choice C is correct. This question tests Rule 1.1. Under the Rule, a lawyer is required to provide competent representation to a client, which requires knowledge and skill reasonably necessary for the representation. Comment [3] to the Rule provides an exception for emergency situations, during which a lawyer may give advice or assistance in a matter in which the attorney does not possess the skill ordinarily required, where referral to or consultation or association with another lawyer would be impractical. In such situations, the attorney should limit the assistance to what is reasonably necessary in the circumstances to avoid doing something that could place a client's interest at risk. Here, the client was facing death, and the attorney did not have time to contact a probate attorney. The only assistance the attorney provided to the client was to write down the client's wishes. Because the attorney limited her assistance to that which was reasonably necessary in the emergency situation, she would not be subject to discipline.

Answer choice A is incorrect. Although there is a general requirement that attorneys provide competent representation, as explained above, there is an exception for emergency situations.

Answer choice B is incorrect. Under normal circumstances, the attorney would be expected to

---

consult with another competent attorney, but in an emergency situation, an attorney may provide assistance to a client that is reasonably necessary in the circumstances.

Answer choice D is incorrect. Although the client signed the will, the attorney could still be subject to discipline for failing to provide competent representation, absent an exigent circumstance.

ANSWER 227

CONFLICTS OF INTEREST

The correct answer is C. This question tests Rule 1.7. Under this Rule, a lawyer is generally prohibited from representing a client if the representation involves a concurrent conflict of interest. A concurrent conflict of interest exists if (1) the representation of one client will be directly adverse to another client or (2) there is a significant risk that the representation of one or more clients will be materially limited by the lawyer's responsibilities to another client, a former client or a third person, or by a personal interest of the lawyer. Notwithstanding a concurrent conflict of interest, a lawyer may represent a client if (1) the lawyer reasonably believes that the lawyer will be able to provide competent and diligent representation to each affected client; (2) the representation is not prohibited by law; (3) the representation does not involve the assertion of a claim by one client against another client represented by the lawyer in the same litigation or other proceeding before a tribunal; and (4) each affected client gives informed consent, confirmed in writing. Here, a concurrent conflict of interest exists because the litigator has been retained by the insurance company to represent the insured client, and there is a significant risk that his representation of the insured client will be materially limited by the insurance company's settlement instructions. The litigator may represent the insured client, though, because he believes he can provide competent representation to both parties, the representation is a common one and not prohibited by law, neither party is asserting a claim against the other in litigation, and both the insurance company and the insured client provided written informed consent.

Answer choice A is incorrect. While it would have probably been in both the insured client's and the insurance company's best interests to settle for the lesser amount, the litigator was bound by the insurance company's instructions, to which the insured client gave written informed consent.

Answer choice B is incorrect. The insurance company was also the litigator's client; so he was bound by the client's wishes to settle.

Answer choice D is incorrect. While the litigator was bound by the insurance company's instructions to settle, the controlling issue is whether the insured client provided written informed consent to the dual nature of the representation and the limitations on the representation of the insured client.

ANSWER 228

THE CLIENT-LAWYER RELATIONSHIP

Answer choice B is correct. This question tests Rule 1.16(c). Under this Rule, a lawyer must comply with applicable law requiring notice to or permission of a tribunal when terminating representation. When ordered to do so by a tribunal, a lawyer must continue representation notwithstanding good cause for terminating the representation. Here, the attorney had good cause to withdraw because the businessman used the attorney's advice to commit the crime for which the businessman is in court. The court, though, has ruled that the attorney may not withdraw. Because of the court's ruling, the attorney must continue to represent the businessman.

Answer choice A is incorrect. The facts indicate that the businessman would have no trouble securing adequate representation if the attorney were to withdraw, and the attorney agreed to provide the subsequent attorney with all relevant work product; so it is unlikely that the withdrawal would have a material adverse impact on the businessman's interests.

Answer choice C is incorrect. Although an attorney has the general right to withdraw if the client has used the attorney's services to commit a crime (Rule 1.16(b), that right is subject to Rule 1.16(c), which requires that an attorney continue the representation of a client, notwithstanding good cause to withdraw from representation, if the court refuses to permit the withdrawal.

Answer choice D is incorrect. While it would be important for the attorney to make arrangements for a smooth transition of representation, the court has ruled that he may not withdraw.

ANSWER 229

CONFLICTS OF INTEREST

Answer choice A is correct. Under Rule 1.11(a), (1) a lawyer who has formerly represented a client in a matter or whose present or former firm has formerly represented a client in a matter shall not thereafter (a) use information relating to the representation to the disadvantage of the former client except as the Rules would permit or require with respect to a client, or when the information has become generally known; or (b) reveal information relating to the representation except as the Rules would permit or require with respect to a client; and (2) a lawyer who has formerly served as a public officer or employee of the government shall not otherwise represent a client in connection with a matter in which the lawyer participated personally and substantially as a government officer or employee, unless the appropriate government agency gives its informed consent, confirmed in writing, to the representation. Here, the attorney worked both personally and substantially in preparing the attorney general's opinion while employed by the attorney general's office. The fact that she was a paralegal at the time is irrelevant because Rule 1.11(a) covers any government employee, not just attorneys. Because of the depth of her participation, the attorney cannot appropriately participate in the litigation challenging the opinion, unless she receives the informed written consent of the attorney general's office.

Answer choice B is incorrect. While the attorney substantially and personally participated in preparing the challenged opinion, she can avoid discipline if she receives the informed written consent of the attorney general's office.

Answer choice C is incorrect. As noted above, the job description is irrelevant in determining whether there is a conflict with the new employer.

Answer choice D is incorrect. A former employee of one government agency can still be subject to discipline for a conflict of interest when moving to another government agency.

ANSWER 230

LITIGATION AND OTHER FORMS OF ADVOCACY

Answer choice B is correct. This question tests Rule 3.1. Under this Rule, an attorney must not bring or defend a proceeding, or assert or controvert an issue therein, unless there is a basis in law or fact for doing so that is not frivolous. One such basis includes a good faith argument for an extension, modification, or reversal of existing law. Here, the current statute does not include toy poodles as a dangerous dog breed; however, the attorney believes in good faith that the statute should be extended to include the breed. Therefore, although there is no current basis in law for bringing a claim on the boy's behalf, which would normally result in a violation of the above Rule, the attorney's good faith belief that the statute should be extended would provide protection from a violation of the Rule.

Answer choice A is incorrect. Although it is true that the boy likely deserves to be compensated for the injuries, the statute does not currently provide a cause of action for attacks by toy poodles; therefore, the claim would normally need to be brought under a negligence theory.

Answer choice C is incorrect. Although the current statute does not provide a cause of action for the boy, the attorney has a good faith belief that the statute should be extended to include toy poodles, and, thus, would not be subject to discipline.

Answer choice D is incorrect. An attorney will not be subject to discipline for bringing a frivolous claim just because the claim is unlikely to be successful.

ANSWER 231

COMMUNICATIONS WITH PERSONS OTHER THAN CLIENTS

The correct answer is D. This question tests Rule 4.3. Under this Rule, when a lawyer is dealing on behalf of a client with a person who is not represented by counsel, a lawyer must not state or imply that the lawyer is disinterested. Here, the attorney was hired by the doctor, and she worked on his behalf to negotiate the sale. The seller was unrepresented, and the attorney told the seller that she was going to be a disinterested intermediary. Because the attorney indicated that she would be disinterested to an unrepresented party, she would be subject to discipline.

Answer choice A is incorrect. The fact that the seller received the asking price despite the misrepresentation by the attorney does not shield the attorney from discipline for the misrepresentation.

Answer choice B is incorrect. The attorney advised her client truthfully, but she behaved improperly when she advised the seller that she was impartial.

Answer choice C is incorrect. The attorney did not have an obligation to require her client to negotiate for a lower amount.

ANSWER 232

CONFLICTS OF INTEREST

The correct answer is C. This question tests Rule 1.12(a). Under this Rule, a lawyer generally must not represent anyone in connection with a matter in which the lawyer participated personally and substantially (1) as a judge or other adjudicative officer or law clerk to such a person or (2) as an arbitrator, mediator, or other third-party neutral, *unless* all parties to the proceeding give informed consent, confirmed in writing. Here, the attorney was employed as a law clerk to the judge who presided over the initial trial, and the attorney participated substantially in the matter because he researched and drafted the opinion. Because the attorney did not get the informed written consent of all of the parties involved, he would be subject to discipline.

Answer choice A is incorrect. The Rule covers law clerks as well as judges.

Answer choice B is incorrect. The Rule requires the attorney to get informed consent, confirmed in writing. The mere lack of objection does not satisfy this requirement.

Answer choice D is incorrect. The attorney clearly feels that he is competent to represent the contractor, and the facts indicate that he had represented clients successfully in three other cases.

ANSWER 233

THE CLIENT-LAWYER RELATIONSHIP

Answer choice B is correct. This question tests Rule 1.2(a). Under this Rule, the lawyer, within the limits imposed by law and his or her professional obligations, is required to abide by a client's decision concerning the objectives of the representation and shall consult with the client as to the means by which they are to be pursued; a lawyer may take such action on behalf of the client as is impliedly authorized to carry out the representation; a lawyer shall abide by a client's decision whether to settle a matter; and in a criminal case, a lawyer shall abide by the client's decision, after consultation with the lawyer, as to a plea to be entered, whether to waive jury trial and whether the client will testify. Here, despite the defense attorney's advice to the contrary, the wife decided that she would like to waive her right to a jury trial. Although the defense attorney may disagree with his client's wishes, he is required by the Rule to abide by her decision with respect to the jury trial.

Answer choice A is incorrect. The Rules do not stipulate how many times an attorney is required to advise a client on a particular matter. Here, the wife acknowledged that she understood the advice; so it does not appear that the defense attorney would need to advise the wife on multiple occasions.

Answer choice C is incorrect. The Rules acknowledge that attorneys and their clients may disagree about the means to be used to accomplish a client's objectives, but Rule 1.2(a) is explicit in directing attorneys to abide by client wishes regarding waivers of jury trials, even if that decision is in direct contradiction to an attorney's advice.

Answer choice D is incorrect. Regardless of whether the outcome of a case is in a client's favor, an attorney is obligated by the Rules to abide by a client's wishes. A favorable outcome does not shield an attorney from discipline for disregarding a client's express orders.

ANSWER 234

CLIENT CONFIDENTIALITY

The correct answer is B. This question tests Rule 1.6(a). Under this Rule, a lawyer must never reveal information relating to the representation of a client unless (1) the client gives informed consent, (2) the disclosure is impliedly authorized in order to carry out the representation, or (3) the disclosure is permitted under the Rules. According to Comment [5] to the Rule, unless a client instructs his or her lawyer to restrict information to specific lawyers in the firm, the lawyer may reveal confidential information to other lawyers in the firm in the course of the firm's practice. Here, the attorney was planning to be out of the country for two weeks and made arrangements with a partner in his firm to cover the client's case while he was gone. Although the attorney did not get the client's informed consent to disclose the information to his partner in the firm, he had the client's implied consent, pursuant to Comment [5] to the Rule, because the client did not instruct the attorney to restrict the disclosure, and the disclosure was in the course of the firm's business.

Answer choice A is incorrect. Even if an attorney knows that another attorney is fully competent to represent a client, he must have either the client's informed or implied consent before disclosing the client's confidential information to another attorney.

Answer choice C is incorrect. In this situation, the attorney had the client's implied consent to share the client's file with the partner; so it was not necessary for the attorney to get the client's written consent.

Answer choice D is incorrect. The Rules do not specify which events in an attorney's life provide sufficient justification for an attorney to ask another attorney in his firm to handle a case.

ANSWER 235

LITIGATION AND OTHER FORMS OF ADVOCACY

The correct answer is D. This question tests Rule 3.7(a), which provides that a lawyer cannot act as an advocate at a trial in which the lawyer is likely to be a necessary witness unless (a) the testimony relates to an uncontested issue; (b) the testimony relates to the nature and value of legal services provided; or (c) the lawyer's disqualification would be a substantial hardship to the client. Here, the attorney is the only person who witnessed the driver typing on his phone before the crash; so his testimony is likely to be necessary in the case. The driver claimed his innocence; so the issue is contested, thereby rendering the first exception inapplicable. The testimony would relate to the accident and not the provision of services; so the second exception does not apply. Finally, the cell phone records were available to help establish the driver's negligence; so the third exception does not apply. Because there are no applicable exceptions, the Rule would prohibit the attorney from representing the cyclist.

Answer choice A is incorrect. The Rule generally prohibits an attorney from acting simultaneously as advocate and necessary witness, unless one of the three exceptions set forth in the Rule applies. As noted above, there are no applicable exceptions.

Answer choice B is incorrect. The Rule does not permit a client to consent to the attorney acting as both a witness and a representative.

Answer choice C is incorrect. The Rule does not provide an absolute bar to an attorney testifying if he or she is a witness, but the situation must fall within one of the three exceptions set forth in the Rule.

ANSWER 236

COMPETENCE, MALPRACTICE, AND OTHER CIVIL LIABILITY

The correct answer is A. This question tests Rule 1.1. Under the Rule, a lawyer is required to provide competent representation to a client, which requires knowledge and skill reasonably necessary for the representation. Comment [3] to the Rule provides an exception for emergency situations, during which a lawyer may give advice or assistance in a matter in which the attorney does not possess the skill ordinarily required, where referral to or consultation or association with another lawyer would be impractical. In such situations, the attorney should limit the assistance to what is reasonably necessary in the circumstances to avoid doing something that could place a client's interest at risk. Here, although the attorney had only limited knowledge of criminal law, his nephew was in an emergency situation, and the attorney provided limited assistance until he could secure competent representation for his nephew. The attorney will not be subject to discipline for such conduct.

Answer choice B is incorrect. Although the attorney acted correctly in quickly securing competent representation for his nephew, the Rule would not have permitted him to represent his nephew without the requisite knowledge and skill, absent the emergency situation.

Answer choice C is incorrect. Because the nephew was in an emergency situation, the attorney was permitted to represent him without being competent in criminal law.

Answer choice D is incorrect. Because the nephew was in an emergency situation, the attorney was permitted to represent him without having recent criminal law experience.

ANSWER 237

LITIGATION AND OTHER FORMS OF ADVOCACY

Answer choice C is correct. This question tests Rule 3.4(f). This Rule provides that a lawyer must not request a person other than a client to refrain from voluntarily giving relevant information to another party unless (1) the person is a relative, employee, or other agent of a client; and (2) the lawyer reasonably believes that the person's interests will not be adversely affected by refraining from giving such information. Here, the prosecutor directed the pharmacist to refrain from voluntarily giving the public defender certain relevant prescription information. The pharmacist was not related to the teenager (and clearly was not an employee or other agent of the teenager); so the exception under the Rule does not apply.

Answer choice A is incorrect. The prescription records were relevant to prove that the teenager possessed the pills legally.

Answer choice B is incorrect. Although the prosecutor reasonably believed that withholding the documentation would not harm the pharmacist's interest, the exception does not apply because the pharmacist was not related to, or an employee or other agent of, the teenager.

Answer choice D is incorrect. The prosecutor is permitted to counsel a person other than the client to refrain from voluntarily disclosing relevant information to another party if the exception in the Rule is satisfied; in any event, providing such advice is not the same as helping a party to falsify testimony.

ANSWER 238

LITIGATION AND OTHER FORMS OF ADVOCACY

The correct answer is A. This question tests Rule 3.5(b). Under this Rule, a lawyer must not communicate *ex parte* with a judge, juror, prospective juror, or other official during the proceeding, unless authorized to do so by law or court order. Here, the defense attorney did, in fact, communicate with the judge without the plaintiff's counsel being present, but he notified the plaintiff's counsel of his plans prior to initiating the conversation. Because he provided such notice, the defense attorney would not be subject to discipline.

Answer choice B is incorrect. Being a friend of the judge does not provide an excuse for engaging in *ex parte* communications.

Answer choice C is incorrect. The Rule does not require that the other party be present as long as the other party is notified of the intention to communicate and the substance.

Answer choice D is incorrect. While it is probably socially unacceptable to engage in such behavior, the Rule does not prohibit it.

ANSWER 239

COMMUNICATIONS WITH PERSONS OTHER THAN CLIENTS

Answer choice A is correct. This question tests Rule 4.2. Under Rule 4.2, in the course of representing a client, a lawyer must not communicate about the subject of the representation with a person the lawyer knows to be represented by another lawyer in the matter, unless the lawyer has the other lawyer's consent or is authorized to do so by law or a court order. Here, although the former partner was represented, and the attorney communicated with him, the communication was not about the subject of the representation but rather about the upcoming theater season. The prohibition is specific to communications about the subject of the representation; so the attorney is permitted to discuss other matters.

Answer choice B is incorrect. Rule 4.2's prohibition on communicating with a person represented by counsel about the subject of the representation applies even if the represented person initiates the communication. In this instance, however, the attorney and the former partner were discussing matters outside of the representation; so the communication was appropriate.

Answer choice C is incorrect. Although the former partner was represented by counsel, the communication was not inappropriate because it was about matters outside of the representation.

Answer choice D is incorrect. Since the former partner and the attorney did not discuss the subject of the representation, the attorney's conduct was not inappropriate, and the rules do not prohibit contact that has the appearance of impropriety.

ANSWER 240

SAFEKEEPING FUNDS AND OTHER PROPERTY

The correct answer is D. This question tests Rule 1.15. Rule 1.15(a) provides that when a lawyer holds property of clients or third persons in connection with a representation, the lawyer must keep that property separate from his or her own. Rule 1.15(c) provides that a lawyer must deposit into a client trust account legal fees and expenses that have been paid in advance, and those funds may be withdrawn by the lawyer only as the fees are earned or expenses incurred. Here, the attorney properly placed the client funds in a separate account, but he withdrew them immediately to pay firm bills, prior to earning any of the fees, and, thus, would be subject to discipline.

Answer choice A is incorrect. Although the attorney eventually earned the fees, he had not earned the fees at the time that he withdrew the client funds to pay firm bills.

Answer choice B is incorrect. While the attorney complied with the Rule regarding the depositing of client funds into a separate client trust account, he violated the Rule by withdrawing the funds prior to earning them.

Answer choice C is incorrect. An attorney is permitted to accept fees prior to earning them, but he must deposit them into a separate client trust account and only withdraw them as he earns them.

ANSWER 241

CONFLICTS OF INTEREST

The correct answer is C. This question tests Rule 1.8(d). Under this Rule, prior to the conclusion of representation of a client, a lawyer cannot make or negotiate an agreement giving the lawyer literary or media rights to a portrayal based in substantial part on information relating to the representation. Here, the lawyer negotiated with the client for the media rights prior to the jury verdict, which is prior to the conclusion of the representation; so the attorney would be subject to discipline.

Answer choice A is incorrect. The timing of the negotiations for media rights, not the amount of the rights given, determines whether the lawyer is subject to discipline.

Answer choice B is incorrect. While the arrangement was beneficial to both parties, the lawyer should have waited until after the conclusion of the representation before negotiating for the rights.

Answer choice D is incorrect. While the lawyer's ability to represent the client was not adversely impacted by the negotiation of the movie deal, the timing of the negotiations was still prohibited by the Rule.

ANSWER 242

THE CLIENT-LAWYER RELATIONSHIP

Answer choice D is correct. This question tests Rule 1.2(a). Under this Rule, the lawyer, within the limits imposed by law and his or her professional obligations, is required to abide by a client's decision concerning the objectives of the representation, and shall consult with the client as to the means by which they are to be pursued; a lawyer may take such action on behalf of the client as is impliedly authorized to carry out the representation; a lawyer shall abide by a client's decision whether to settle a matter; and in a criminal case, a lawyer shall abide by the client's decision, after consultation with the lawyer, as to a plea to be entered, whether to waive jury trial and whether the client will testify. This mandatory obligation in criminal cases does not extend to civil cases. Here, the developer told the lawyer that she would like to testify, but when the time came to call her to the stand, the lawyer felt that the case would not be served by her testimony. In a criminal case, the lawyer would have been obligated to call the developer to the stand, but because this case was a civil case, the lawyer was not required to abide by that wish if he felt that he did not need to in order to carry out the representation.

Answer choice A is incorrect. While Rule 1.2(a) requires a lawyer to abide by a client's wish to testify in a criminal case, that same compulsory obligation does not apply in a civil case.

Answer choice B is incorrect. The outcome of a case does not determine whether a lawyer will be subject to discipline for disregarding a client's wish to testify.

Answer choice C is incorrect. While the lawyer acted correctly when he abided by his client's determination to not settle, the key issue in this question is whether or not he was obligated to call the client to the stand to testify.

ANSWER 243

CLIENT CONFIDENTIALITY

The correct answer is D. This question tests Rule 1.6 regarding the disclosure of confidential client information. Generally, an attorney may not disclose information relating to the representation of a client unless (1) the client gives informed consent, (2) the disclosure is impliedly authorized in order to carry out the representation, or (3) the disclosure is permitted by any of the enumerated exceptions in Rule 1.6(b). In particular, Rule 1.6(b)permits an attorney to disclose confidential information if he reasonably believes that doing so is necessary (1) to prevent reasonably certain death or substantial bodily harm; (2) to prevent the client from committing a crime or fraud that is reasonably certain to result in substantial injury to the financial interests or property of another and in furtherance of which the client has used or is using the attorney's services; (3) to prevent substantial injury to the financial interests or property of another that is reasonably certain to result or has resulted from the client's commission of a crime or fraud in furtherance of which the client has used the attorney's services; (4) to secure legal advice about the attorney's compliance with the Rules; (5) to establish a claim or defense on behalf of the attorney in a controversy between the attorney and the client, to establish a defense to a criminal charge or civil claim against the attorney based upon conduct in which the client was involved, or to respond to allegations in any proceeding concerning the attorney's representation of the client; (6) to comply with other law or a court order; or (7) to detect and resolve conflicts of interest arising from the attorney's change of employment or from changes in the composition or ownership of a firm, but only if the revealed information would not compromise the attorney-client privilege or otherwise prejudice the client. In this case, the husband has not consented to the disclosure, and none of the enumerated exceptions in Rule 1.6(b) apply. The attorney, however, would be permitted to disclose this information if she had implied authority to do so, but the joint representation of two clients does not alone confer such implied authority.

Answer choice A is incorrect. As discussed above, the joint representation of two clients does not necessarily confer implied authority to disclose confidential information.

Answer choice B is incorrect. For the exception in Rule 1.6(b)(3) to apply, it must be the case that the client committed a crime or fraud and used the attorney's services in the process. Concealing a child born out of wedlock would not satisfy this requirement.

Answer choice C is incorrect. An attorney may engage in joint representation if the attorney meets the requirements of Rule 1.7(b): (1) the lawyer reasonably believes he will be able to provide competent and diligent representation to each affected client; (2) the representation is not prohibited by law; (3) the representation does not involve the assertion of a claim by one client against another client represented by the lawyer in the same litigation or other proceeding before a tribunal; and (4) each affected client gives informed consent, confirmed in writing.

ANSWER 244

CLIENT CONFIDENTIALITY

Answer choice D is correct. Pursuant to Rule 1.18(a), a person who discusses with a lawyer the possibility of forming a client-lawyer relationship with respect to a matter is a prospective client. Furthermore, as set forth in Rule 1.18(b), if, after consultation, no client-lawyer relationship forms, a lawyer who has had discussions with a prospective client must not use or reveal information learned during the consultation, except as otherwise permitted by the Rules. The Comment to Rule 1.18 states that a person who unilaterally discloses information to an attorney without a reasonable expectation that the attorney is willing to discuss the possibility of forming an attorney-client relationship is not a prospective client within the scope of Rule 1.18(a). Here, the doctor approached the attorney at a cocktail party while inebriated, disclosed the information and had no reasonable expectation of forming an attorney-client relationship. Because the doctor would not be considered a prospective client, the attorney can represent the patient without any conflict.

Answer choice A is incorrect. While the attorney received damaging information from the doctor, the doctor was not a prospective client, and the attorney did not owe him the duties owed to a prospective client.

Answer choice B is incorrect. The facts do not indicate that the doctor had a reasonable expectation of forming an attorney-client relationship, and the discussion never turned to that subject.

Answer choice C is incorrect. Although the doctor was discussing the facts publicly instead of in the attorney's office, the attorney would have still owed a duty of confidentiality to the doctor if the doctor had been a prospective client.

ANSWER 245

THE CLIENT-LAWYER RELATIONSHIP

Answer choice B is correct. The question tests Rule 1.2(d), which provides that a lawyer shall not counsel a client to engage, or assist a client, in conduct that the lawyer knows is criminal or fraudulent, but a lawyer may discuss the legal consequences of any proposed course of conduct with a client and may counsel or assist a client to make a good faith effort to determine the validity, scope, meaning, or application of the law. Perjury is considered unlawful conduct for which the perpetrators can be subject to criminal liability. Here, the attorney learned that his client had committed perjury while testifying at her deposition, and he counseled his client to commit perjury again by telling the same lie at the actual trial. Because the attorney counseled his client to commit a crime and assisted in its commission, he can be subject to discipline.

Answer choice A is incorrect. An attorney will not be disciplined for his client's criminal activities if the attorney did not know about them and did not assist in their commission.

Answer choice C is incorrect. The client lied under oath both times, and the attorney assisted the client in committing perjury, which would subject him to discipline.

Answer choice D is incorrect. While an attorney is charged with zealously representing his client, the Rules expressly prohibit an attorney from advising a client to commit a crime.

ANSWER 246

COMMUNICATIONS WITH PERSONS OTHER THAN CLIENTS

Answer choice A is correct. This question tests Rule 4.1. Rule 4.1 provides that in the course of representing a client, a lawyer must not knowingly (1) make a false statement of material fact or law to a third person or (2) fail to disclose a material fact when disclosure is necessary to avoid assisting a criminal or fraudulent act by a client, unless disclosure is prohibited by the Rule of Confidentiality. An attorney can violate this Rule by affirming a statement by another person that the attorney knows is false. Here, the agreement contained a statement that the attorney was only representing the businessman when in fact she was also providing representation to the corporation. Both parties signed the agreement, thereby affirming the statement, and the attorney, knowing that the statement was false, signed an affirmation of the truth of the statement. By affirming the representation, the attorney violated Rule 4.1.

Answer choice B is incorrect. According to Rule 1.9(a), an attorney can represent a new client whose interests are adverse to a former client if the former client gives informed consent, confirmed in writing. Here, the corporation provided informed written consent to the representation.

Answer choice C is incorrect. Although the attorney received informed written consent from the corporation to represent the businessman, the attorney is still subject to discipline for affirming a false statement by another person.

Answer choice D is incorrect. Although the attorney did not use the information she received in the prior representation in representing the businessman, the attorney is still subject to discipline for affirming a false statement by another person.

ANSWER 247

COMMUNICATION ABOUT LEGAL SERVICES

Answer choice B is correct. This question tests Rule 7.1. Under this Rule, a lawyer cannot make false or misleading communications about the lawyer or the lawyer's services. A communication is false or misleading if it contains a material misrepresentation of fact or law, or omits a fact necessary to make the statement considered as a whole not materially misleading. Here, the attorney was a solo practitioner, but her advertisement provided a firm name that suggests, through the use of the word "associates," that there are other attorneys in the firm. The use of that name makes the advertisement false and misleading, which violates Rule 7.1.

Answer choice A is incorrect. The Rules permit attorneys to indicate a specialty in advertisements as long as the statement is not false or misleading.

Answer choice C is incorrect. The attorney is required to include the name and office address of at least one lawyer or law firm responsible for the content (Rule 7.2), but that alone does not keep the attorney from violating Rule 7.1 if the statement is otherwise misleading.

Answer choice D is incorrect. An attorney may state that he or she specializes in a particular area if that statement is not false or misleading; however, this does not address the issue. Here, the attorney was a solo practitioner, but her advertisement provided a firm name that suggested, through the use of the word "associates," that there were other attorneys in the firm. The use of that name makes the advertisement false and misleading, even if the attorney intended to work exclusively on tax law matters.

ANSWER 248

JUDICIAL CONDUCT

The correct answer is B. This question tests Code Rule 2.9(A)(1). Under this Code Rule, a judge is generally prohibited from initiating, permitting, or considering *ex parte* communications, or other communications made to the judge outside of the presence of the parties or their lawyers, regarding a pending or impending matter, but the Rule provides an exception, when circumstances require it, for scheduling, administrative, or emergency purposes that do not deal with substantive matters. In order for these *ex parte* communications to be permitted, the judge must (1) reasonably believe that no party will gain a substantive, procedural, or tactical advantage as a result of the *ex parte* communication and (2) make provision promptly to notify all other parties of the substance of the *ex parte* communication and afford them an opportunity to respond. Here, an emergency situation arose, the *ex parte* communication was purely for scheduling purposes, the *ex parte* communication afforded neither party an advantage, and the plaintiff's counsel was promptly notified of the *ex parte* communication and given an opportunity to respond. Because all of the elements of the Code Rule were satisfied, the judge would not be subject to discipline.

Answer choice A is incorrect. The availability of the assistant does not factor into whether the communication was proper under the Code Rule.

Answer choice C is incorrect. While the communication was *ex parte*, the type of communication fell within an exception to the general prohibition on such communications.

Answer choice D is incorrect. Asking another judge to make an *ex parte* communication on one's behalf would not make the communication legitimate.

ANSWER 249

JUDICIAL CONDUCT

Answer choice A is correct. This question tests Rule 8.2(a). This Rule states that a lawyer must not make a statement that the lawyer knows to be false or with reckless disregard as to its truth or falsity concerning the qualifications or integrity of a judge, adjudicatory officer, or candidate for election or appointment to judicial or legal office. Here, the tax attorney expressed her opinion of a candidate for a school board election. This office is not a judicial or legal office; so the statements would not be inappropriate.

Answer choice B is incorrect. Honest and candid opinions are permitted under the Rules in evaluating the professional or personal fitness of persons being appointed to judicial office and to public legal offices. In any event, the tax attorney's statements are proper because the election is for a school board and not a judicial or legal office.

Answer choice C is incorrect. It appears that the remarks were not made with reckless disregard as to their truth or falsity, but rather were honest and candid opinions. In any event, as noted above, the statements are permitted because of the type of election.

Answer choice D is incorrect. The Rules explicitly permit attorneys to make honest and candid opinions about elections or appointments to judicial office and to public legal offices.

ANSWER 250

REGULATION OF THE LEGAL PROFESSION

Answer choice A is correct. This question tests Rule 5.5(a), which provides that a lawyer must not practice law in a jurisdiction in violation of the regulation of the legal profession in that jurisdiction, or assist another in doing so. Here, the attorney assisted the realtor in the unauthorized practice of law because the attorney provided information to the realtor that the realtor, in turn, used to provide legal advice to her seller client. By assisting the realtor in the unauthorized practice of law, the attorney violated Rule 5.5(a).

Answer choice B is incorrect. The facts indicate that the attorney was a general practitioner; so he was likely fully qualified to provide the information.

Answer choice C is incorrect. Even if the information was available on the internet, the attorney provided legal advice to his client that his client, in turn, used to provide legal advice to her seller client.

Answer choice D is incorrect. The violation here stems from the attorney assisting the realtor in the unauthorized practice of law. The fact that the attorney originally provided the advice does not excuse the violation of the Rule.

ANSWER 251

REGULATION OF THE LEGAL PROFESSION

Answer choice D is correct. This question tests Rule 5.4(a)(2). Under this Rule, a lawyer or law firm is not permitted to share legal fees with a non-lawyer except that an attorney who purchases the practice of a deceased, disabled, or disappeared attorney may, pursuant to the provisions of Rule 1.17 governing the sale of a law practice, pay the agreed-upon purchase price to the estate or other representative of that attorney. Here, the facts indicate that both the husband and the solo practitioner complied with the rules governing the sale of a law practice, and the solo practitioner purchased the practice from a disabled attorney; so the Rule is satisfied, and the solo practitioner would not be subject to discipline for sharing earned legal fees with the non-attorney husband.

Answer choice A is incorrect. As explained above, the Rule permits an attorney to purchase a deceased, disabled, or disappeared attorney's practice and to pay the purchase price to a representative of such attorney from the earned legal fees.

Answer choice B is incorrect. The Rules do not require that the attorney from whom the practice is purchased be deceased.

Answer choice C is incorrect. Regardless of whether the purchase price is reasonable, the purchasing attorney cannot pay the legal fees to a non-attorney if the specific conditions of the Rule are not met.

ANSWER 252

CONFLICTS OF INTEREST

Answer choice B is correct. This question tests Rule 1.8(g). Under this Rule, an attorney who represents two or more co-clients must not participate in making an aggregate settlement of the civil claims of or against the clients, or in a criminal case an aggregated agreement as to guilty or nolo contendere pleas, unless each client gives informed consent, in writing signed by the client. According to the Comment to the Rule, the attorney's disclosure must include all material terms of the settlement, including what the other clients will receive or pay if the settlement or plea offer is accepted. Here, the attorney did not disclose to each partner that the other would be paying a different amount of the settlement. Because the attorney did not disclose the material terms of the settlement, he would be subject to discipline.

Answer choice A is incorrect. The client makes the ultimate decision as to whether to settle a case; so the attorney would not be subject to discipline for abiding by his clients' decision to settle here.

Answer choice C is incorrect. As noted above, the client determines whether to settle a case; so whether the settlement is more or less beneficial is irrelevant to whether the attorney will be subject to discipline.

Answer choice D is incorrect. Although the partners provided written consent, the consent was not fully informed because the attorney did not disclose all of the material terms of the settlement to each partner.

ANSWER 253

CONFLICTS OF INTEREST

The correct answer is C. This question tests Rule 1.8(a). Under this Rule, an attorney cannot enter into a business transaction with a client or knowingly acquire an ownership, possessory, security, or other pecuniary interest adverse to a client, unless (1) the transaction and terms on which the lawyer acquires the interest are fair and reasonable to the client, fully disclosed, and transmitted in writing to the client in a manner that can be reasonably understood; (2) the client is advised in writing of the desirability of seeking, and is given a reasonable opportunity to seek, the advice of independent counsel in the transaction; and (3) the client provides informed consent, in a writing signed by the client, to the essential terms of the transaction and the lawyer's role in the transaction, including whether the lawyer is representing the client in the transaction. Here, the attorney did not comply with any of the requirements of the Rule because he did not fully disclose the provision in the agreement that was advantageous to him, he did not advise the businessman to seek the advice of independent counsel, and he did not get the businessman's written, signed informed consent.

Answer choice A is incorrect. Because the transaction was between the attorney and a client, the attorney was obligated to comply with the Rule, even if there was consideration for the agreement.

Answer choice B is incorrect. Although advising the businessman to review the agreement was a prudent choice, the attorney had further obligations to comply with under the Rule for the transaction to be considered appropriate.

Answer choice D is incorrect. Although an attorney's use of his or her expertise to a client's detriment is inappropriate, the attorney' conduct in this case was improper because he did not comply with the requirements under the Rule for entering into a business transaction with a client. In fact, the client might have discovered the attorney's improper conduct had the attorney complied with the Rule.

ANSWER 254

THE CLIENT-LAWYER RELATIONSHIP

Answer choice A is correct. This question tests Rule 1.16(c). Under this Rule, a lawyer must comply with applicable law requiring notice to or permission of a tribunal when terminating representation. When ordered to do so by a tribunal, a lawyer must continue representation notwithstanding good cause for terminating the representation. Here, the attorney was justified in withdrawing from representation because the college student did not comply with the agreement between the two of them (Rule 1.16(b)), and the attorney complied with the local requirement that he provide notice to the tribunal of his intent to withdraw from his representation of the college student. The judge, after reviewing the situation, ruled in favor of permitting the attorney to withdraw. Because the attorney was justified in withdrawing, and the judge permitted the withdrawal, he may withdraw at the end of the thirty days.

Answer choice B is incorrect. Although the fee agreement and the Rules permit the attorney to withdraw if the college student does not comply with the agreement, the attorney would not be permitted to withdraw if the judge had not permitted the withdrawal.

Answer choice C is incorrect. It does not appear that the withdrawal will have a material adverse impact on the college student's interests because he will have representation through a public defender. Moreover, the judge ruled that the withdrawal was permissible.

Answer choice D is incorrect. The Rule and the related Comment expressly permit an attorney to withdraw for nonpayment of fees.

Made in the USA
Las Vegas, NV
26 January 2021